Table of Contents

Southwestern BC
Regions 2 & 3

Fishing Mapbooks

come see us at
www.backroadmapbooks.com

British Columbia
Total Area... 944 735 km²
Population...4 113 487
Capital...Victoria
Largest City...Vancouver
Highest Point...Mount Fairweather
4 663 meters (15 299 ft)
Tourism info...1.800.HELLO.BC
www.hellobc.com

Acknowledgements

Published by:

Mussio Ventures Ltd.
Unit 106- 1500 Hartley Ave,
Coquitlam, BC, V3K 7A1
P. (604) 521-6277   F. (604) 521-6260
E-mail: info@backroadmapbooks.com
www.backroadmapbooks.com

Backroad Mapbooks

DIRECTORS
Russell Mussio
Wesley Mussio
Penny Stainton-Mussio

ASSOCIATE DIRECTOR
Jason Marleau

VICE PRESIDENT
Chris Taylor

COVER DESIGN & LAYOUT
Farnaz Faghihi

COVER PHOTO
Allcanadaphotos.com

CREATIVE CONTENT
Russell Mussio
Wesley Mussio

PROJECT MANAGER
Andrew Allen

PRODUCTION
Rhianna Beauchamp,
Shaun Filipenko
Oliver Herz, Justin Quesnel
Dale Tober

SALES / MARKETING
Joshua Desnoyers
Chris Taylor

WRITER
Trent Ernst

Library and Archives Canada Cataloguing in Publication

Ernst, Trent
Southwestern BC fishing mapbook [cartographic material] : region 2,
Lower Mainland, region 3, Thompson Nicola / Trent Ernst. -- 2nd ed.

(Fishing mapbooks)
Includes index.
ISBN 978-1-897225-00-4

1. Fishing--British Columbia--Lower Mainland--Maps. 2. Fishing-
-British Columbia--Lower Mainland--Guidebooks. 3. Lower
Mainland (B.C.)--Bathymetric maps. 4. Lower Mainland (B.C.)--
Guidebooks. I. Mussio Ventures Ltd. II. Title. III. Series.

G1172.S68E63E74 2008   799.109711'3   C2008-906561-1

Copyright © 2011 Mussio Ventures Ltd.

Acknowledgement

We would like to thank everyone for their support and encouragement to resurrect the Fishing Mapbook series. This book is a collaboration of many organizations and people and is intended to be a resource that can and will be used by all anglers on southern BC. First off, this is a big thank you to the Freshwater Fisheries Society of BC, in particular Brian Chan. If he doesn't know about a lake in the Southern Interior, it isn't worth knowing. Then there is Trent Ernst. He took over the writing and research of the lakes and streams and has really learned to fish out impressive information. Of course we can not forget the helpful team of mappers, editors and graphics people at Backroad Mapbooks. These are the people who pieced everything together in such a convenient, yet comprehensive package. Thank you Andrew Allen, Rhianna Beauchamp, Joshua Desnoyers, Farnaz Faghihi, Shaun Filipenko, Oliver Herz, Justin Quesnel, Chris Taylor, and Dale Tober.

When doing our research, we had to consult numerous people who live and play in the area. Many times we were looking for the owner of a store, but got someone who was much more knowledgeable. We apologize when we forgot to ask your names.

Here are some of the people who have helped us, though:

Rios Sdrakas at Rivers Edge Fishing in Sechelt provided us with information on most everything we needed to know about fishing on the Sechelt Peninsula. And, since he recently moved to Sechelt from Squamish, we asked him a bunch of questions about that area, too. Clint Goyette at Valley Fishing Guides knows most everything about lakes and rivers from Squamish to the boundary of Region Two. He's at www.valleyfishing.com. Sam Sansalone at Powell River Outdoors was our go-to guy for the Powell River area. Bill and Myron at Westside in Salmon Arm knew an awful lot about the remote areas north of Adams Lake. Bert at Winner's Edge in Lillooet was very helpful in setting us up with people who knew about the lakes in that area, especially John at Bridge Side Forest in Lillooet. Finally, Mel at Surplus Herby's gave us lots of good information on river fishing around Kamloops.

Also a special thanks goes out to our advertisers for supporting the product line as well as helping out with information for the book, and they are: Berry's Bait & Tackle, BC Parks, Fred's Custom Tackle, Freshwater Fisheries Society, Hatch Match'r Fly & Tackle, Michael & Young, Pacific Angler, Rivers Edge, Sea Run Fly & Tackle & Surplus Herby's.

The maps and charts are courtesy of Backroad Mapbooks. However, they had to source Fisheries for the templates for the Lake Depth Chart Maps as well as Geogratis and the Ministry of Sustainable Resources for the source data for the overview maps.

Finally we would like to thank Allison, Devon, Jasper, Nancy, Madison and Penny Mussio for their continued support of the Backroad Mapbook Series. As our family grows, it is becoming more and more challenging to break away from it all to explore our beautiful country.

Sincerely,

Russell and Wesley Mussio

Disclaimer

Help Us Help You

A comprehensive resource such as Fishing Mapbooks for Southwestern BC could not be put together without a great deal of help and support. Despite our best efforts to ensure that everything is accurate, errors do occur. If you see any errors or omissions, please continue to let us know.

All updates will be posted on our web site: www.backroadmapbooks.com

Please contact us at:
Mussio Ventures Ltd.
Unit 106- 1500 Hartley Ave,
Coquitlam, BC, V3K 7A1

Email: updates@backroadmapbooks.com
P: 604-521-6277 toll free 1-877-520-5670
F: 604-521-6260 , www.backroadmapbooks.com

Welcome

Welcome to the second edition of the Southwestern BC Fishing Mapbook. Those of you familiar with our previous edition will find this book a radically different experience. This book is the latest in our continuing quest to produce the perfect fishing guide. The biggest change you will notice is the inclusion of bathymetric charts for all the lakes that we have included. This means that we have not included every single lake that is fishable, choosing instead to focus on the best.

Of course, different people have different definitions of what defines the perfect fishing experience. Some people love fast and furious action. They'd rather snag 100 small fish in a day than spend time waiting around for the big one. Others would rather sit patiently waiting for The One. Some people prefer bar fishing for salmon, sitting with a dozen other anglers and shooting the breeze; catching a fish is almost secondary to the experience. Still others enjoy the pure fly-fishing experience, standing knee deep in a fast flowing mountain stream searching for trout and the experience is sullied somehow if there is another angler within 5 kilometres.

As a result, there is a vast diversity in the lakes and rivers we present here, from urban fishing lakes where catchable-sized rainbow provide fast and furious action to hike-in lakes that are at least a day's walk from the nearest road and where the trout might see only a handful of anglers all season.

The other major change with this book is that we've re-drawn the boundaries to include lakes and streams in the Thompson Nicola. This effectively doubles the size of the area covered, but not to worry; we've also (more than) doubled the size of the book.

Southwestern BC is a vast area, stretching from the Lower Mainland north past Pemberton and east to Manning Park, then north to include Merritt, Kamloops and Wells Gray Provincial Park. The waterbodies in this area are comprised of two fishing regions: Region 2 and Region 3.

Region 2 offers some of the most scenic lakes in the province. The wet climate, spectacular coastal mountains and the deep, dark lakes makes the scenery as much of the fishing experience as the fishing. To compliment the surroundings, there is an abundance of small trout allowing fishermen of all ages to enjoy a successful outing. Whether you are an ardent fly fisherman or prefer the ol' fashion bait and bobber, there is surprisingly good lake fishing very close to the urban centres.

In addition to the lakes, we have included a sampling of some of the best rivers in Region 2. The Fraser is arguably the world's most important salmon river, the Pitt offers some of the best river fishing in the world, and the Vedder/Chilliwack is easily the most popular fishing river in the province. Add to these three a handful of other rivers, and you have some of the best river fishing in the world.

Region 3, on the other hand, is not known for its river fishing. While the Thompson is considered the best steelheading river in the world, it is the exception that proves the rule. But the lake fishing here is unbelievable. The Bonaparte Plateau is a world class trout fishing destination, and the lakes here offer some of the finest fishing around. Due to the abundance of nutrient rich alkaline waters in this region, fish are faster growing and achieve larger sizes then the coastal lakes.

In choosing any waterbody, a review of the fishing regulations is a must. The lakes and streams are heavily regulated to ensure that the fish stocks are not significantly depleted and remain healthy for years to come.

Since a lot of the lakes require you to weave your way through a maze of backroads, we recommend you pick up a copy of the *Vancouver, Coast & Mountains Backroad Mapbook* and the *Thompson Okanagan BC Backroad Mapbook*. These books have detailed maps along with descriptions on everything from camping areas to other fishing opportunities. They are the perfect compliment to the Fishing Mapbook series.

History

The Fishing Mapbook Series evolved from research done when creating the Backroad Mapbook Series. The authors and researchers really enjoy exploring and fishing new lakes but didn't always know where to start. After stumbling across the depth charts for a few lakes, they learned how to read a lake a lot quicker and have been able to fish that much more effectively.

In their travels, they get a chance to explore a lot of new lakes and streams. The visual information provided in the depth charts and river maps help the researchers find the best place to fish time and time again. They figured if they found these charts that useful, other anglers would too.

Mussio Ventures Ltd. was not the first company to see the value of depth charts. Other companies were producing individual lake charts and selling them for a premium. In typical entrepreneurial fashion, Russell and Wesley Mussio took it one step further. Rather than selling individual charts, they put several lakes in a single book and added valuable information on everything from directions and facilities to fishing tips and stocking information. They also priced the book reasonably.

Today, the series have evolved into even bigger books and now cover the more popular streams in the area. Working with key people in the industry has also helped gain more valuable insight into fishing the various lakes and rivers covered in each book.

Russell & Wesley Mussio - Founders of Backroad Mapbooks

Regional Boundaries

Lake Chart Classifications:

⁺⁺⁺	Rocks	▢	Sandbar
☙	Swamp / Marsh	▢	Provincial Park
→	Stream	▱	Lake
▬▬▬	Highway	———	Side Road
═══	Main Road	-----	Old Road/Trail
┼┼┼	Railways	━━━	Management Zones

Recreational Activities and Miscellaneous

Wheelchair	Hiking	Dock/Wharf	Anchorage
Parking	Boat Launch	Beacons	Viewpoint
Swimming	Biking	Waterfall	View
Paddling	Picnic Area	Lodge / B&B	Community
Float Plane Access		Resort	Dam
Highway, Primary		Point of Interest	
Highway, Secondary		Truck Only Campground	
Highway, Trans-Canada		Trail or Water Access Campsite	
		Trailer and Tent Campground	

Conservation Officer Service District Offices

Chilliwack:	1-800-731-6373
Powell River:	604-485-3612
Sechelt:	1-800-731-6373
Surrey:	1-800-731-6373
Squamish:	1-800-731-6373
Clearwater:	250-674-3722
Kamloops:	250-371-6281
Lillooet:	250-256-4636
Merritt:	250-378-8489

Regions 2 & 3 - Lower Mainland & Thompson

Fish and Wildlife Regional Office

Surrey: 10470-152nd St.,V3R 0Y3, 604-582-5200

Fraser Valley Trout Hatchery

Abbotsford: 34345 Vye Rd,V2S 4N2, 604-504-4709

Fish and Wildlife Regional Office

Kamloops: 1259 Dalhousie Dr.,V2C 5Z5, 250-371-6200

Clearwater Trout Hatchery

Clearwater: 40 East Old N. Thompson Hwy,V0E 1N0, 250-674-2580

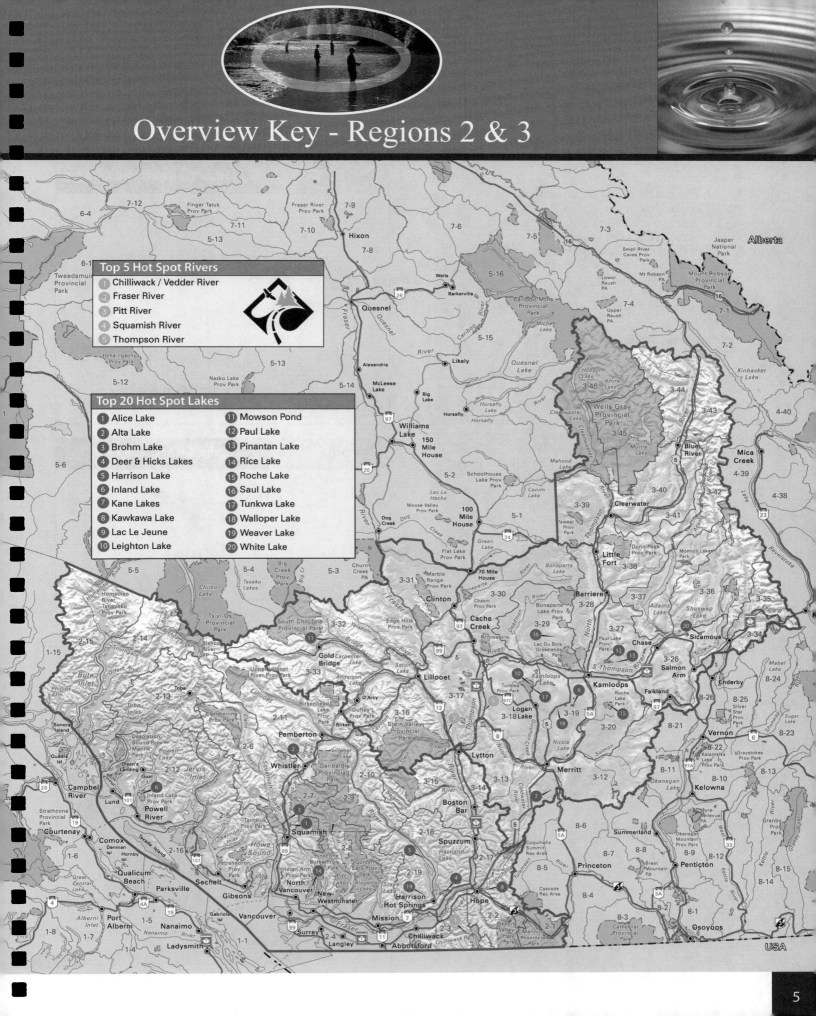

Top 5 Hot Spot Rivers

1. Chilliwack / Vedder River
2. Fraser River
3. Pitt River
4. Squamish River
5. Thompson River

Top 20 Hot Spot Lakes

1. Alice Lake
2. Alta Lake
3. Brohm Lake
4. Deer & Hicks Lakes
5. Harrison Lake
6. Inland Lake
7. Kane Lakes
8. Kawkawa Lake
9. Lac Le Jeune
10. Leighton Lake
11. Mowson Pond
12. Paul Lake
13. Pinantan Lake
14. Rice Lake
15. Roche Lake
16. Saul Lake
17. Tunkwa Lake
18. Walloper Lake
19. Weaver Lake
20. White Lake

How to use this Mapbook

Fish Species

The book begins with a rather elaborate section on the main sportfish species in the region. In it we give pointers on how to identify and fish for these sometimes elusive fish. These tips should not be overlooked, as they are an accumulation of many years of personal experience and research. Of course there are many anglers out there that know a lot more than we do, but few sources put it all together in such a convenient, compact package. Whether you are new to the area or new to fishing or have fished these holes for years, we guarantee that following these tips will help you find more fish.

The Lakes (Bathometric Charts)

The lake fishing section of this book features all of the favourites as well as some of those lesser know lakes that can produce that lifetime fishing memory. With so many lakes to choose from, the task was indeed a challenge to try to get that right mix in our book.

Similar to this book's predecessors, Fishing BC Okanagan and Kootenays, we have highlighted many of the better lakes with depth charts. These charts, if read properly will help you pinpoint the likely areas on a lake to start fishing. These charts show the contours of the lake and help readers figure out where the shoals, drop-offs, hidden islands or basically any sort of water structure that will likely hold fish is located. Reviewing these charts before visiting the lake for the first time could reveal where to find the fish. At the very least, they will help you know where to start fishing.

We have also included the fish species and whether they are stocked or not for each listing. In some cases we even tell you how and what to fish with. If there are no fishing tips included under the individual listing, you can refer to the front or back of the book to refresh yourself on tactics and fly patterns of the prominent species in that lake. Of course, when you get to the lake and there are other anglers there do not be shy to ask where to fish and what to use. Most people are more than willing to help out.

Rivers & Streams

The river or streams section is new to the series, but follows the similar pattern of including fish tips, access and facilities for each stream that is highlighted. Of course, the river maps are a popular feature that include fishing pools and popular access points where possible.

Fishing Tips & Techniques

Near the back of the book this is another excellent resource to refer to. In this section, we give pointers on how to fish using the various lake and stream fishing techniques, as well as some useful fishing tips. Constant referral to this section will help anglers new and old to the sport.

Overview Map and Index

There are also handy planning tools such as the Overview Map and an Index. If you know the waterbody you are planning on visiting, you simply turn to the lakes or river section and find the listing you are interested in. Alternatively, you can look it up in the index to see what page it is listed on.

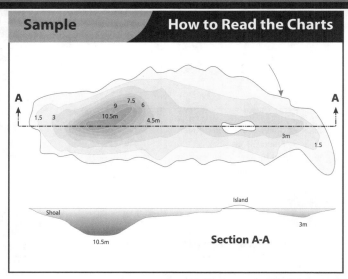

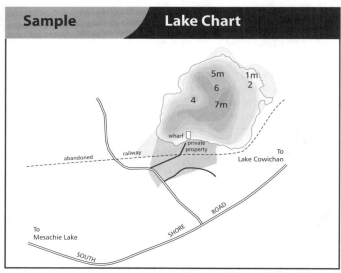

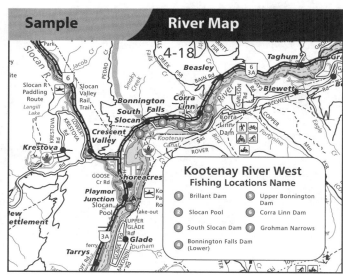

Fish Species

Southwestern BC has a good variety of species of fish and some of the most important salmon and steelhead runs in the world. The breadth and variety of fish species that can be found here is a testament to how good the fishing can be. We have listed the main sportfish found in the region, along with tips on how and when to fish for each species.

Burbot (Ling Cod) are a large bottom feeder that used to be a common sportfish. Over fishing has drastically affected the numbers and size and many lakes are now catch and release only for this tasty fish. Ling cod are an ugly fish that is easily recognized by their large mouth and long brown body with sharp fins. Jigging near creek mouths can produce the odd cod to 4 kg (10 lbs) in the larger water bodies. However, in the southern Interior, they are most frequently caught through the ice.

Chinook are the largest of the Pacific Salmon. They can reach an impressive 27 kg (60 lbs) on occasion. These fish are recognized by their black mouths and spots on their back. They enter the Fraser as early as March and various runs carry through to November. June to early September is usually the peak period in most rivers.

The classic bar fishing set up for big rivers like the Fraser is a 10 foot or longer rod, a level wind reel with at least 30 pound test, rod holder and lawn chair. Cast into about 2 m (4 to 8 ft) of water with the current slow enough that rig will hold up. You rig should consist of a barrel swivel 30 cm (12-16 in) above the weight. The main line should hold the large lead weight with a wire standoff. The lure is often a #8 red Spin-N-Glo suspended just off the bottom. Don't forget the bell and the lawn chair.

In smaller rivers, casting or drift fishing with cured roe into deep holes seems to be the most effective methods. If trout are cleaning the hook of bait, switch to lures, wool (white, red or pink) or flies. Lures of choice include a Kitimat spoon or Spin-N-Glos. Woolly Buggers, Egg Sucking Leeches or Marabou Eggs dead drifted are good flies to try.

Chum salmon can be found in most rivers from late September until late November. Often referred to as dog salmon, they prefer fast, shallow water and colour quickly when they enter fresh water. They are the second largest Pacific Salmon, averaging 5–9 kg (12-20 lbs). Flies such as a '52 Buick (a small, green shrimp imitation) or big Marabou flies (green, pink or orange) with or without bead heads work well on a slow steady retrieve. You will need heavy gear to fish these strong, acrobatic fish. Alternatively, float fishing with pink worms or bottom bouncing wool or lures with pink in them can also be very effective.

Coho are the most prized of all river run salmon. These silver fish are identified by their white mouths and spots on their tail and their acrobatic nature makes them a joy to catch. They average 2-5 kg (5-10 lbs). On most rivers, you can use lighter line, while smaller floats and lighter weights are essential since Coho are easily spooked. Look for them to run quickly from the deep pools and structure when the water raises and clarity of the river is reduced.

Coho can be caught by drift fishing wool or bait (salmon eggs or roe). Spincasters should try size 4 or 5 spinners (Blue Fox or Mepps) cast upstream and worked through slower edges of pools. Spoons such as Gibbs Ironhead, Pen Tac's BC Steel and a Little Cleo with 2/0 hook are other popular spincasting gear. Coho will only chase moving flies, Rolled Muddlers and Harrison Fiords are local favourites. Working with a size 4 to 8 gold or silver Muddler Minnow, Mickey Finn or beaded Woolly Bugger can also be dynamite. Try olive colours on bright days and brighter colours on darker days.

Cutthroat Trout get their name from the red slash under their jaw. You will find both resident and sea run cutthroat in rivers and lakes. Resident cutthroat are usually found in the 25–50 cm (10–20 in) range. They are predatory fish that feed extensively on kokanee, sculpins and sticklebacks. If baitfish aren't present, they will survive quite nicely on insects. The most productive times of the year to fish for cutthroat are during the salmon fry migration from March through May and the stickleback spawn in July through September. A fly imitating a baitfish is a good choice when baitfish are present. Muddler Minnow or Wool Head Sculpin are two such patterns to try. Cast around the drop-off areas as the cutthroat tend

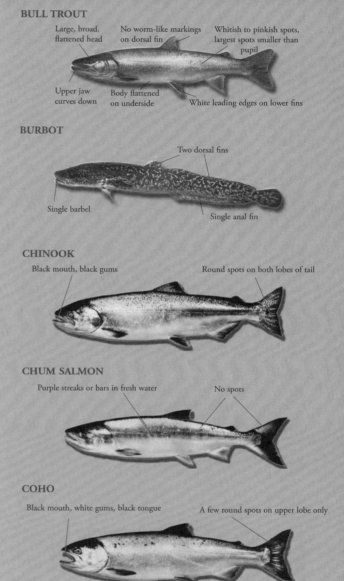

to cruise the near shore area in search of baitfish.

Sea-run cutthroat are often bigger and run in schools, chasing spawning salmon. In the spring they feast on the salmon fry. Look for feeding activity and cast across the current slightly downstream. Fly-anglers should use a floating line with a long leader and weighted fly. During the fall, they'll grab salmon eggs or anything close. Attractor patterns, such as Woolly Buggers and sparkle leeches are good bets in winter when food is scarce. Fishing the estuaries or beaches is an art that requires good knowledge of when the tides are moving. It is also essential to match the size and colour of the eggs the cutthroat are chasing.

Dolly Varden & Bull Trout are often-confused with bull trout. They are both members of the char family and recognized by the pinkish spots on the body. Dollies are more common in coastal areas and can reach up to 6.5 kg (14 lbs) in bigger lakes and the sea run stream version have been known to

Fish Species

CUTTHROAT TROUT

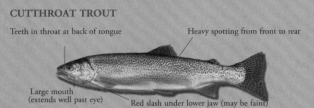

Teeth in throat at back of tongue

Heavy spotting from front to rear

Large mouth (extends well past eye)

Red slash under lower jaw (may be faint)

DOLLY VARDEN

No worm-like markings on dorsal fin

Oval, snake-like body

Whitish to pinkish spots, largest spots smaller than pupil

Head does not dominate body

White leading edges on lower fins

EASTERN BROOK TROUT

Red spots with blue halos

Worm-like markings on back and dorsal fin

Pinkish-orange paired fins edged in white

KOKANEE

No distinct black spots on sides

Long anal fin (13 or more rays)

LAKE TROUT

Worm-like markings on back and dorsal fin

Tail deeply forked

top 9 kg (20 lbs). Bull trout are also noted for having a large head and are found in bigger Interior lakes and streams. Both prefer cold, clean water and spawn in fall.

Their primary diet is insects, eggs and small fish. Troll a green or orange Flatfish or a Krocodile lure. Trolling plugs or larger lures on a downrigger with a flasher can produce big fish. Fishing the creek mouths with bait balls (a large cluster of worms or cured roe) suspended near the bottom can be deadly. Also, jigging with a bucktail and flasher in the winter or spring near a large creek mouth can be very successful.

These fish are slow growing and particularly vulnerable to over fishing. As a result, tough regulations have been imposed in an effort to maintain the resource.

Eastern Brook Trout are actually char that were first introduced into BC in the early 1900s. They are found in many of the cooler streams and smaller mountain lakes, as they can survive harsher conditions than other trout. Easily identified by the large number of speckles (and sometimes called speckled trout), they are good fighters and very tasty.

Brookies feed on insects and shrimp. Fly-fishing is a popular method using chironomids in the spring and various nymph patterns in summer. During their fall spawning period, attractor type flies like a Doc Spratley or Woolly Bugger can be very effective. Spincasters should try a small Deadly Dick tipped with worm or Flatfish. They are also a popular fish for ice fishing with bait, as they typically remain quite active through the winter.

Kokanee (a word that means 'red fish') are actually landlocked sockeye salmon. They are easily recognizable by their slim silver bodies and forked tail. Kokanee turn a brilliant red when they spawn in the late summer. In the plankton-rich interior lakes, they can reach 3 kg (5 lbs), although that is rare.

Kokanee are best caught on a Willow Leaf with a short leader and a Wedding Band or Dick Nite and maggot. Troll as slow as possible and in an "S" pattern so your line, will speed up or slow down and change depths as you round the bend. This entices the fish to bite. Trolling with one ounce of weight or less, which takes the lure to 5–15 m (15 to 45 ft), is the most productive. An exciting alternative is to try to catch kokanee on a fly. In the spring, chironomids and mayflies can yield surprising results.

Lake Trout are another misnamed char. They are only found in large, deep and cold lakes. They grow very slowly but often reach sizes in excess of 10 kg (25 lbs), since they live longer than most other fish species. Fish to 3 kg (5 lb) are quite common. Lakers are a fall spawning fish and are recognized by their forked tail, long head and large snout as well as an abundance of spots. Lake trout are not great fighters, but they do have a lot of mass, and there's something special about catching a fish that big.

Lakers are best caught on the troll with silver spoons or spinners, which imitate the fish's main food source, the minnow. These fish stay near the surface during the early spring and late fall when the water temperatures are cold. In the summer, the fish retreat to the depths of the lake so it is best to troll deep during summer months. A downrigger helps. Ice fishing for the big fish can be quite effective, although the big lakes rarely freeze in BC. During winter, lakers can be found closer to the surface and they readily hit small spoons tipped with minnows.

Largemouth Bass are found in the shallow, low-lying lakes, mostly tucked up against the US border. These waterbodies are often too warm to support extensive trout populations, and have been stocked (usually illegally) to provide an alternative fishery. In lakes with largemouth bass, top water lures and flies can create a frenzy of action. Plastic jigs or any minnow imitation lure or fly can also be productive. Largemouth bass generally grow larger than its cousin, the smallmouth bass.

Pink Salmon are the smallest of the Pacific Salmon and rarely reach over 2.5 kg (5 lbs). Also known as humpies, they develop a large, prominent hump and hooked mouth in freshwater. Pinks fade quickly in fresh water, so it is best to fish them closer to the estuary to find bright, hard fighting fish. They are the perfect fish to learn how to fly-fish with due to their preference for shallow water with medium currents. They return every two years (2009, 2011, etc in BC). The peak of the run usually occurs in early September. Fly-fishing for pinks has become very popular. Getting them to bite, as opposed to fowl hooking them, requires drifting a fly or lure dead slow allowing it to bump along the bottom. Use anything with pink in it.

Rainbow Trout are native to many streams and lakes in British Columbia. Due to their hardy nature and the fact they are an excellent sportfish, they are stocked throughout the province. Rainbow get their name from the colourful strip they get when spawning in the spring. The mainstay of their diet in many lakes and rivers are small shrimp (scuds), leeches and insects, but they will also eat small baitfish if given the opportunity. During spawning season, they are quite fond

of free-floating eggs.

The fish varies in size depending on the waterbody and strain you catch. The Kamloops area is famous for its Pennask strain, which are hard fighting acrobats that like to leap high into the air to shake the lure. These fish range from 0.5–2.5 kg (1–5 lbs) really like their insects, and are part of the reason the Kamloops area is one of the world's great fly-fishing destination. Chironomids are popular early in the season, but are replaced by mayflies, damselflies, dragonflies and then caddisflies later in the season. Attractor type patterns, such as Woolly Buggers or Doc Spratleys, are also popular. Trout tend to stay hidden in the depths during the day and you will have to fish deeper with a leech or a nymph pattern. In the late evenings, though, top water fishing with dry flies like a Tom Thumb or Elk Hair Caddis offers great excitement.

Also found in the area are the Blackwater strain of rainbows. They are piscivorous, meaning they eat other fish. As a result, they grow big fast. These fish can hit 4.5 kg (10 lbs) or more and what they lack in spirit they make up for in size. The best way to catch these big trout is to use lures that imitate small baitfish. For spincasters, this means a variety of spoons and spinners, while fly anglers usually use patterns like a Muddler Minnow.

Trolling is a popular way to catch trout. Lake trolls with Wedding Band, a silver Dick Nite or Flatfish, Kwikfish or Krocodile spoons or spinners such as Mepps or Panther Martin can all entice the rainbow to bite. Tipping the hook with bait, single eggs or Powerbait is often the trick. Even fly anglers have taken to dragging around a leech or nymph pattern in order to cover more water. But on many lakes, a simple hook with bait and bobber can work just as well as any other method.

Sockeye are good eating and are generally easy to catch. They run in schools and can reach 7 kg (15 lbs) in size, but generally less than half that size. They have diamond-like scales and prominent eyes that make them one of the easiest salmon to identify. Look for them to begin entering the rivers in June, but it is not until late July that the bigger runs arrive. The sockeye fishery lasts until mid-September.

Sockeye prefer current seams and riffles on downstream sides of gravel bars. During early morning and evening they can be in less than 1.5 m (4 ft) of water, but go deeper in the day. Bottom bouncing is the preferred fishing method. A 9-foot rod with a level wind reel and 15 lb test is all you need. Use light enough weight to bounce every three feet or so. Fish the slots between fast and slow water in no more than a few feet of water, using either fluorescent wool or a size 12 green Spin-N-Glo.

In addition to bottom bouncing from shore, anglers can have luck drift fishing by using a float and bait (pink krill or Ghost Shrimp). Fly-fishing for sockeye requires an 8-weight rod with short leaders (5-7 ft) and 10-12 lb tippet on high density sink tip lines. Cast the fly directly across the current allowing it to sink and skip on the bottom. Small size 8 green flies are preferred, although in murky waters you will need bigger flies with a bit of sparkle.

Steelhead are the most prized sportfish in British Columbia and can get as large as 9 kg (20 lbs). They are a sea-run version of rainbow trout known for their acrobatics and fight. Steelhead are notoriously difficult to catch. The trick is to vary the presentation depending on the season and water conditions. Steelhead like slow presentations so the quicker the water, the bigger the lure.

They hold in shallow water close to shore. Fish close to the bottom and cast above holding areas. Drift fishing with a float suspending a ¼" pencil lead weight above a short leader of about 30–50 cm (12–20 in) with 1/0–#4 hooks is the most common method. However, many anglers bottom bounce. Wool (pink or orange) and a single egg is the most popular attractor. Popular lures include Corkys, Spin-N-Glos, Gooey Bobs and Colorado Spinners.

Fly-fishing for steelhead, especially in the Thompson River, is incredibly popular. Marabou patterns like the Popsicle, small Muddler Minnows or weighted leech patterns are popular. Floating lines and long leaders with a dry fly like a Grease Liner can produce the fish of a lifetime. In deeper pools, work a weighted stonefly

LARGEMOUTH BASS

Large wide lower jaw slightly longer than the upper jaw

The anal and pelvic fins are green to olive with some white

PINK SALMON

White mouth, black gums

Large oval spots

Tiny scales

Dirty white belly in fresh water

RAINBOW TROUT

Small black spots mostly restricted to above the lateral line

Radiating rows of spots on tail

No teeth in throat at back of tongue

SOCKEYE

Large scales

Small black speckles

No spots

STEELHEAD

Fork length 50 cm or more

No teeth in throat at back of tongue

or size 10 Glo Bug along the bottom using a sink tip line and short leader.

Steelhead are heavily regulated and regulations are subject to change on short notice.

Whitefish are a silvery fish with large scales. They spawn in the fall and give a good fight even in the winter. They can reach 50 cm (20 in) but average half that. They are not a popular fish, because they are quite boney and they don't offer the same acrobatics as trout. They feed mainly on insects and will readily strike spinners, spoons or other shinny lures. Fly-fishing can also be effective, especially in the spring during the mayfly hatch.

Message From Brian Chan

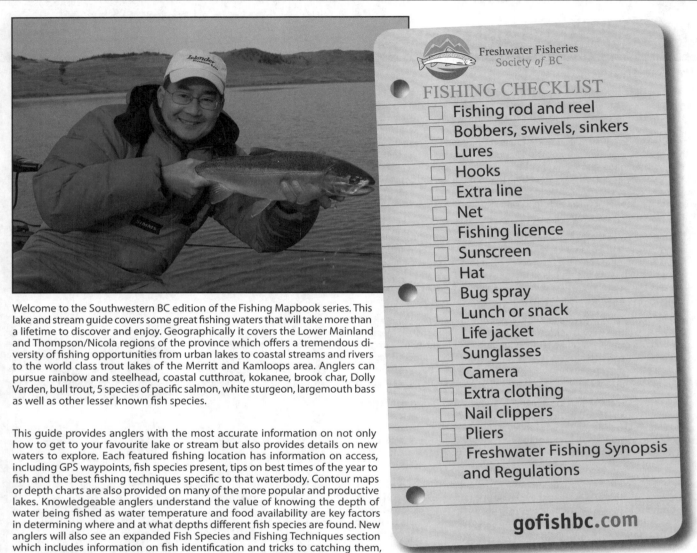

Welcome to the Southwestern BC edition of the Fishing Mapbook series. This lake and stream guide covers some great fishing waters that will take more than a lifetime to discover and enjoy. Geographically it covers the Lower Mainland and Thompson/Nicola regions of the province which offers a tremendous diversity of fishing opportunities from urban lakes to coastal streams and rivers to the world class trout lakes of the Merritt and Kamloops area. Anglers can pursue rainbow and steelhead, coastal cutthroat, kokanee, brook char, Dolly Varden, bull trout, 5 species of pacific salmon, white sturgeon, largemouth bass as well as other lesser known fish species.

This guide provides anglers with the most accurate information on not only how to get to your favourite lake or stream but also provides details on new waters to explore. Each featured fishing location has information on access, including GPS waypoints, fish species present, tips on best times of the year to fish and the best fishing techniques specific to that waterbody. Contour maps or depth charts are also provided on many of the more popular and productive lakes. Knowledgeable anglers understand the value of knowing the depth of water being fished as water temperature and food availability are key factors in determining where and at what depths different fish species are found. New anglers will also see an expanded Fish Species and Fishing Techniques section which includes information on fish identification and tricks to catching them, choosing the right rod and reel or fly gear, as well as common fishing methods and tackle. There is even proper fish handling techniques in this section.

The Freshwater Fisheries Society of BC has partnered with Backroad Mapbooks on the production of the Fishing Mapbook series, as one of our strategic objectives is to inform and educate the public about fish and recreational fishing. Guidebooks are an important tool in achieving this goal. Other Society activities include delivering Learn to Fish programs for children and families, developing community fisheries within urban areas through our Fishing in the City program, promoting the Fishing Buddies program to help attract even more new and lapsed anglers to sport fishing and improving access to fishing waters. Our major responsibility is delivery of the provincial fish stocking program and many of the lakes covered in this guide are stocked on a regular basis to ensure a sustainable recreational fishery. Up to date stocking records for all waterbodies stocked in the province and additional information on other society activities is available our website www.gofishbc.com.

This Fishing Mapbook covers a range of fishing locations from easily accessible small stocked lakes to popular Lower Mainland rivers to more remote lakes and streams to waters that are only accessible by walking. Detailed information is also provided on a number of quality river fisheries that should be on every angler's "must fish" list. The southwest area of the province provides a tremendous diversity of fishing opportunities so that day trips to weekend getaways to summer long vacations are all possible. This guidebook will be an important part of planning your fishing trips for many years to come so get out and Go Fish BC!

Brian Chan
Fishing Ambassador
Freshwater Fisheries Society of BC

| Location: 30 km north of Chase |
| Elevation: 412 m (1,351 ft) |
| Surface Area: 13,760 ha (34,000 ac) |
| Max Depth: 397 m (1,302 ft) |
| Mean Depth: 169 m (554 ft) |
| Way Point: 51° 10′ 00″ N, 119° 35′ 00″ W |

Adams Lake

Fishing

Adams Lake is a popular fishing and vacation destination north of Chase. It is a big, beautiful lake that is approximately 63 km (39 mi) long and up to 3.2 km wide. It is second deepest lake in BC next to Quesnel Lake and feed by many tributaries including the Upper Adams River, Momich River and Bush Creek. Anglers will find good fishing for rainbow and kokanee as well as deeper holding bull trout and lake trout and the odd whitefish. Linked to the famous Adams River, there are also Chinook, Coho and of course sockeye in the big lake, although there is no fishery for salmon in Adams Lake.

Being a big cold lake, Adams Lake is best trolled. It is not the most productive lake, but there are some big fish to be found. Bull trout over 8 kg (18 lbs) and rainbow in the 40-60 cm (16-24 in) range are not uncommon. Most anglers prefer to fish for the rainbow by trolling Apex or Flatfish lures. However, there is some success with flies like bucktails, Doc Spratleys and whatever is hatching. Rainbow are usually found closer to the surface depending on the wind. If there is a nice chop on the lake, use lighter weight, but if it is calm use heaver weight or a downrigger.

If you are looking for the bigger bull and lake trout, you will need to get deeper. Frog pattern Apex on a downrigger have been known to lure some big fish here. Similarly, the kokanee also hold deeper than on most lakes.

The better action is usually found around the river and creek mouths, especially in fall. Other hot spots include working the middle between Honeymoon Bay and the Momich River or even the log booms at the south end of the lake

A word of warning, if the wind picks up get off the lake quickly. The steep, narrow valley funnels the wind making for very hazardous conditions on the water.

Directions

Resting north of Chase and east of Kamloops, Adams Lake is found off Highway 1. Look for signed turn off and follow the Squilax- Anglemont Road north to Holdings Road. Continue another 10 km or so to the south end of the long lake and the small mill town of Adams Lake. Beyond here, the road turns to gravel and takes you past Bush Creek, Skwaam Bay and so on. It is about 72 km to the north end of the lake, where it is possible to loop south on the east side of the lake to access more recreation sites and the mouth of the Momich River. Beyond the Momich, the road starts to deteriorate.

Note this is an active industry area. Use caution when travelling the gravel roads and yield to logging trucks.

Facilities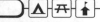

Although there is a bit of development at the south end of the lake, most of the north end is surrounded by Crown land. Visitors will find a store with basic supplies and boat launch in town as well as a number of parks and recreation sites from which to base your stay. Perhaps the most popular is the **Adams Lake (Bush Creek) Provincial Park site** near the south end of the lake offering 33 sites, a nice beach and boat launch. There are also boat access only marine parks at **Spillman Beach**, **Poplar Point** and **Refuge Bay** as well as the **Momich River Campsite** at the northeast end of the lake.

The impressive recreation site system offers sites at **Skwaam Bay**, **Sandy Point**, **Honeymoon Bay**, **Rocky Point**, **Gordon Bay** and **Tsikwustum Cree**k. These sites range in size from 4 campsites to 30 sites and offer boat launches and good shore access. Sandy Bay and Honeymoon Bay are two of the more popular and bigger sites with plenty of room for RV's.

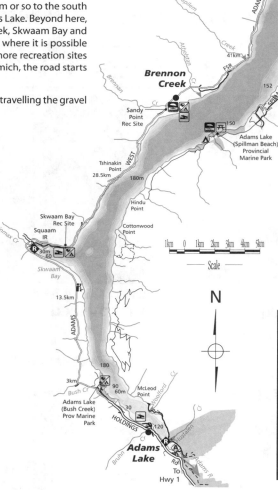

www.backroadmapbooks.com

Alice Lake

Location: 13 km (8 mi) north of Squamish
Elevation: 190 m (623 ft)
Surface Area: 11.48 ha (28.4 ac)
Max Depth: 16.8 m (55 ft)
Mean Depth: 9.8 m (32 ft)
Way Point: 49° 46' 44.2" N, 123° 7' 15.6" W

Fishing

Alice Lake is a very popular recreation lake with a large, grassy picnic site and two sandy beaches. It is a good place to bring a family to try to catch a small trout in the spring or swim and sunbath in the summer.

The lake has Dolly Varden as well as rainbow and cutthroat. The fish, particularly the rainbow, remain small (a 30 cm/12 inch fish would be a good-sized catch) but numerous.

The lake is stocked with catchable-sized rainbow for the family fishing weekend in spring, but by summer, the surface becomes quite warm, while the deeper waters suffer from low oxygen levels. This makes the fish extremely sluggish and even if you were to find one willing to take to your lure, it wouldn't put up much of a fight. Fishing is best left to the spring or fall during which time casting a fly, bait fishing or trolling a small lure are good choices. The best time to fly-fish is during the black ant hatch in May. That is not to say that other fly patterns do not work throughout the spring and into the fall.

A trail circles the lake allowing for access to shore fishing. Shore fishing has been improved by the Parks Branch, who have made a number of deadfall trees into floating wharfs ideal for casting. The man-made wharf at the east end is a good spot to try but it is closed to fishing from May 15 to September 1.

Small spoons and spoons work well for spincasting, as does a rubber grub on a small hook. Remember, the fish are small here, so use light tackle. Trolling a fly behind a rowboat or float tube is another popular method used here.

The pothole lake is deepest in the middle and has fairly murky water. The small inflow creeks near the drop-off on the south side of the lake are worth trying.

Area Indicator

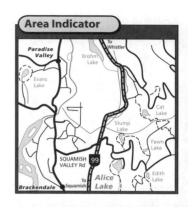

Alice Lake			
Fish Stocking Data			
Year	Species	Number	Life Stage
2011	Rainbow Trout	500	Catchable
2010	Rainbow Trout	500	Catchable
2009	Rainbow Trout	500	Catchable

Directions

Alice Lake is easily located off of the Sea to Sky Highway (Highway 99). Simply follow the signs north of Squamish. The lake is about 800 metres off the main highway. Turn right to access the day use area or stay left to reach the campground.

Facilities

Alice Lake Provincial Park s a beautiful park that offers over 100 campsites, including 55 with electric hook-ups. Most of the sites can hold trailers/campers but there are some walk-in sites reserved for tenters. The campsites are located in a second growth hemlock/cedar forest nearby to the lake. There are flush toilets, outhouses, hot showers and firewood available for the camper. Other facilities in the park include a picnic area, a wharf and two beaches. Reservations are recommended.

Other Options

Stump, **Edith** and **Fawn** Lakes all require a short hike from Alice Lake with Stump Lake being the best of the walk-in lakes. Fawn, unfortunately is reported to be barren as it is no longer stocked. The **Four Lake Walk**, a 6.5km (2–3hr) well developed trail, leads past the lakes providing a leisurely stroll through a second growth forest and easy access for fishermen. The trail, except for a short uphill climb to the bench where Edith and Fawn Lakes are located, has little elevation gain.

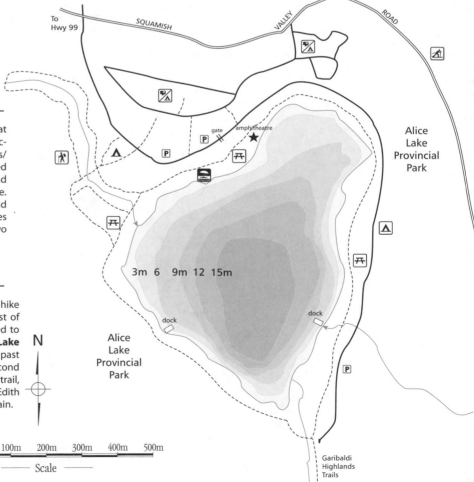

Alice
Lake
Provincial
Park

To Hwy 99

SQUAMISH VALLEY ROAD

gate
amphitheatre

3m 6 9m 12 15m

dock

dock

Alice
Lake
Provincial
Park

N

Garibaldi
Highlands
Trails

100m 0 100m 200m 300m 400m 500m
— Scale —

Location: 54 km (33 mi) southwest of Clearwater
Elevation: 1,246 m (4,089 ft)
Surface Area: 157 ha (389 ac)
Max Depth: 17.7 m (58 ft)
Mean Depth: 6.7 m (22 ft)
Way Point: 51° 13' 43" N, 120° 21' 5" W

Allan Lake

Area Indicator

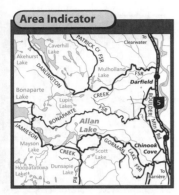

Fishing

Found on the Bonaparte Plateau, Allan Lake is a medium sized lake that is best known for its whitefish. While we wouldn't call Allan Lake ugly, it is not one of the prettiest lakes up on the plateau. And compared to trout, whitefish are not the most popular sportfish. While they are a scrappy fighter and quite tasty eating, they are a boney fish and most people just don't want to go through the hassle of deboning them.

That's two strikes against the lake. Fortunately, for those anglers who like fishing for whitefish (and there are a few, judging by the crowds the lake attracts in the summer), the aggressive fish offer a good fishing experience throughout the year.

The lake is fairly deep, getting down to 15 metres (50 feet) at its deepest point, with a large, shallow, tree-filled bay that starts in the lake's northeastern corner. While the Allan Lake Recreation Site is found at the south end of the bay, whitefish generally prefer to stick to deeper water and anglers will need a boat or float tube to get out to the main body of the lake.

There are some good shoals towards the southwest end of the lake, as well as a nice drop-off. This is the usual starting point for fishing the lake. In the spring, fly anglers can catch the whitefish cruising these shoals during the many hatches the lake features: chironomid, mayflies, damselflies and dragonflies. Later on in the year, the fish do like to retreat to deeper water and are best caught using a deep jig or trolling with a downrigger.

Whitefish have small, tender mouths and are usually caught using small hooks. Try using size #0 Mepps or Blue Fox with bait, trolling very slowly. Whitefish are not known for their solid hits. Given the chance, a whitefish will slowly suck the bait off your hook, making it sometimes difficult to detect when you have a hit. Once snagged, though, whitefish put up a determined fight.

In winter, ice fishing for whitefish is quite popular. Jigging a Williams Whitefish spoon can be effective.

Directions

Allan Lake is located on the Bonaparte Plateau. To get to the lake, take the Yellowhead Highway (Highway 5) to Barriere. On the north side of the Thompson River bridge, turn onto Westsyde Road and at the first major intersection turn right/north. This road turns into the Gorman Lake Forest Service Road. You will pass Gorman Lake itself and then at about 17.5 km (10.9 miles), turn right onto the unmarked Scott Lake Forest Service Road. From here, it is only a couple kilometres to the recreation site at the southeast end of the lake.

The lake is about 20 km (12 miles) from the highway. The road is passable with a 2wd vehicle, but RVs are not recommended.

Facilities

The **Allan Lake Recreation Site** rests on the southeast end of the lake in a shallow, tree-filled bay. There is space for about 6 groups and a handful of picnic tables. There is a cartop boat launch and a dock. The site, like the lake itself, is functional but not exactly attractive. Even so, it is often full, especially on summer weekends.

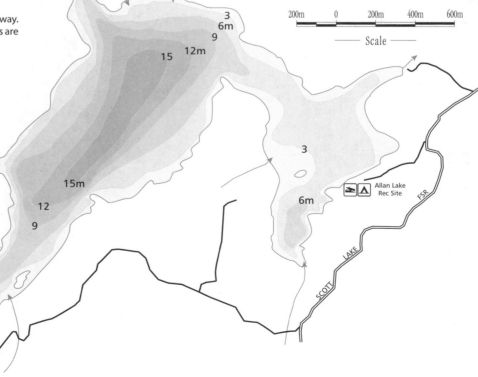

N

200m   0   200m   400m   600m

Scale

3
6m
9
12m
15

15m

12
9

6m

3

Allan Lake
Rec Site

3

6m

SCOTT LAKE FSR

www.backroadmapbooks.com

Location: 13 km (8 mi) northeast of Maple Ridge
Surface Area: 1,643.6 ha (4,061 ac)
Elevation: 125 m (410 ft)
Max Depth: 159 m (522 ft)
Mean Depth: 71.3 m (234 ft)
Way Point: 49° 20′ 7″ N, 122° 24′ 34″ W

Alouette Lake

Area Indicator

Alouette Lake			
Fish Stocking Data			
Year	Species	Number	Life Stage
2010	Cutthroat Trout	5,218	Yearling
2010	Rainbow Trout	84,575	Catchable
2009	Cutthroat Trout	9,508	Catchable

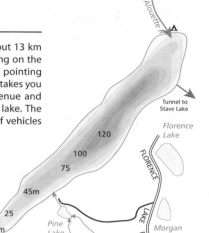

Directions

Alouette Lake is a large lake located about 13 km northeast of Maple Ridge. When travelling on the Lougheed Highway, you will see a sign pointing the way to the provincial park. The route takes you along Dewdney Trunk Road, to 132 Avenue and then finally along Fern Crescent to the lake. The road is paved all the way and all types of vehicles can access the lake.

Golden Ears
Provincial Park

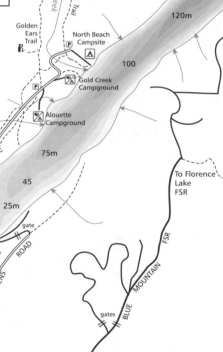

Fishing

This large multi-use lake is also used as a reservoir to produce hydroelectric power. It is damned at the south end and is subject to drawdown as water is piped from the north end into nearby Stave Lake.

Despite its popularity for boating and swimming, the lake is not known for its fishing, despite an intensive cutthroat trout and rainbow trout stocking program and a lake fertilization project that was initiated in 1998 to improve productivity.

The lake has a variety of species—cutthroat trout, rainbow, kokanee, Dolly Varden and lake trout—but it is a big lake and the fish can be hard to find. Therefore, the fishing pressure is comparatively light.

This is the only lake in the Lower Mainland that holds lake trout, remnants of a stocking program in the 1960s. Every year, some lunkers are caught weighting up to 15 kg (33 lbs). The most popular method of fishing is setting up downriggers with larger baitfish imitations such as an Apex, small hoochies, Lyman plugs, Hotshots, or large Flatfish, which are usually trolled 20 metres (60 ft) or deeper.

The rainbow and cutthroat tend to be in the 0.5–1 kg (1–2 lb) range, while the dollies can reach 2 kg (5 lbs). For cutthroat and rainbow try lake troll combinations trailed by worms, Flatfish, or other minnow imitations. Early season trolling with Woolly Buggers, leech patterns and Muddler Minnows on medium to fast sinking fly lines can also be successful. When fishing for kokanee use Wedding Bands and worms or Dick Nite spoons on a slow troll. Work along the drop-offs, at one of the creek estuaries or in one of the many bays.

The deep, deep lake does not warm significantly in the summer so fishing remains steady throughout the year. But the fish tend to be closer to the surface in the spring and fall.

Shore fishing is very limited due to the steep, uninviting shoreline.

Facilities

Golden Ears Provincial Park is a massive park protecting the west side of Alouette Lake. The park is noted by rugged and remote mountain terrain to the north and its multi-use area to the south. Next to Alouette Lake are three different camping areas (Alouette, Gold Creek and North Beach) with over 400 campsites. Within the campgrounds are full facilities including sani-stations, showers and toilets. There is also a picnic area and boat launch at the south end of the lake that also offers a nice swimming beach. An extensive multi-use trail network leads through the southern portion of the park.

© Mussio Ventures Ltd.

Location: 3 km (1.8 mi) southwest of Whistler

Alpha & Nita Lakes

© Mussio Ventures Ltd.

Nita Lake

Elevation: 638 m (2,093 ft)
Surface Area: 11.4 ha (28 ac)
Max Depth: 21.6 m (71 ft)
Mean Depth: 8.8 m (29 ft)
Way Point: 50° 06'00" N, 122° 59' 45" W

Alpha Lake

Elevation: 632 m (2,073 ft)
Surface Area: 15.18 ha (37.5 ac)
Max Depth: 11.6 m (38 ft)
Mean Depth: 4.3 m (14 ft)
Way Point: 50° 05' 33" N, 123° 00' 16" W

Area Indicator

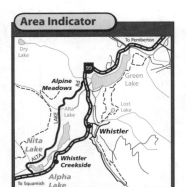

Fishing

Found within the municipality of Whistler, these two lakes are not as busy as one might think. Of the two, Alpha is more popular due in part to big trout that it produces on occasion.

Alpha Lake is a highly productive lake that is stocked annually with catchable rainbow. It also holds good populations of kokanee and Dolly Varden. Springtime finds fish in shallow water, around the beaver ponds at the south end and off the dock around the mouth of Jordan Creek. In June and July, the fish are more spread, while August evenings are known to product good results right off the Jordan Creek dock or rocks of Pine Point Park. If you are fly-fishing from shore try a half-back or green caddis larvae pattern. Spincasters also do well casting small spoons.

Alpha has more structure than most Whistler Lakes. When trolling the west side (the side with the BC Rail line) towards Pine Point Park be aware of old pilings, as many lures have been lost on these submerged structures. The island in the middle of the lake is privately owned, but the drop-off on both sides of the island are hot spots.

There are no real discernible insect hatches on the lake in early spring, so trolling the 3–5 m (10–16 ft) depth with leeches, green Woolly Buggers, a Panther Martin or Wedding Band tipped with a worm is usually the order of the day.

You can also try fly-fishing with small black chironomids in the early season, with the southeast and southwest bays being most productive. Hot days in May bring on the black ant hatch. Caddisfly provide some great evening dry fly-fishing action in late June or early July. Fly patterns such as the Tom Thumb or a Parachute Midge are also good evening bets at this time of year.

Nearby Nita Lake is harder to access and as a result doesn't see as much pressure. Unlike Alpha, it doesn't have a park and shoreline access is limited due to private residences. However, a new fishing dock is in the works. The lake is stocked annually with catchable rainbow, which complement the natural kokanee population. Like Alpha, the small lake has an electric motor only restriction, but most people use tubes to get out onto the water. The best time to fish is in June, right after the lake is stocked.

Directions

These two popular lakes are found in the heart of the Whistler Valley. Access to Alpha Lake is fairly easy, as it sits right beside Highway 99. The best access is from Alpha Lake Park at the southwest end off Lake Placid Road. Nita Lake is also found off Lake Placid Road. However, instead of continuing to Alpha Lake Park, turn right on Karen Creek then another quick left on Drew Drive. That road will lead to the southern shores of the lake.

Facilities

Pine Point and Alpha Lake Parks are small parks that offer picnic facilities and beach access. There is also a casting dock near Jordan Creek on Alpha Lake and one in the works for Nita. The paved **Valley Trail** also provides decent shore access to the lakes.

Nita Lake

To Whistler

To Squamish

dock

19
13m
7

P

Nita Lane

Sea to Sky Highway

99

N

Trail

Valley

DREW Dr

LK PLACID Rd

KAREN CRES

To Squamish

ALTA

LAKE Rd

100m   0   100m   200m   300m   400m   500m
Scale

Alpha Lake

(WESTSIDE)

OLD GRAVEL Rd

LAKE

ALTA

3m
7
10

10
7
3m

dock

Alpha Lake Park

Valley Trail

LAKE PLACID Rd

TAYLOR Rd

To Squamish   Sea to Sky Highway   99

| Nita Lake | | | |
| Fish Stocking Data | | | |
Year	Species	Number	Life Stage
2010	Rainbow Trout	1500	Catchable
2009	Rainbow Trout	1000	Catchable

| Alpha Lake | | | |
| Fish Stocking Data | | | |
Year	Species	Number	Life Stage
2010	Rainbow Trout	500	Catchable
2009	Rainbow Trout	500	Catchable

Alta Lake

Location: Whistler
Elevation: 641 m (2,103 ft)
Surface Area: 100 ha (246 ac)
Max Depth: 24 m (80 ft)
Mean Depth: 9.5 m (31 ft)
Way Point: 50° 06' 54" N, 122° 58' 53" W

Fishing

Before Whistler was Whistler, it was known as Alta Lake, taking its name from this lake, which defines the western boundary of the municipality. The lake drains both east to Lillooet Lake and west to the Cheakamus River.

Great fishing can be found off the public docks that exist at five municipal parks around the lake, with late evenings being very productive. Rainbow, kokanee or bull trout up to 1 kg (2 lbs) as well as cutthroat up to 2.5 kg (5.5 lbs) entice anglers.

To help bolster the fishery, the Freshwater Fishery Society of BC stocks the lake every few years with 4,000 catchable, sterilized cutthroat. Some of these cutthroat reach 46 cm (18 in) within the first year, while reports of fish up to 69 cm (27 in) are caught each year. Rainbow fishing also improved after the cutthroat stocking, with fish up to 50 cm (20 in) in size.

Alta Lake is a fly-angler's paradise. April/early May offers exceptional chironomid fishing off the east side docks. June and July sees action spread out over the lake, with the north end weeds producing regularly. Early season also sees a sizeable caddisfly hatch in the weeds.

During late summer evenings, casting a Tom Thumb or Elk Hair Caddis from any of the docks surrounding the lake can produce a frenzy of action. As does the black ant hatch for those who time it right. This usually happens on the first day over 27° C in May or June. Go deep with type 7 sinking line.

Fishing picks up again in late September and October at the docks with fish returning to shallow water as the impulse to feed before winter returns. Leeches in black, green or brown are local favourites. Rolled Muddler patterns in pink or gold are also effective, while Doc Spratleys in red or black are other favourites.

For spincasters, try the early part of the year by trolling Flatfish, small Apex or Hildebrandt lures from the surface down to the midwater level. As the season progresses try a Dick Nite spoon or any flashy metal lure trolled deep.

Wind can play havoc with smaller craft and there is a maximum 12 km/hr speed restriction on the lake. Anglers should also note the catch and release, single barbless hooks and bait ban restrictions.

Facilities

There is no shortage of public facilities around Alberta Lake. The paved Valley Trail provides walking or biking access to many of the day-use parks as well as the impressive **Fairhurst Fishing Dock in Alta Lake Park** on the west side of the lake. There are numerous park facilities on Alta Lake such as picnic tables, barbecues, washrooms, volleyball courts, seasonal concessions and canoe rentals. **Blueberry Park** also offers a few docks to cast from, while small boats can launch at Carleton Way in the Alta Vista subdivision. For overnight accommodation, the popular tourist town of Whistler has an endless supply of hotels.

Directions

Alta Lake is the largest of the lakes in the Whistler Village area. The lake is seen from Sea to Sky Highway (Highway 99) as you are heading north of Whistler Creekside to the Whistler Village. Just before the village of Whistler, turn left on Hillcrest Drive and follow it for about 300 metres (1000 feet) to the lake.

Alta Lake			
Fish Stocking Data			
Year	Species	Number	Life Stage
2010	Cutthroat Trout	350	Yearling
2009	Cutthroat Trout	1,000	Yearling

Area Indicator

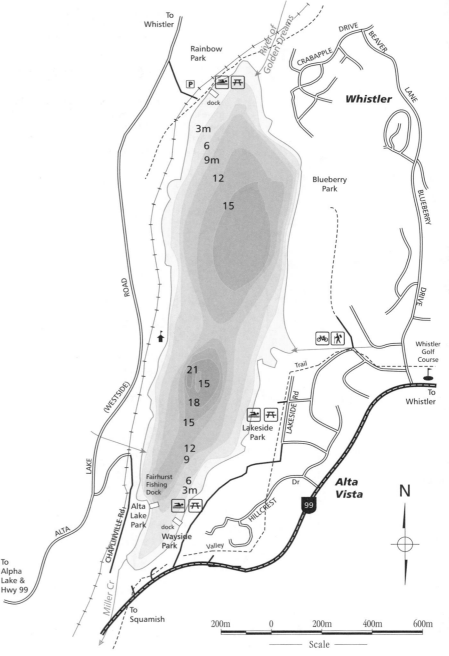

Location: 17 km (10 mi) south of Barrière
Elevation: 1,091 m (3,579 ft)
Surface Area: 56 ha (139 ac)
Max Depth: 15 m (48 ft)
Mean Depth: 4.6 m (15 ft)
Way Point: 51° 2′ 5″ N, 120° 8′ 11″ W

www.backroadmapbooks.com

Badger Lake

Area Indicator

Fishing

Badger Lake is ideal for a vibrant fishery because it has dark, nutrient rich waters ideal for insect and plant life. In fact, Badger Lake once produced trophy rainbow in the 4.5 kg (10lb) range. It was even a practice lake for the 1993 World Fly Fishing Championship.

These days, the fish in the lake are substantially smaller, but can still reach 1.5 kg (3.5 lbs). The reasons the fish are smaller are many and varied. However, it is most likely the fact that the lake was overstocked in the mid 1990s. With too much competition for food, the fish didn't grow as quickly.

To counteract this, fisheries removed the trophy designation for a number of years. Since anglers were allowed to catch and keep the daily limits, the population was thinned and fisheries have once again put the trophy designation back on the lake. It is hoped that the lake will once again start producing monster rainbow.

For fly fishermen, the lake is best fished during the green sedge hatch in mid-June and the spring mayfly hatch. Early spring chironomid pupa fishing is also fairly effective. This is followed by a fairly large sedge hatch in mid-June.

Later in the spring and into the fall, try a caddis fly, leech or dragonfly pattern. Caddis hatch in late June and early July and fishing an Elk Haired Caddis during the evening can provide fast action. Leech patterns are especially effective in the fall when the fish are feeding heavily in preparation for the upcoming winter.

The lake is ice-free in early May until November and not as susceptible to summer doldrums as other lakes in the area. Focus your efforts around the island and try casting towards one of the many shoals that line the lake. Trolling a fly is another good bet.

Trolling the lake with lures is fairly difficult as the lake is shallow except in the area north of the island. Also, there are a lot of deadheads and debris in the lake that are certain to grab your gear. Spincasters can work the shoreline casting a small green or silver Flatfish, Blue Fox, Deadly Dick or Frisky Fly near the fallen logs where the fish tend to hang out. Also, since the water is murky, fish come right into the shallows to feed so try casting right near shore.

Across the lake from the rec site is a small stream that leads to Spooney Lake. You can try fishing around here, or you could even work your way up to the smaller lake, which produces smaller fish.

Directions

Head north on Highway 5 for about 22.5 km from Kamloops and take the Vinsulla-Knouff Lake Road heading to the right. The road winds its way up from the Thompson River Valley past Knouff and Little Knouff Lakes before reaching Badger Lake. Badger Lake is about 8 km from Knouff, with the last few kilometers being best left to trucks.

An alternative route is to take the Badger Lake Forest Service Road south of McClure. This road is much rougher but shorter.

Facilities

The **Badger Lake Recreation Site** is a fairly open 18 unit, user maintained site which has seen some recent improvements. There is a decent boat launch here for those willing to trailer in boats, while the area is also popular with ATV and Trail Bike Riders.

Badger Lake			
Fish Stocking Data			
Year	Species	Number	Life Stage
2005	Rainbow Trout	1,277	Fingerling

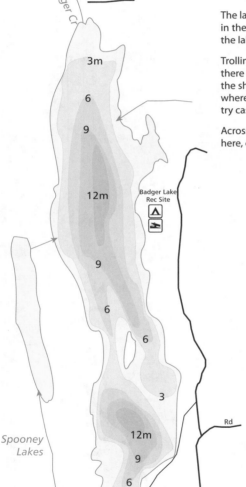

100m 0 100m 200m 300m 400m 500m
Scale

N

© Mussio Ventures Ltd.

Big OK Lake

Location: 30 km west of Logan Lake
Elevation: 1,524 m (5,000 ft)
Surface Area: 34 ha (84 ac)
Max Depth: 12 m (40 ft)
Mean Depth: 6.7 m (22 ft)
Way Point: 50° 28' 00" N, 121° 7' 00" W

www.backroadmapbooks.com

Fishing

Tucked in behind the Highland Valley Mine west of Logan Lake, Big OK or Island Lake offers some of the finest fly fishing for trophy rainbow in the region. It's clear waters, shoals and submerged island creates an abundance of prime casting locations.

The man-made lake is surrounded by a mix of pine and deciduous forests offering a good mix of cover including stumps, boulders and aquatic plants for the trout to hide. A huge sunken island located near the middle of the lake is another good area to work. Averaging 2 m (6 ft) in depth, it soon drops off to a 12 m (40 ft) hole on the south end of the lake. The northwest and northeast corners contain pockets of deep water, while the earthen dam makes up most of the southwest end. Water is only able to pass over the overflow on the west side of the dam at high water.

Managed as a quality lake Big OK produces big rainbow trout. Fish over 3.5 kg (8 lbs) are not unheard of, while 1.5 kg (3 lb) trout are common. Prolific chironomid, mayfly and sedge hatches along good populations of freshwater shrimp ensure these trout get enough food to grow big. This is an artificial fly only catch and release fishery with a limited season. With the exception of electric motors, no motor boats are permitted.

Big OK is a moody lake and can be tough fishing some days. Prepare to put a bit of time learning the tricks on this trophy lake. Start by looking for what is hatching, alternatively drifting leeches near the weeds and bulrushes can be rewarding. Earlier in the year chironomids under a strike indicator are the method of choice, while caddis flies can create a frenzy of action later in summer. Once you learn the tricks of the lake, you will be rewarded with beautiful fish in a near perfect wilderness setting.

Area Indicator

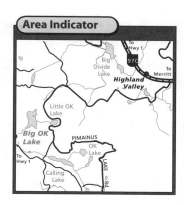

Directions 🅐 ✈

Big OK lake is accessed from Highway 97C between Logan Lake and Ashcroft. Travel west past the Highland Valley Copper Mine and tailings pond to Laura Lake Road. Turn left. The pavement ends here and from this point on the road passes through Highland Valley Copper Mine property. The junction of Big OK and Calling Lake are well marked from this point on. Travel 4.2 km on the Laura Lake Road staying straight while passing along the lower end of the tailing pond dam. At 18.4 km turn right and right again at 20.4 km. The recreation site at the north end of the lake is 100 metres down this rough and rocky access road.

Note that the access through the mine property can be altered at any time. Be sure to follow signage or ask at the office if you are unsure.

Facilities ⛺ 🏕 🚻

Big OK (Island) Lake Recreation Site offers visitors seven campsites and a cartop boat launch in two different areas at the north end of the lake. With rough road access and limited space, motorhomes or trailers are not recommended. It is also worth noting that hazardous pine beetle infected trees have been removed resulting in a fairly open site that is prone to the wind.

There is also an informal camping area at the southeast corner of the lake.

Other Options 🅐 🎣 ⚓ 🏃

Little OK Lake, Calling Lake and **Trojan Pond** are a few nearby options. Little OK and Calling Lake are stocked on occasion and provide fishing for smaller rainbow than Big Ok. Trojan Pond is a private lake in the mine site that can be accessed for a fee.

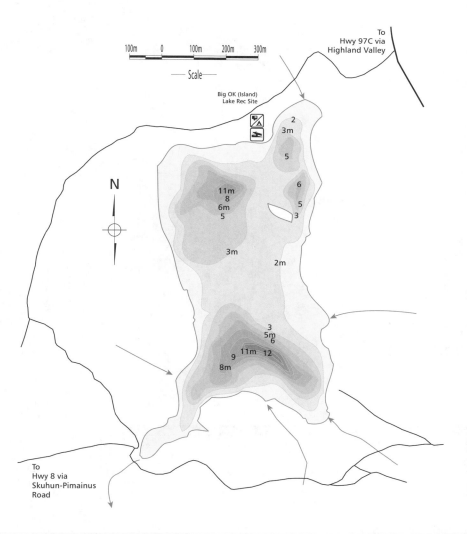

To
Hwy 97C via
Highland Valley

100m   0   100m   200m   300m

— Scale —

Big OK (Island)
Lake Rec Site

2
3m

5

6

11m
8
6m
5

5
3

3m

2m

3
5m
6

9 11m 12
8m

N

To
Hwy 8 via
Skuhun-Pimainus
Road

Birch & Phinetta Lakes

Birch Lake

Elevation: 1,126 m (3,694 ft)
Surface Area: 240 ha (593 ac)
Max Depth: 37.8 m (124 ft)
Mean Depth: 20.1 m (65.9 ft)
Way Point: 51° 27' 15" N, 120° 30' 13" W

Area Indicator

Fishing

The Birch Lake Group is found just off Highway 24 west of Little Fort. It is comprised of Birch Lake, Phinetta Lake and Tortoise Lake. The lakes are at a reasonably high elevation, which means that the water does not warm up as much here as at lower elevation lakes. In turn this means that the lakes are not as prone to the summer doldrums, especially the deeper Birch Lake.

Birch is the largest and most popular of the three lakes. It holds good numbers of rainbow, which grow over 2 kg (to 5 lbs), but are usually much smaller. Trolling is by far the most popular method of fishing although fly anglers certainly should not be discouraged because there are soon nice shoals particularly at the east and the west ends of the lake.

Trolling lures (Flatfish, Deadly Dick or Krocodile), flies (leech, dragonfly, Doc Spratley, Muddler Minnow) or lake trolls (Willow Leaf or Ford Fender) is your best options. For fly fishermen wishing to cast a line, chironomid pupae, mayfly or damselfly nymphs, sedges and leech patterns are your best bets as long as you match the hatch.

Of the three, Birch Lake offers the best summer fishing as the combination of deep water and high elevation keep the fishing here strong. However, at this time anglers should wait until later in the day after the sun is no longer shining directly on the lake for better action. The trout become bolder under the cover of dusk and are more willing to come out of the depths into the shallows or even to the surface during a hatch.

There is also a fishery for burbot. Jigging in the depths of the lake is the best method of catching these good eating fish.

Please note there is a 10 hp engine power restriction on Birch.

Phinetta Lake is the smallest of the group. It is not very deep and hard to troll, but it is a good fly-fishing lake. This is because the lake has many shoals that are ideal for insect growth. Like Birch Lake, chironomid pupae, mayfly or damselfly nymphs, sedges and leech patterns are the flies of choice so long as you match the hatch. Spincasters should throw a small spoon or spinner towards the shallows that line the lake.

N

100m 0 100m 200m 300m

Scale

Phinetta Lake

Birch Lake

Phinetta Lake

Elevation: 1,122 m (3,681 ft)
Surface Area: 28 ha (68 ac)
Max Depth: 16.2 m (53.1 ft)
Mean Depth: 4.4 m (14.4 ft)
Way Point: 51° 28' 21.8" N, 120° 29' 37.7" W

Directions

To reach this chain of lakes, follow Highway 24 northwest from Little Fort and you will soon find the Eakin Creek Road (the old Highway 24) heading off to the west. The old highway brings you right by the northern shores of Phinetta Lake. A side road immediately past Phinetta Lake brings you south to Birch Lake.

Alternatively, you can follow Highway 24 west past Long Island lake towards Lac des Roches. The Eakin Creek Road rejoins the highway halfway between these two lakes. It is a short jaunt south on the road before meeting Phinetta Lake.

Facilities

Birch Lake has cartop boat launch facilities as well as a resort. There is random camping, but no developed recreation site. Nearby **Phinetta Lake Recreation Site** actually offers two separate sites. One is located at the north end and the other camping area and boat launch is located at the east end of the lake. The easy highway access makes this a nice place for a picnic and to cast a few lines.

Other Options

Tortoise Lake is found south of Birch Lake. It, too, is a good fly-fishing lake, although spincasting can work well. There are several bays on the lake that offer ideal casting areas. There are also numerous shoals that line the lake for fly casters. Try the same fly patterns as the other lakes.

Birch Lake			
Fish Stocking Data			
Year	Species	Number	Life Stage
2010	Rainbow Trout	5,000	Yearling
2009	Rainbow Trout	10,000	Yearling

Phinetta Lake			
Fish Stocking Data			
Year	Species	Number	Life Stage
2010	Rainbow Trout	8,200	Yearling
2009	Rainbow Trout	8,000	Yearling

Birkenhead Lake

Location: 24 km (15 mi) north of Pemberton
Elevation: 636 m (2,087 ft)
Surface Area: 408.75 ha (1,010 ac)
Max Depth: 38.4 m (126 ft)
Mean Depth: 21.6 m (71 ft)
Way Point: 50° 32' 14" N, 122° 41' 30" W

Fishing

Located north of Pemberton, Birkenhead Lake is a beautiful turquoise-coloured mountain lake, surrounded by the rugged coastal mountains. The lake contains fair numbers of rainbow, bull trout, kokanee and Rocky Mountain whitefish.

Trolling is the mainstay of the fair sized lake. Try working a Flatfish or a gang troll with a Wedding Band and worm. The best fishing is in the early summer or fall. Because the lake is deep, it does not warm significantly in the summer and fishing stays steady throughout the ice-free season.

While the western shore of the lake accessed by a trail (you would cover about 16 km if you were to hike the whole thing and back again), there are only a few places where the shoreline is open enough to fish from, so even fly casters do better with a boat. Try working a green Doc Spratley along the drop-off, casting towards the shore and retrieving towards the deeper water. The water is extremely clear and it is possible to watch the fish rising to your fly.

Most people have good luck fishing where the streams flow into the lake, and there are plenty of creeks that flow into the lake, especially towards the northern end of the lake. However, one of the best spots is where Sockeye Creek flows into the lake. There is a rustic campsite a few hundred metres north, which is accessible by canoe or along the Wilderness Trail.

While the lake is not huge, it is long and narrow and prone to strong winds. The winds blow fairly constantly, which makes using float tubes difficult and dangerous.

Note that it is catch and release only for bull trout. There are no Dolly Varden in the lake, so if you're not sure, it's a bull trout.

Directions

Birkenhead Lake is set in a steep valley capped by rugged mountain peaks. The lake is found north of Pemberton on the Blackwater Lake Road. To reach the lake, head east from Pemberton to Mount Currie on Highway 99. Watch for signs pointing northward towards D'Arcy along the Pemberton Portage Road. The paved road leads along the Birkenhead River and then past Gates Lake. At about the 41 km (25.5 mile) mark, the Blackwater Lake Road heads northwest off the paved road. Watch for the sign pointing the direction to Birkenhead Lake Provincial Park and follow that road. Blackwater Lake is the first lake on the left. Birkenhead Lake is at the end of the road. From the turn-off, it is a 17 km (10.5 mile) drive along a gravel road. The nearest communities are D'arcy, Pemberton and Mt Currie.

Area Indicator

Facilities

Birkenhead Lake Provincial Park is a popular destination due to its spectacular scenery. The campground is at the north end of the lake and has over 90 campsites, together with a picnic area, wharf, concrete boat launch and a sandy beach. There are even canoe and kayak rentals available on-site. Unfortunately, the walk-in campsites are now closed. Anglers can also take advantage of the well-established trail system. Be sure to be bear aware in this remote wilderness park.

Location: 9 km (5.5 mil) east of Pemberton
Stream Length: 57.3 km (35.6 mi)
Geographic: 50° 28' 53" N, 122° 43' 28" W

www.backroadmapbooks.com

Birkenhead River

Fishing

Draining the unnamed mountains west of Birkenhead Lake into Lillooet Lake, the Birkenhead is a lovely river found northeast of Pemberton. It can also be a pleasure to fish as it does not see the Lower Mainland crowds that many of the streams further south do.

The river sees fair returns of Chinook, sockeye and Coho. In fact, the sockeye return here was once considered one of the strongest this side of the Adams. Unfortunately, returns have been down dramatically over the last few years and the river is currently closed to salmon fishing in July and August when the sockeye return. Further, like nearly all rivers in the region two, the river is catch and release only for all species of salmon.

In addition to the salmon, the river has good populations of rainbow trout, cutthroat trout and bull trout. Of the three non salmon species, the river is best known for its bull trout fishing. These trout can get to 4 kg (8 lbs), although are usually about half that size. Still, even a 2 kg bull trout can put up a heck of a fight. Those interested in rainbow will find a decent population; however, cutthroat are a little more difficult to find.

Like most rivers in this region, the Birkenhead is unfishable during the spring run-off, which lasts until about June. After which, fly anglers can try streamers and nymphs. Starting in August or so, dry flies like a Hare's Ear or an Elk Hair Caddis can be a lot of fun. For spincasters, a variety of spoons and spinners will work well.

When the salmon are spawning, the trout like to avail themselves of a bit of caviar au naturel. While there is a ban on bait fishing in the Birkenhead, fly anglers will do well with egg patterns.

The river is a walk and wade river only. While some paddlers have successfully navigated the river, it is full of snags and sweepers, especially above the Owl Creek Bridge. Fortunately, the river is right beside the Pemberton Portage Road and is easily accessible from the road for most of its length. However, anglers should take precautions during the salmon season. In addition to spawning salmon, there are plenty of berries lining the banks of the river. Needless to say, this is bear heaven for both grizzly and black bear.

Directions

The Birkenhead River runs parallel to the Pemberton Portage Road for much of its length. The Pemberton Portage Road was a key link in the Douglas Road during the Gold Rush. These days the road is paved but is not a numbered highway. To get to the road, take the Sea to Sky Highway (Highway 99) east of Pemberton towards Mount Currie. Watch for the signs pointing north towards D'Arcy. East of Mount Currie, the Highway 99 parallels the lower section of the river.

Facilities

The **Owl Creek and Spetch Creek Recreation Sites** provide convenient camping spots near the river. There is also a private campground and basic supplies available at Mount Currie, while Pemberton offers even more services including a local tackle shop. The **Fee Creek Spawning Channel** is another interesting place to visit during the fall salmon spawning season.

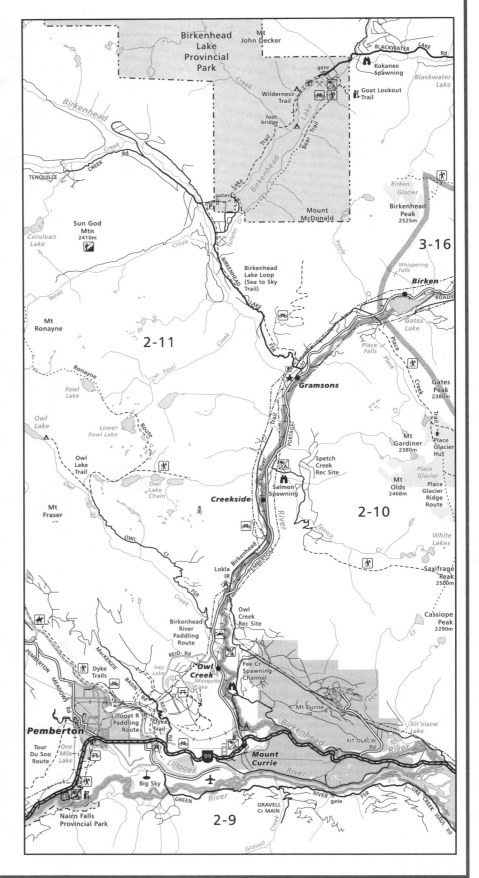

Blackwater Lake

Location: 39 km (24 mi) northeast of Pemberton
Elevation: 731 m (2,398 ft)
Surface Area: 15.24 ha (37.7 ac)
Max Depth: 9.1 m (30 ft)
Mean Depth: 5.2 m (17 ft)
Way Point: 50° 33' 41.3" N, 122° 35' 7.4" W

Fishing

Blackwater Lake is a dark water lake, which is stocked annually by the Freshwater Fishery Society of BC with rainbow. The rainbow tend to be pan-sized but they are fairly plentiful making the fishing decent so long as the lake did not winterkill the previous year. They are also known for being quite feisty, making them fun to catch.

The shore is fairly bushy and it is nearly impossible to cast from the shore to deeper water. There is a day-use area with a floating dock at the north end of the lake, but is tucked away in a little cove and fishing off the dock does not work well. A second dock at the south end of the lake, part of the forest service site, sticks out into the lake and can be fished off of. Here the lake, the drop off is only about 10 metres (30 feet) from shore.

But anglers who can get out onto the water will have more luck than those stuck on the dock. Since the lake is not that deep, it is rather difficult to troll in a boat. However, some fly anglers have had good luck doing long retrieves or slow trolls from a float tube.

Fly-fishermen should use an attractor type pattern (Woolly Bugger or Doc Spratley). Red Carey Specials seem to produce well on the lake. Spincasters do well with small spoons or spinners with a worm cast near the drop-offs. However, the fish can be extremely particular at times and won't take anything you throw at them.

Focus your fishing efforts to the early spring and later in the fall as the lake suffers from the summer doldrums. If you do fish the lake in the summer, stick around the deeper water near the southeast end of the lake. Also, fish tend to be photophobic, so fishing the shady areas of the lake in the morning or evening tends to produce better than fishing at midday.

Area Indicator

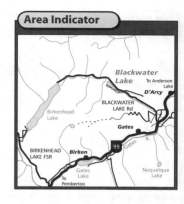

Facilities

Blackwater Lake Recreation Site is located at the southeast end of the lake and provides a picnicking site, dock and six campsites located in a brushy/treed area next to the lake. The road from the Blackwater Lake Road to the recreation site is fairly rough and RVs are not recommended. Many people who fish here chose to stay at **Birkenhead Lake Provincial Park**, located at the north end of Birkenhead Lake about 7 km (4.4 miles) past Blackwater Lake. The provincial park has over 90 campsites and a sandy beach.

Blackwater Lake Fish Stocking Data			
Year	Species	Number	Life Stage
2008	Rainbow Trout	2,000	Yearling
2007	Rainbow Trout	2,000	Yearling
2006	Rainbow Trout	2,000	Yearling

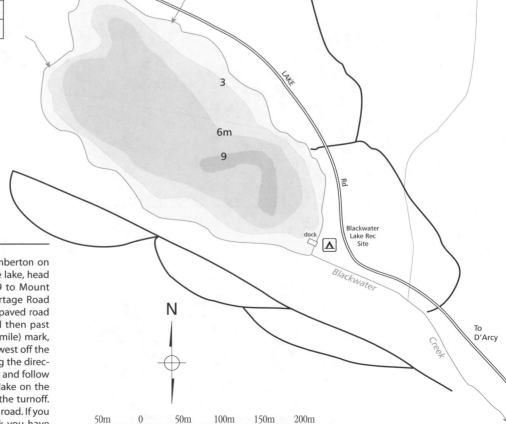

Directions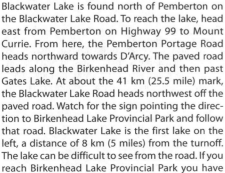

Blackwater Lake is found north of Pemberton on the Blackwater Lake Road. To reach the lake, head east from Pemberton on Highway 99 to Mount Currie. From here, the Pemberton Portage Road heads northward towards D'Arcy. The paved road leads along the Birkenhead River and then past Gates Lake. At about the 41 km (25.5 mile) mark, the Blackwater Lake Road heads northwest off the paved road. Watch for the sign pointing the direction to Birkenhead Lake Provincial Park and follow that road. Blackwater Lake is the first lake on the left, a distance of 8 km (5 miles) from the turnoff. The lake can be difficult to see from the road. If you reach Birkenhead Lake Provincial Park you have gone too far.

Location: 22 km (13 mi) southeast of Kamloops
Elevation: 1,048 m (3,438 ft)
Surface Area: 38 ha (94 ac)
Max Depth: 13.7 m (45 ft)
Mean Depth: 7.4 m (24 ft)
Way Point: 50° 30' 6.9" N, 120° 8' 1.5" W

www.backroadmapbooks.com

Bleeker Lake

Area Indicator

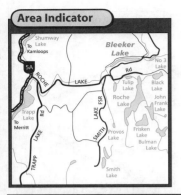

Bleeker Lake Fish Stocking Data			
Year	Species	Number	Life Stage
2011	Rainbow Trout	3,000	Yearling
2010	Rainbow Trout	3,000	Yearling
2009	Rainbow Trout	5,000	Yearling

Fishing

Bleeker Lake is located near Roche Lake Provincial Park. While it is only a couple kilometres from the park, it is a couple hundred metres lower in elevation. In the early season, while the much more famous Roche Lake is still ice-bound, Bleeker Lake is often ice-free, making a nice alternative. And, while Roche Lake is closed to ice fishing, Bleeker is not. However, there is an aerator in the lake that creates dangerous thin ice conditions.

Before spring turnover, the trout can be found cruising the shallows of the lake looking for food. This can be a highly productive time to fish the lake as the fish are often bolder and less selective about what they will eat. Once the lake hits spring turnover, fishing is basically a wash for about a week. Spring turnover can come on quickly here; the fishing can be hot in the morning and by afternoon, nothing.

The murky, nutrient-rich waters of Bleeker Lake allow rainbow to grow over 3 kg (6 lbs). This is a double edged sword as the fish grow quickly, but there is also a lot feed that makes the fish a little pickier. Anglers need to present their offerings just right to trick these plump fish.

Fishing is also difficult from shore as the lake is covered with thick aquatic vegetation around its entire shoreline. Fishing is restricted to the middle of the lake making a float tube or boat essential to fish the lake. However, you will need to get here after spring turnover and before the weed growth gets too thick.

The weeds make trolling a near impossibility but it also provides lots of places for insects to grow. While it can be difficult to keep your lures free of weeds when spincasting or fly-fishing with a sinking line, using a floating line can produce quite well. Try using a shrimp, leech or dragonfly pattern. The most common diet for the local fish is shrimp.

In the summertime, the water warms, aquatic vegetation is rapidly growing and there is significant drawdown for irrigation purposes. This makes fishing virtually hopeless. It is not until the fall that fishing begins to pickup. Even in fall, though, the weeds make fishing difficult. But savvy anglers know that the 3,000 or so Pennask trout that were stocked in the lake in spring are usually reaching a catchable size by now. So if you don't mind fighting your way through the weeds, September and October can be productive months.

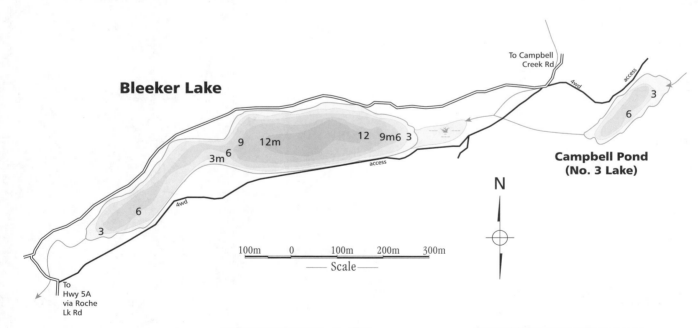

Directions

Bleeker Lake is found north of the Roche Lake Provincial Park and to the east of Highway 5A between Kamloops and Merritt. To get to the lake, take the Roche Lake Road turnoff from Highway 5A. When you reach the park, the Bleeker Lake Road heads off to the north where it reaches the southern shore of the lake. Follow this road past the lake before turning right on a rough road that follows the north side of the lake. A 4wd vehicle is recommended, as the Bleeker Lake Road is rough in places.

Facilities

Facilities at the lake are quite limited. There is an opportunity to launch small boats and that's about it. If you are planning on spending the night, best to find a campsite in nearby **Roche Lake Provincial Park.**

www.backroadmapbooks.com

Bolean Lake & Area

Location: 66 km (41 mi) southeast of Kamloops
Elevation: 1,459 m (4,786 ft)
Surface Area: 78 ha (193 ac)
Max Depth: 12 m (39.4 ft)
Way Point: 50° 32' 16.7" N, 119° 30' 6.9" W

Fishing

Arthur, Bolean and Spa lakes are three prime fishing destinations that are nestled in the rolling Spa Hills outside of Falkland. Surrounded by fir and spruce, they offer a wild experience not found at the region's busier lakes. The lakes do not see as much fishing pressure and the area is full of wildlife, including deer, moose and black bears.

The higher elevation means cooler temperatures, which in turn mean the lakes fish well all summer long and escape the doldrums common to lower elevation lakes.

Of course, the higher elevation means that the lakes are not ice-free until later than lower elevation lakes, often not until mid-May or so. However, once the fishing starts, it doesn't slow down.

Arthur Lake is the largest of the three, but not by much. There are enough insect hatches and other food sources, such as leeches, to help rainbow grow to more than 0.7 kg (1.5 lbs). Cast or troll Flatfish in various colour combinations, Dick Nite lures and Panther Martin spinners. Fly patterns that imitate chironomid or caddis pupae and adult patterns along with leeches and dragonflies are all effective at various times of the open water season.

While many of the southern interior lakes don't have good spawning habitat, all three of these lakes have streams, which allow the rainbow trout to reproduce naturally. As a result, none of these lakes are stocked and the fishing can vary from year to year, depending on how water levels affect the spawning creeks. Some years see more trout than other years.

Bolean Lake itself is rather unique as it has a pothole at the northwestern end of the lake. Although you wouldn't know it because the water is a tea colour, the rest of the lake is rather shallow. There are a lot of small rainbow in the lake, but some have been caught to 1.5 kg (3 lbs). Cast near the drop-off around the pothole except in early spring and late fall when the fish are cruising the shallows. Fly casters should try caddis, dragonfly or leech patterns here. The lake is not that suitable for trolling, except for around the pothole with a Wedding Band or small lure with a worm.

Area Indicator

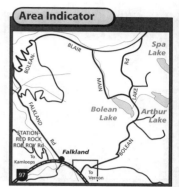

Directions

From Kamloops, travel east for about 27 km on the Trans Canada Highway to Highway 97. Drive down Highway 97 for 45 km to Falkland. Just past Falkland, turn left on Silvernails Road and take the left fork at km 1.3 onto Bolean Lake Road (Ord Road). The road switchbacks up the hill for about 8.5 km before the resort sign directs you towards the southwest end of the lake. The recreation site is found just past the resort.

To reach Arthur Lake, stay on the main road for 4 km past the turnoff to Bolean Lake. Keep right at the 12.6 km and 13.8 km forks. The recreation site at Arthur Lake is just past the 15 km marker.

Spa Lake is found even further along this road. Avoid the temptation to follow one of the many side roads and you should eventually reach the northwest side of the lake and the recreation site.

Facilities

Recreation sites, found at each of these lakes, offer camping and boat launches of various states. Of the three, **Bolean Lake Recreation Site** is the most popular with five sites in a treed area and cartop boat launch. There is also a private resort on Bolean Lake.

Arthur Lake North Recreation Site is a little more difficult to access and offers three sites and a rustic launching area. Similarly, Spa Lake has a user-maintained site with space for about five groups and a cartop boat launch.

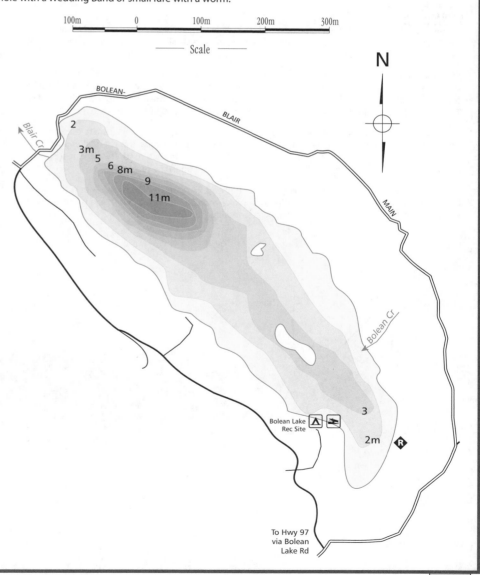

Location: 80 km (50 mi) north of Kamloops
Elevation: 1,176 m (3,858 ft)
Surface Area: 3,367 ha (8,321 ac)
Max Depth: 98 m (321.5 ft)
Mean Depth: 40.3 m (132.2 ft)
Way Point: 51° 15' 30" N, 120° 32' 25" W

www.backroadmapbooks.com

Bonaparte Lake

Area Indicator

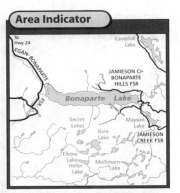

Fishing

Set at the north end of the high Bonaparte Plateau, this beautiful green lake is the largest lake on the plateau. It is also one of the more popular fishing lakes in an area filled with popular fishing lakes.

While the lakes up here aren't famous for their big fish, Bonaparte Lake is an exception. The lake contains lots of kokanee, which the trout like to feed on. Rainbow in the 5.5 kg (12 lb) range and occasionally up to 9 kg (20 lbs) are caught annually, although most of the fish are around the 1–1.5 kg (3–4 lb) range. There may not be a lot of trout, but if you find one, chances are it will be pretty big.

From one end to the other, Bonaparte Lake is 18 km (11 miles) long 2 km (1.2 miles) wide and 100 metres (330 feet) deep. Many of the techniques that work at the hundreds of small lakes in the region will not work here. Trolling is the mainstay of the lake with plugs and spoons like Apexes, Rapalas and Krocodile lures working the best when trolled deep (9–27 m/30–90 ft) with a long leader. Try to imitate the kokanee that the trout seem to feed on. Fly anglers are best to visit the many nearby smaller lakes. The big lake has a rocky bottom, with few weeds to attract insects.

Trolling a Spin-N-Glo or Willow Leaf with maggots easily catches the small kokanee. A Dick Nite also works for the kokanee.

Because of the kokanee, fishing remains active throughout the summer months. For trout, the fishery is best in early spring or late fall when they are closer to the surface. Ice fishing with bait and a hook can also be productive.

Be warned, the lake is susceptible to sudden, strong winds and big waves. There is also a 10 mph speed limit for boats.

During the winter, Bonaparte Lake is reported to offer some of the best ice fishing around.

Directions

Getting to the big lake is as much the adventure as the fishing. A copy of the Backroad Mapbook for the Thompson Okanagan is recommended since there are several routes that will get you here. All require a long drive on many dusty, teeth rattling miles on a mainhaul logging roads.

From the north, follow Highway 24 for about 45 km to Bridge Lake. Look for the North Bonaparte Road branching south. This road soon meets up with the Eagan-Bonaparte Forest Service Road (3300Rd) on the left. Follow this road south, past the Eagan Lake Resort and the branch road to Sharpe Lake. The road will eventually bring you to the west end of the lake where you will find the recreation site.

From Kamloops, take Westsyde Road north along the North Thompson River for 22 km to the Jamieson Creek Forest Service Road. Following the Spruce Wilderness Lodge signs, this road takes you north for about 55 km before eventually meeting the Bonaparte Hills branch road. This road leads along the northeast side of the big lake. The main access here is through the resort.

You can also access the lake from the west off Highway 97 near 70 Mile House along the North Bonaparte Road. From the east, the Darlington Creek Forest Service Road climbs the hill to the new Powder Lake Forest Service Road, which links to the Jamieson Creek Road.

Facilities

Bonaparte Lake has a few resorts together with the **Bonaparte Lake Recreation Site** to choose from. Located at the northwest end of the lake, the large open grassy area has room for about five units as well as a good gravel launch. For roofed accommodations, the lakeside resorts include **Bonaparte Lake Resort, Spruce Wilderness Lodge** and **Thunderbird Lodge.** In addition to cabins and campsites, boat rentals and last minute supplies can be found here.

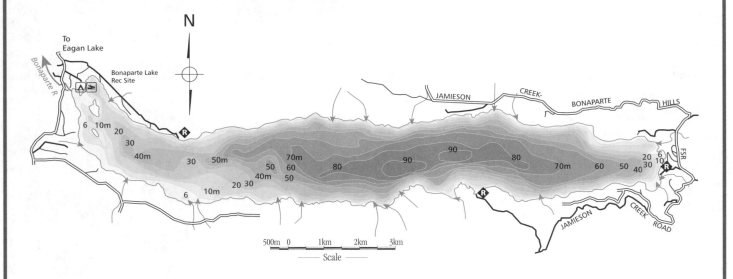

www.backroadmapbooks.com

Brohm Lake

Location: 19 km (12 mi) north of Squamish
Elevation: 272 m (892 ft)
Surface Area: 12.67 ha (31.3 ac)
Max Depth: 23.8 m (78 ft)
Mean Depth: 11.2 m (37 ft)
Way Point: 49° 49' 27.2" N, 123° 8' 10.2" W

Fishing

Brohm Lake is a popular fishing lake alongside the Sea to Sky Highway north of Squamish. The small lake is stocked annually with rainbow trout, albeit not heavily anymore (250 catchable annually in 2007 and 2008). The lake also has a brown bullhead, Dolly Varden and a natural population of cutthroat trout.

Because it is so easy to get to, the lake receives fairly heavy pressure. The bottom of the lake drops of quickly and shore fishing is certainly a possibility here, especially along the eastern shore. However, most people who come here bring a small cartop boat or a float tube.

The lake features a good chironomid hatch and fly-fishers can do very well during the hatch. Another popular pattern, especially later in the year, is a scud pattern, as the lake has plenty of freshwater shrimp. Fly-fishing from shore at Brohm Lake is difficult, as there is not much room for back casting. If you are a fly angler, you will probably want to bring a small boat or float tube. Microleeches, dressed in black, olive or brown with some flashing are the typical patterns used by local anglers. The fly can either be retrieved slowly, or suspended under a strike indicator.

For shoreline anglers, there are rocky ledges where you can sit and fish in the southeastern corner of the lake, but the noisy highway behind you can often ruin the experience. However, it is a short walk away from this area to places where the forest is thick enough to muffle the noise from the road.

When fishing from shore, a simple worm and bobber set-up can work wonders. Because the fish don't get big here, use a hook between size 4 and 8. Bait such as deli shrimp, dew worm, single eggs, maggots will also work well. However, spincasting using lures will allow you to cover more ground and can attract the larger, more aggressive fish. Try working a small spoon.

Brohm Lake is a small, low elevation lake and the fishing does slow down in summer before picking up again in fall. The lake's cutthroat are very small and finding one to 25 cm (10 inches) is a nice catch. They average about 20 cm (8 inches) in size.

Facilities

From the parking lot, an easy 5km (3 mile) trail circles the lake with minimal elevation gain along the way. The trail provides access to the picnic area next to Brohm Lake and is used for shore fishing as well as wildlife viewing. There is also a launch for hand carried boats found a short distance from the parking lot.

There is no camping at the lake, but **Cat Lake Recreation Site** or **Alice Lake Provincial Park** to the south both provide nice places to overnight.

Directions

Brohm Lake is a small, scenic lake north of Squamish. You can see the lake on the left hand side of the Sea to Sky Highway (Highway 99) as you drive north towards Whistler. The turnoff to the parking lot is about 5.5 km (3.3 miles) past the turnoff to Alice Lake Provincial Park.

The southern part of the lake is very shallow with lots of reeds and a foot bridge across the lake. The northern part of lake, which is reach by a short trail from the parking lot off the highway, is where everyone fishes.

Area Indicator

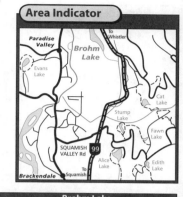

Brohm Lake			
Fish Stocking Data			
Year	Species	Number	Life Stage
2010	Rainbow Trout	250	Catchable
2009	Rainbow Trout	250	Catchable

To Whistler

Brohm Lake Rec Site

Brohm Lake Interpretive Trails Parking Lot

Rock Bluff Loop

23
18
14 9 5m

Bridge

wooden bridge

To Squamish

200m   0   200m   400m   600m
Scale

N

Location: 15 km (9 miles) south of Squamish
Elevation: 137 m (449 ft)
Surface Area: 2.6 ha (6.4 ac)
Max Depth: 10 m (33 ft)
Mean Depth: 4.2 m (14 ft)
Way Point:49° 38' 39.9" N, 123° 12' 27.0" W

www.backroadmapbooks.com

Browning Lake

Area Indicator

Browning Lake Fish Stocking Data			
Year	Species	Number	Life Stage
2011	Rainbow Trout	3,000	Catchable
2010	Rainbow Trout	4,000	Catchable
2009	Rainbow Trout	4,000	Catchable

Fishing

Located alongside the Sea to Sky Highway, Browning Lake is one of the most easily accessible, family-friendly fishing spots in the Lower Mainland. It is a tiny lake, but every year it is stocked with several thousand catchable-sized rainbow trout by the Freshwater Fisheries Society of BC to help maintain the fast fishery.

Catching a fish in Browning Lake requires a minimal amount of tackle and knowledge. The lake is very small and the surrounding area is not heavily vegetated allowing for fairly easy shore casting. The northern and southern shores are better locations due to the drop-off.

A good tip for fishing Browning is to look for fish before you actually select a place to start fishing. Telltale circular rings left on the surface by rising fish are a sure sign of fish in the area and a great place to start fishing.

If you are using spinning gear you should try fishing bait on the bottom or with a float. The advantage of a float or bobber is that you can adjust your fishing depth and for kids it is easier and more exciting to see the effects of a bite when the float bobbles and disappears. Try common baits like worms, fish eggs or Powerbait which is offered in a multitude of colors and scents. Spin fishermen should also try casting small lures such as a Krocodile, Mepps Silver Fox or Panther Marten. This is a very effective way to cover a large amount of water in an effort to entice a bite.

Fly-fishermen also do well at Browning Lake with standard offerings such as chironomids, leeches, Doc Spratleys and Tom Thumbs. If you plan on fly-fishing you are best advised to bring some form of non-motorized watercraft like a float tube or pontoon boat. This allows you to access portions of the lake's shoreline that can't be fished from shore.

It is not uncommon to see dozens of anglers around the shores of this lake, especially right after it is stocked. The first stocking is usually around mid- April. These fish are almost always fished out by the end of the year so finding a fish bigger than 30 cm (12 inches) is rare.

Directions

Browning Lake is located in Murrin Lake Provincial Park right next to the Sea to Sky Highway (Highway 99). From the south, the lake is about 3 km (1.8 mi) past Britannia Beach. Watch for Browning Lake right beside the highway on the west side. It is the only lake next to the highway south of Squamish and north of Lions Bay.

The access point to the lake is at the northeast end of the lake were there is a large parking lot. A short walk from the parking lot brings you to the lake past a series of rock bluffs, which are used by rock climbers.

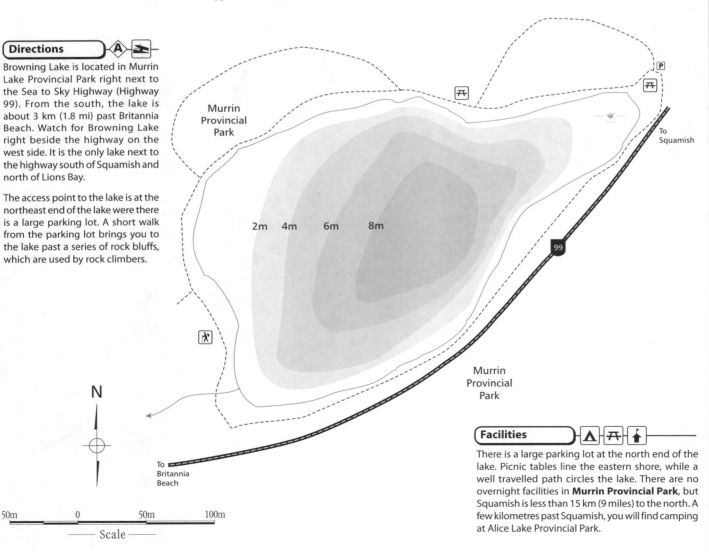

Facilities

There is a large parking lot at the north end of the lake. Picnic tables line the eastern shore, while a well travelled path circles the lake. There are no overnight facilities in **Murrin Provincial Park**, but Squamish is less than 15 km (9 miles) to the north. A few kilometres past Squamish, you will find camping at Alice Lake Provincial Park.

www.backroadmapbooks.com

Buntzen Lake

Location: 8 km (5 mi) north of Port Moody
Elevation: 126 m (413 ft)
Surface Area: 151 ha (373 ac)
Max Depth: 65 m (213 ft)
Mean Depth: 30 m (98 ft)
Way Point: 49° 21' 11" N, 122° 51' 21" W

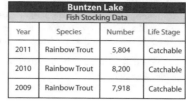

Buntzen Lake Fish Stocking Data			
Year	Species	Number	Life Stage
2011	Rainbow Trout	5,804	Catchable
2010	Rainbow Trout	8,200	Catchable
2009	Rainbow Trout	7,918	Catchable

Area Indicator

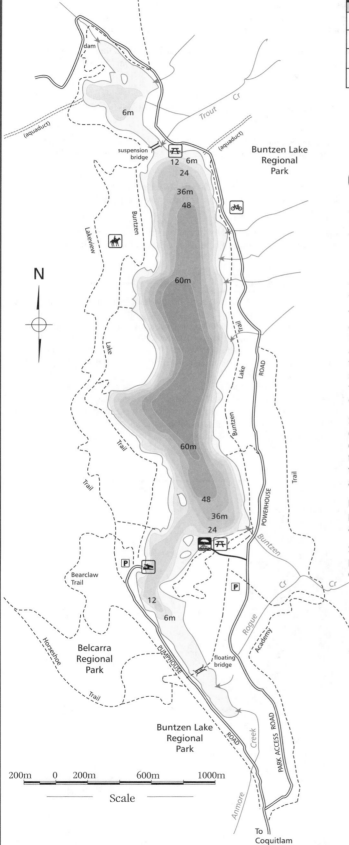

Fishing

Buntzen Lake, located approximately 30 km (18 miles) from Vancouver, is a very deep BC Hydro reservoir. The lake is 4.8 km long and was formerly known as Lake Beautiful. While the scenic qualities of the lake haven't changed, the name has. It was the first hydroelectric generating facility in the area and was brought online in 1903. The lake is subject to sudden water level fluctuations.

Buntzen Lake contains rainbow, cutthroat, Dolly Varden and kokanee averaging 20–30 cm in size. Some of the cutthroat can reach 1 kg (2 lbs), while the rainbow are usually slightly smaller.

The lake used to be stocked with cutthroat, but hasn't been for over a decade. The cutthroat seem to have developed a self-sustaining population. However, the lake is still stocked quite heavily with rainbow trout, to the tune of six or more times annually. The stocked rainbow are catchable and as a result, fishing is fast and furious for a couple weeks after the lake is stocked. When the lake is not freshly stocked it is best fished in the spring and in the fall when the fish are found closer to the surface. Anglers will need to be a bit more patient or work the fringe hours of the day during the summer.

Since no power boats are allowed at the lake, it is best to bring a float tube or canoe and try spincasting or fly-fishing the edges of the lake. The lake has steep drop-offs resulting in very little shoal areas to work. This does make shore fishing fairly easy as it is possible to cast into the deeper water from shore. A trail circles the lake providing good access for shore fishing and there are a couple docks and a floating bridge as well.

Fly-fishers will usually find the docks and floating bridge too crowded to back cast properly. It is better to work the lake from a boat or a tube, or find an open spot along the shoreline. Trolling a microleech can be extremely effective.

Spincasters can have great success off the docks and bridge. Try using a small spoon, pausing frequently in your retrieve. Bait fishing works well, too, using dew worm, deli shrimp, roe and artificially scented bait.

Directions

Located northwest of Port Moody, Buntzen Lake is immensely popular among sunbathers and fishermen. The lake is easily accessed by taking Ioco Road north off of the Barnett Highway (Highway 7A). A right off Ioco Road onto Sunnyside Road brings to you to the lake. Be sure to follow the park signs as there are a few tricky turns en route.

Facilities

Despite the short drive from downtown Vancouver, **Buntzen Lake Regional Park** retains a wilderness quality. It is a popular site, not just with anglers, but with picnickers and trail enthusiasts. The park offers a large picnic area and beach, a good gravel boat launch, floating dock and an incredible trail system.

Location: 16.5 km (10 mi) northwest of Whistler
Elevation: 1,200 m (3,937 ft)
Surface Area: 120 ha (295 ac)
Max Depth: 53 m (174 ft)
Mean Depth: 21.6 m (71 ft)
Way Point:50° 11′55″N, 123° 11′14″W

www.backroadmapbooks.com

Callaghan Lake

Area Indicator

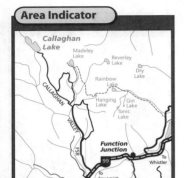

Fishing

Callaghan Lake is a beautiful mountain lake located in the high country northwest of Whistler. The valley is undergoing many changes in preparation for the 2010 Olympics, but those changes are happening lower in the valley and do not affect the lake itself, although access over the next few years will certainly change.

The lake itself is quite large and provides decent fishing for rainbow trout to 0.75 kg (1.5 lbs). The lake is a high elevation lake and is often not accessible, let alone fishable, until early summer. However, once the fishing starts it continues unabated by the heat of the summer through into fall.

Callaghan Lake was actively stocked up until 2003, but has not been stocked since then. The rainbow trout seem to have developed a self-sustaining population. In addition to the rainbow, the lake also holds Dolly Varden and kokanee.

Spring run-off carries glacial mud and till into the lake, making the water quite murky. As a result, the fishing is quite spotty until the water clears up. Once that till settles, the waters become exceptionally clear, as there is very little algae growth in the lake due to the cold, glacier fed waters.

Trolling is the primary method of fishing although spincasting and fly-fishing should not be ruled out. Fly-fishermen should focus on imitating a chironomid pupae or freshwater shrimp as those two insects/invertebrates are the most common in the lake.

Shore fishing is tough because three sides to the lake are defined by steep, forest-covered slopes. However, there are rapid drop-offs, so if you can find a place to cast, you should be able to get your gear out far enough to get in deeper water.

Directions

Callaghan Lake is located northwest of Whistler and is one of the most scenic lakes in the whole region. Access into the area has changed with the Olympic development. To find the lake follow the Sea to Sky Highway (Highway 99) south of Whistler and north of Brandywine Falls Provincial Park to the paved Callaghan Valley Road. Follow this for about 8.5 km. Right before you get to the Olympic Nordic Venue, the old Callaghan Lake Forest Service Road heads off to your left, crosses a small bridge, and then makes its way up to the lake. The road is deactivated and cross-ditched, but can usually be navigated by 2wd vehicles with a high clearance. Given the snow accumulation, the lake is not usually accessible until mid June-early July.

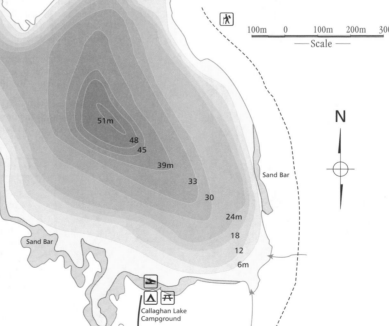

100m   0   100m   200m   300m
— Scale —

N

Facilities

Callaghan Provincial Park is year round backcountry destination. There is a former recreation site situated at the south end of the lake that is not much more than a large parking lot with room for 4 to 6 camping units and an undeveloped cartop boat launch. Tenters will find the campsite especially uninviting, as there is no longer tenting allowed in the adjacent forest and meadows. However, the dramatic setting of Callaghan Lake makes up for the campground as the lake is surrounded by some rugged peaks together with a glacier and a beautiful waterfall. And there is no fee for camping at the lake.

The recreation site receives moderate use from mid-June to October. Note that the mosquitoes can be unbearable at times.

www.backroadmapbooks.com

Calling Lake

Location: 50 km (31 mi) southwest of Kamloops
Elevation: 1,564 m (5,131 ft)
Surface Area: 30 ha (74 ac)
Max Depth: 8.2 m (26.9 ft)
Way Point: 50° 27' 34.7" N, 121° 6' 1.3" W

Fishing

Near Logan Lake's Highland Valley Copper Mine are two prime fishing lakes. While many anglers are familiar with Big OK Lake, its neighbour Calling Lake is often neglected. The lake is stocked annually with about 6,000 rainbow trout. Although these fish average 0.7 kg (1.5 lbs) when caught, they occasionally reach up to 1.5 kg (3 lbs).

Calling Lake is a high elevation lake. Although it seldom suffers the dreaded doldrums in summer, it is an irrigation reservoir. This means water levels can drop if the summer season is unusually hot or dry, which has the same general effect as the summer doldrums.

Calling is an average sized lake. It's big enough to give anglers room to explore, but not so big that small boats, pontoon boats or float tubes will feel out of place. Since it's a bit of a journey to reach, this lake does not get much fishing pressure.

The lake is stained with tannins, giving the lake tea-coloured water and lily pads and the shoreline is marked by tree stumps and open grassy areas. It is relatively shallow and has extensive shoals, which supports a wide variety of aquatic vegetation. Unfortunately, the lake is fairly shallow and prone to winterkill on harsh winters.

Fly-fishers do well throughout the year by matching the hatch. Calling has good populations of chironomids, leeches, caddis flies and scuds (freshwater shrimp).

Early in the morning or late into the day, try casting small dry flies around the edges of the beds of lily pads. Rainbow–especially the older, wiser and larger fish–don't like to venture very far into the shallows when it is bright out, but become quite bold when the sun is no longer hitting the lake.

Trollers go with the usual pieces of hardware like small Flatfish. Reports suggest Flatfish, spinners or small lures with flashes of black and red are very productive at this lake.

Directions

From Kamloops, drive to Logan Lake via the Coquihalla Highway and Meadow Lake Road (Exit 336). Continue through Logan Lake, past the Tunkwa Lake Road intersection and west past the Highland Valley Copper Mine. Turn left on Laurel Lake Road at the intersection with Landon Road. The road becomes gravel and passes through mine property. The junctions to Calling Lake and Big OK Lake are well marked. Drive about 20 km (12 miles); passing the lower end of the mine's tailing pond and Big OK Lake. Drive over the dam on the unnamed lake southeast of Big OK and continue for 2 km to Calling Lake.

Facilities

The **Calling Lake Recreation Site** has space for four groups at the campsites and a boat launch at the north end of the lake. It is a popular site for fishing and hunting and is often used as a base for fishing nearby Big OK or Island Lake.

Other Options

Nearby **Big OK (Island) Lake** is a popular fly-fishing lake. The lake produces well for rainbow to 1.5 kg (3 lbs) and even larger. Many would argue that it is one of the best fly-fishing lakes in the region. It is an artificial fly, catch and release only lake. It is a moody lake but when it is on, the fishing is spectacular.

Area Indicator

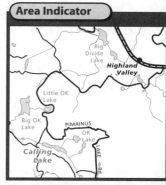

Calling Lake			
Fish Stocking Data			
Year	Species	Number	Life Stage
2010	Rainbow Trout	6,000	Fry
2009	Rainbow Trout	6,000	Fry

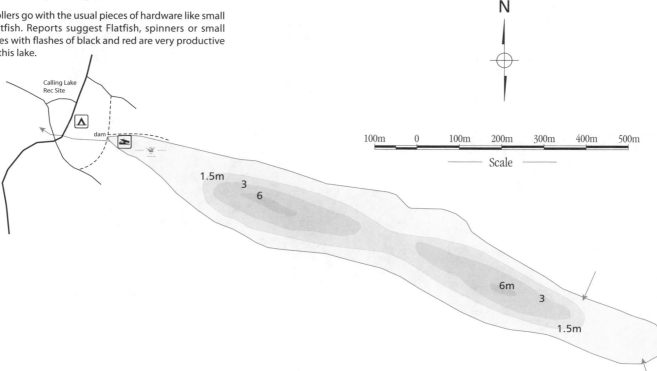

Location: 22 km (13.5 mi) southeast of Kamloops
Elevation: 1,051 m (3,448 ft)
Surface Area: 113.2 ha (279.6 ac)
Max Depth: 7 m (23 ft)
Mean Depth: 5.5 m (18 ft)
Way Point: 50° 33' 19.0" N, 120° 5' 43.1" W

www.backroadmapbooks.com

Campbell Lake

Area Indicator

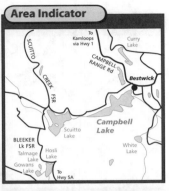

Campbell Lake			
Fish Stocking Data			
Year	Species	Number	Life Stage
2008	Rainbow Trout	5,000	Yearling
2007	Rainbow Trout	5,000	Yearling
2006	Rainbow Trout	5,000	Yearling

Fishing

Campbell Lake is a sprawling lake southeast of Kamloops. Anglers who fish here usually add it to their list of favourite lakes and nearly all who fish it regularly have "best day ever" stories to tell.

Nestled in the grasslands of Barnhartvale, the long, narrow Campbell is 2.5 km (1.5 miles) long running in an east to west direction. The lake can get windy, making it difficult (but not impossible) to fish from a float tube.

The lake has two main arms, to the east and west and two large bays to the north and south. Each section offers unique fishing structures to accommodate a variety of fishing styles.

Trollers like to target the deep hole at the east end of the lake, as well as the holes in the middle. With a maximum depth of 7 metres (22 feet), the holes are shallow enough to make a fish finder valuable. Troll large Ford Fender flashers ahead of small green or black and red Flatfish with a worm. Also try Mepps and other inline spinners. Trolling over the expansive mud shoal at the west end is productive when trout are cruising.

However, Campbell Lake is a fly-angler's dream. The big shoals in the west, east and north bays are popular, as are the deep hole and drop-offs at the east end. This lake is big enough that finding the schools is often the first key to success.

Chironomids and mayflies are tremendous producers at the lake, but the standard still water flies will produce when the time is right. There is a big hatch of "bomber" chironomids in August and anglers who take advantage will become instant converts.

In the summer, the key to success is to get your fly or lure quickly through the heavy algae blooms to the clear water, which is often 3–4 metres (6–9 feet) below the surface. The trout often swim just beneath the bloom, which provides protection, shade from the sun and tends to keep the water cooler.

Autumn fishing is spectacular right up to the first ice. Small maroon leeches in shallow water are a hot ticket at this time of year since the fish are starting to bulk up for winter and will take a nice big, easy leech any day. Trolling general attractor patterns like Woolly Buggers or Doc Spratleys can also produce well. Dark colours like black and maroon seem to work best.

The Freshwater Fisheries Society of BC has been stocking the lake since 1995 with sterile triploid rainbow trout. These fish do not reproduce and grow much larger than average trout. Averaging 1 kg (2 lbs), fish have been pulled out of here as big as 4 kg (8 lbs).

Directions

Access to Campbell Lake is via a 14 km traverse of the Sciutto Lake Forest Service Road, which joins the Robbins Range Road 4 km south of Barnhartvale Road. Barnhartvale Road joins the Trans Canada Highway (Highway 1) 8 km east of Kamloops. Sciutto Lake Road is rough in places but generally good, even in wet conditions. In dry conditions the road is good enough to allow fifth-wheel campers and small boat trailers passage.

Facilities

The **Campbell Lake Recreation Site** rests on the southwest shore of the lake. The enhanced site offers 32 campsites, a nice day-use area and a boat launch for small trailered boats.

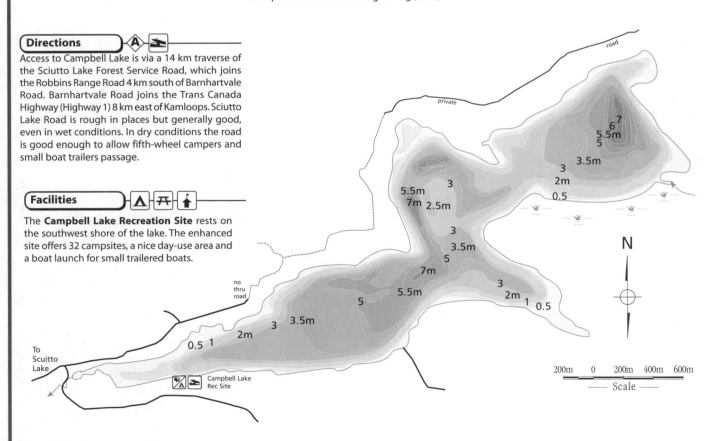

www.backroadmapbooks.com

Location: North Vancouver
Stream Length: 29.17 km (18 miles)
Geographic: 123° 08' 00" Lon - W   49° 19' 00" Lat - N

REGION 2

Capilano River

Capilano River

Fishing

On a good day, you can get from Downtown Vancouver to the Capilano River in ten minutes. Dropping down into the Capilano River valley–at least in places–there are no houses visible, no sound of traffic and no obvious signs of development. There's just the river, plenty of fish and the thick coastal rainforest.

Oh. You will also find dozens, if not hundreds of other anglers…sorry.

Its success as a fishing river is due in no small part to the Capilano Hatchery. You see, the Capilano shouldn't be a good fishing river. In the 1950s, the Cleveland Dam was constructed, effectively blocking off 95% of spawning habitat. However, in 1969 the Capilano Hatchery was built and the hatchery continues to supply most of the Coho, Chinook and steelhead that now live in the river.

The Cap can be a frustrating river to fish. Anglers tell stories of casting into pools where they literally see hundreds of fish, yet come away with nothing. But if you pick the right place and use the right technique you can easily turn this frustration into pure excitement.

The best place to fish is at the river mouth in Ambleside Park. This is one of, if not the, most productive place in the Lower Mainland for Coho. And starting in June, anglers line up along the banks of the river trying to catch these feisty, but skittish salmon. Coho congregate here when the river is low, waiting for the water to rise.

Fishing here during low tide is much more effective, as is using a pair of waders to get out onto the shallow tidal flat. Try working Colorado spinners, Crocodile spoons, Buzz Bombs and a variety of jigs. However, the fish can be extremely particular so don't invest all your energy in one lure. If you're not having success with a green Buzz Bomb (which is one of the most successful lures), try switching to something different. Silver colours also seem to work well.

The rest river features a number of steep walled canyons. To get from one area to the next can involve a very long hike up and around. Two of the most popular angling locations are Cabin Pool, near the hatchery and just below the Trans Canada Highway. Most of the fishable stretches have nice gravel bars that you can fish from, except in extremely high water. It is not recommended to fish here during high water for both safety and success reasons.

Fishing the shallower whitewater sections can be more effective than fishing the pools as the fish are easier to find. Use a long rod, a float and some wool. Green is the most effective colour, but pink and orange have also been used to good effect.

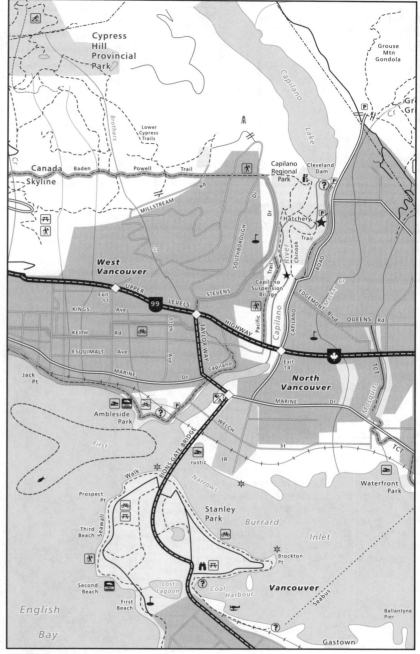

Facilities

The **Capilano River Hatchery** is found just below the Cleveland Dam and provides an amazing display of the various fish anglers are trying to catch. Most of the river is protected by day-use parks (**Ambleside Park and Capilano River Regional Park**), where you will find washroom and picnic facilities along with numerous trails. There is also the ever popular **Capilano Suspension Bridge** to give you a much different perspective of the river.

For supplies and services, the cities of North and West Vancouver are both nearby. Anglers will find tackle shops, restaurants and plenty of accommodations to sample.

Directions

The Cap can be accessed from a variety of places. Ambleside Park is off of Marine Drive in West Vancouver, while the Capilano Road parallels the river for most of its length. Trails line most of the river and can be picked up from Ambleside Park near the mouth or the Capilano River Regional Park in the upper sections.

Capilano River			
Fish Stocking Data			
Year	Species	Number	Life Stage
2006	Steelhead	69,902	Fry
2006	Steelhead	10,492	Smolt
2005	Steelhead	6,287	Fry
2005	Steelhead	10,123	Smolt

Location: 8 km (5 mi) north of Squamish
Elevation: 348 m (1,142 ft)
Surface Area: 6 ha (16 ac)
Max Depth: 43 m (141 ft)
Mean Depth: 17 m (54 ft)
Way Point: 49° 47' 56.4" N, 123° 6' 34.8" W

Cat Lake

Area Indicator

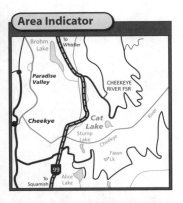

Cat Lake
Fish Stocking Data

Year	Species	Number	Life Stage
2009	Rainbow Trout	2,314	Fry
2008	Steelhead	2,169	Parr
2007	Steelhead	2,933	Yearling

Fishing

This tiny lake is located in the shadow of Garibaldi Park north of Squamish. Because it is farther off the highway than some of the other lakes in the Sea to Sky Highway corridor and because you have to walk in to get to the lake, it does not see the same level of usage as lakes like Alice, Brohm and Browning.

Cat Lake is a low productivity lake that is currently being stocked with rainbow trout. However, the Freshwater Fishing Society of BC is currently evaluating its stocking plans for the lake, which might not continue.

Because the lake is so small though, most of the fish have been caught a few times and are starting to become wary. As a result, the fishing here can be slow, especially later in the year. The fish also tend to be on the small side.

The lake is set in a thick, lush forest that creates a sense of intimate remoteness but makes shore fishing difficult, though not impossible. The lake bottom does drops off rapidly allowing spincasters to cast in a few places. Unfortunately, fly casters will find few places where they don't wind up snagging trees on the back cast. There is a dock at the recreation site, which is popular to fish off of. However, most anglers bring a float tube or canoe and get out on the lake.

Casting from the deeper water into the shallows is more productive. This way you can slowly retrieve your fly or lure across the drop-off where the fish like to hang out and skirt into the shallows to nab food and, if you're lucky, your lure. Vary your speed and depth to figure out where the fish are hanging.

Despite the lake's size and relatively low elevation, fishing remains good from late March all the way to early November. The lake is surprisingly deep and is often sheltered from the direct sun by the thick trees and surrounding mountains, so it does not warm up as much as one would expect.

Directions

Cat Lake is a pretty little lake found just off the Sea to Sky Highway (Highway 99). To reach the lake, take the Cheekeye River Forest Service Road heading east. The road is about 3 km from the turnoff to Alice Lake Provincial Park, just north of the mileage sign that says "Whistler 42 km". Once on the forest service road, stay right at the major junction and before the road swings uphill, take the side road down to the lake, which leads off to the right. A gate, which is usually closed on weekends, prevents access to the shores of the lake so you may have to hike your gear in a short distance.

Facilities

The side road from the Cheekeye River Forest Service Road leads to a parking spot above the lake and the **Cat Lake Recreation Site**. From there, a short, steep hike downhill brings you to the camping area next to the lake. There are 36 walk-in sites nestled in the trees here. A wharf offers a tie up for your small boat or a place to cast a line. Those that prefer drive to camping, or do not like the bears that frequent Cat Lake, can always head back to Alice Lake Provincial Park.

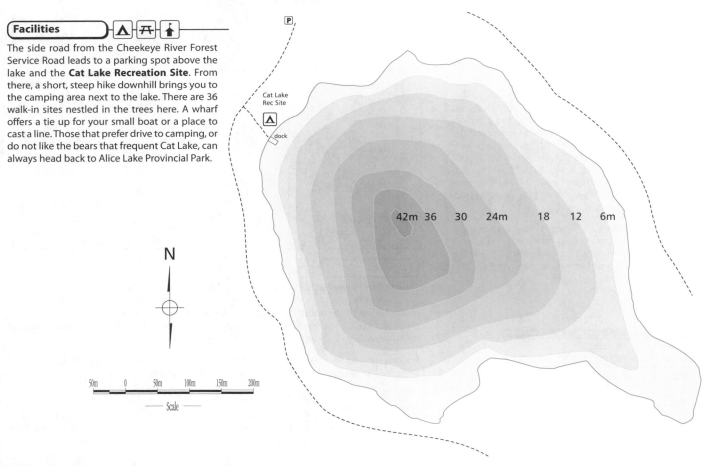

www.backroadmapbooks.com

Caverhill Lake

Location: 24 km (15 mi) northeast of Barrière
Surface Area: 542 ha (1,339 ac)
Elevation: 1,397 m (4,583 ft)
Max Depth: 40.2 m (131.9 ft)
Mean Depth: 14 m (45.9 ft)
Way Point: 51° 20′ 35″ N, 120° 24′ 46″ W

Fishing

Caverhill Lake is one of the larger lakes in the Nehalliston Plateau, but the many bays and arms give the appearance of a small, fly-fishermen friendly lake. The ice leaves the lake by mid-May and the open water fishing runs all the way to the end of October. Since the lake does not warm significantly in the summer months, fast fishing for small trout is common for the entire ice-free season.

The lakes in this area are not stocked, but are naturally reproducing. These Kamloops rainbow trout are famous for their strength, stamina and aerial displays. The trout can grow to 1 kg (2 lbs).

The cool, well-oxygenated water and abundant shallow areas provide an ideal habitat for food sources and are prime feeding areas for the trout. The main food sources for the fish here are scuds, or freshwater shrimp and leeches. The lake also has some hatches, including chironomids, mayflies, cinnamon caddis flies, damselflies and dragonflies. Terrestrials also work well, especially black and brown ants.

Chironomids are also a significant food source. Maroon or red coloured bloodworm patterns are excellent imitations of the larval stage of these insects. Try bloodworm patterns tied on #14-2X and #12-2X hooks. Chironomid larvae should be fished within inches of the bottom of the shoal and the easiest way to present them is under strike indicators.

Chironomid pupa come in a wide variety of colours but the most common species are black, green or brown. At this elevation, the most intense pupal emergences occur from late June through August but smaller hatches occur throughout the entire open water season. The best colours to try are: black with red wire rib, black with silver wire rib, green with gold wire rib and brown with natural copper wire rib.

Some dry fly patterns that should be part of your arsenal on the lake are Tom Thumbs, Humpies, Grey Wulffs and Adams. Wet flies to try are Carey Specials, Halfbacks, Fullbacks, Doc Spratleys, leeches and everyone's favourite the Woolly Bugger.

Other leech patterns such as the Little Fort Leech, Maroon Ruby Eyed Leech and Black Rabbit Strip Leech in various colour combinations are all effective. Common leech colours are black, dark brown, mottled green and brown and maroon.

Spincasters can do well by trolling a small lure such as a Flatfish or Deadly Dick. Lake trolls also produce.

Area Indicator

Directions A

Approximately 14 km north of Barrière on the west side of Highway 5, follow the Darlington Creek Forest Service Road as it winds up a series of switchbacks out of the Thompson River Valley to the southeast corner of the Nehalliston Plateau. There are many side roads, but if you stay on the main road you should reach the south end of the lake after a total of 23 dust filled kilometers. There is a large parking lot here that is used by the Caverhill Lodge to access the lake. Most cars can manage the road. If preferred, the Darlington Creek Road continues along the western shore of the lake.

Facilities

The **Caverhill Lodge** is a boat access only resort open from June to October. The resort has rustic cabins, boat launch, boat rentals and camping. There is no other development on the lake of any kind.

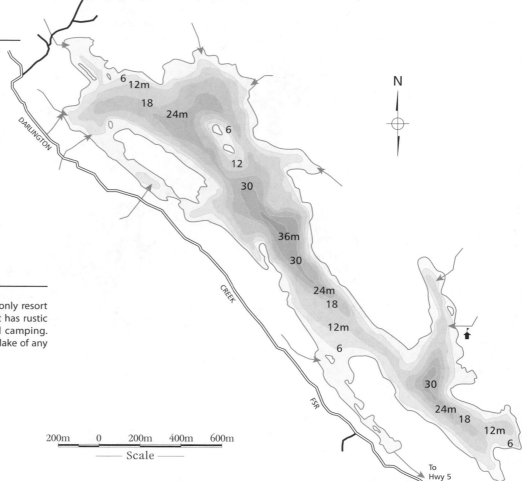

200m   0   200m   400m   600m
— Scale —

Location: 7 km (4 mi) south of Whistler
Elevation: 833 m (2,733 ft)
Surface Area: 469 ha (1,159 ac)
Max Depth: 119 m (390 ft)
Mean Depth: 58 m (191 ft)
Way Point: 50° 0' 36" N, 122° 55' 18" W

www.backroadmapbooks.com

Cheakamus Lake

Area Indicator

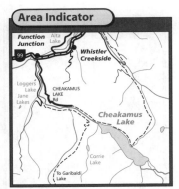

Fishing

Cheakamus Lake is another stunning mountain lake that is worth fishing simply for the scenery. The turquoise coloured lake is surrounded by rugged snow-capped peaks and tall pine trees. The fact the lake is only accessible by trail and has a couple backcountry campsites adds to the appeal.

The lake holds good numbers of rainbow in the 20–30 cm (8–12 in) range and the odd Dolly Varden that grows to 4 lbs (2 kg). People have breathlessly reported catching small lake trout here, but they are almost certainly incorrectly identified dollies.

The lake is very deep and the water drops off rapidly from shore. However, the forested shoreline limits fly-fishing or spincasting from shore. Anglers will need to bring a float tube or canoe to effectively work the lake, which only adds to the difficulty of accessing the lake. Although it is possible to use a canoe cart along the trail, it is still a 3.2 km (2 mile) hike from the parking lot to the lake. This last point is one reason why the lake does not receive much fishing pressure.

The lake is found at a relatively high elevation meaning the fishing season starts a little later here than elsewhere. By mid-May/early June the lake is ready to be fished and it remains cool through summer until the snow starts to fly in early November.

Watch for signs near the north end of the lake demarking the river and the lake, as regulations are quite different in the lake.

Directions

To reach the lake, follow the Sea to Sky Highway (Highway 99) to Function Junction where the Cheakamus Lake Road begins. The gravel road leads southward to the trailhead and parking lot, some 8 km from the highway. Signs point the way wherever there is a junction so it is near impossible to get lost. A car can reach the parking lot.

From the parking lot, a well-used trail meanders initially through a boulder field and some slide alders before entering into a forested area along the Cheakamus River. Overall, it is 3.2 km (2 mi) one-way trek to the campsite located at the west end of Cheakamus Lake. The trail is used by mountain bikers as well as hikers. Packing or rolling in a canoe or kayak to the lake is not out of the question as the trail is very good.

Facilities

Cheakamus Lake is found in **Garibaldi Provincial Park** south of Whistler. At the south end of the lake is a rustic campsite, which is set in a second growth fir/cedar forest next to the lake. There are several tenting pads, a small wharf, a very rough boat launch and some bear caches at the site. Another backcountry campsite, called the **Singing Creek Campsite**, is found on the northern shores near the estuary to Singing Creek. It also has a few lakeshore camping pads for tenters.

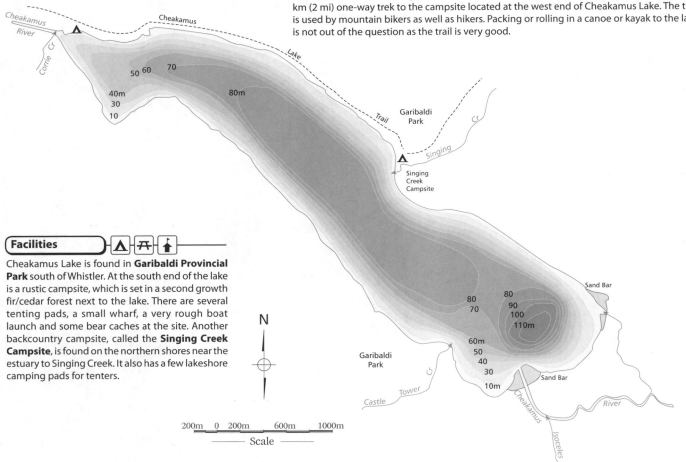

200m   0   200m   600m   1000m
— Scale —

Cheakamus River

Location: 12 km (7.5 mi) north of Squamish
Stream Length: 68.4 km (42.5 mi)
Geographic: 123°9′00″W, 49°49′00″N

Fishing

It is an image that many anglers won't forget: a railway tanker car laying in the Cheakamus River, spilling sodium hydroxide into the water. The date was August 5, 2005. Within a few days the water quality was back to normal. However, the caustic chemical had a devastating effect on the fish population. Steelhead stocks, already down to annual returns of only about 150 fish, were nearly devastated, with 70–90% of juveniles affected. Chinook saw approximately 50% of the 2005 spawning population affected. Resident populations of rainbow trout, cutthroat trout and bull trout were also affected.

That was three years ago. While there is still environmental monitoring happening on the Cheakamus, the river is returning to a state of normalcy. 20,000 smolts were released in 2007 and 2008 to enhance and supplement the 2009 and 2010 steelhead returns. These fish will be allowed to spawn, to determine the effectiveness of the program before the fishery will reopen. And resident trout have started spreading into the areas where populations were wiped out.

The Cheakamus is a gorgeous emerald green river, except when rapids turn the water a frothy white. Only the lowest 17 km (10.5 miles) of the river are salmon bearing. A waterfall at the head of the Cheakamus Canyon presents a natural barrier to salmon spawning upstream.

About 10 km (6 miles) upstream from the waterfall is another barrier, this one the man-made BC Hydro Dam. Below the dam (including the section below the waterfall), you will find lots of rainbow in the 20–25 cm range (8–10 inch), although there are occasionally trout caught to 40 cm (16 inches). Above the dam, the average catch is smaller. Finding a fish bigger than 20 cm (8 inches) is difficult and finding one larger than 35 cm (14 inches) is nearly impossible.

Like all the rivers in the Lower Mainland area, the Cheakamus is basically unfishable during spring freshet, which doesn't usually end until July, with the best times to fish starting in August and continuing to October. There is good nymph and dry fly-fishing above Paradise Valley. There are some good hatches of mayflies and caddis flies. Czech Nymphs, Hare's Ears and Elk Hair Caddis patterns work really well.

The river also has plenty of bull trout. The best time to catch bull trout is in winter, starting in October and continuing to May. Work streamers, popular flies and anything that imitates fry.

There are hatchery Coho in the river, which you can currently catch and keep. Remember, there is a voluntary head recovery program in effect. Call 1-866-483-9994 to find the nearest recovery depot.

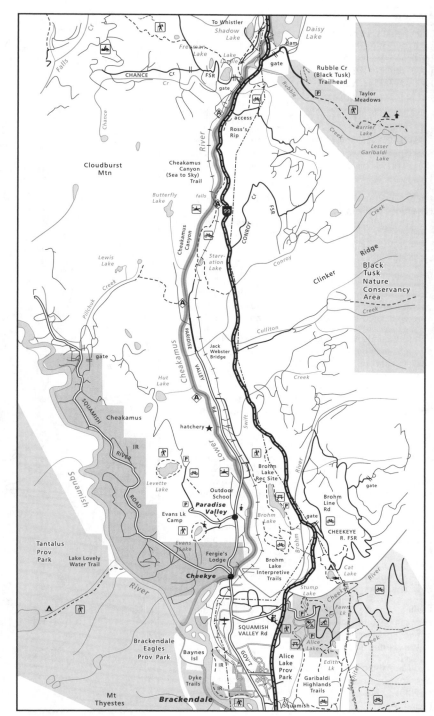

Facilities

There is a formal camping area at the **Cal-Cheak Confluence Recreation Site** north of Daisy Lake. South of the canyon there are a few informal sites at the end of Paradise Valley Road. There is also a fish hatchery found along the road. Framing the river, both Whistler and Squamish offer all manner of services including tackle shops.

Directions

From Squamish, the Paradise Valley Road parallels the Cheakamus until the start of the canyon. Here there is some foot access to the river, but it is difficult. Between the Cheakamus Canyon and Function Junction in Whistler, the river plays tag with the Sea to Sky Highway (Highway 99). At Function Junction, the Cheakamus Road follows the river southeast, almost to Cheakamus Lake. Access is good throughout.

Cheakamus River Fish Stocking Data			
Year	Species	Number	Life Stage
2008	Steelhead	17,618	Smolt
2007	Steelhead	6,679	Smolt
2007	Steelhead	14,081	Fingerling

Location: 15 km (9.3 mi) west of Agassiz
Stream Length: 31 km (19 mi)
Geographic: 121° 56' 9" W, 49° 17' 55" N

Chehalis River

Fishing

The Chehalis is a beautiful river, spending much of it's time navigating the steep, mountainous terrain west of Harrison Lake. It enters the Fraser Valley right before it flows into the Harrison River, just above the Lougheed Highway Bridge. It is a medium sized river that continues to be a popular fishery.

Unfortunately, because most of the river is hard to access, the portions that are easily accessible are usually packed. However, there are some nice places along the river where, if you're willing to put in a bit of work to get there, you will have the place all to yourself.

The Chehalis has a late run of Coho that starts in September and runs through early December. The Hatchery Hole is one of the most popular spots, as are the Easter Seals Run and the Gun Barrel Run. The Easter Seal Run is found just below the Morris Valley Bridge. From here, it is possible to follow the river all the way down to the Harrison confluence…at lease in low water.

The Chehalis blows out easily when it rains, but it also clears up quickly. People have got stranded on the wrong side of the river when the water levels rose too quickly, so keep an eye on the water levels.

In mid-June a small run of summer steelhead passes through here. These summer –run steelhead average 3.5 kg (7 lbs) and are famous for their fight. The steelhead continue to trickle through into September, when the Coho begin to appear. There is also a small Chinook fishery in July and early August, but anglers have had little luck catching these fish except after a good rain.

The low water of early fall and the extreme popularity of this river can make fishing here on a weekend a less than pleasant experience. Unless you enjoy fishing in a crowd try working further upstream or visit during week days. Also bear in mind that the best time to fish is when the river has got a little bit of colour, but isn't blown out.

Above the Morris Valley Bridge, the Chehalis enters a deep, steep walled canyon. Although there are trails heading up along the canyon, getting down to the water can be difficult. If you can find a pool to call your own, you're in luck. Two is a crowd here, so you might have to look long and hard to find your own pocket of water.

In winter, there is a second run of steelhead. Again, the river can be tough to fish, as the water is either too low or two high. The best time to fish the river is when it is a little warmer and raining gently.

If you are fishing for steelhead, work wool in pink, peach or orange, with or without a Jensen egg. Because the steelhead here are not overly large, try using lighter gear.

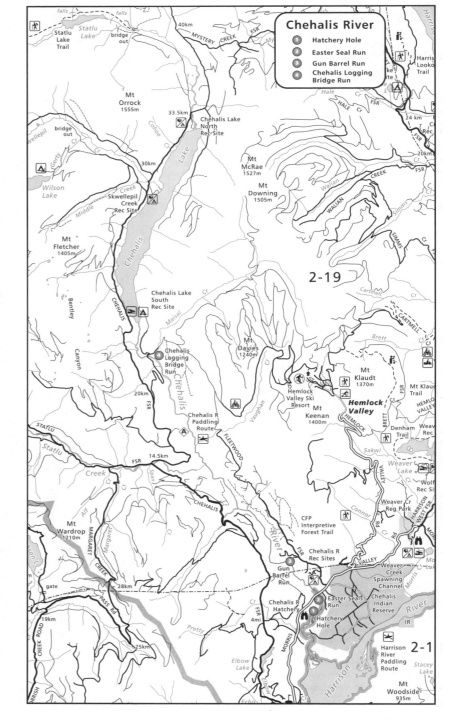

Directions

Take the Lougheed Highway (Highway 7) to the Morris Valley Road turnoff, just west of Harrison Mills. The road crosses the Chehalis River 6.7 km from the turnoff. Just before you hit the bridge, you will pass the Chehalis Hatchery.

Facilities

In addition to the Chehalis River Hatchery, the **Chehalis River Recreation Site** is found at the Morris Valley Bridge. Anglers will find space for about 50 groups as well as good access to the river here. There are also number of other recreation sites in the area.

Chehalis River			
Fish Stocking Data			
Year	Species	Number	Life Stage
2011	Steelhead	51,233	Smolt
2011	Cutthroat Trout	3,000	Smolt

www.backroadmapbooks.com

Chilliwack Lake

Location: 20 km (12 mi) east of Chilliwack
Elevation: 621 m (2,037 ft)
Surface Area: 1,210 ha (2,990 ac)
Max Depth: 114 m (374 ft)
Mean Depth: 67 m (220 ft)
Way Point: 49° 3′ 17″ N, 121° 24′ 58″ W

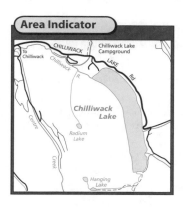

Area Indicator

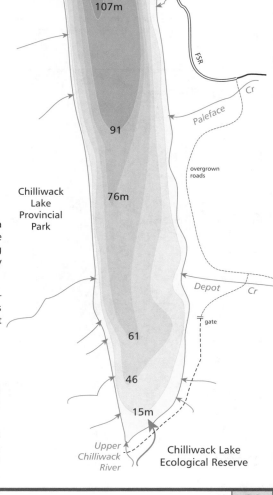

Fishing

Chilliwack Lake is a 9 kilometre long lake found at the head of the Chilliwack River Valley southeast of Chilliwack. It is an extremely popular recreation lake and home to a provincial park.

The big lake contains some big cutthroat and Dolly Varden (to 2 kg/4.5 lbs) along with smaller rainbow, plenty of kokanee and even steelhead. Alternatively, the lake does hold species like black crappie and whitefish, which are rarely fished for but can provide an interesting alternative to the other species.

Since the lake is glacier fed, the waters remain cold, yet clear throughout the summer meaning fishing does not decline over the summer months. Try bottom fishing for the dollies with cured salmon roe or trolling plugs or large Flatfish on a downrigger with a flasher. The rainbow and kokanee are caught on a lake troll with a Wedding Band.

If you are not able to bring a boat to the lake, try shore fishing near one of the inflow creeks or where the Upper Chilliwack River enters the lake at the north and leaves the lake at the south end. Bait and bobber suspended near the bottom or spincasting may work. Fly-fishing is limited but there is a prolific carpenter ant hatch in May. Dry fly-fishing can be great at this time.

However, trolling is your best bet as you can cover more ground and effectively work the drop offs. Try trolling a plug, gang troll or larger spoon. Working around the mouths of creeks will improve your chances of finding all sportfish species.

Directions

The lake is accessed by the Chilliwack Lake Road. Take the Vedder Road exit off the Trans Canada Highway at Chilliwack. Follow this road south through Sardis to the Chilliwack River Bridge. Before the bridge, take a left on the Chilliwack River Road and drive all the way to Chilliwack Lake along the river. The road is paved except the last few kilometers before the lake. The direction is clearly marked and the drive is very scenic with many stops of interest.

After reaching the north end of the lake, you can turn right into the Chilliwack Provincial Park camping area or continue south along the lake. The road–now the Chilliwack Forest Service Road–follows the lake on the eastern shores, gradually deteriorating the farther you get from the pavement. It is still possible to drive your car all the way to the south end.

Facilities

Chilliwack Lake Provincial Park surrounds Chilliwack Lake. The popular park has over 140 treed campsites together with a boat launch, picnic area and beach. The campground is usually full throughout the summer due to its proximity to Chilliwack and its scenic surroundings.

The park was recently expanded, swallowing up the Paleface Recreation Site, the Depot Creek Recreations Site and Sappers Provincial Park. While these sites still provide access to the lake, camping is prohibited in these areas, although development plans are in the works and these areas may be reopened.

Location: 8 km (5 mi) south of Chilliwack
Stream Length: 63.6 km (39.5 mi)
Geographic: 49° 4′ 44″ N, 121° 45′ 27″ W

www.backroadmapbooks.com

Chilliwack/Vedder Rivers

Fishing

This is easily the most popular river in the Lower Mainland, offering nearly year-round fishing in a beautiful setting that seems remote, but is quite easy to access.

Despite the two names, this is one river. The Chilliwack River drains Chilliwack Lake and the Chilliwack Valley, becoming the Vedder at Vedder Crossing. Above the bridge, it is the Chilliwack. Below, it is the Vedder.

The river is closed year-round to fishing above the confluence with Slesse Creek and just to confuse the issue, anglers usually refer to the fishable waters as the Vedder. Between the Slesse Creek confluence and the Vedder Crossing Bridge, the river is closed May 1–June 30. Below the bridge, the river is closed to angling for the month of June.

Whether you call it the Vedder, the Chilliwack or the Vedderwack, the fact remains that there are 36 km (22 miles) of fishable water from Slesse Creek to the Fraser. The lowest sections of the river has been diked and straightened (and given yet another name: the Vedder Channel) and the entire section is accessible by trail.

Because this section is without any form of rapids, the fish zip through this section quickly and start to pool up near the end of Wilson and Lickman Roads. There is a parking lot at the end of Lickman Road.

Above Vedder Crossing, the river is a typical mountain river, featuring runs of whitewater and deep, calm pools. There are boulders and rapids, but no falls to block the fish as they make their way upstream.

The Vedder is one of the best steelhead rivers in the province and when the fishing is on, the river can be extremely crowded. Too many anglers in too short a space can cause conflicts and occasionally, fist fights. Usually fouled lines cause these kerfuffles; try and control your cast and don't allow your float to drift downstream.

Anglers tend to congregate around a handful of popular stretches of water, but with a bit of exploration, intrepid anglers can usually find a stretch of water that no one (or almost no one) is fishing.

When the river opens on July 1, anglers can catch the tail end of the summer run Chinook, although success is very dependant on the year. In summer, it is best to fish for resident populations of rainbow and cutthroat trout, Dolly Varden and Rocky Mountain whitefish.

Coho enter the system in late September and the run peaks in late October, although you can still find Coho until early December, right around the time the steelhead start returning.

When the Coho first enter the river, fresh roe seems to work the best. Wool ties and corkies for the faster water and spinner blades and spoon for the slower water work great. They become harder to catch after the second run of Chinook, transplanted from the Harrison River and known for having white

Continued >>

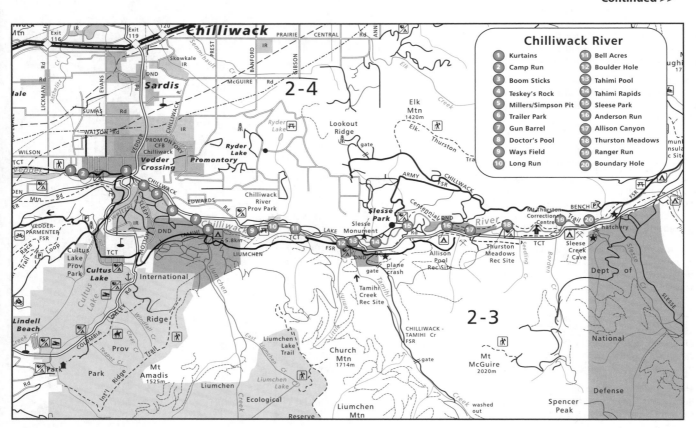

Chilliwack River

1	Kurtains	11	Bell Acres
2	Camp Run	12	Boulder Hole
3	Boom Sticks	13	Tahimi Pool
4	Teskey's Rock	14	Tahimi Rapids
5	Millers/Simpson Pit	15	Sleese Park
6	Trailer Park	16	Anderson Run
7	Gun Barrel	17	Allison Canyon
8	Doctor's Pool	18	Thurston Meadows
9	Ways Field	19	Ranger Run
10	Long Run	20	Boundary Hole

Location: 8 km (5 mi) south of Chilliwack
Stream Length: 63.6 km (39.5 mi)
Geographic: 49° 4' 44" N, 121° 45' 27" W

Chilliwack/Vedder Rivers

Fishing   Continued >>

flesh, enters the river. These big brutes show up starting in early October and run until November. They generally muscle the smaller Coho out of the best holding pools and have been known to destroy gear. They average 9 km (20 lbs) and can pull smaller anglers right into the water. Wool ties in red, red and white or peach, as well as big corkies and Spin-N-Glos fished with a float are all popular. Roe is also popular, but usually unnecessary, as these guys will hit most anything. You will find them holding in deep, fast runs and at the bottom of pools.

The first run of winter steelhead enters the Chilliwack in November and steelheading continues until May when there is a fly-fishing only season. This is the most productive steelhead stream in the region and is heavily enhanced by hatchery fish.

Steelhead like roe, but will also take to pink, peach or orange wool, spoons or spinners. The fish average around 6 kg (12 lbs), but can get to 9 kg (20 lbs) or more. As a result, heavier gear will be more effective.

When the water is very low, the fish don't like entering the shallow Vedder Canal as it offers little protection and few holding pools. Salmon and steelhead queue up at the mouth of the Vedder Canal, moving in and out of the mouth of the canal during the evening or when the water is murkier. This can be a great place to fish, although you will have to hike a short way down the dike roads that line the river here.

There is a clay bank, about 6 km (4 miles) below Slesse Creek, which dissolves when it rains. This leaves the waters below a murky and muddy. At this time, the fish, especially Coho, prefer to move and fishing can be quite good until the waters clear.

On top of the closures noted above, it is catch and release for all wild salmon. The strong appeal of the Chilliwack/Vedder is the fact that most of the runs have been enhanced with hatchery fish, which you are allowed to keep (check the regulations for limits).

Directions

The Trans Canada Highway crosses the Vedder Cannel between Abbotsford and Chilliwack. There are countless backroads in the area that lead to the canal. One of the easiest is to take Exit 116 off the Trans Canada and follow Lickman Road south to the cannel. Keith Wilson Road also leads to the river.

Exit 119 leads to Vedder Road and the infamous Vedder Crossing. Again there is a popular parking area here or you can follow the paved Chilliwack Lake Road upstream and pick the hole of choice. Beyond the bridge that crosses the river near Tamihi Creek the main road continues east, while a lesser used logging road branches west. Both provide good access to generally quieter holes than those found closer to Chilliwack.

Facilities

There are no shortage of recreational facilities in and around the river. West of Vedder Crossing there are a couple private campsites, a few informal campsites and numerous parking locations. East of the crossing, there are countless recreation sites and parks. Camping is offered at **Tamihi, Allison Pool and Thurston Meadows Recreation Sites** just to name a few. You will also find anything else you need in Chilliwack and Sardis, just north of Vedder Crossing. Be sure to stop in at Fred Custom Fly & Tackle before heading out to find out what is working best.

Chilliwack/Vedder River Fish Stocking Data			
Year	Species	Number	Life Stage
2008	Steelhead	96,847	Fry
2007	Steelhead	94,309	Smolt
2006	Steelhead	113,825	Smolt

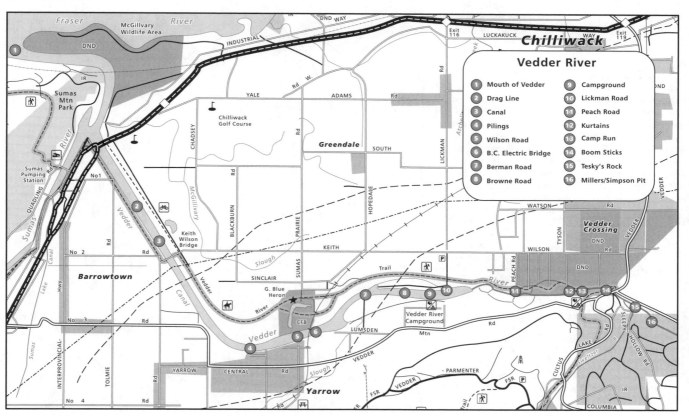

Clearwater River:
Location: North of Clearwater
Stream Length: 119.6 km (74.3 mi)
Geographic: 51° 54' 19" N, 120° 9' 43" W

Clearwater & Mahood Rivers

Fishing

The Clearwater is a gorgeous catch and release river that has its headwaters deep in Wells Gray Provincial Park. For most people, the river starts where it flows out of Clearwater Lake because here it is road accessible, but its headwaters are found at the north end of the park, flowing through Hobson Lake before flowing into Clearwater Lake. The Mahood River, on the other hand, is what you see is what you get, a short, 5.5 km (3.4 mile) stretch of water that drains Mahood Lake into the Clearwater. Together, these two rivers offer some of the best trout fishing in the area.

The Clearwater is known as a drifting river. Floating this section in a dory or canoe is a beautiful and relaxing way to fish here. It is also possible to walk and wade the river, sampling here and there as you move from pool to pool. The best time to fish here is summer, starting in late July and carrying on until September.

The main stem of the Clearwater has lots of rainbow trout, as well as a fair number of Dolly Varden. In summer, salmon begin spawning up the Clearwater. Currently, you are allowed to fish for Chinook in the Clearwater during the month of August, except from Murtle River downstream to the 35 km post to protected Mahood River Salmon. As always, check the regulations before heading out, as in-season changes are quite common.

The Mahood River is known for its huge stone fly hatch. Fish come down out of the lake and into the river to feast on the hatch. Working both dry stone fly and wet nymph patterns can be extremely effective on the river.

Like most great fishing rivers, these two rivers have some very strict regulations on them, the most notable being that they are both catch and release. Bait isn't allowed on the Mahood and is only allowed in certain areas at certain times on the Clearwater. Check the regulations for complete details.

Directions

Found about 120 km north of Kamloops on the Yellowhead Highway (Highway 5), anglers are better off accessing the rivers from the Clearwater River Road on the west side of the river. To get onto this road, turn north on the Clearwater Village Road, then immediately left onto the Old Highway 5. After 1.2 km turn right onto Camp 2 Road, then right again onto Musgrave Road, which becomes the Clearwater River Road. Note that this road is known for sudden mudslides, rock fall, flooding and washouts that can block the road for days. Be prepared for emergencies.

There is also no bridge crossing of the Mahood, but there is a good trail system along this river. To access points further north along the Clearwater, you will need to follow the much more popular Clearwater Valley Road that leads into Wells Gray Provincial Park. Follow the signs and look for the many day use sites and trail systems along the valley.

Facilities

There is no shortage of facilities in the Clearwater Valley. There are some rustic campsites available along the Clearwater River Road, as well as walk-in sites on Mahood Lake. On the east side of the river, there are vehicle accessible campsites, numerous day use sites and countless trails to help explore the rivers.

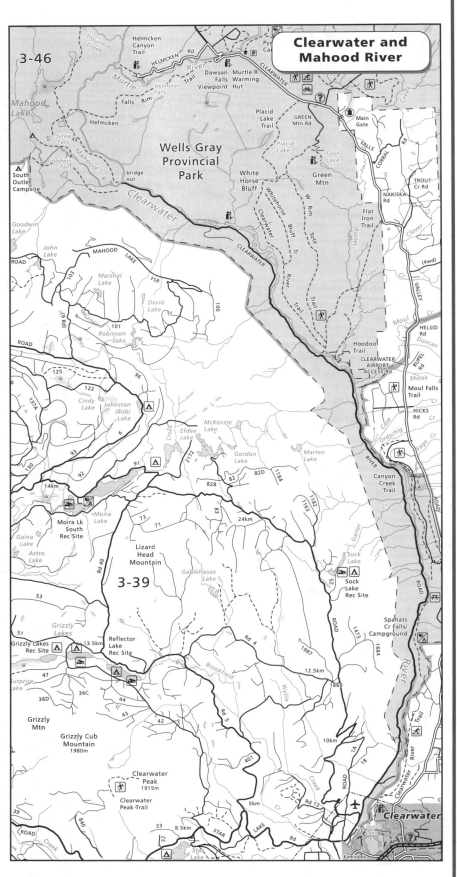

Clearwater Lake

www.backroadmapbooks.com

Location: 67 km (42 mi) north of Clearwater
Elevation: 685 m (2,247 ft)
Surface Area: 3,326 ha (8,218 ac)
Max Depth: 197 m (646.3 ft)
Mean Depth: 101.6 m (333.3)
Way Point: 52°15'N, 120°12'W

Fishing

Clearwater Lake has long been a popular destination for visitors to Wells Gray Provincial Park. The lake is surrounded by majestic mountains with numerous waterfalls cascading down the hillsides. Canoeists, kayakers and anglers all enjoy the peace and tranquility this wild lake has to offer.

Stretching over 22 km (13 miles) long, it is a deep lake with a lot of places for the fish to hide. As a result, trolling is the most effective way to find the rainbow trout, lake trout and bull trout that reside here. Patient anglers may be rewarded with bull trout up to 3 kg (6.5 lbs) and lake trout that can top 6 kg (13 lbs) in size, but most of the success is for rainbow trout in the 1 kg (2 lb) range.

Most anglers work either the north or south ends where the Clearwater River enters and leaves the big lake. The trout congregate in these regions and will readily strike lures or flies that resemble baitfish. Try working a green or orange Flatfish or a Krocodile lure in these areas. Trolling plugs or larger lures with a flasher can also produce, while jigging with a bucktail and flasher in the spring near the outflow of the river can be very successful.

Other good areas to work are around prominent points and around the larger creek mouths such as Barella Creek and Angus Horne Creek. These are the areas that the fish like to hang out in because the creeks wash in oxygen and a variety of insects and other feed. Fishing the creek mouths with bait balls (a large cluster of worms or cured roe) or grasshoppers suspended near the bottom can also be very effective.

Fly anglers will find trolling a leech pattern or Woolly Bugger along the shoal areas at either end of the lake is a good place to start. Again streamer patterns that resemble baitfish can be worked in these areas as well as around the creek mouths.

There are special regulations in place for outlet of Clearwater Lake so anglers need to check regulations.

Directions

Found north of the town of Clearwater, the big lake is easily found at the end of the Clearwater Valley Road. The scenic road snakes next to the river all the way north to the lake. Anglers hauling in boats will want to ignore the campsite and continue onto the boat launch area. It is about 71 km to the end of the road, with only 43 km of that being paved and the rest being a well-maintained gravel road suitable for all vehicles.

Facilities

Found in the heart of Wells Gray Provincial Park, the lake makes up part of the popular Clearwater/Azure Canoe Route. In addition to the **Clearwater/Falls Creek Campground** at the south end, there is a good boat launch onto the lake. The 80 unit campground is open from mid-May to the end of October and available on a first come, first serve basis. Once on the lake, there are also 12 boat/canoe accessible campsites on either side of the lake. There is space for about 33 groups between them.

Other Options

Alice Lake is a small lake that lies on the north side of the Clearwater Valley Road. A picnic area and elaborate trail system are also in the area. Anglers will find good fishing for rainbow trout with the best fishing occurring from mid June to late fall. It is a great family lake with trout that average 30 cm (12 in). A boat or tube is needed to access the water.

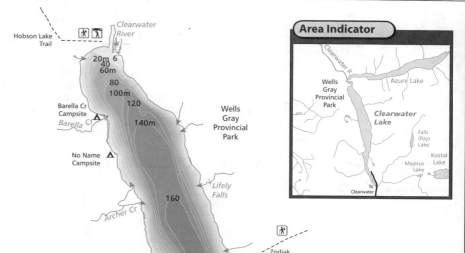

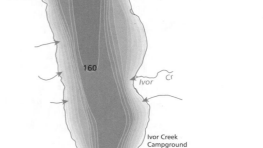

Area Indicator

N

500m 0 1km 2km 3km
Scale

Location: Coquitlam South
Elevation: 148 m (485 ft)
Surface Area: 5 ha (12 ac)
Max Depth: 4 m (12 ft)
Mean Depth: 2 m (5 ft)
Way Point: 49° 15' 36.1" N, 122° 51' 29.2" W

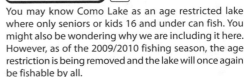

www.backroadmapbooks.com

Como Lake

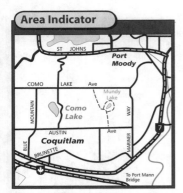

Area Indicator

Directions

Como Lake is an urban lake in the heart of Coquitlam. It is surrounded by Como Lake Park and is located off Gatensbury Road. To get to the park, take the North Road exit off the Trans Canada Highway and follow that to Austin Avenue. Turn right onto Austin Avenue and follow it for about 2.5 km (1.5 miles). Turn left onto Gatensbury Road and watch for the park to your right. Gatensbury Road can also be accessed from the north, from Como Lake Avenue.

Como Lake			
Fish Stocking Data			
Year	Species	Number	Life Stage
2011	Rainbow Trout	3,499	Catchable
2010	Rainbow Trout	6,189	Catchable
2009	Rainbow Trout	6,284	Catchable

Fishing

You may know Como Lake as an age restricted lake where only seniors or kids 16 and under can fish. You might also be wondering why we are including it here. However, as of the 2009/2010 fishing season, the age restriction is being removed and the lake will once again be fishable by all.

That doesn't mean that this won't still be one of the best places for youngsters to fish. Easy access, lots of nearby facilities and two fishing docks make this a great place for kids to learn about fishing. The lake, though quite shallow, has broad, open shores and is quite easy to fish from the shore. This makes it a popular place to learn the basics of fly-fishing, as there is lots of space to practice back casting.

The lake is stocked frequently (usually seven or eight times a year), with catchable sized rainbow trout. The best time to fish is right after the lake is stocked, as the fish are extremely willing to take to almost anything you throw at them. For about two weeks after the lake is stocked, the fishing is fast and furious, but slowly the fastest and most furious trout are fished out of the lake, while the rest start to become a little more discerning in what they will chase.

In addition to the rainbow, people still occasionally pulled out cutthroat trout (which were last stocked in the lake in 1993), brook trout (which were stocked in the lake way back in 1916), brown catfish and carp.

The lake is easily fished using a traditional bobber and bait setup but using small spoons can produce well too. And while it is possible to get out onto the water using a float tube, most people don't bother. The lake is relatively shallow and shore fishing is quite easy particularly if you cast a bobber and bait from one of the two docks or off the rocks at the northeast end of the lake.

One of the busiest times to fish the lake is during the Como Lake Fishing Derby, which is usually held in May by the Port Coquitlam and District Hunting and Fishing Club.

Facilities

Como Lake Park is a typical urban park with no camping but a lot of day use facilities. There is a parking lot at the north and south ends of the lake. A jogging track circles the lake and there is a large playground on the west side of the lake. Two docks and several beaches line the lake. There are plenty of restaurants, hotels, gas stations and other facilities in the surrounding area.

Other Options

There are a variety of other fishing lakes in Coquitlam and surrounding area. These include **Buntzen Lake** in Anmore, which holds cutthroat trout, rainbow trout, kokanee and Dolly Varden as well as **Lafarge Lake**, which holds stocked rainbow and brown catfish. Both these lakes are written up elsewhere in this book.

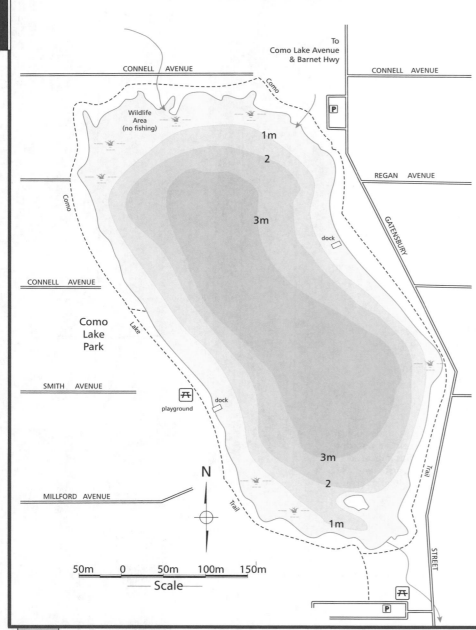

www.backroadmapbooks.com

Courtney Lake

Location: 18 km (11 mi) southeast of Merritt
Elevation: 1,005 m (3,297 ft)
Surface Area: 74 ha (183 ac)
Maximum Depth: 11.8 m (39 ft)
Mean Depth: 4.1 m (13.4 ft)
Way Point: 50° 0' 23" N, 120° 36' 13" W

Fishing

Courtney Lake is a pretty, clear lake with large marl shoals and great visibility. Anglers often overlook this lake because it is so close to the highway, but the lake has some great seasonal hatches and is a near perfect fly-fishing lake. In fact, it is managed as a trophy lake and anglers can only keep one fish a day. There are also seasonal closures, no bait and single barbless hooks restrictions.

The lake is not very deep with two holes, one near the north end and one near the south end of the lake. It is too shallow to troll effectively so it is best to spincast or fly-fish off one of the many shoals. Cast towards the marshy area with a dragonfly or damselfly nymph works very well. Also, minnow imitation flies or lures can produce.

Red-sided shiners were illegally introduced to the lake in the past and when fisheries came and eradicated the fish, they were re-introduced again. Red-sided shiners tend to eat a lot of the same food as the rainbow trout do but they also provide a good source of food for the Blackwater strain of rainbow that were stocked in the lake. These fish were specifically stocked to keep the shiner population down. Blackwater rainbow, while not as famous as the Gerrard strain, are also piscivorous and can grow quite big. It doesn't happen every day, but finding fish to 4.5 kg (10 lbs) is not uncommon and 7 kg (15 lb) fish are occasionally caught here.

The big fish tend to hang out along the drop offs and trolling with a Muddler Minnow or other streamer pattern can often attract the monsters. Caddisfly patterns can also attract significant attention. Trout feed on the pupae but it is the adults that see the most exciting surface fishing action of the season. Good pupal imitations include Fullbacks, Stillwater Caddis Pupae, Cary Specials and Knouff Lake Specials. Effective adult patterns include Tom Thumbs, Goddard Sedges, Elk Hair Caddis and Humpies.

In the fall, black and olive leech patterns, especially Woolly Buggers also do a great job of attracting the attention of the trout.

Gear anglers will want to have a variety of gear along at this lake. Popular alternatives include Mepps spinners in red, gold or silver, silver Flatfish, silver Krocodiles or Dick Nites in brass or silver.

The low elevation lake gets quite warm in the summer. Anglers looking to fish here will find that the fishing is much better in spring and fall.

Area Indicator

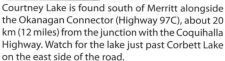

Courtney Lake			
Fish Stocking Data			
Year	Species	Number	Life Stage
2010	Rainbow Trout	6,000	Yearling
2009	Rainbow Trout	5,000	Yearling

Directions

Courtney Lake is found south of Merritt alongside the Okanagan Connector (Highway 97C), about 20 km (12 miles) from the junction with the Coquihalla Highway. Watch for the lake just past Corbett Lake on the east side of the road.

Facilities

There is a day-use area with a boat launch and dock on Courtenay. Virtually next door you will find the **Corbett Lake Resort**. For those looking to camp in the area can follow the **Kane Valley Road** to choose from one of many sites in the popular recreational area.

Other Options

Nearby **Corbett Lake** is managed as a trophy fly-fishing lake. It is a private lake that is selectively stocked to ensure the fishery is good and the fish can reach nice sizes. It is well known for its excellent spring chironomid hatch and a good mayfly hatch.

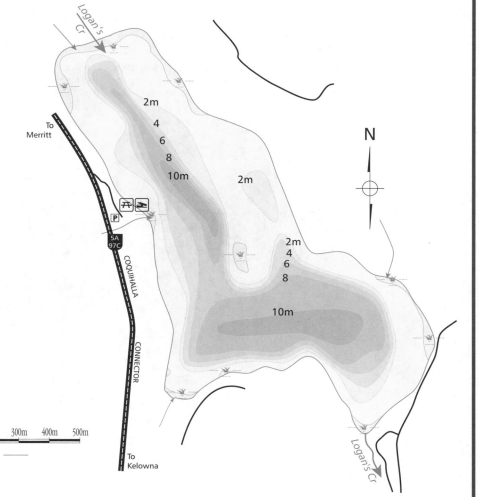

100m   0   100m   200m   300m   400m   500m

— Scale —

Location: 4 km (2.5 mi) south of Bridge Lake
Elevation: 1,143 m (3,750 ft)
Surface Area: 138 ha (340 ac)
Max Depth: 23 m (75 ft)
Mean Depth: 18 m (59 ft)
Way Point: 51° 27' 14.3" N, 120° 45' 35.9" W

www.backroadmapbooks.com

Crystal Lake

Area Indicator

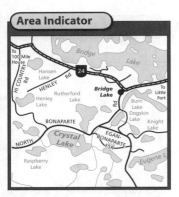

Crystal Lake			
Fish Stocking Data			
Year	Species	Number	Life Stage
2010	Rainbow Trout	35,000	Yearling
2009	Rainbow Trout	34,795	Yearling

Fishing

Crystal Lake is a sensitive wilderness lake, famous for its large insect hatches and trophy sized rainbow trout. As the name suggests, it has crystal clear water making it a better alternative for those with a float tube or small boat.

The lake produces well beginning after ice-off in the early part of May and the fishing remains good until into the early part of the summer. The summer doldrums soon hit and the fishing falls off until late September, picking up again in September and October.

The largest known trout hooked and landed here weighed 6.3 kg (14 lbs) but the average catch weighs 1–2 kg (2–4 lbs), which is still a good-sized fish.

In an effort to protect and enhance the fishing here, BC Fisheries and the Ministry of Environment in conjunction with the Crystal Waters Guest Ranch have developed a spawning channel on the guest ranch property.

Even with the spawning channel, the lake is heavily stocked, to the tune of 25,000 Blackwater rainbow and 10,000 Pennask rainbow in 2008. For the last couple years, the fish that have been stocked are non-reproducing triploid, which grow larger faster.

While the lake is known as a great fly-fishing lake, this is not the only way to fish here. You will see trollers, spincasters as well as fly-fishers hooking on to the trout. If you are fly-fishing, use a long leader because of the clear water and match the hatch. Chironomid, midge, sedge, dragonfly and damselfly patterns all produce depending on the hatch. Because the lake lives up to its name, you will need a long leader, as the fish tend to be quite wary during the day, often staying deep to escape the bright sunlight. On early summer evenings, the trout will rise during the hatches and dry fly fishing can be extremely fun.

Trollers can try working a lake troll, but Flatfish, spoons and spinners also work quite well.

There are some open areas around the shore, but because the bottom generally falls away quite slowly, shore fishing is not usually productive. The best place to try is right around the recreation site.

Facilities

The **Crystal Lake Recreation Site** sits on the northern shore of the lake and offers a cartop boat launch and about a dozen campsites. The site is nicely treed and the road is good enough for cars and RVs to reach the lake.

For a little more luxury, why not check out **Crystal Waters Guest Ranch.** It is one of BC's great guest ranches and they obviously care about the fishery with their spawning channels. Found at the west end of Crystal Lake, the feature log cabins, a lodge and a variety of watercraft for guests.

Directions

The best way to reach Crystal Lake is from the north off Highway 24. About 45 km along the highway, look for the North Bonaparte Road branching south. Follow this road for about 5 km to reach the northern shores of the lake.

You can also access the lake along the North Bonaparte Road from 70 Mile House off of Highway 97. Although the road is a good gravel road, this route is a lot bumpier and dustier.

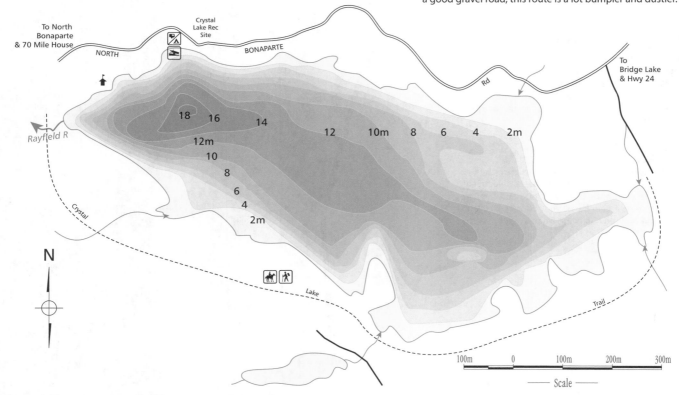

Cultus Lake

www.backroadmapbooks.com

Location: 13 km (8 miles) south of Chilliwack
Elevation: 47 m (154 ft)
Surface Area: 627 ha (1549 ac)
Max Depth: 42m (137 ft)
Mean Depth: 32 m (105 ft)
Way Point:49° 3′ 6″ N, 121° 59′ 13″W

Fishing

Cultus Lake is a popular recreation lake accessed by paved road south of Chilliwack. Home to a provincial park, private campgrounds, marinas, water slides, motels, go-charts, mini-golf and restaurants this is a popular summer destination for Lower Mainland residents.

Well known for its water sports, during the 'off season' fishing is quite good. Trolling in the early spring into May or late fall can produce some large cutthroat and Dolly Varden. In fact, some of the fish approach 50 cm (20 inches) or 2.5 kg (5 lbs). There are also small rainbow and the odd whitefish in this natural reproducing lake.

The lake stays relatively cool in the summer months allowing fish to remain active throughout the ice-free year. Shore fishing is possible since the water drops off fairly rapidly. Try working the five main inflow creeks, around Main Beach or in Maple Bay where the fish tend to congregate. However, the big lake is better trolled. For the bigger fish, try with minnow fly patterns, a Woolly Bugger or trolling with big lures and flashers. Lake trolls with small lures and bait as well as using bait (worm or single egg) and bobber is also effective.

Directions

Cultus Lake is located some 13 km (8 miles) south of Chilliwack. There are two ways to get to the lake that are both well signed. From the west, take the Trans Canada Highway (Highway 1) to the No. 3 Road exit towards Yarrow and Cultus Lake. Keep right at the fork, make a quick right onto Tolmie Road and then left, back onto No. 3 Road. Turn left onto Yarrow Central Road, which turns into Vedder Mountain Road. Follow this to Cultus Lake Road. Turn south and watch for the provincial park to your right.

From the east, take the Vedder Road exit off the highway and follow it south until it turns into Vedder Mountain Road. Turn south on Cultus Lake Road and watch for the provincial park signs to your right.

Facilities

Cultus Lake is an extremely popular recreation area with the **Cultus Lake Provincial Park** being just one of the attractions. The park offers over 280 campsites, beautiful beaches, picnic areas and trails. The campgrounds are open between April and mid-October and reservations through www.discovercamping.com are highly recommended. Paved boat launches are found at Jade Bay (open year round) and Maple Bay (seasonal). Also in the area are private campgrounds, marinas, water slides, motels, go-charts, mini-golf and restaurants.

Other Options

In the mountains east of Cultus Lake is **Liumchen Lake.** You will need an ATV and good navigational skills to reach the trailhead. The difficult access results in little fishing pressure and a good summer fishery for trout that are rumoured to reach 35 cm (14 inches).

Area Indicator

Cultus Lake Provincial Park

15m
30
35

40m

Entrance Bay Picnic Area & Campground

Jade Bay

Windfall

To Vedder Crossing

EDMESTON Rd

40m

Delta Grove Campground

Honeymoon Bay

Clear

Honeymoon Bay Campgrounds

Delta Grove Campground

giant douglas fir

Cultus Lake Provincial Park

Frost Cr

40m
35

30
15m

Maple Bay Picnic Area & Campground

Lindell Beach

amphitheatre

Maple Bay

N

400m   0   400m   800m   1200m

Scale

Deadman & Vidette Lakes

Deadman Lake

Elevation: 860 m (2,821 ft)
Surface Area: 45 ha (111 ac)
Max Depth: 22.5 m (73.8 ft)
Way Point: 51° 7' 29.1"N, 120° 52' 52.9"W

Vidette Lake

Elevation: 876 m (2,874 ft)
Surface Area: 35 ha (86 ac)
Max Depth: 32.9 m (107.9 ft)
Mean Depth: 14.6 m (47.9 ft)
Way Point: 51° 9' 32" N, 120° 53' 39"W

Area Indicator

Vidette Lake

Deadman Lake

N

Fishing

This pair of lakes is found in the beautiful Deadman River valley, northwest of Kamloops.

Deadman Lake is the better of the two lakes with reasonably good fishing for rainbow and kokanee that reach 1 kg (2 lbs) in size. The lake is fairly deep and is easily trolled. Fertile shoals are located near the north and south ends of the lake as well as around the island at the southeast end of the lake.

Nearby Vidette Lake is easily the prettiest lake in the scenic Deadman Valley. However, the scenery is often better than the fishing here.

It too is a deep lake, but it is much longer stretching 3 km along the valley. The rainbow are generally smaller (in the 20–30 cm/8-12 in range) and there are also good numbers of kokanee in the lake.

Fly anglers are often enticed by the prolific hatches in the region. Leech, shrimp, damselfly nymph and dragonfly patterns all work depending on the hatch. The favorite flies for the area are the Tom Thumb, Doc Spratley or Carey Special.

By far the most effective way to fish the kokanee in both lakes is to troll a Wedding Band and worm or maggot. Dick Nites, tiny Spin-n-Glos and Mepps spinners can meet with success. Alternatively, you can cast a dry fly (the best one is a Grey Gnat). The kokanee tend to be small but you may be lucky enough to catch a fish in the 1 kg (2 lbs) range. During the summer, kokanee stay near the surface of the lake, unlike the rainbow.

In the winter months, ice fishing is popular particularly for kokanee. Bait such as maggots, worms or corn on a hook and weight are productive.

Directions

The access into these remote lakes will discourage most fishermen from sampling the productive waters. The Deadman-Vidette Road leads north from the Trans Canada just west of the Deadman River Bridge, about 50 km west of Kamloops. The road follows the Deadman River for what appears like an eternity until you reach Skookum Lake, the first of five lakes in the valley. Beyond Skookum, the road becomes much rougher. It is about 47 km to Deadman Lake and another 6 km to Vidette Lake.

Facilities

The **Deadman Lake Recreation Site** is located on the eastern shore of the lake and offers four treed camping sites and a place to hand launch small boats. The **Vidette Lake Recreation Site** is a smaller, two unit site that offers rustic lakeshore camping at the northeast end of the lake.

Further north, the **Vidette Gold Mine Resort** offers year-round accommodation as well as a wide array of services including a fly-fishing school and canoe and rowboat rentals.

Deep Lake

Location: 12 km (7.5 mi) north of Kamloops
Elevation: 557 m (1,827 ft)
Surface Area: 5 ha (12 ac)
Max Depth: 12.8 m (42 ft)
Mean Depth: 5.2 m (17.1 ft)
Way Point: 50° 47′ 42.4″ N, 120° 20′ 45.8″ W

www.backroadmapbooks.com

Fishing

Deep lake is a gem of a lake tucked in the hills above Kamloops. The small lake holds large populations of rainbow and brook trout, in a location sure to guarantee a quiet day on the water.

This lake is not easy to get to. In fact, the only way to access Deep Lake is on foot, via a trail that will challenge anyone's fitness. Deep Lake may be only 12 kilometres north of Kamloops city centre but don't be fooled by its proximity to the city. Once there, it will feel like you're in the middle of nowhere. The lake is set at the bottom of a sprawling grassland basin. A steep hillside rises to the west of the lake, blocking out signs of nearby civilization and Ponderosa pine, sagebrush, bright yellow arrowleaf, balsamroot and bunchgrass surround the rest of the lake. This is big sky country and if you are willing to make the effort to get there, you will feel like you stumbled onto a movie set for an old fashioned western. Who knows who will come riding up over the rise?

Deep Lake is not very big. A strong arm could pitch a rock from one side to the other at parts of the lake. The lake is ideal for spinning gear, as its quickly rising banks make fly-casting challenging for most anglers. A good spinning rod can throw a spinner halfway down the lake.

Ultra-light gear–short rods and reels loaded with four to six-pound test line–is ideal, but don't forget to bring a bit of bait as a small worm dangled beneath a bobber is tempting for trout. Mepps spinners in various sizes and colours are a good bet.

Fish the shallows at both ends.

Fly-fishers who want to take full advantage of their gear should pack a float tube. The usual stillwater patterns, from chironomids to leeches, can all be successful.

The lake is stocked with eastern brook and rainbow trout on an alternate-year basis. In 2006, the Freshwater Fisheries Society of BC released 2,000 brook trout fry.

Deep Lake is a wonderful family lake. The ability to fish from shore makes it fun for the kids and the half hour hike should tire young legs. Exercise, isolation, spectacular surroundings and a unique fishery make Deep Lake a winner on all fronts.

Directions

To get to Deep Lake from downtown Kamloops, take Tranquille Road to Eighth Street. Drive north for about 10 km (6 miles) on Westsyde Road to Ida Lane. Turn west and follow this road to a black arch and trailhead sign. The newly established **Grasslands Community Trail** starts here and leads to the south end of Deep Lake and all the way to McQueen Lake Forest Service Road. This trail follows an old road and can be walked or biked (no motorized vehicles allowed). It should take about half an hour to walk over the ridge to the lake. It is also possible to loop around the west side of the lake on an old road/trail.

Facilities

The lake is found in **Lac Du Bois Grasslands Protected Area**. Walk-in camping is permitted in the park, but there are no facilities provided. There are recreation sites north of the park, at **Isobel** and **Pass Lakes**, but most people will probably just head back into Kamloops, where all services are found.

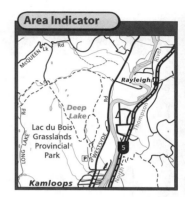

Area Indicator

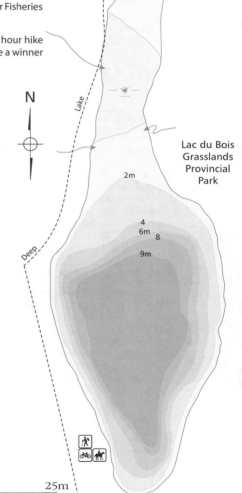

Lac du Bois Grasslands Provincial Park

Trail to Westsyde Rd via Ida Lane

Deep Lake Fish Stocking Data			
Year	Species	Number	Life Stage
2011	Rainbow Trout	1,500	Fingerling
2010	Brook Trout	2,000	Fingerling
2009	Rainbow Trout	1,500	Fingerling

25m   0   25m

Scale

Location: 11 km (6.8 mi) northeast of Harrison Hot Springs

Deer, Hicks & Trout Lakes

Area Indicator

Fishing

This trio of lakes is located in Sasquatch Provincial Park near Harrison Hot Springs. The lakes offer excellent year-round fishing and are easily accessible.

The biggest of the three lakes is Hicks Lake. It is the hub of the provincial park and is quite busy in summer. There are several sportfish present here, including cutthroat and rainbow trout, kokanee and lake whitefish. Cutthroat and rainbow trout in the lake average about 0.5 kg (1 lb) and kokanee are a little smaller but provide an excellent pan-fry opportunity. The lake whitefish can reach up to 3 kg (6 lbs) but are less common. Rocky shorelines and a small, rehabilitated outlet creek provide natural spawning opportunities for the native cutthroat, rainbow, kokanee and whitefish populations.

Of all the species, cutthroat trout are the most frequently caught fish. The lake is typical of many mid-elevation coastal lakes with overhanging or downed trees providing cover for fish and habitat for food. The best place to fish is around the small island or at the mouth of one of the four bays.

There is no seasonal angling closure and the lake usually doesn't freeze in the winter; however, summer months can be busy with other users. The best fishing for bait anglers is in the early spring, from February to April and for trollers and fly-fishers, from April to early July and again from September to November. Trolling, bait and spincasting and fly-fishing are all successful methods of catching cutthroat, rainbow and kokanee. For trout, try trolling close to shore or around the two small islands located at the north end of the lake.

Worms, small Flatfish or spoons trolled behind a small Willow Leaf are all reliable producers. Still fishing with worms, single salmon eggs or Powerbait on the bottom or with a float can also be effective especially in the winter or early in the spring.

Fly-anglers should try small black, brown or green chironomids in sizes 12–16 earlier in the spring and then switch to small micro leeches in the same colours in sizes 8–14 during late spring and early summer. Your best bet for kokanee is to fly-fish with chironomids or troll with a Wedding Band and worm or a pink or red coloured spoon such as a Dick Nite or Hildebrandt at shallower (between 5–8 m/15–25 ft) water depths. Kokanee are most active in the early morning or late afternoon.

Deer Lake has both rainbow and cutthroat in the 20–35cm (8–12 in) range. The lake is best fished by boat although shore fishing along the road is possible. Since the fish are plentiful, they are easily caught using a number of methods. For example, casting from shore using a bobber and bait (worm or salmon flies) is effective. Also, trolling a Willow Leaf and worm is effective as is casting an attractor type fly (Doc Spratley, Woolly Bugger or Royal Coachman). Boaters should be wary that the lake can be quite windy in the spring and fall.

The lake is quite shallow near the boat launch and slowly gets deeper, with the deepest part of the lake being near the south end of the lake. These sharp transitions make for prime holding areas for trout later in the year, especially as there is both an inflowing and outflowing stream at this end of the lake. In the spring, people have reported lots of success towards the north end of the lake, where there are plenty of weeds and lily pads.

There is a trail along the southwest side of the lake, which provides some access for shore fishing. Another place to try is off the point near the boat launch, although it is still quite shallow here.

The lake has plenty of brown or olive coloured scuds and fly anglers should try working these patterns. Another options is to try a dry line with a Knouff Lake Special and strip it quickly, giving it a few moments to rest between strips. A fast retrieve seems to be more effective here than a slow retrieve, but it seems to depend on the day, the weather and the person doing the fishing. Doc Spratleys can also work well.

Nearby Trout lake is the smallest of the bunch and is the least fished, probably due to the fact there is no campsite here. The shallow lake can be one of the most productive lakes in the area since it has plenty of small rainbow trout that take easily to flies.

The lake should be fished from a canoe or float tube as shore fishing is limited by the bushy and marshy shoreline. The lake is a very low elevation lake and this, coupled with its small size mean that the water here gets warmer in summer than the other two. Fishing tends to slow down in summer but is quite good in spring or fall.

There are various motor restrictions on all of the lakes. Hicks Lake has a maximum 10 hp motor restriction, while Deer Lake has an electric motor only restriction. Engines of any kind are not allowed on Trout Lake.

Deer Lake

Elevation: 196 m (643 ft)
Surface Area: 54 ha (133 ac)
Max Depth: 8 m (26 ft)
Mean Depth: 4 m (13 ft)
Way Point: 49° 22' 1.5"N, 121° 40' 26.8"W

Directions

Sasquatch Provincial Park is an easy two hour drive east of Vancouver, along the Lougheed Highway (Highway 7). Follow this highway almost to Agassiz, where Highway 9 heads north to the town of Harrison Hot Springs. From here, follow the park signs and Rockwell Drive northeast for about 11 km (6.8 mi) to the park entrance. The last 5 km (3 mi) within the park is a well maintained gravel road.

Facilities

Found in **Sasquatch Provincial Park**, these three lakes offer a good selection of facilities. In addition to 177 campsites spread out between Deer and Hicks Lakes, there are host of other amenities including picnic areas and beaches, playgrounds and amphitheatres, boat launches and docks, as well as an elaborate trail system around the lakes for shore anglers. The campgrounds are almost certainly full during the summer weekends, but you can reserve a space through www.discovercamping.com.

Other Options

There are two other places to try in the park. **Beaver Pond** is a tiny pond north of Hicks that produces well for rainbow and cutthroat to 40 cm (16 inches). A tube or waders is a must. **Moss Lake** is accessed by a 1.5 km hike, which keeps most anglers out. But if you're willing to pack a float tube, the action can be pretty constant for cutthroat to 35 cm (14 inches).

Deer, Hicks & Trout Lakes

Elevation: 211 m (692 ft)
Surface Area: 128 ha (316 ac)
Max Depth: 55 m (180 ft)
Mean Depth: 23 m (75 ft)
Way Point: 49° 20' 31"N, 121° 42' 1"W

Hicks Lake

Elevation: 86 m (282 ft)
Surface Area: 13 ha (32 ft)
Max Depth: 6 m (19 ft)
Mean Depth: 3 m (10 ft)
Way Point: 49° 20' 55.9" N, 121° 44' 21.6"W

Trout Lake

Deer Lake			
Fish Stocking Data			
Year	Species	Number	Life Stage
2010	Cutthroat Trout	3,360	Yearling
2009	Cutthroat Trout	1000	Catchable

Deer Lake

N

100m 0 100m 200m 300m 400m 500m

— Scale —

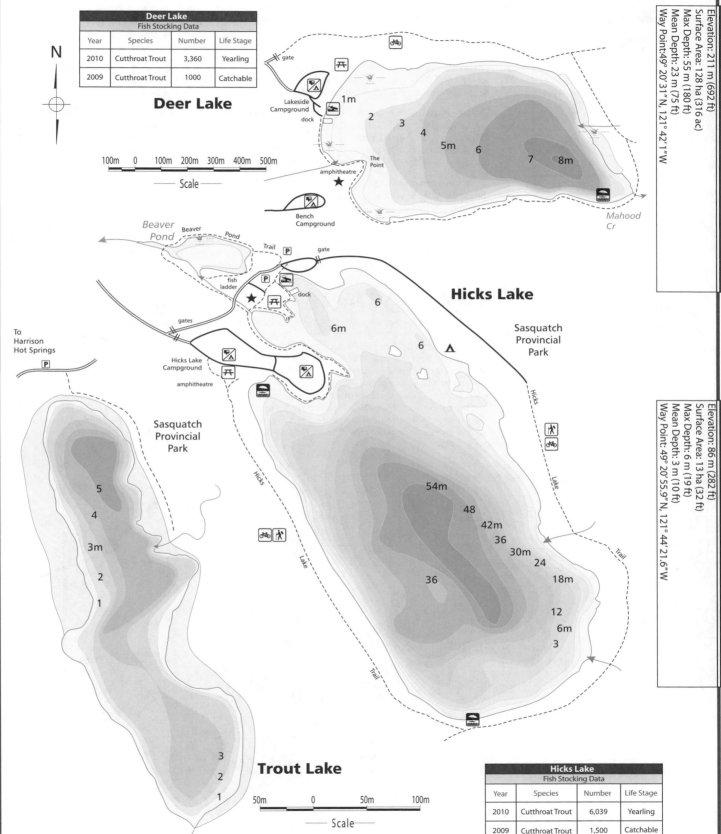

Hicks Lake			
Fish Stocking Data			
Year	Species	Number	Life Stage
2010	Cutthroat Trout	6,039	Yearling
2009	Cutthroat Trout	1,500	Catchable

Hicks Lake

Trout Lake

50m 0 50m 100m

— Scale —

Location: Burnaby
Elevation: 25 m (82 ft)
Surface Area: 35 ha (86 ac)
Max Depth: 6 m (20 ft)
Mean Depth: 3 m (10 ft)
Way Point: 49° 14' 11.3" N, 122° 58' 18.5" W

www.backroadmapbooks.com

Deer Lake - Burnaby Area

Area Indicator

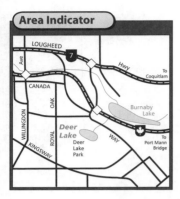

Fishing

Deer Lake Park is located in the city of Burnaby, right near City Hall. It is accessible by public transit and is a green oasis in the heart of the city. The lake from which the park gets its name is a popular destination for sunbathers, trail enthusiasts, wildlife watchers and, of course, anglers.

The lake is best known for its stocked rainbow trout but is one of the few places in the Lower Mainland where you can find black crappie. This helps maintain the fishery here, as the crappie become active in the summer, at the same time the rainbow trout are not hitting lures with their usual vigor.

The lake is usually stocked several times a year (in 2007, it was stocked four times) with pan-sized catchable rainbow. Right after the lake has been stocked is a perfect time to bring kids to the lake to teach them how to fish. This is because for about two weeks after the lake is stocked, the trout are willing to hit most anything you throw at them. After they've been caught a few times (and after the most willing victims have been pulled out of the lake), the fish become more wary.

While some people like to get in a belly boat and kick over to the Royal Oak Avenue side of the lake, most of the rainbow like to stick around the boathouse dock, where they are released. This makes them fairly easy to find, although the dock can get quite crowded right after a release.

Black crappie are usually found in sloughs, warm water lakes or swamps. The fish school together so if you catch one, chances are you will catch a few more. They bite on just about any bait. A small spinner, nymph fly pattern or tiny bass jig also work. Wheel them in slowly as they have small, soft mouths. Crappie are a warm water fish and become most active in July and August when the water is warm.

Directions

Deer Lake is located in Deer Lake Park in Burnaby. Take the Kensington exit off the Trans Canada Highway south to Canada Way. Turn easy on Canada Way and then south on Sperling Avenue. There park is signed and there is a parking lot just off Sperling.

Facilities

Deer Lake Park is a popular retreat for city dwellers. In addition to a comprehensive system of trails on the north and west side of the lake, there is a popular beach and picnic area on the east end of the lake. Here you will find boat rentals in the summer and your typical urban park amenities (washrooms, playground, etc), as well as some not-so-typical ones. (In the summer there are often open-air concerts here and the park is home to the Shadbolt Centre for the arts and the Burnaby Village Museum.) There is no camping here, but there are plenty of hotels and restaurants a short drive from the lake.

Other Options

While **Burnaby Lake** is located nearby, it is not known as a great fishing lake, although that may change with habitat improvements taking place. Instead, pop over to Coquitlam, where you will find **Lafarge Lake**. In 2008, a new fishing pier was built here, to provide better access for anglers. The lake is stocked regularly (up to ten times a year) with catchable-sized rainbow and fishing is fast and furious following a release.

Deer Lake			
Fish Stocking Data			
Year	Species	Number	Life Stage
2011	Rainbow Trout	1,600	Catchable
2010	Rainbow Trout	500	Catchable
2009	Rainbow Trout	1,600	Catchable

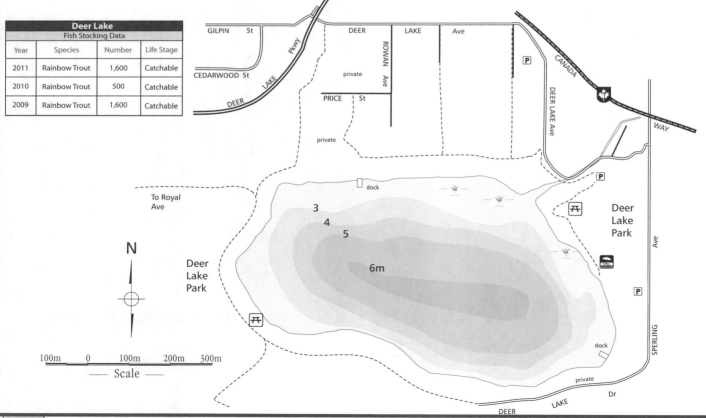

Duffey Lake

Location: 35 km (22 mi) northeast of Pemberton
Elevation: 1,121 m (3,678 ft)
Surface Area: 367 ha (907 ac)
Max Depth: 84.4 m (276.9 ft)
Mean Depth: 37.8 m (124 ft)
Way Point: 50° 24' 17" N, 122° 18' 23" W

Fishing

Duffey Lake is one of those lakes burned into the consciousness of outdoorsy types who live in the Lower Mainland. It helps that the route between Cache Creek and Pemberton gets its name from the lake.

But while the lake is often thought about, it does not get visited as frequently as you would expect. It is at least a three hour drive from either location. The lake is too far for a day trip and since the park is currently advertised as day-use only, it is not a prime destination for campers, either.

For those willing to make the journey, they will find a beautiful mountain lake right next to the highway. From the boat launch at the east end of the lake, you can see straight down the lake, with steep sided cliffs rising on the north side and glaciers to the west.

Duffey Lake is very deep, with some points exceeding 84 metres (275 feet). This and the high elevation keep the water quite cool, even in summer.

However, the lake is not known for offering the greatest fishing, despite the low pressure it receives. The BC Parks website is somewhat ominous, when it says there are "some fish still available in the lake."

The lake, given its size, is best trolled. The lake contains rainbow and bull trout that can reach 2 kg (4 lbs) but average less than half that, usually. The lake also holds some lake trout and mountain whitefish.

Try trolling a lake troll such as a Ford Fender with a Wedding Band and worm. A Flatfish (silver or frog colour) or Krocodile can also be productive especially for the bull trout.

For something different, you can try casting around the mouth of one of the many incoming creeks. The three big creeks are Cayoosh Creek, at the west end of the lake, Van Horlick Creek, about 1 km east on the southern shore and Steep Creek, about halfway down the lake.

To fish the creeks, try anchoring about 30 metres (100 ft) offshore and cast across the current of the stream. Some lures that work are a Blue Fox and a Hot Shot. This is a good area for fly-anglers, too.

Facilities

Duffey Lake Provincial Park is a large 2,379 hectare park encompassing the entire lake and some of the surrounding mountains. The old Duffey Lake East Recreation Site is part of the park and is located right next to Highway 99 at the northeast end of the lake. However, BC Parks is not advertising the site and the park is currently considered a day-use park. There are plans to build a new 40-50 unit campsite at the west end of the lake, but nothing yet. The boat launch at the east end of the lake is still available, although it is a rough gravel launch with very little parking for vehicles.

Directions

This large lake is located northeast of Pemberton right next to the Sea to Sky Highway (Highway 99), the so-called "Duffey Lake Road". To find the lake, head east from Pemberton on Highway 99 for about 35 km. Continue east past Mount Currie and soon you will reach the northwest end of Lillooet Lake. The highway switchbacks uphill from Lillooet Lake alongside Joffre Creek before heading east to Duffey Lake.

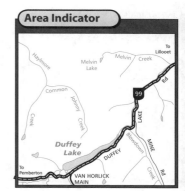
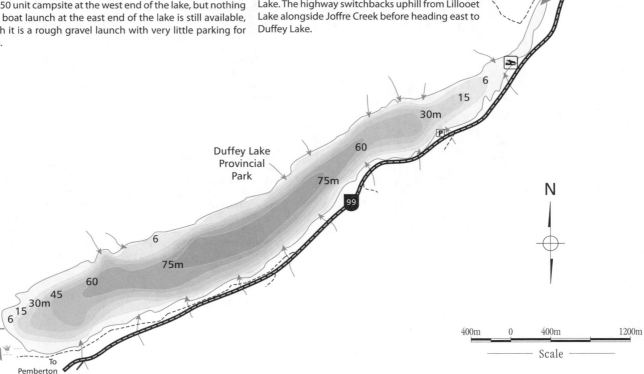

Location: 25 km (15.5 mi) west of Kamloops
Elevation: 1,187 m (3,894 ft)
Surface Area: 24 ha (59 ac)
Max Depth: 11 m (36.1 ft)
Mean Depth: 6.7 m (22 ft)
Way Point: 50° 39' 14.6" N, 120° 42' 26.2" W

Duffy Lake

Area Indicator

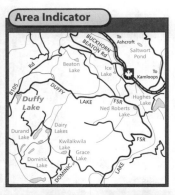

Duffy Lake			
Fish Stocking Data			
Year	Species	Number	Life Stage
2011	Rainbow Trout	3,500	Yearling
2010	Rainbow Trout	3,500	Yearling
2009	Rainbow Trout	3,500	Yearling

Fishing

Duffy Lake is a small lake west of Kamloops. While the lake is a reasonably popular fishing destination (along with the nearby Dairy Lakes), this area is a popular destination for motorcyclists. In fact, the Greater Kamloops Motorcycle Association looks after the recreation site at the lake. If you are looking for a secluded getaway, this is not your lake.

If you are looking for a small lake with extensive shoals, one that offers good fishing for stocked rainbow and don't mind the sound of an occasional two-stroke engine, then Duffy Lake is for you.

The lake is stocked annually with 3,500 rainbow that can reach 2 kg (4 lbs) in size. However, the average fish is quite small. It is not very deep and has nice drop-offs and shoals ideal for fly-fishing and trolling.

Of the two, fly-fishing is definitely more productive. That is because the water is clear and the fish tend to spook when a boat motor passes by. Spincasters willing to drop anchor and cast usually have better success.

While the lake is fairly high in elevation allowing for a decent the summer fishery, the best time to fish here is in late May and early June. There are days where a fisherman can easily limit out during this time.

For the fly angler, try a shrimp, dragonfly or mayfly pattern depending on the hatch. Casting from the deep water to the shoals, then slowly retrieving, or even kicking very slowly backwards if you are in a float tube helps you work the shoals better.

A popular place to fish this lake is at the head of a bay at the south end of the lake. Work around the drop-off here. People in float tubes or small boats can work their way slowly along the eastern shore, working towards the back bay along the edge of the drop-off.

In the spring, there are some good chironomid hatches, while in the fall, scuds and black or maroon leeches work well. Halfbacks, fullbacks and Doc Spratleys are also good choices.

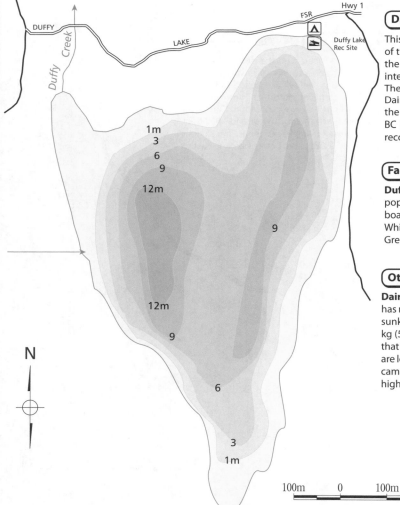

Directions

This small lake is located off the Dairy Lake Forest Service Road south of the little community of Cherry Creek. To reach the lake, head west on the Trans-Canada Highway (Hwy 1) from Kamloops past the Coquihalla interchange. About 6 km later, the Greenstone Road leads to the south. The second major intersection leading to the west on this road is the Dairy Lake Road. That road continues west and eventually branches into the rougher Duffy Lake Road. A 4wd vehicle, The Thompson Okanagan BC Backroad Mapbook and a GPS with the BC Backroad GPS Maps are recommended to help find the lake.

Facilities

Duffy Lake Recreation Site is set below Greenstone Mountain. It is a popular dirt biking area that offers 52 campsites together with a cartop boat launch. There is a fee to camp here from mid-May until mid-October. While in the area, be sure to explore the extensive network of trails around Greenstone Mountain.

Other Options

Dairy Lakes are about 15 minutes south of Duffy Lake. The bigger lake has nice shoals along the south and east sides of the lake as well as a large sunken island just out from the recreation site. There have been some 2.5 kg (5 lb) fish out of here, but the average is much smaller. Fly anglers say that the Knouff Special seems to work quite well here. Other flies that work are leeches, dragonfly nymphs, scuds, a '52 Buick and Mayfly patterns. The campsite is usually full despite the rough road into it. Dairy Lakes rest at a higher elevation than Duffy and take a few more days to defrost.

N

100m   0   100m   200m   300m

Scale

www.backroadmapbooks.com

Dunn Lake

Location: 25 km (15 mi) south of Clearwater
Elevation: 460 m (1,509 ft)
Surface Area: 374 ha (924 ac)
Max Depth: 84.1 m (275.9 ft)
Mean Depth: 54.8 m (179.8 ft)
Way Point: 51° 26' 9" N, 120° 7' 43" W

Fishing

Dunn Lake is a somewhat bigger lake set below Mt. Fennell. The lake is known for its crystal clear water surrounded by scenic mountains. Anglers will find rainbow trout, Dolly Varden, lake trout and kokanee.

While the fish are generally small, there have been reports of 11 kg (25 lb) lake trout coming out of here. However, lakers are hard to come by in the lake. They like to stay deep and since Dunn Lake is up to 84 m (276 ft) deep in places, they can be hard to reach. The two most common ways of fishing for lake trout are jigging or trolling. Jigging just off the bottom with a ¾ ounce to ounce and a half bright yellow or white baited jig can be effective. However, jigging in depths much deeper than 24 metres (80 feet) can be difficult, as there is just so much line out. Better to troll using a downrigger using a baited spoon like an Apex, or a large Rapala plug. As a rule of thumb, the later in the year, the deeper you should troll. Lake trout are often found in the shallows of the lake in spring, just after ice off, but slowly make their way deeper as the summer progresses.

Because lake trout are so hard to find, few people fish for them. Instead, most people here are fishing for rainbow, which are usually less than 1 kg (2 lbs). Trolling is also the prime method of fishing for rainbow, which are best taken using a lake troll (Willow Leaf with Wedding Band and bait) or small lure (Panther Martin, Deadly Dick or Mepps).

For the kokanee, a lake troll worked slowly is a good bet. Trolling in a slow S pattern causes the lure to flutter and behave much more randomly, making it more attractive to these landlocked sockeye. For dollies, a lure such as a Krocodile or green Flatfish is a good bet.

Fly-fishing is tough here. Use a long light leader for best success.

Given the depth of the lake, the water does not warm significantly in the summer so fishing remains active throughout the ice-free season.

Directions

From Little Fort and Highway 5 north of Kamloops, take the ferry across the North Thompson River. Once on the east side of the river, head north on the Windpass Road and follow this road up and over to the Dunn Lake Road, some 6 km later.

Alternatively, the Dunn Lake Road connects the towns of Barrière in the south with Clearwater in the north. It is paved for most of its length but there are stretches north of the lake that are not.

Facilities

The **Dunn Lake North Recreation Site** is found at the north end of the lake. The semi-open grassy site has room for about six units as well as a boat launch. In addition to fishing and canoeing on the lake, there are horseback and motorized trails in the area to explore.

The **Dunn Lake Resort,** at the south end of the lake, offers rustic cabins and a nice campground set in an old growth cedar stand. There are boat rentals and a boat launch as well.

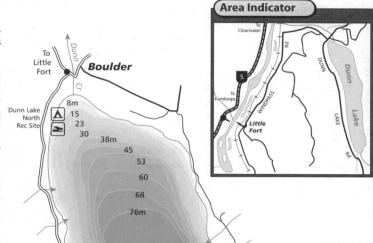

Area Indicator

N

200m 0 200m 600m 1000m

Scale

Location: Clearwater
Elevation: 412 m (1,352 ft)
Surface Area: 58 ha (143 ac)
Max Depth: 41 m (134.5 ft)
Mean Depth: 13.6 m (45 ft)
Way Point: 51° 39' 4.4" N, 120° 3' 24.8" W

www.backroadmapbooks.com

Dutch Lake

Area Indicator

Dutch Lake
Fish Stocking Data

Year	Species	Number	Life Stage
2010	Kokanee	3,050	Fry
2010	Rainbow Trout	3,000	Yearling
2009	Rainbow Trout	3,000	Catchable
2009	Kokanee	2,999	Fry

Fishing

Dutch Lake is found within the town of Clearwater. It gets its name from a pair of German, or "Deutch" homesteaders who resided near the lake. Over time, "Deutch" became "Dutch" and as a by-product, the lake has become a popular tourist destination for folks from Holland.

More than 50 years ago, Dutch water lilies were planted in the lake. These lilies create a magnificent flowering display in summer. The lilies also provide some coverage for the brook trout, kokanee and rainbow trout that live in the lake. Kokanee and rainbow are stocked here annually (sometimes more than annually), while brook trout were stocked in the lake until 2006. They have been stocked in the lake since 1998 and have historically been all female triploid, which means they do not reproduce. Expect to find fewer and fewer brook trout over the next few years, unless the Freshwater Fisheries Society of BC decides to stock the lake again.

The kokanee and rainbow are also triploid fish, which means they are genetically modified to be sterile. This means that the fish do not reproduce and pour all that repressed sexual energy into growing bigger faster.

Being so close to town, the fishing pressure here can be pretty heavy. The stocking keeps the levels of fish strong and the lake is a good family recreation lake, ideal for young children looking to catch their first small fish. Almost by design, the water drops off fairly rapidly from shore allowing virtually anyone a good chance to fish from shore. In particular, children are able to cast a bobber and worm from shore.

Despite the low elevation, the lake is deep enough to maintain an active fishery, even in the heart of the summer. Trolling a lake troll with a Wedding Band and worm or a Flatfish is a good choice. For fly anglers, concentrate your efforts around the west side of the island located near the east end of the lake. There are some nice shoals in that area. Mayfly, shrimp or chironomid patterns are the most effective.

In the winter, the lake offers decent ice fishing using bait (worm, maggots or corn) and a hook.

Directions

Dutch lake is located off the north side of Highway 5 before entering the town of Clearwater. Follow the Old North Thompson Highway for a short distance to the lake and park access road.

Facilities

Dutch Lake Park is a nice retreat for local residents offering a picnic area, several trails and good access to the lake. For those looking to stay on the lake will find the **Dutch Lake Resort & RV Park** offers cabins and campsites as well as a restaurant. They even maintain a working sternwheeler (the Yukon Queen) that takes passengers on half-hour rides around the lake.

Other Options

There are a number of good fishing lakes near Clearwater. These include **Surprise Lake, Grizzly Lakes** and **Reflector Lake** north of Clearwater in the shadow of Grizzly Mountain. The latter two lakes have recreation sites on them with boat launches. All three lakes offer good fishing for rainbow trout. A copy of the Backroad Mapbook for the Thompson Okanagan will help you find these and other good fishing lakes in the area.

N

To Little Fort

100m 0 100m 200m 300m 400m 500m

— Scale —

East Barrière Lake

Location: 25 km (15 mi) east of Barrière
Elevation: 632 m (2,074 ft)
Surface Area: 994 ha (2456 ac)
Max Depth: 100 m (328.1 ft)
Mean Depth: 48 m (157.5 ft)
Way Point: 51° 16' 50" N, 119° 47' 21" W

Fishing

East Barrière Lake is one of the last undeveloped lakes in the interior of British Columbia, but that is changing. The lake is found in a narrow valley surrounded by mountains. Recently, a waterfront development has sprung up on the lake. While there have always been a few cottages and retreats here (including a Scouts wilderness retreat), the new development will see an entire cottage community on the shores of the lake. How that will change the ambiance here remains to be seen.

Historically, the lake hasn't seen as much pressure as the Bonaparte Plateau Lakes and is still a good option if you want to get away from the crowds.

The lake is a low elevation lake and in the heart of summer, the water can get shockingly warm for such a deep lake. Some years, the water has been as warm as 27°C (80°F). This is much too warm for a cool water species like rainbow trout, which are the most popular game fish here.

But it is also a deep lake–over 90 metres (295 feet) in places. That keeps the water below the surface layer quite cool and the fishing can remain quite active, even in the heart of summer.

Well, active is a relative term. Because the lake is so big, the fish have lots of places they can go and even when the fishing is on, don't expect fast and furious action. However, big lakes have a tendency to produce big fish and this lake is no exception. The average size rainbow is 1 kg (2 lbs), while catches to 4 kg (8 lbs) are not unheard of. The lake also holds nice sized bull trout, burbot, Dolly Varden, Mountain Whitefish and kokanee.

Because it is a big lake, trolling is the primary method of fishing. Rainbow take lake trolls as wells as a variety of plugs and lures such as the Kamlooper, Rapala, Flatfish or Apex. Dollies can be fished effectively at the river estuaries using a bait ball. Trolling with a Flatfish or a Krocodile at the 9–27 metre (30–90 foot) level is also effective.

If you are fishing the kokanee, try a Willow Leaf with Wedding Band or Dick Nite and worm trolled near the surface (3–9 m/10–30 ft deep) on a very slow troll. Trolling in an "S" manner slows the lure even further while enticing the fish to bite because of the speed fluctuation of the lure.

Fly anglers can have good success fishing at the estuaries of inflowing creeks, around the many shoals, or in the lake's shallow bays.

Directions

To get to East Barrière Lake, your best option is to head to Barrière on Highway 5, north of Kamloops. Follow the paved Barrière Lakes Road east. At the intersection with the South Barrière Lake Road, stay straight. This will bring you straight to the lake.

The East Barrière Lake Forest Service Road continues along the southeast side of the lake. It leads past several private cottages and the occasional place where you could theoretically access the lake for shore fishing.

Facilities

On the northwestern shores of the lake, the **East Barrière Lake Recreation Site** is an enhanced site that offers an improved boat launch and 16 campsites. The forested site has a nice beach for swimming and there are a few trails in the area to explore. There is a fee to camp here from mid-May until mid-October.

Beyond the recreation site, there is a boat access scout camp and a few private cottages and little other development on the lake…yet.

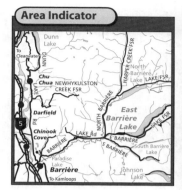

Area Indicator

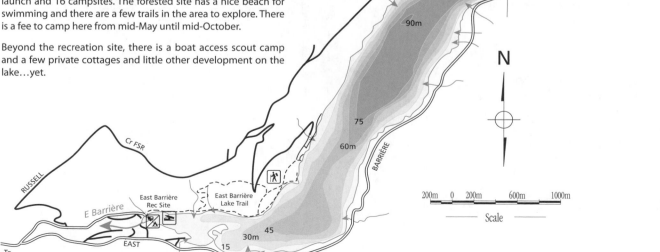

Location: 12 km (7.5 mi) south of Kamloops
Elevation: 1,025 m (3,363 ft)
Surface Area: 27 ha (66 ac)
Max Depth: 11.6 m (38 ft)
Mean Depth: 5.8 m (19 ft)
Way Point: 50° 34' 22.9" N, 120° 21' 2.3" W

Edith Lake - Kamloops Area

Area Indicator

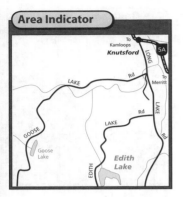

Fishing

Edith Lake is found in open rangeland with mostly wide-open shores and only a few trees. The 27 hectare lake is extremely productive and grows big brook and rainbow trout. Because the lake is stocked with triploid (sterile) fish and because the lake has a lot of food for the fish to eat, the fish grow quickly. A fingerling stocked in the spring is usually close to 1 kg (2 lbs) by the fall. The lake was one of the first lakes in the area stocked with triploid rainbow, which can get up to 4.5 kg (10 lbs) here. The brookies also reach impressive sizes here.

The open shore provides easy access for shore fishermen with a set of waders. The lake is fairly low in elevation and the ice starts to break in early April before freezing up again in late November. This is one f the longest open water seasons of lakes in the area and as an added bonus, is open to ice fishing, too.

However, the low elevation means the lake gets quite warm in the summer and a green plankton bloom covers the surface of the lake with a green scum for most of the summer.

The eastern brook trout are best caught by casting a small lure like a Deadly Dick or a green Flatfish with a worm. Fishing a traditional bobber and worm can also work well.

In the fall, the brook trout spawn. They begin congregating in the shallows and become extremely aggressive. Fishing an attractor type pattern like a red, black or yellow Doc Spratley or Woolly Bugger can yield unbelievable results. Colourful micro-leech patterns are also popular, as the brook trout really seem to like fattening up on leeches. Spincasting at this time can be productive, too.

The lake has four distinct bays with shallow water where there is a proliferation of insects and invertebrates. The fish are often found near these areas, usually cruising along the drop-off. Try working around the drop-off, either by trolling slowly or by casting from deep water into the shallow water and retrieving across the break.

Fly anglers looking for rainbow, try working a floating line with a strike indicator and a chironomid pattern early in the spring and nymph patterns a little later on. For faster action, stick closer to the launching sites on the west side of the lake. The north shore seems to produce the bigger fish.

That said, fishing here is often an exercise in patience and changing gear or fly patterns to see if you can figure out what works. When the fish are biting, it is a magical experience. If they're not…well, there is always tomorrow.

Directions

Edith Lake is easily accessed from the good 2wd Edith Lake Road. From Kamloops, take Highway 5A south toward Merritt. At the tiny community of Knutsford, head south on Long Lake Road for 3.5 km to the Edith Lake Road turnoff. From here it is 4.3 km to the north end of Edith Lake. There is random parking next to the lake.

Facilities

There are no facilities at the lake, but people just pull up a camper or tent trailer. There are at least three places where you can launch a cartop boat and small trailer boats.

Edith Lake			
Fish Stocking Data			
Year	Species	Number	Life Stage
2011	Rainbow Trout	3,000	Yearling
2010	Rainbow Trout	11,712	Catchable
2010	Brook Trout	4,500	Fingerling
2009	Brook Trout	7,500	Fingerling
2009	Rainbow Trout	4,500	Fingerling

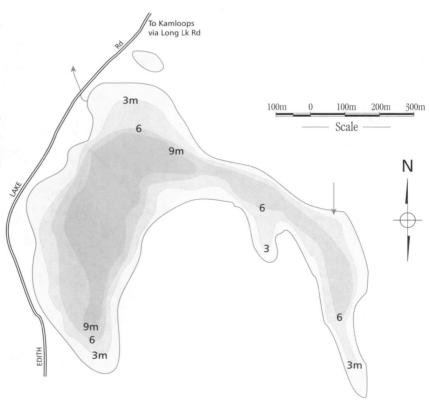

Elbow Lake

www.backroadmapbooks.com

Location: 8 km (5 mi) northwest of Chilliwack
Elevation: 176 m (577 ft)
Surface Area: 20 ha (49 ac)
Max Depth: 22 m (72 ft)
Mean Depth: 10 m (33 ft)
Way Point: 49° 16' 32" N, 121° 57' 55" W

Fishing

Elbow Lake is a small lake found on the way to Chehalis Lake. The water is a beautiful emerald green colour and is well protected from the strong winds of the Fraser Valley. The small, steep-sided lake is fairly low in elevation making for a fine early and late season fishery for rainbow trout.

Elbow Lake offers plenty of small rainbow and has recently been stocked with catchable sized fish by the Freshwater Fisheries Society of BC to help keep the lake quite productive. The easy access and stocked fish help make this a great family fishing lake.

The lake is pretty enough, though is not tucked back far enough in the mountains to have the same stunning scenery as Chehalis Lake. While the east side of the lake is bushy and steep and nearly impossible to angle from shore, the Chehalis Forest Service Road runs along the lake's west side, opening it up. Even better, the water quickly drops off, making it easy to fish from shore here. However, passing vehicles can kick up quite a cloud of dust.

There is no boat launch, but it is possible to hand launch a boat. Trolling along the drop-off on either side of lake with a Willow Leaf and worm or wet fly produces small rainbow. Given that the lake is sheltered from winds, fly-fishing is also popular. Float tubes also work well on the lake.

Fly-fishers have reported having success here with red bellied Tom Thumbs and water boatman patterns, while spincasters say that a red Wedding Band with nice big fat gooey dew worm work wonders. In fact, the fish in the lake lack discrimination and will usually take well to most anything you decide to toss at them, at least early in the year after the stocking. Spincasters working from shore will find that a float and worm, or other bait will produce quite well. Casting small spoons can also prove effective.

The does get quite warm in summer resulting in a slower fishery. It is best fished between March to May and again in September to November.

Directions

Elbow is a small lake found along the Chehalis Forest Service Road north of Harrison Mills. This road is found almost immediately off the Morris Valley Road, which branches north from the Lougheed Highway (Highway 7) at Harrison Mills. If you cross the Harrison River Bridge, you've gone too far. Turn left again at the first junction, which puts you on the Chehalis Forest Service Road. At 2.9 km along the good gravel road, you will come to the south end of the lake. The lake can easily be accessed by car.

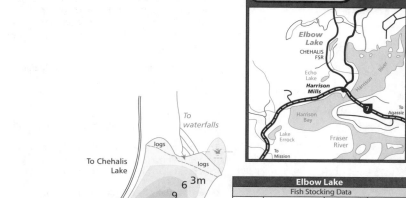

Area Indicator

Elbow Lake
Fish Stocking Data

Year	Species	Number	Life Stage
2011	Rainbow Trout	400	Catchable
2010	Rainbow Trout	400	Catchable
2009	Rainbow Trout	433	Catchable

To waterfalls

To Chehalis Lake

logs

6 3m
9
12m

15
18

21m

18
15

15m

CHEHALIS FOREST SERVICE ROAD

12
9
6m
3
logs

Elbow Cr

To Hwy 7

N

50m 0 50m 100m 150m
Scale

Facilities

There are no developed facilities at the lake but there is a gravel parking area at the south end of the lake. Visitors have cut out several camping spots next to the shoreline and near the gravel parking area. Unfortunately, it is not a maintained campground and some people don't feel the need to take care of it. The site is starting to get beat up and covered with litter; if you do go, leave the place in a better state than you found it in.

There are a number of alternate camping spots in the nearby area, including **Kilby Provincial Park**, just east of the Lougheed Highway/Morris Valley Road junction, as well as a bunch of recreation sites farther north along the Morris Valley/Harrison West Forest Roads.

Location: 24 km (15 mi) northeast of Logan Lake
Elevation: 1,463 m (4,800 ft)
Surface Area: 65 ha (161 ac)
Max Depth: 9.3 m (30.5 ft)
Mean Depth: 5.2 m (17.1 ft)
Way Point: 50° 32′ 31″ N, 120° 37′ 58″ W

www.backroadmapbooks.com

Face Lake

Area Indicator

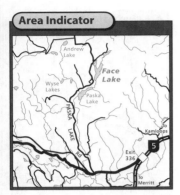

Fishing

When the water is cool, fishing is hot for trout and other cool water species and when the water is hot, the fishing cools down. Based on this simple fishing equation, Face Lake will offer some of region three's hottest fishing in summer. At 1432 m (4700 ft) the lake is just shy of a mile above sea level, which has earned the lake the alias "Mile High Lake". The high altitude means the water never warms up during the heat of the summer.

Face Lake has dark, tannic water and lily pads around the shorelines, typical of many high-altitude lakes. There is a large population of rainbow trout due to the natural creek spawning. However, the high numbers of fish mean they seldom grow big. Expect plenty of trout in the 0.5 kg (1 lb) range with the occasional fish reaching 1 kg (2 lbs).

But lots of fish means fast action for anglers and, because the lake isn't ice free until late in the spring, the fish here are usually more than willing to strike at anything and everything offered.

The fast action means this lake is friendly to various types of anglers: from experienced fly-anglers to young beginners wielding a spinning rod with a worm and bobber. It is one of the best lakes for fly-fishers to test new patterns. Flies that fail to attract attention from trout here may not be ready for more serious action elsewhere.

Green is usually the magic colours for flies here, working some standard patterns like damsels and scuds and attractor patterns like Woolly Buggers, Carey Specials, halfbacks and Doc Spratleys. However, sometimes the fish have a thing for reds, too.

Finding the bigger fish can take a bit of work. While the younger, smaller fish are willing to hit most anything, the older, wiser trout that have survived a season or possibly two are often less willing to come up from the deeper sections of the lake. They generally wait for the low light periods of late evenings and early mornings to feed.

Trollers find success with the usual methods and hardware. Experiment with combinations of lures, trolling speed and depth. Lessons learned in this classroom could improve odds elsewhere.

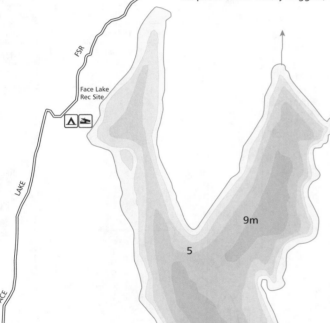

Directions

When travelling the Coquihalla Highway between Merritt and Kamloops, keep your eyes open for the exit to Logan Lake. This exit, which is Exit 336 or the Meadow Creek Road, leads west. At about the 8 km mark, turn north onto Paska Lake Road, which is well signed. Continue down this road for 10.2 km (6.2 miles), passing Paska Lake before reaching the south end of Face Lake. The road beyond the resort is rough and may require a 4wd vehicle.

Facilities

At the south end of Face Lake are the **Mile High Lodge** and the **Face Lake Recreation Site.** The resort offers both cabins and campsites along with boat and canoe rentals. The access into the 2 unit recreation site and the rustic launching site further north is a little rough and may deter some.

Other Options

Dominic Lake is a nearby lake worth investigating. The higher elevation lake offers a good summer fishery for rainbow that top 0.7 kg (1.5 lbs).

Face Lake Fish Stocking Data			
Year	Species	Number	Life Stage
2010	Rainbow Trout	4,000	Fry
2009	Rainbow Trout	4,000	Fry

N

— Scale —
100m   0   100m   200m   300m

To Hwy 5
Exit 336 via
Meadow Lake Rd

Flash & Thunder Lakes

Elevation: 1,242 m (4,075 ft)
Surface Area: 13 ha (32 ac)
Max Depth: 4 m (13 ft)
Mean Depth: 1 m (3 ft)
Way Point:49° 2'25" N, 120° 51'42"W

Flash Lake

Fishing

Flash and Thunder Lakes are part of the Lightning Lake Chain in Manning Park. They are lake two and lake four in the lake chain, respectively and are relatively popular destinations for hikers as well as anglers from late June through to October.

Flash Lake is best known for holding the largest rainbow in the park with the average being 25–30 cm (10–12 in) on years when the fish are not winterkilled. The fish come readily to a fly, bait or small lure.

The lake is not very deep and has expansive shallow areas good for insect and invertebrate growth. Because the lake is so shallow, shore fishing is fairly tough but you can usually get towards the deeper water if you try near the middle of the lake off the northern shoreline.

Try casting a good trout fly like a Royal Coachman or Grizzly King in the early morning or late in the evening when the fish are rising. A Doc Spratley, Carey Special or nymph pattern are also good choices. For the spincaster, most small lures with some bait will produce.

Thunder Lake is about an hour's walk down the trail from Flash Lake. It holds plenty of small rainbow, averaging 20 cm (8 inches) best caught with bait or fly-fishing.

Facilities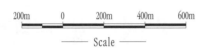

There are no facilities at either lake, outside of the trail that links the two of them. However, there is a backcountry campsite between the two, at Strike Lake. There is also drive-in camping at nearby Lightning Lake.

Area Indicator

Flash Lake

Manning Provincial Park

Scale
200m 0 200m 400m 600m

N

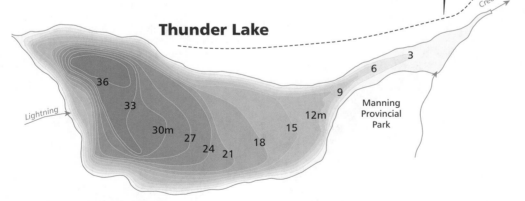

Thunder Lake

Manning Provincial Park

Elevation: 1,170 m (3,839 ft)
Surface Area: 33 ha (82 ac)
Max Depth: 38 m (125 ft)
Mean Depth: 17 m (56 ft)
Way Point:49° 1'15.7" N, 120° 56'25.4"W

Thunder Lake

Directions

To access the lakes, drive to the Manning Park Lodge on the Crowsnest Highway (Highway 3) east of Hope. At the lodge, turn right and follow the signs to the day-use area at Lightning Lake along the Gibson Pass Road. Park your vehicle and begin the hike on the Lightning Lake Chain Trail along the northern shores of Lightning Lake. The trail is well maintained and has little elevation gain. Once past Lightning Lake, Flash Lake will appear within a few hundred meters. Thunder Lake is about an hour's walk beyond Flash Lake.

Other Options

There are two other lakes in the Lightning Lake Chain. **Lightning Lake** is described in more detail later in the book, while nearby **Strike Lake** also contains many small rainbow. The fishing in all four lakes is quite similar to tactics that work in Lightning or Flash will work here.

Location: 58 km (36 mi) southeast of Pemberton
Elevation: 994 m (3,261 ft)
Surface Area: 154 ha (380 ac)
Max Depth: 46 m (151 ft)
Mean Depth: 18 m (59 ft)
Way Point: 49° 50' 24" N, 122° 23' 45" W

Area Indicator

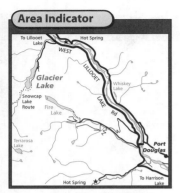

Fishing 🐟

This pair of lakes was once fairly inaccessible, but logging roads, built in the 1990s have made getting to these lakes easier. However, the lakes are found of the Harrison West Forest Service Road, one of the loneliest stretches of roads to be found so near to the Lower Mainland. The best access is via Pemberton, which means that, while the lakes are less than 100 km from downtown Vancouver as the crow flies, it's nearly three times that distance to drive. So despite the improved access to these high elevation lakes, the fishing remains strong here.

The lakes are set just outside of Garibaldi Provincial Park's eastern boundary, so close that Glacier Lake's western shore actually defines the boundary. The scenery in this area is remarkable and for many people, the natural beauty found here makes the difficult access more worthwhile.

Both lakes feature a rapid drop offs making shore line fishing a possibility. However, getting out onto the lakes with a boat or float tube will improve your mobility and allow you to cover much more water than you could trying to beat your way around the lakes.

Fire Lake is the harder of the two to access and you will need to hike about a kilometre to access the lake, which has plenty of small rainbow averaging 30 cm (12 inches) that come readily to a fly or lure in the summer and fall. The best location to fish is towards the shoals located at the northwest end of the lake. There are two inflow creeks near the small island together with some nice shoals. Working chironomid patterns off the shoal areas early in the season can be productive. Chironomids can be a variety of colours depending on the week, the day, even the time of day. Having a dip net or a throat pump will help you figure out what colour the fish are feeding on. Chironomids tend to hatch quite deep in Lower Mainland lakes, so be prepared to fish down deep. Trolling a leech pattern is never a bad idea pretty well all season long, but can work particularly well in autumn. Other attractor patterns like Doc Spratleys and Carey Specials can be used, too.

Trolling is the most popular way to catch the fish. Lake trolls, spinners, spoons and plugs have all been known to produce, especially tipped with powerbait or a worm.

Spincasters can work a variety of small gear. Casting almost any small spinner or spoon with some bait (worms are preferred) can prove successful, but watch for bait restrictions. Favorites are the Panther Martin (silver or black), Mepps Black Fury or Blue Fox. As for lures, a Deadly Dick, small Dick Nite, Flatfish or Kamlooper also work well.

There is a trail that circles the lake.

Continued>>

Facilities ⛺ 🍱 🚹

There are no developed facilities at either lake, although there seems to be more of an established backcountry campsite on the eastern shores of Glacier Lake. Both lakes are frequented by trail enthusiasts looking to explore the remote northwest side of Garibaldi Provincial Park.

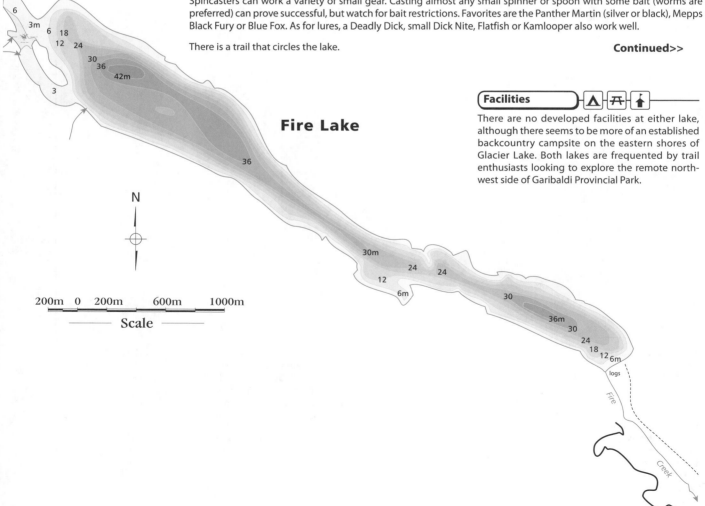

Fire Lake

N

200m 0 200m 600m 1000m
Scale

Fire & Glacier Lakes

Location: 54 km (33.5 mi) southeast of Pemberton
Elevation: 292 m (958 ft)
Surface Area: 212.7 ha (525.6 ac)
Maximum Depth: 29 m (95.1 ft)
Mean Depth: 16.4 m (53.80 ft)
Way Point: 49° 53′ 4″ N, 122° 26′ 50″ W

Fishing   Continued

Nearby Glacier Lake provides fairly good fishing for rainbow trout, kokanee and Dolly Varden throughout the spring and fall. Trolling is your best bet, although fishing the shoreline with a fly or small lure can be effective. Despite its proximity, Glacier Lake lies in a valley, more than 600 metres (2,000 feet) below Fire Lake. As a result the fishing starts here sooner. Fly-fishermen and spincasters should try near the inflow creek near the south end of the lake or near the small island in the middle of the lake.

Kokanee are best taken using a small Willow Leaf trolled. Kokanee usually feed on plankton, so a large pattern will frankly scare them off. Trolling too fast will also scare the kokanee off; the usual accepted speed is about 5 kmph (3 mph). Of course, trolling in a straight line at a constant speed will do little to entice the kokanee. Rather, troll in large, slow S-Curves, occasionally varying your speed. The more random the pattern, the more curious the kokanee become. Use a rubber snubber to absorb the shock from the initial strike. Kokanee have tender mouths, and if you set the hook too hard, it can tear the hook right out, which is bad for the fish.

Directions A

To reach these lakes involves a long drive from Pemberton or a long drive up the Harrison West Forest Service Road. However, the Harrison West Road is infamous for having sections that will destroy even the heartiest of 4wd, so the better route is via Pemberton.

Continue northeast on Sea to Sky Highway (Highway 99) until you reach the north end of Lillooet Lake. Take the main logging road (In-Shuck-Ch Forest Service Road) all the way to the south end of the Lillooet Lake. Here you will find Little Lillooet Lake and a bridge over the narrows. Turn right at the bridge and head south along the Lillooet River via the Lillooet West Forest Service Road to the second road heading up Snowcap Creek around the 23 Mile sign post. This road leads up the creek to Glacier Lake.

To reach Fire Lake, continue down the Lillooet West Road to the Fire Lake Road. It is about 78 km from Highway 99 to the Fire Lake Road junction. Mining activity in the area may limit access, but reports are they will escort you to the trailhead if you report in at the office near Tipella.

These lakes are not easy to find and it is highly recommended that you bring along a map as well as a high clearance 4wd vehicle. The Vancouver, Coast and Mountains Backroad Mapbook and Backroad GPS Map for BC are excellent resources when exploring these and other backcountry lakes.

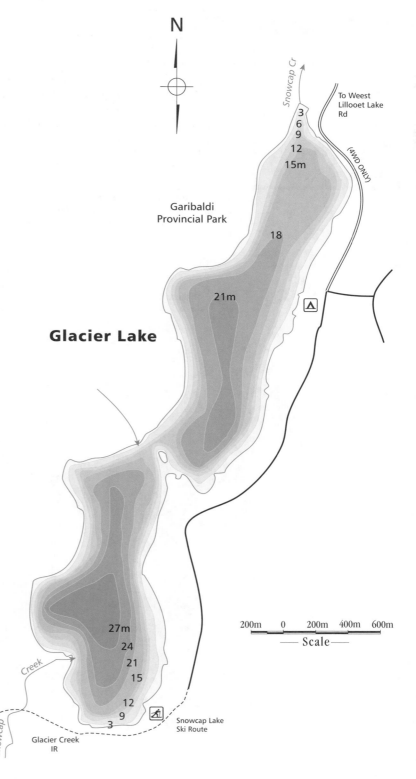

N

Snowcap Cr

To Weest Lillooet Lake Rd

(4WD ONLY)

3
6
9
12
15m

Garibaldi Provincial Park

18

21m

Glacier Lake

200m   0   200m   400m   600m
Scale

27m
24
21
15
12
9
3

Snowcap Lake Ski Route

Creek

Snowcap

Glacier Creek IR

Location: 29 km (18 mi) east of Chilliwack
Elevation: 1,360 m (4,462 ft)
Surface Area: 16 ha (40 ac)
Max Depth: 16 m (53 ft)
Mean Depth: 7 m (23 ft)
Way Point: 49° 6' 49.5" N, 121° 24' 53.0" W

www.backroadmapbooks.com

Flora Lake

Area Indicator

Fishing

One of a series of hike-in lakes in the Chilliwack River Valley, Flora Lake offers good fishing and a nice atmosphere for camping. The lake does not receive a lot of fishing pressure due to the difficult trail access so it is a nice getaway from the crowds of the Lower Mainland.

Those who do make the trip rave about the stunning scenery, the crystal clear water and the size of the fish. While the lake holds plenty of small rainbow that average 20–25 cm (8–10 inches), there have been reports of fish coming out of here to 50 cm (20 inches).

Regardless of your fishing method, the smaller rainbow are generally willing to bite just about anything. Since so few people make it up to the lake, the fish are not lure shy. Small spinners are often better than fly-fishing for the smaller fish. However, the larger rainbow are a lot wilier, but can often be taken in the early evening on a dry fly. A Tom Thumb or Elk Hair Caddis are good bets.

The lake has crystal clear water and is best fished with a float tube, although many people will think twice about carrying a tube such a long way, especially if they are carrying camping gear, too. There is a nice shoal area at the northwest end of the lake and along the eastern banks, which is worth fly-fishing or spincasting.

Directions

Take the Vedder Road exit off the Trans Canada Highway at Chilliwack and follow this road south. You will pass through Sardis and soon come to the Chilliwack River Bridge. Before the bridge, take a left on the Chilliwack River Road and drive all the way to Chilliwack Lake along the river.

As you near Chilliwack Lake, there is a short gravel side road that leads north to the former Post Creek Recreation Site. Here you will find the trailhead for this steep, difficult 14 km (8.7 mile) return trail, which climbs steadily to a pass at 1,770 metres before dropping down to the lake at 1,356 metres. Thus, the elevation gain on the trail is 1,500 metres (4,921 feet) to the pass. Adding to the challenge are several large landslides on the way to the lake, which require hikers to scramble over, under and around some large boulders.

Facilities

There are no developed facilities but there are some openings next to the lake where it is possible to camp. An old miner's cabin is found nearby to the lake. Expect to spend at least one day camping at the lake, as it is nearly impossible to hike to the lake in a day and back and still get any fishing done.

Other Options

From Flora Lake, it is possible to hike to the northwest to **Lindeman and Greendrop Lakes** along a rough, poorly marked route. Both lakes are described in more detail later in this book and are rumoured to house rainbow over 45 cm (18 in) in size.

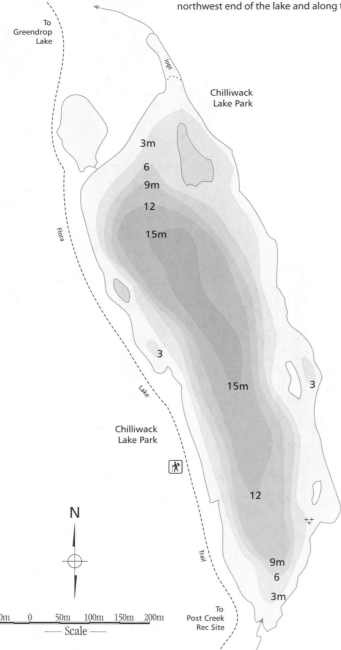

Francis Lake

Location: 17 km (10.5 mi) northwest of Agassiz
Elevation: 395 m (1,296 ft)
Surface Area: 4 ha (10 ac)
Max Depth: 15 m (49 ft)
Mean Depth: 6 m (20 ft)
Way Point: 49° 20' 38.8" N, 121° 51' 2.5" W

Fishing

Francis Lake is one of several lakes found to the west of Harrison Lake off of the Harrison West Forest Service Road. It is a small lake, with lots of rainbow trout to 30 cm (12 inches) best caught by fly-fishing or spincasting.

Shore fishing is somewhat limited because there are expansive shoals surrounding the east and south end of the lake where the road access is. If you are restricted to fishing from shore, it is best to hike around to the south west corner of the lake and cast from there.

The lake is not particularly suited to trolling. However, fly anglers can work a long retrieve, or can drag a scud or nymph pattern behind them as they kick around the lake in a tube. The lake has two deep pockets, one towards the southwest end and one near the northwest end of the lake. Those two pockets are where you should try fishing in the summer months after the water begins to warm.

Earlier and later in the year there are ample shoals and shore cover that are great for insect rearing. Fly anglers can try trolling Doc Spratley flies, a small leech or damselfly imitation on a slow sinking line. Spincasters can have success with a small Flatfish or similar. Alternatively, bottom fishing with bait always seems to provide some success.

Directions

To reach Francis Lake you will need to find the Harrison West Forest Service Road from the Lougheed Highway (Highway 7). To find this road, look for the Morris Valley Road when you reach Harrison Mills. Stay on the main road and just past the side road to the Weaver Creek Spawning Channels is where the forest service road begins. The access road leading to Francis Lake is located about 6.5 km down the Harrison West Forest Service Road. It immediately begins climbing away from the main road and is best accessed with a 4wd vehicle. About 3 km along the spur road, the lake will appear in front of you.

Facilities

Francis Lake Recreation Site is comprised of about four campsites in an open area next to the eastern shore of the lake. A gravel boat launch for non-motorized boats is found towards the south end of the lake.

Other Options

There is certainly no shortage of other good fishing lakes in the area. **Grace Lake** is found to the south and offers rainbow. **Morris Lake** is found even further south on a steep road leading just east of the Weaver Creek Spawning Channel. The lake has a large channel leading from the outlet to Harrison River as well as a few cutthroat. **Weaver Lake** lies to the northwest and is one of the more popular lakes in the area. It has good numbers of rainbow and cutthroat as well as a scenic recreation site complete with a beach and boat launch. All of these lakes are described in more detail elsewhere in the book.

Area Indicator

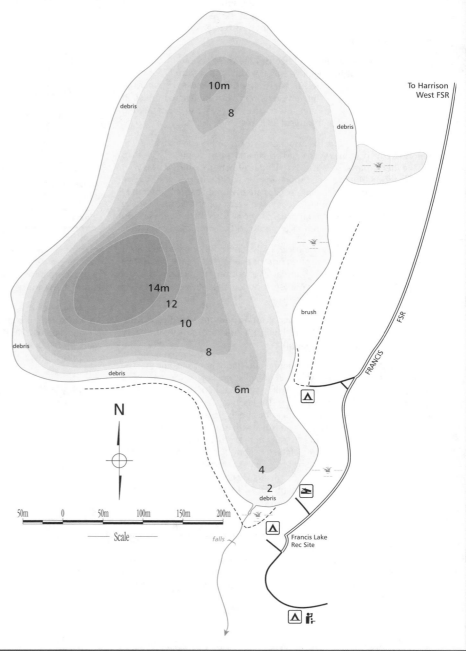

To Harrison West FSR

10m
8
debris
debris
14m
12
10
8
6m
brush
4
2
debris
debris
debris
N
falls

50m 0 50m 100m 150m 200m
Scale

Francis Lake Rec Site

FRANCIS FSR

Francis Lake			
Fish Stocking Data			
Year	Species	Number	Life Stage
2010	Rainbow Trout	500	Yearling
2009	Rainbow Trout	500	Yearling

REGION 2

Fraser River

Location: Lower Mainland
Stream Length: 1,375 km (854 mi)
Geographic: 122° 6′ 00″W, 49° 8′ 00″ N

www.backroadmapbooks.com

Fraser River

Fishing

The Fraser River is BC's longest river, finding its headwaters in Mount Robson Provincial Park near Alberta and flowing 1,375 km (854 miles) through the heart of the province. It drains fully 1/3 of the province and over half the people who live in BC live within 50 km of the river. The Fraser is the most important salmon-bearing river in the province and possibly the world. For the purposes of this book, we are only going to focus on the section of the river below Hope.

The Fraser is a huge river and techniques that work on smaller rivers don't stand a chance on the Fraser. It is home to large runs of Chinook, Coho, sockeye, chum and pink salmon. Adding to the mix are sea-run cutthroat as well as resident rainbow and dollies. The lower reaches of the Fraser are also home to a small but thriving catch and release sturgeon fishery.

The first salmon to enter the Fraser River are Chinook. These are the largest of the five species of salmon found in BC and begin working their way upstream as early as March. These are the red springs, so-called because of their distinctive red-coloured flesh. Early in the year, the river is murky and deep. On a good day, visibility might be 30 cm (12 inches). Try a big spoon or drifting roe.

As the water drops, bar fishing becomes the most common technique for catching Chinook and, while it isn't the most active form of fishing, it is one of the most productive. To bar fish for Chinook, use a medium to heavy rod, between ten and twelve feet long, with anywhere from 10 lb to 30 lb test line. Rods are either a surf rod or bait cast rod. Reels need to be able to hold at least 200 yards of 25 lb test.

Using a 6–8 inch spreader bar attached to the mainline, tie a 6 inch piece of mono to the bottom with a snap swivel attached to a piece of lead. To the spreader bar, attach a 36–40 inch leader. Attached to the leader is your terminal tackle. The most common are Spin-N-Glos, from size #2 to size #00. The two most popular Spin-N-Glos are the green cap/chrome body and the red cap/chrome body. Some people add salmon beads to space the hook back away from the spinner. The hook is often baited with salmon roe or ghost shrimp, while others prefer to add scent to the Spin-N-Glo.

Bar fishing is most popular below the Mission Bridge, where the river is slow and deep and there are often dozens of anglers on each bar. Above the bridge, bar fishing is still popular, as is bottom bouncing with wool ties, corkies and Spin-N-Glos. Anglers tend to concentrate at places like Gill Road, Herrling Island and Scale Bar.

By mid-August, the bulk of the Chinook found here are white fleshed and bound for the Harrison and Vedder River. These fish are massive and every year, fish to 22 kg (50 lbs) are caught.

Sockeye begin entering the river in June but it is not until mid-July that the bigger runs arrive. By the first week of August, sockeye fever is rampant and literally thousands of anglers will line the banks of the popular bars. That is of course, if there is an opening. The last few years have seen smaller returns and the popular sport fishery has been closed. When open, the sockeye fishery lasts until mid-September with most of the action taking place between Chilliwack and Hope, where there are literally dozens of places to access the river. Some of the most popular are Island 22, Pegleg, Jones Creek, Herrling Island and Scales Bar. The most common method of fishing for sockeye is bottom bouncing a weight swinging 6 to 10 feet of leader and a piece of fluorescent wool off the bottom. Colour really does not matter.

Following the sockeye into the Fraser in mid-September are the Coho and chum. Coho are quite popular and are either bar fished with Spin-N-Glos in the lower river and bottom bouncing wool ties or corkies in the upper river. The lower river can be productive in mid-October as the Coho enter the Harrison and Chilliwack/Vedder systems. You will see the odd fly angler out there looking to entice a Coho into striking a big Rolled Muddler or Harrison Fiord.

Chum, on the other hand, are not all that popular despite there size and power. They are caught in both the mainstem and side channels of the Fraser mainly during October. These are aggressive fish that can be caught by float fishing or bottom bouncing.

Pink show up in large numbers from late July to late September on odd-numbered years. They take willingly to bait and bottom bouncing wool similar to sockeye but don't really put up much of a fight. For added challenge, try taking a pink on the fly.

Sturgeon, which can exceed 450 kg (1,000 lbs), are also caught throughout the river system by using a large weight, hook and bait (salmon roe or lamprey). The largest populations are between Agassiz and Maple Ridge with the bite dependent upon the tides. They seem most active when the sockeye run in late August but should continue to bite into December. Although fishing the deep holes and back eddies can produce a fish of a lifetime, it is essential to have the right gear. We recommend using a guide. The fishery is catch and release only.

Sea-run cutthroat trout are another popular fishery with fish that can get up to 50 cm (20 in). They are best caught from March into May and again in October when they follow the chum. Fly-fishing with fry patterns and floating line is very popular in the many backwaters east of Mission to Herrling Island including Dewdney Slough, Maria Slough, Nicomen Slough, Pumphouse Slough and the mouths of the Stave and Harrison Rivers.

The river even holds resident rainbow and Dolly Varden, but these are rarely angled for. The best time to try for these is in the winter near the hard to reach tributaries.

Note: the openings on the river change frequently during the season. It is your responsibility to know when and what is open to fishing. Visit http://www.env.gov.bc.ca/fw/fish/regulations/ before heading out.

Facilities

Considering the river flows through the most populated area in the province, there is no shortage of facilities in and around the big river. There are countless parks and boat launches at various points along the river. Two of the more popular parks with boat launches in the Fraser Valley include **Island 22 Regional Park** and **Kilby Provincial Park**.

For people looking to camp, there is camping at **Derby Reach Regional Park** in Surry, **Brae Island Park** in Fort Langley, **Dewdney Nature Park** in Mission, **Island 22Park** in Chilliwack and **Kilby Provincial Park** in Harrison Mills. Motels, hotels and fishing retailers are also readily available in most centres including Agassiz, Chilliwack, Hope, Maple Ridge and Mission.

Fraser River			
Fish Stocking Data			
Year	Species	Number	Life Stage
2011	Cutthroat Trout	4,000	Smolt

Location: Lower Mainland
Stream Length: 1,375 km (854 mi)
Geographic: 122° 6′ 00″ W, 49° 8′ 00″ N

Fraser River

Directions A

There are literally dozens, if not hundreds, of places to access the river between Vancouver and Hope. Downstream of New Westminster, the river sees a lot of commercial traffic, but some possible access points include Garry Point Park in Richmond and No. 2 and No. 1 Road Piers in Steveston. Further upstream there are too many locations to mention.

Here's a breakdown of some of the river's most popular hot spots and access points:

Bowman's Bar: Located on the southeast side of Nicomen Island it is one of the most all-around productive spots.

Co-op Bar: This one is above the Mission Bridge and accessible via the Matsqui Trail on the Matsqui side of the river.

Grassy Island: Marks the mouth of the famous Vedder Canal. When water levels are low on the Vedder, salmon and steelhead hold here until night. There is a trail down to this pool from Highway 1.

Herrling Island: Easily accessed off the Trans Canada Highway this is one of the more popular and productive salmon hot spots on the big river.

Island 22: Off Cartmell Road in Chilliwack, the boat ramp here is one of the busiest on the river.

Jones Creek Bar: Accessed from Exit 153 on the Trans Canada Highway, this is a popular sockeye and pink location that requires crossing a side channel to get to.

Mountain Bar: This boat access only site at the foot of Harrison Hill between Queens Island and the mouth of the Harrison. It is rumoured to be one of the best salmon holes on the Fraser.

Queen's Island: Located opposite Island 22 and Island Park, on the north side of the river, this one requires a bit of a hike to get to. Cutthroat are found in the middle channel while salmon run up the main channel.

Pegleg Bar: Located at the end of McSween Road, across from the mouth of the Harrison, this is one of the best-known bars.

Ridgedale Bar: Found off the Matsqui Trail in Ridgedale.

Scales and Landstrom Bars: Located near Hope, both of these bars are popular salmon bars with Chinook and sockeye being the most popular to fish here.

Standard Gaz Bar: Just below the Mission Bridge in Abbottsford, in Matsqui Trail Regional Park.

Strawberry Island: Found south of Nicomen Island, this is a popular location for salmon, cutthroat and sturgeon.

Wellington Bar: Like a few other local favourites, this bar is found off Athey Road. Salmon and cutthroat run in the area, while the smaller channels are popular with fly anglers.

Wingdam Bar: This hike-in bar is located just upstream of Deroche Landing on the north side of the river.

Note: If travelling the river on a boat, please be wary of water conditions, debris and unmarked hazards. Fluctuating water levels can expose gravel bars and snags in a matter of minutes. Never assume the passage you took upstream or downstream are still a safe route.

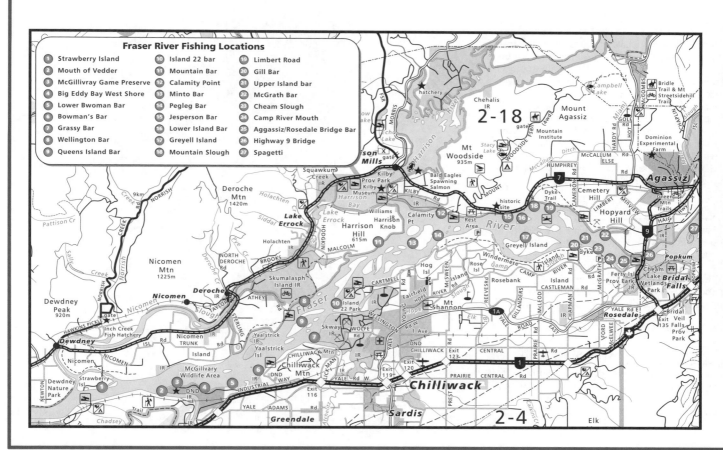

Fraser River Fishing Locations

1 Strawberry Island	10 Island 22 bar	19 Limbert Road
2 Mouth of Vedder	11 Mountain Bar	20 Gill Bar
3 McGillivray Game Preserve	12 Calamity Point	21 Upper Island bar
4 Big Eddy Bay West Shore	13 Minto Bar	22 McGrath Bar
5 Lower Bwoman Bar	14 Pegleg Bar	23 Cheam Slough
6 Bowman's Bar	15 Jesperson Bar	24 Camp River Mouth
7 Grassy Bar	16 Lower Island Bar	25 Aggassiz/Rosedale Bridge Bar
8 Wellington Bar	17 Greyell Island	26 Highway 9 Bridge
9 Queens Island Bar	18 Mountain Slough	27 Spagetti

Location: 24 km (15 mi) northeast of Squamish
Elevation: 1,477 m (4,846 ft)
Surface Area: 994 ha (2456 ac)
Max Depth: 259 m (850 ft)
Mean Depth: 121 m (397 ft)
Way Point: 49° 56' 2" N, 123° 1' 8" W

Garibaldi Lake

Area Indicator

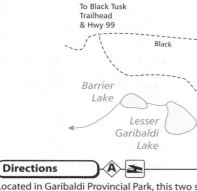

Fishing

The scenic Garibaldi Lake provides excellent fishing for small rainbow beginning at ice off in July and extending until the snow begins to fall in late October.

This has long been a destination for anglers. The lake holds a native population of cutthroat trout, but near the end of the 1920s, rainbow trout were stocked in the lake, packed in on horseback. That was enough, as the trout took to the alpine lake. While most of the fish you will find here are small (to 30 cm/12 inches), there are rumours that fish have been pulled out of here to 55 cm (21 inches).

If possible, bring in a float tube so you can get out past the drop-offs and cast towards shore. If you don't want to pack in a float tube up the long trail, don't worry. Shore fishermen also have good success. When the ice is off, just about anything works at this lake. This is because the rainbow are vigorously feeding during the four open water months, trying to bulk up for the long cold winter. Bait and bobber, fly-fishing or spincasting all work.

The lake is fed by glaciers and is quite cold, even on the hottest days. The glacial flour makes the water a lovely colour, but reduces visibility. Darker coloured patterns seem to work better than lighter coloured ones. Fly-fishers will find this a great dry fly-fishing lake and most traditional patterns (Tom Thumb, Elk Hair Caddis or mosquitoes) seem to do well. The lake also has a good chironomid hatch to look for.

The shallowest part of the lake is towards the west end so it is best to focus around there. Fishermen with a float tube should hang around the shoreline as the water depth drops off rapidly and the trout tend to congregate around the drop-offs, cruising into the shallow water to eat

Directions

Located in Garibaldi Provincial Park, this two spectacular sub-alpine lake is accessed by the steep but well maintained Black Tusk Trail. To reach the trailhead, look for the signs off Highway 99 north of Squamish. Before you come to Daisy Lake, a paved road leads off the highway to the right. This side road switchbacks up the mountain to a large parking lot next to Rubble Creek. From the parking lot, it is a 9 km (5.5 miles) return trail to Garibaldi Lake. You will pass Lesser Garibaldi Lake on the way. The trail is best taken in July-October and provides fantastic views of surrounding glacier and mountaintops as you climb 940 m (3,085 ft) to the lake.

Facilities

For overnight travellers, there are two options to choice from. **Taylor Meadows Campground**, which is located about 500 metres west of the lake, has 40 tent pads together with a covered cooking shelter. The **Garibaldi Lake Campground** is at the west end of Garibaldi Lake and has 50 sites as well as a covered cooking shelter. Both sites are open from May 1st to the middle of November depending on snow accumulation. There is a fee to camp.

Other Options

Lesser Garibaldi Lake is found en route to the bigger lake and is stocked occasional with rainbow that can grow as large as 35 cm (14 in). Due to its elevation, it also provides fishing in the summer and fall.

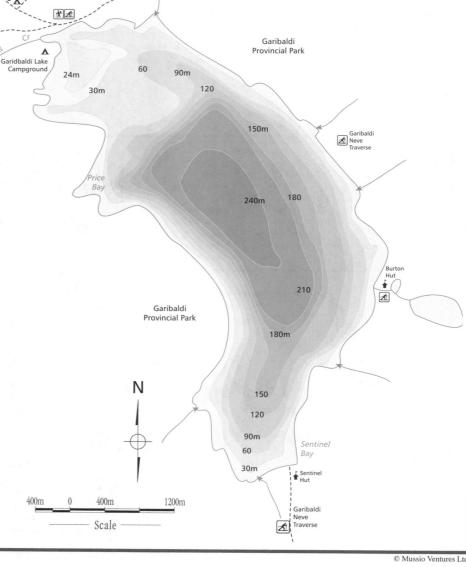

www.backroadmapbooks.com

Glimpse Lake

Location: 48 km (30 mi) northeast of Merritt
Elevation: 1,172 m (3,845 ft)
Surface Area: 95 ha (235 ac)
Max Depth: 21.3 m (69.9 ft)
Way Point: 50° 14′ 53.5″ N, 120° 16′ 8.2″ W

Fishing

Glimpse Lake is found north of Douglas Lake and east of Nicola Lake in cattle country. It is an easily accessible and highly productive lake, with plenty of small rainbow and the occasional few in excess of 1.5 kg (3 lbs). There are cabins and summer homes along the northwest shore of the lake, as well as the Little Beaver Creek Ranch.

The lake features steep drop-offs and shallow weedbeds, especially at the east end of the lake. The shoreline has plenty of reeds that result in a profusion of freshwater insects. The lake even has a hatch of speckled mayflies, which are not all that common in the region.

The big draw, though, is a large hatch of caddisflies. The best times to fish here is late spring and early summer, with early May to mid-June and then again from mid-September until ice-up being the most productive months. The caddis hatch usually happens around the last week of June. Try fishing the pupal and adult stages of an olive caddis. Other patterns that work well are black leeches, Woolly Buggers, a Raymond's Golden Shrimp, or an olive damselfly nymph. If you are working around the reeds, try working a green damselfly or dragonfly nymph.

Spincasters should use light gear with small spoons and spinners like a black and yellow Panther Martin. Mepps and Blue Fox spinners are other popular brands. All are best cast towards the reeds. Because of all the trees and reeds and weeds around the edge of the lake, shore fishing is difficult.

Trollers can also have good luck using a small lake troll like a Willow Leaf. However, the lake is tough to troll unless you focus around the deep part near the west end of the lake. An electric motor only restriction is in effect at the lake.

Being a somewhat developed lake, there is decent access during winter. As a result, ice fishing is fairly popular. The usual tricks of jigging or fishing with bait such as worms, maggots, corn or Powerbait is most effective.

Area Indicator

Directions

To reach the lake, begin on Highway 5A from either Kamloops or Merritt. Near the north end of Nicola Lake, past the Quilchena Hotel, you will find the Douglas Lake Road. Drive east on the road for about 7 km and immediately after the hydro station, turn north on the Lauder Road. This road is a good gravel road that stretches about 12 km before reaching the south end of Glimpse Lake. Most vehicles should have no trouble driving here.

Facilities

The lake has a pair of managed recreation sites with fees: **Glimpse Lake North** and **Glimpse Lake Southwest Recreation Sites**. The northern site has 17 campsites, while the southern campsite has eight sites in a semi-open forest. There are cartop boat launches and wharfs at both, but most prefer to launch at the bigger launching site at the north end of the lake by the cabins. Both sites are RV accessible and open from the start of May until the end of September.

The **Little Beaver Creek Ranch** at the north end of the lake provides first class lodging and dining. There are also several private cottages around the lake.

Glimpse Lake Fish Stocking Data			
Year	Species	Number	Life Stage
2011	Rainbow Trout	12,000	Yearling
2010	Rainbow Trout	15,000	Yearling
2009	Rainbow Trout	15,000	Yearling

Other Options

If the fish are not biting at Glimpse Lake, try **Blue Lake**, located to the northeast. The road access is a bit rougher and the fish are notoriously difficult to catch. But patient anglers will be rewarded with larger rainbow. Rustic camping as well as a cartop boat launch is available at the lake.

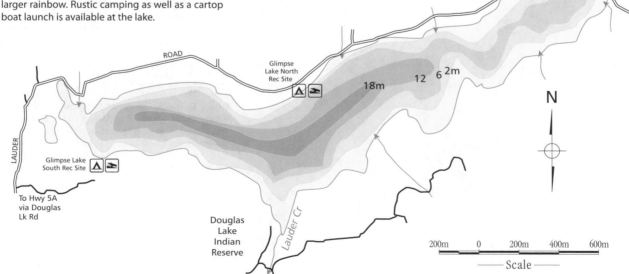

Location: 8 km (5 mi) northwest ofBarrière
Elevation: 1,162 m (3,812 ft)
Surface Area: 20 ha (49 ac)
Max Depth: 10.4 m (34.1 ft)
Mean Depth: 3.8 m (12.5 ft)
Way Point: 51° 13' 28.2" N, 120° 15' 44.5" W

Gorman Lake

Area Indicator

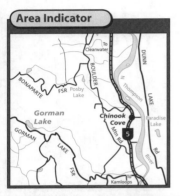

Gorman Lake Fish Stocking Data			
Year	Species	Number	Life Stage
2010	Rainbow Trout	4,000	Fry
2009	Rainbow Trout	4,000	Fry

Fishing

Found in the high country of the Bonaparte Plateau north of Kamloops, Gorman Lake sits in a forest of lodgepole pine and Douglas fir that is home to moose, deer and wolves.

Gorman Lake is a popular choice for many anglers because, not only does its recreation site serve as a good base, but it offers excellent fishing throughout the open water season. The lake is popular with trollers despite the fact that the edges of the lake are swampy, making it difficult (but not impossible) to launch a boat.

There are two deep holes in the lake: one in the middle and one at the south end. Try spinners, Willow Leafs or Ford Fenders with Wedding Bands, and Flatfish all tipped with bait. Work around the edge of these holes, passing back and forth over the drop-off. Don't troll too fast and don't troll in a straight line.

With ample shoals to explore, especially between the two deep holes, this lake is ideal for fly-fishing. Trolling flies, such as a dragonfly or leech pattern on a sinking line, slowly along the edges of the drop offs can entice those hiding trout. Due to the lake's high altitude, insect hatches (especially caddis flies) occur later than you might expect.

Trout dart up from the deeper water into the shoals to grab an insect or invertebrate and then head back to the safety of the drop-off. Cast from deep water and retrieving slowly over the drop off. In the spring, smaller insect patterns produce well, while in fall, larger patterns like leeches, nymphs and Woolly Buggers work better.

Of course, bigger is relative; the largest fish you will find here are about 1 kg (2 lbs) with the average size catch being half of that. Don't use patterns that are to big, lest the trout ignore them completely.

The high altitude also means the fishing action never slows down. Cool temperatures keep the lake from suffering the hot weather doldrums common in lower elevation lakes.

The Freshwater Fisheries Society of BC releases 4,000 Pennask rainbow trout into this lake annually. Pennask fish are known for their hard fight and acrobatic nature.

During the wildfires of 2003, flames engulfed forested areas near Gorman Lake. The burned areas are recovering well and attracting moose, deer and bear in large numbers – an added bonus when seeking the true Bonaparte wilderness experience.

Directions

From Kamloops, travel north on Highway 5 to Barrière. Turn west (left) onto Westsyde Road, the first left past the bridge over the North Thompson River. This paved road switchbacks out of the valley before meeting the Gorman Lake Forest Service Road. Follow this decent gravel road north to the lake, but watch for logging trucks.

Facilities

The **Gorman Lake Recreation Site** rests in open, grassy area next to the lake. There is room for a couple groups and an area to hand launch small boats. Bring bug spray.

Other Options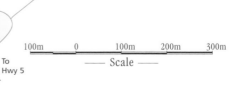

Other lakes in the area worth visiting include **Scott, Allan, Dunsapie, Mayson, Windfall, Windy** and **Whitewood Lakes**. These lakes all hold rainbow trout to 1 kg (2 lbs) and offer fishing similar Gorman. Several remote walk-in or fly-in lakes are also nearby and can be found by using the Backroad Mapbook for the Thompson Okanagan area.

N

2m
3
5
6 8
8m

Gorman Lake
Rec Site

GORMAN

LAKE

9m
8
6 5m
3
2m

100m   0   100m   200m   300m
—— Scale ——

To
Hwy 5

FSR

Grace Lake

Location: 15 km (9.3 mi) northwest of Agassiz
Elevation: 105 m (345 ft)
Surface Area: 6 ha (15 ac)
Max Depth: 15 m (49 ft)
Mean Depth: 6 m (20 ft)
Way Point:49° 19′ 57.8″ N, 121° 51′ 47.6″ W

Fishing

Grace Lake is a small lake found on the west side of Harrison Lake. The lake holds many rainbow in the 30–35 cm (12–14 inch) range. The lake has expansive marshy areas with lots of logs and mud around the perimeter of the lake, making shore fishing difficult. If you don't have a boat or float tube, try working the east end of the lake, where you may be able to cast out to the deeper water.

The lake is quite pretty, but the real reason people come here to fish is because it is one of the first lakes to start to warm up in the early season; insects start to hatch here earlier than at many lakes, meaning the trout start to rise and fly-fishers will have more luck. Of course, that is a double-edged sword and by summer, the lake is too warm to fish with any great success. By fall, the fishing starts to improve.

The small lake has an abundance of aquatic invertebrates and insects do to its expansive shallows. Therefore, this lake is known as a good fly-fishing lake. Favourites include leeches, halfbacks or the versatile Tom Thumb. In addition, the chironomid hatch in March is often good.

Trolling is restricted not only by the size of the lake but also because of an electric motor only restriction. Casting a bait and bobber or spincasting small spinners and lures from a boat should not be ruled out.

Area Indicator

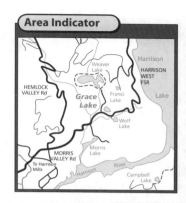

Directions

Grace Lake is one of several lakes found to the west of Harrison Lake off of the Harrison West Forest Service Road. From the Lougheed Highway (Highway 7), you turn north on the Morris Valley Road at Harrison Mills. Stay right at the first major junction and avoid the temptation to head left on the Hemlock Valley Road at the next major intersection. Just past the side road to the Weaver Creek Spawning Channels is where the forest service road begins.

The recreation site and access to Grace Lake is found after passing over Weaver Creek and the Weaver Lake Forest Service Road. Look for a small open area on the left side of the main road.

Other Options

Within a short distance of Grace Lake are a number of other good fishing lakes: **Francis Lake** has many rainbow trout to 30 cm in size best caught by fly-fishing or spincasting. The lake has an electric motor only restriction as well as a recreation site. **Morris Lake** has a few cutthroat to 50 cm which can be caught by spincasting or fly-fishing. Try worms, roe or flies. **Weaver Lake** has good numbers of rainbow and cutthroat that reach 50 cm but average around 30 cm. Trolling with a fly or Wedding Band and worm is popular although the lake is well suited to spincasting or fly-fishing. All of these lakes are described in more detail in this book. Unfortunately, nearby **Wolf Lake** is reported barren.

Grace Lake			
Fish Stocking Data			
Year	Species	Number	Life Stage
2010	Rainbow Trout	500	Catchable
2009	Rainbow Trout	500	Catchable

Facilities

Grace Lake Recreation Site is large enough to hold six groups among the trees and rocky outcrops next to the lake. In addition to a floating wharf, there is a short trail around west end of the lake. The site is also a designed staging area for newly established motorized trails in the area. Also new is the ability to reserve sites by calling M.G.C. Campsite Management Inc. at (604)796-0102, on Mon/Tues/Wed between 6-9 pm. Camping is available all year, but a host and fees are charged during long weekends and between May 1st and the Labour Day long weekend in September.

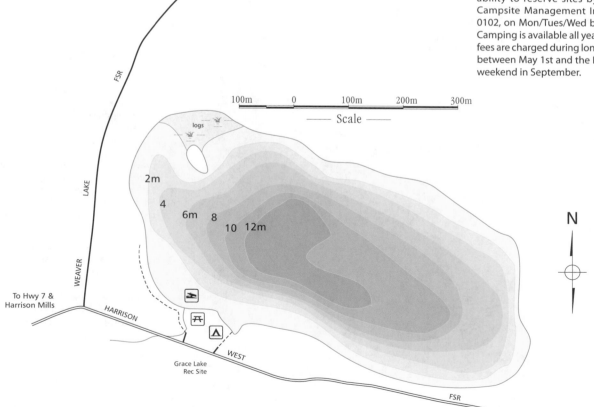

Location: 3 km (1.8 mi) north of Whistler
Elevation: 634 m (2080 ft)
Surface Area: 205 ha (507 ac)
Max Depth: 40 m (131 ft)
Mean Depth: 14 m (46 ft)
Way Point: 50° 9' 3" N, 122° 56' 4" W

www.backroadmapbooks.com

Green Lake - Whistler Area

Area Indicator

Fishing

Green Lake takes its name from its emerald-coloured waters. The mid size lake is found just north of Whistler, alongside the highway and is home to some big bull trout that are rumoured to reach 5 kg (11 lbs). It is also home to some very nice rainbow trout and kokanee.

The fishing here is nearly as spectacular as the setting and a recent regulation change to catch and release, single barbless hook and a bait ban has made the fishing even better.

This is the deepest lake in the Whistler area but still has a fair amount of shoal area. When fishing Green Lake, try the shoals and inlets and you will find the fish. A popular fishing location is the Fitzsimmons Creek fan near the floatplane dock. This area can be accessed from the Valley Trail near the Nicklaus North Golf Course Clubhouse, but beware the sudden drop-off when wading. Nineteen Mile Creek, on the opposite side of the bay, is another productive area that brings in feed for hungry trout.

The River of Golden Dreams inlet is popular with fly anglers. Wade the mouth of the river or follow the drop- off past the Edgewater Lodge for great fishing action. The shallow areas in front of the abandoned Parkhurst homes on the east side can also provide some good chironomid fishing for rainbow.

Also try the outlet near Green River especially in late summer. Float tubes are not recommended near this outlet because of the strong current. The wind can also get quite strong on the lake, so take care with small boats in general.

When selecting your fishing gear for trout remember that they are generally fish eaters. Fish eaters like larger offerings so when fly-fishing try a large green zonker or Muddler Minnow. If fishing with spinning gear or trolling try a large minnow imitation Flatfish or Apex plug.

There are also a large number of kokanee in the lake, which seem to respond to those who troll along the drop-off for the length of the lake. Try lures such as a Wedding Band or a Dick Nite spoon.

200m 0 200m 600m 1000m

Scale

Emerald Estates

Alpine Meadows

Trudy's Landing

To Pemberton

Green River

N

Parkhurst Town Historic Site

24m

18

12

6m

Green Lake Park

Loop

37m

24

30

24

18m

12

Green Lake Air Base

6m

River of Golden Dreams

Nineteen

Mile Cr

boat rentals

NICKLAUS

N BLVD

Nicklaus North Golf Course

Fitzsimmons Cr

To Whistler

Directions

Green Lake is located alongside The Sea to Sky Highway (Highway 99), approximately 3 km (1.8 mi) north of Whistler Village. Public parking is limited in the south, but there are multiple access points provided via the Valley Trail. The best boat launch is at the north end in the Emerald Estates subdivision on Summer Lane. Boaters should be aware of the boating restrictions and floatplane traffic during the summer.

Those looking to access the River of Golden Dreams by foot can enter at Nicklaus North subdivision and head north down Golden Bear Place to park at Fishermans Loop. A short jaunt on the Valley Trail leads to the mouth of the river. It is also possible to launch at the car park and drift down to the lake.

Facilities

Green Lake Park is on Lakeshore Drive, just south of the official boat launch. There are washrooms and the shore is suitable for hand launching small boats or canoe. There are no camping faculties at the lake, but Whistler, to the south, provides just about everything you could possibly want.

© Mussio Ventures Ltd.

Green Timbers Lake

www.backroadmapbooks.com

Location: Surrey
Elevation: 97 m (318 ft)
Way Point: 49° 10′ 44″ N, 122° 49′ 14″ W

Fishing

Green Timbers Lake is an urban lake found in Surrey's Green Timbers Lake Park. The stocked lake is fishable year round, except on those rare occasions when it is frozen over in mid-winter. While the lake does suffer from the summer doldrums, brought on by warm waters, summer evenings can still be productive.

The lake is stocked with catchable-sized rainbow trout multiple times a year. The lake is very small and swimming, boating and even float tubes are not allowed in the lake. ("The lake is reserved for ducks and other waterfowl," says the Green Timbers website.) Therefore, shore fishing is the only way to fish the lake. There is a small pier that can be fished from, but it can be extremely busy.

The east side of the lake is quite open and there is enough room for fly-fishers to fish here. This is a popular area and you need to look behind for walkers passing within range before you back cast…. The northern and southern ends are the deepest portions of the lake, where fishing is best, but don't offer the same space for fly-fishers.

Bait fishing with a float or bottom rig is the easiest method to catch fish here. Because the lake is stocked with catchable sized fish, the fishing is often fast and furious shortly after stocking and the fish are fairly indiscriminate about what they eat. A worm, deli shrimp, single eggs or scented artificial bait will all produce. Spincasting with small lures like a Panther Martin or Mepps Black Fury will also work, but the shoreline can get crowded, making even spincasting difficult.

The average weight of most stocked rainbow trout is less than half a pound, but occasionally the Fraser Valley Trout Hatchery will release larger trout that weigh up to 3.5 kg (8 lbs) into the lake. These big fish are formerly brood stock, so they aren't all that tasty, but imagine pulling one of these monsters out of here, especially on light gear….

The lake is managed as a catch and keep lake. There are no regulations as to the size you can keep, but fishing is only allowed during park hours. The limit in Green Timbers is one fish per day per fisher.

Stocking is not done on a tight schedule. The hatchery determines when and how many fish based on their criteria. The average is every three months through the peak season.

Directions

Green Timbers Lake is located in the Green Timbers Urban Forest in Surry. The parking lot is found on the 14600 block of 100 Avenue. To get to the lake from the Trans Canada Highway, take the 152 Street/108 Avenue exit towards Surrey City Centre, heading south on 152 Street. Turn right on 100 Avenue and follow the road to the parking lot. It is a five minute walk from the lot to the lake.

From the Patullo Bridge in New Westminster, simply follow the King George Highway to 100 Avenue and turn left. Watch for the parking lot on your right.

Facilities

Green Timbers Lake Park is an urban oasis set in a protected forest. There are trails, a fishing dock and washroom facilities, but little else in the park itself. Of course, the park is minutes away from Surrey Centre, where you will find most anything you need.

Green Timbers Lake			
Fish Stocking Data			
Year	Species	Number	Life Stage
2011	Rainbow Trout	1,700	Catchable
2010	Rainbow Trout	6,562	Catchable
2009	Rainbow Trout	5,328	Catchable

Area Indicator

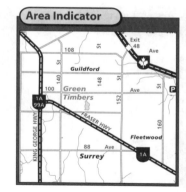

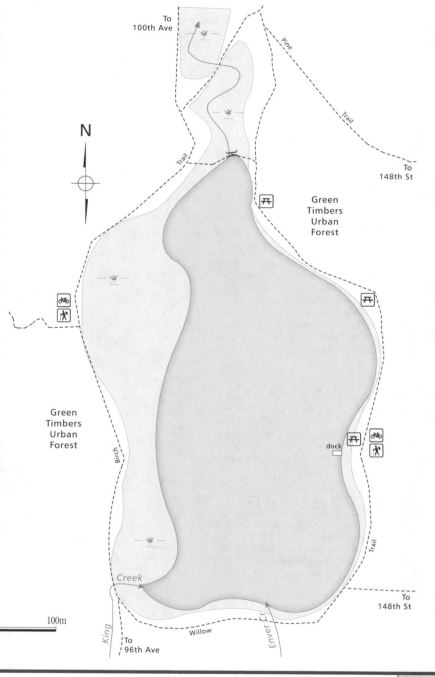

Scale
50m   0   50m   100m

Location: 28 km (17.4 mi) east of Chilliwack
Elevation: 952 m (3123 ft)
Surface Area: 21 ha (52 ac)
Max Depth: 48 m (157 ft)
Mean Depth: 18 m (59 ft)
Way Point: 49° 8' 33.2" N, 121° 25' 45.7" W

Greendrop Lake

Area Indicator

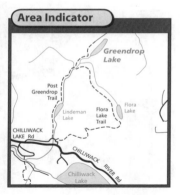

Fishing

Greendrop Lake is one of several hike-in lakes in the Chilliwack River Valley that offers good fishing for small trout from early June into the fall. Despite the good fishing, the lake seems to get more attention from hikers rather than anglers.

The lake has good numbers of rainbow best taken by fly-fishing from a float tube. Working from a float tube allows you to cast towards shore and more effectively work the drop off. Of course, the difficult hike in deters all but the most determined from hauling in a float tube.

The deep waters and elevation ensure that the water temperature remains cold throughout the summer. The rainbow average 20–30 cm (8–12 inches) and it is a rare catch indeed if you find one bigger than that. Regardless of your fishing method, the smaller rainbow are generally willing to bite just about anything.

The lake has crystal clear water so be careful not to spook the fish when approaching the lake. However, the water level drops off fairly quickly from shore allowing you to cast past the drop-offs. Stick around the north and southern shoreline for the deeper water if you can't pack a float tube into the lake. Shore casting around the outflow creek where the trail reaches the lake is tough because of the shallow water.

Fly-fishing can be fantastic throughout the season. Fly-anglers will find mayflies are very productive on mountain lakes, while site fishing with dry flies is a lot of fun. Patterns like a Royal Coachman, Adams, Elk Hair Caddis or mosquito will keep the trout hoping. Alternatively, wet flies such as a Doc Spratley, a chironomid or a variety of nymph patterns are also worth a try.

Spincasters can do worse that bait (worm or single egg) and bobber. Most small spinners like a Panther Martin or Mepps Black Fury also work.

Directions

Greendrop Lake is a popular hike-in lake found in the Chilliwack Lake Provincial Park. From the Trans Canada Highway at Chilliwack, head south on the Vedder Road. You will pass through Sardis and soon come to the Chilliwack River Bridge. Before the bridge, take a left on the Chilliwack River Road and drive all the way to Chilliwack Lake along the paved road, which follows the river.

As you near Chilliwack Lake, there is a short gravel side road that leads north to the Post Creek Recreation Site. Here you will find the trailhead for this 6 km (3.6 mile) one-way hike to Greendrop Lake. The trail begins by rising sharply from the Chilliwack River Valley before reaching Lindeman Lake. Greendrop Lake is an additional 3 km one way from the north end of Lindeman Lake.

Facilities

There is a rustic camping site at the southwest end of Greendrop Lake, which can be used as a base camp for overnight fishing trips. It is possible to hike to the lake and back in a day, allowing you the option to spend the night at the recreation site or at Chilliwack Lake.

Other Options

On your way to Greendrop Lake, you may wish to try **Lindeman Lake**. It is a cold emerald green lake that also has good numbers of rainbow trout. This lake, along with nearby **Flora Lake** are described in more detail elsewhere in this book.

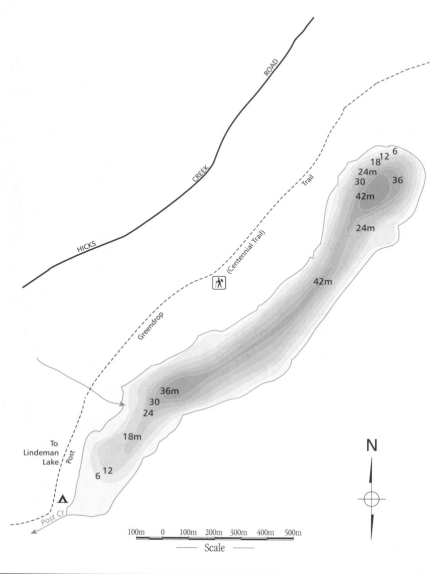

100m 0 100m 200m 300m 400m 500m

Scale

N

www.backroadmapbooks.com

Gun Lake

Location: 80 km (49.7 mi) north of Pemberton
Elevation: 883 m (2,897 ft)
Surface Area: 535 ha (1,322 ac)
Max Depth: 103 m (337.9 ft)
Mean Depth: 49.4 m (162.1 ft)
Way Point: 50° 52' 25" N, 122° 52' 19" W

Fishing

Although not small, Gun Lake is the smallest of three large lakes found in the Bridge River Valley Area. This area marks the transition from the glacial covered Coastal Mountains to the dry, arid interior. Across the Bridge River Valley to the southwest are towering glacial peaks, while behind Gun Lake is the rugged South Chilcotin Provincial Park. It is a beautiful location, set in a lush forest and surrounded by towering mountains.

The scenery will help occupy your mind as you wait for a nibble here. The fishing, while not terrible, is not fast and furious, either. The lake fishes like a coastal lake and despite the lake's rather large size, the rainbow here only get to about 1 kg (2 lbs). The lake does produce larger bull trout and Dolly Varden, to about 4 kg (8 lbs) and a fair number of small kokanee.

The rainbow are the most common catch here and are stocked annually. Anywhere from 10,000 to 35,000 fish have been stocked annually over the last five years.

It should be noted that in 2006, Blackwater rainbow were stocked in the lake for the first time. These fish are piscivorous, meaning they feed on smaller fish. In Gun Lake, that means redside shiners and small kokanee. It also means that there is a good chance that people are going to start pulling bigger rainbow out of the lake soon.

Trolling is the mainstay of the lake. Try a Willow Leaf and Weeding Band tipped with bait trolled near the outflow creek or near the drop-offs for both the rainbow and kokanee. A variety of small lures such as the Kamlooper, Mepps or Panther Martin also entice the rainbow to bite. For the kokanee, you may also wish to try a pink colour lure such as a small Spin-n-Glo trolled slowly in an "S" manner.

The bull trout and Dolly Varden prefer larger lures such as a green Flatfish or Krocodile. These two species are cousins of the char family and tend to be found a little deeper than the rainbow and kokanee. Downrigger gear, while not essential, can help get your lure down

The lake is not that great for fly-fishing as it does not have the vibrant hatches of the lakes to the east.

Area Indicator

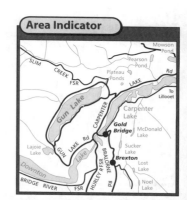

Gun Lake Fish Stocking Data			
Year	Species	Number	Life Stage
2011	Rainbow Trout	20,000	Yearling
2010	Rainbow Trout	20,000	Yearling
2009	Rainbow Trout	20,000	Yearling

Directions

While Gun Lake can be reached from the south, the better access is from the east. Head north from Lillooet on the west side of the Fraser River and take the Bridge River Road heading west after crossing the Bridge River. Follow the Carpenter Lake Road at the first major intersection. This road is an intermittent mix of pavement and gravel and has some amazing (if not scary) vistas as you cross the Yalakom River and travel along the northern shores of Carpenter Lake all the way to Gold Bridge.

From Gold Bridge, a relative short drive on the Gun Lake Road brings you to the south end of the lake. Continue around the west side of the lake to find the boat launch and recreation site.

Facilities

Gun Lake South Recreation Site is a semi-open site found on the western shore of Gun Lake. The open area has space for about eight units and is RV friendly. A good boat launch is located at the south end of the lake near the Lajoie Dam. There are also a number of resorts to stay at in and around the lake.

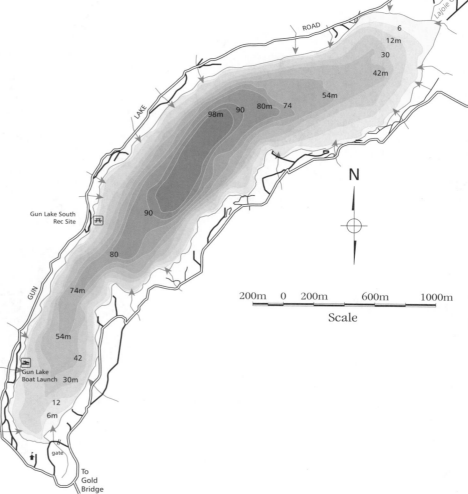

Location: 18 km (11 mi) south of Clearwater
Elevation: 660 m (2,165 ft)
Surface Area: 24 ha (59 ac)
Max Depth: 22.6 m (74.1 ft)
Mean Depth: 13.4 m (44 ft)
Way Point: 51° 30' 10.7" N, 120° 7' 40.4" W

Hallamore Lake

Area Indicator

Fishing

There is a new resort at the north end of Hallamore Lake, though contrary to some of the rumours we've heard, they are not charging people to fish. They are charging a small fee for the public to use the boat launch, but if you would rather save your money, it is possible to access the lake from the south end, where some hand launch boats.

Hallamore Lake is an inviting lake with drop-offs circling the entire lake. The lake is quite deep and the water does not warm enough to make the summer doldrums a problem.

Unlike many of the lakes in the area, there is an inflowing stream that offers great spawning habitat and the fish in the lake are naturally reproducing. They are doing a great job at it. Too good, in fact, as the lake is now nearly over-run with small, slow growing rainbow trout. In 2008, the biggest fish pulled out of the lake was 35 cm (14 inches).

Early in the spring, after a long, cold winter, the fish are starving and fishing can be fast and furious. Trolling a lake troll (Willow Leaf or Ford Fender) with a worm is a good bet as is trolling a fly (Leech, Doc Spratley or Carey Special) or small lure (Mepps, Kamlooper or Panther Martin).

Fly anglers and spincasters can do well focusing at the Axel Creek estuary at the north end of the lake or by trying the outflow area at the south end. The usual hatches common to other lakes in the region occur here.

In the winter, the ice fishing is phenomenal. The best ice fishing usually happens before Christmas, when the oxygen levels are at their highest and the water temperature hasn't dropped. Ice needs to be 15 cm (6 inches) thick before you can walk on it safely, but once the ice is thick enough, winter action can be fast and furious. Because the lake is covered with ice, the fish are much more willing to head into shallower water where the food usually is, without fear of predators. Fishing the shallows at either the north or south end of the lake can be phenomenally productive. Fishing in water 3 metres (10 feet) or less, around structure or overtop weed beds is usually the best place to start. A fish sounder can be helpful, but most people just lie on the ice and watch for fish through the hole. If you haven't seen a fish in 15 minutes, move onto the next hole.

Directions

Hallamore Lake is located north of Dunn Lake near Little Fort and Highway 5. You can access the lake from Little Fort by taking the ferry across the North Thompson River and following Windpass Road to the Dunn Lake Road and heading north to Hallamore Lake. However, the people at Alpine Meadows Resort suggest the easier access is from Clearwater to the north.

Follow Highway 5 north to the Wells Grey Inn in Clearwater. Look for the sign marking the Dunn Lake Road and follow this road south for about 18 km to Hallamore Lake. The last stretch of road is gravel, but most cars can reach the lake.

Facilities

There is an undeveloped camping and launching area at the south end of the lake. But if you're fishing here, it is recommended to start at **Alpine Meadows Resort**. In addition to accommodations and a restaurant, they have boat rentals, a boat launch and a wharf.

To Clearwater
via Dunn Lk Rd

Axel Cr

6m
9
12
15m
18
21

ROAD
LAKE
DUNN

Axel Creek

N

100m   0   100m   200m   300m

— Scale —

Hammer Lake

Location: 30 km (18.6 mi) south of Bridge Lake
Elevation: 1,271 m (4,170 ft)
Surface Area: 68 ha (168 ac)
Max Depth: 9.8 m (32.2 ft)
Mean Depth: 3.4 m (11.2 ft)
Way Point: 51° 14' 30" N, 120° 42' 27" W

Fishing

Hammer Lake vaguely resembles a hammer and thus the name. The "handle" part of the lake is at the deeper south end, while the "head" of the lake is located to the north end.

Hammer Lake is a good fly-fishing and spincasting lake for stocked rainbow. The lake holds redside shiners, which are the prime food source for the Blackwater rainbow that are stocked here. Given the choice, Blackwaters will eat small fish and as a result grow up nice and big. While the average catch here is 2 kg (4 lbs), there have been fish pulled out of here to 6 kg (13.5 lbs).

After ice-off in early May, the lake offers a series of good chironomid hatches right into early June. Use a #10-14 pupae pattern sunk to the bottom and retrieved very slowly. Olive, black, maroon and brown colours all work.

The lake is lined with reeds. Beginning in late June, cast a damselfly or dragonfly nymph into the reeds and hang on. Some days the fly-fishing can be absolutely unbelievable.

For the dry fly fishermen, a good sedge hatch occurs in late June and into early July. Focus on the late evening as that is when the hatch is at its peak and the fish are often jumping feverishly. Green coloured patterns are most consistent producers.

Blackwater like eating small fish, so working a pattern that resembles a redside shiner is usually a good idea. If that isn't working, try a leech pattern, or a searching pattern like a Woolly Bugger or Doc Spratley.

By summer, the water warms and the summer doldrums set in. Fishing becomes incredibly slow except for the odd bite late in the evening or early in the morning. By late fall fishing picks up.

Spincasting can be quite productive using a mix of small spinners and spoons. The lake can also be trolled, as long as you focus along the deeper handle area. In the shallower areas, a surface fly or lure can be trolled, but the action is rarely that great. In fact if you troll too deep here, you will find yourself getting a lot of hits from the weed trout….

An electric motor only restriction applies.

Directions

The lake can be reached from the north, off Highway 24 west of Little Fort. At Bridge Lake, turn south onto the Bridge Lake Business Route and then south again onto North Bonaparte Road and again onto the Eagan Bonaparte Forest Service Road. This long, rough road takes you past Eagan Lake and Bonaparte Lake before reaching Hammer Lake near the 3376 km marking.

Facilities

The **Hammer Lake Recreation Site** is located on the north end of Hammer Lake and has a cartop boat launch and space for about 11 campsites.

Other Options

The 800 pound gorilla in the room here is **Bonaparte Lake**, located just north of Hammer Lake. This big lake is extremely popular and provides big fish. However, as mentioned earlier, it is best suited for trolling. If you are in a float tube or other small boat, you might do better heading west to **Scot Lake** or **Little Scot Lake**. These two lakes are even smaller than Hammer and hold good numbers of naturally reproducing rainbow trout.

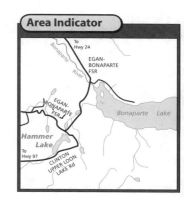

Area Indicator

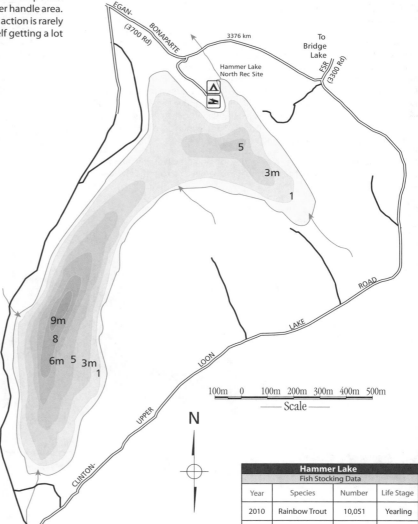

Hammer Lake			
Fish Stocking Data			
Year	Species	Number	Life Stage
2010	Rainbow Trout	10,051	Yearling
2009	Rainbow Trout	10,000	Yearling

Location: 34 km (21 mi) south of Lytton
Elevation: 300 m (984 ft)
Surface Area: 72 ha (178 ac)
Max Depth: 11 m (36.1 ft)
Mean Depth: 5.2 m (17.1 ft)
Way Point: 50° 0' 47" N, 121° 41' 23" W

www.backroadmapbooks.com

Hannah Lake

Hannah Lake (sidebar)

Area Indicator

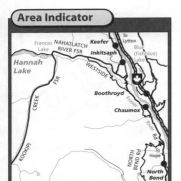

Fishing

Hannah Lake is not known for being a good producer but the area is certainly scenic and well worth the trip. The lake is located in Nahatlatch Provincial Park and surrounded by old growth forests, towering mountain peaks and glaciers.

The lake holds rainbow, bull trout and Dolly Varden, which are usually small. The odd fish grows to 1 kg (2 lbs), but they are usually a quarter that size.

The lake stretches out along the Nahatlatch River Valley and offers a fairly rapid drop off making it possible to cast a line from most of the shoreline. Try using a Krocodile or a Gibbs Croc spoon. Or simply try still fishing with bait such as a worm or deli shrimp under a bobber suspended just off the bottom. Good places to try are the inflow and outflow areas of the Nahatlatch River on the west and east end of lake as well as any of the feeder streams.

Trolling a lake troll or a lure tipped with a worm around the perimeter of the lakes is often the most common fishing method. A lake troll, such as a Willow Leaf, with a Wedding Band and a small piece of bait can produce good results almost anytime of year.

The lake is a low elevation lake. When the water warms up, the trout tend to stay in the deeper, cool water for the better part of the day, coming into the shallows to feed only at night. Fishing late at night or early in the morning, or fishing deep are two options when the lake starts to get warm. You can also try fishing around the mouth of creeks, which bring cool oxygen-rich water into the lake, but you will find that the best time to fish here is in spring and fall.

There is a single barbless hook restriction at the lake.

Directions

Hannah Lake is the second lake in the Nahatlatch River Valley, a popular white-water kayaking area. To reach the lake, drive to Boston Bar on the Trans-Canada Highway (Highway 1). Turn west at the main intersection in Boston Bar, at the sign indicating to North Bend. Continue over the bridge to the west side of the Fraser River and follow the Nahatlatch Forest Service Road and the Nahatlatch Provincial Park entrance. Follow the park directional signs and you will soon be rising out of the Fraser Canyon area to the plateau above the Fraser River. Along the way, you will have numerous views of the Nahatlatch River and perhaps see a whitewater paddler shooting some rapids. The Hannah Lake Campsite is about 26 km from the North Bend School.

Note that access to this area is via an active logging road (usually busy Monday thru Friday) and sections of the road are narrow, hilly and rough. Drive carefully.

Facilities

There are two former recreation sites at either end of Hannah Lake. Now part of **Nahatlatch Provincial Park**, these sites still retain their rustic appeal and are part of a series of campsites in the popular recreational valley. The **Hannah Lake Campground**, which is set at the east end of Hannah Lake at the outflow of the Nahatlatch River, has space for a single group and a hand launch for smaller boats. The campsite is right next to the main road so road traffic noise can take away from the camping experience.

The **Old Ranger Station site** offers an old cabin near the inflow of the Nahatlatch River at the west end of the lake. The cabin, which is very popular, is available on a first come first served basis.

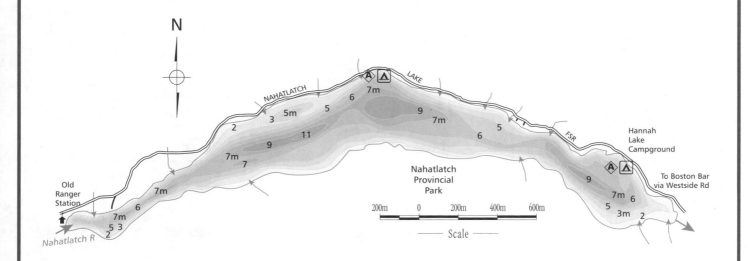

Harbour Lake

www.backroadmapbooks.com

Location: 90 km (56 mi) northest of Chase
Elevation: 848 m (2,782 ft)
Surface Area: 54 ha (133 ac)
Max Depth: 18.3 m (60 ft)
Mean Depth: 7.7 m (25.3 ft)
Way Point: 51° 32' 29" N, 119° 10' 47" W

Fishing

Harbour Lake is located northeast of the Adams Lake in Harbour Dudgeon Lakes Provincial Park. This is remote corner of the province and while there is a logging road past the lake, few people are willing to get this far off the beaten track.

As a result, Harbour Lake does not receive a lot of fishing pressure and it produces well for small rainbow up to 1 kg (2–3 lbs) in size. The lake also holds a fair number of mountain whitefish.

The north and south ends of the lake have some nice shallows near the inflow and outflow creeks ideal for spincasting and fly-fishing. Try throwing a bobber and worm at the creek mouth and you may get lucky. Spinners, such as a Mepps or Gibbs black with orange dots, tipped with a piece of worm are good casting options.

Trollers can work the drop offs along the western and eastern shores of the lake. There is no boat launch, but it is possible to hand launch a boat. A lake troll with a Wedding Band and small piece of bait can produce good results. Also try trolling black/silver speckled Flatfish or Kwikfish, a Dick Nite spoon, or a Luhr Jensen brass needlefish. If desired, a lake troll can accompany these lures.

Whitefish are not the most popular sportfish, but can provide an interesting diversion. You will need light gear and small bait to catch these aggressive fish, which can put up an impressive fight on light and ultra light gear. Whitefish have small mouths and so the lure and hook has to be small, too.

The lake is a fairly low elevation lake and can be fished as early as mid-May. The summer doldrums are not much of a problem as the lake is fairly deep. By early November, the ice is back on the lake.

Area Indicator

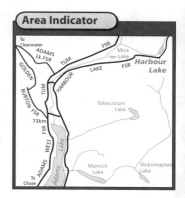

Directions

From the Trans Canada Highway 5.5 km (3.3 miles) northeast of Chase, take the Squilax-Anglemont Road leading north. This paved road links with Holdings Road, which winds gently along the western banks of the Adams River to the south end of the lake. After the mill, the Adams West Forest Service Road takes over. This is a well graded but windy mainhaul logging road that will bring you 72 km to the north end of the Adams Lake. Once at the north end of the Adams Lake, look for the Harbour Lake Forest Service Road, which follows the east side of the Adams River. Harbour Lake is found at the junction with the Harbour Tum Tum Forest Road. You will need to pay attention as the rough side roads to the lake may not be marked.

Due to the long distance of logging road travel, a truck, a GPS and a copy of the Backroad Mapbook for the Thompson Okanagan is highly recommended.

Facilities

A former recreation site and boat launch is found on the east side of the lake near Bower Creek. The site is quite rustic.

Other Options

For a completely different experience, why not try **Adams Lake**? This large lake contains rainbow trout that average 3 kg (8 lbs). There are also some large lake trout, Dolly Varden and kokanee. Although trolling is the most productive method on the big lake, casting from shore can yield some decent results. The north end of the lake has fairly good access and some good areas to cast from.

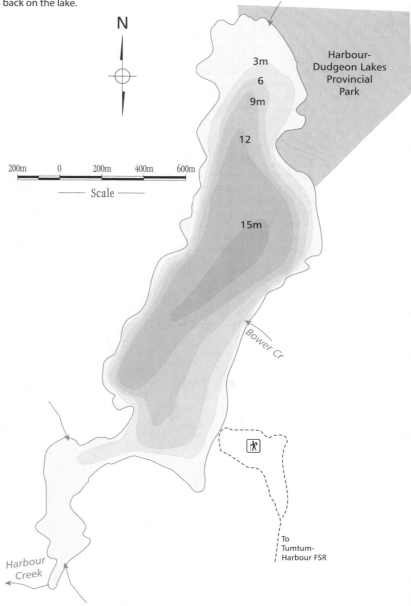

N

Harbour-Dudgeon Lakes Provincial Park

3m
6
9m
12
15m

200m   0   200m   400m   600m
Scale

Bower Cr

To Tumtum-Harbour FSR

Harbour Creek

Location: 15 km (9 mi) southeast of Merritt

Harmon & Englishmen Lakes

Harmon Lake

Elevation: 1,112 m (3,648 ft)
Surface Area: 31 ha (77 ac)
Max Depth: 21 m (68.9 ft)
Mean Depth: 8 m (26.2 ft)
Way Point: 49° 58' 13.2" N, 120° 41' 53.0" W

Area Indicator

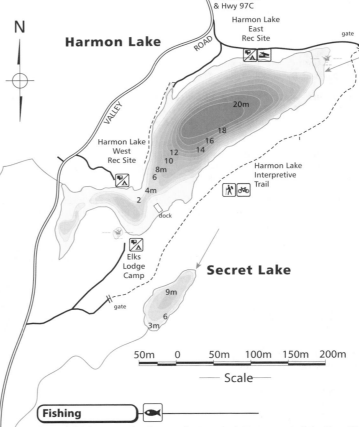

Directions

A

Located on Kane Valley Road, about 9 km southwest of the Coquihalla Connector, these lakes can be accessed of the Coquihalla Highway at the Coldwater turnoff. To avoid extra gravel road travel and the climb out of the Coldwater Valley, it is best to access the lakes from the Connector side. This side of the Kane Valley Road is found about 17 km southeast of Merritt. The good gravel road leads past a number of smaller lakes along the way to Harmon Lake. Englishmen Lake is another couple kilometres further along. Both lakes can be accessed in a car or RV.

Facilities

Harmon Lake is so popular that is actually has two recreation sites with a total of 45 campsites. The East site is much bigger with an improved boat launch. There is a fee to camp here from early May to mid-October. There is also a private campsite at the south end of the lake and a series of trails in the area.

There is a roadside parking area at Englishmen Lake but nothing much else.

Englishmen Lake

Elevation: 1,085 m (3,560 ft)
Surface Area: 2.5 ha (6 ac)
Max Depth: 8 m (26.2 ft)
Mean Depth: 1.5 m (4.9 ft)
Way Point: 49° 57' 18.0" N, 120° 42' 48.9"

Harmon Lake Fish Stocking Data			
Year	Species	Number	Life Stage
2010	Rainbow Trout	6,000	Yearling
2009	Rainbow Trout	6,000	Yearling

Englishmen Lake Fish Stocking Data			
Year	Species	Number	Life Stage
2011	Rainbow Trout	1,000	Catchable
2011	Rainbow Trout	2,000	Yearling
2010	Rainbow Trout	3,000	Yearling/Fry
2009	Rainbow Trout	3,000	Yearling/Catchable

Fishing

Set on a high mountain plateau, the popular lakes are part of the Kane Valley chain of lakes. The Kane Valley itself is a very popular recreational area for a variety of activities including camping, trail riding, cross-country skiing and, of course, fishing.

Harmon Lake is a small body of water surrounded by grasslands and a fir and pine forest. It is populated with red-sided shiners–small, illegally introduced fish that flourish in the insect-rich lakes of the Thompson area. They bear the potential to strip a lake of insects and other food sources from trout. To combat the threat of shiners, the Freshwater Fisheries Society of BC stocks Harmon Lake annually with Blackwater rainbow trout, which feed on the smaller red-sided shiners.

As a bonus, Blackwater rainbow are known for their size and trout between 1 & 3 kg (2 & 6 lbs) are common. While Blackwater trout will feed on insects, they target shiners when insect hatches are less abundant.

There are not a lot of trout here, but they do get to a good size. Lures that imitate red-sided shiners, like Buzz Bombs, Rapalas and small spoons, are successful when insect hatches are on the decline. Troll or anchor down and cast the lures, especially around underwater structures like sunken stumps, trees, weedbeds and drop offs, where shiners congregate.

Fly anglers should use the standard stillwater patterns that trout key in on spring and early summer including chironomids, mayflies and damselflies. Streamer and baitfish patterns are good on days when little else will interest fish. Fish these patterns with combinations of slow and fast strips to mimic the look of a panicked or wounded shiner.

Nearby Englishmen Lake is smaller and less popular, but it is a perfect lake for fishing from a float tube. There is a two fish limit, which can be caught with unbaited, single barbless hooks.

For such a small lake, Englishmen has some pretty big fish, averaging 1.5 kg (3 lbs) but getting up to 4 kg (8 lbs). The lake has some large hatches and is known specifically for its mayfly hatch. The fish also seem to love dragonfly nymphs and micro leech patterns.

Harper Lake

Location: 10 km (6.2 mi) southwest of Chase
Elevation: 683 m (2,241 ft)
Surface Area: 28 ha (69 ac)
Max Depth: 23.2 m (76.1 ft)
Mean Depth: 12.7 m (41.7 ft)
Way Point: 50° 44' 18.2" N, 119° 42' 54.7" W

Fishing

Located just off the Trans Canada Highway, south of the village of Chase, Harper Lake is a popular lake with locals. Not the least of its many qualities is ease of access. The lake is also stocked regularly with rainbow trout to help maintain the fishery.

Early spring is the most popular season for this lake as its relatively low elevation means it is always ice-free on May 1, when the season opens. By this time, it has been ice-free long enough to spark hatches of insects in its warming waters.

Although Harper Lake is slightly tannic and not as productive as other lakes in the region, it has big hatches, making it a great place for fly anglers.

Chironomids are always a solid bet in the early spring. Knowledgeable fly anglers target the shoals at the ends of the lake and around the sides. Strike indicators are often used to keep flies suspended at precise depths, usually between 15 and 45 cm (6 and 18 inches) off the bottom of the lake. Fly fishers should definitely visit the lake in June when the caddis fly hatch is in full swing. A pupae imitation is very effective.

The lake is deep, which makes it popular with trollers. In the summertime, warm water temperatures push trout off the shoals and into the deeper water. Electronic fish finders are good at finding the right trolling depth during the summer. Good fish finders can even locate the thermocline – the band of water that separates the cool depths from the warmer surface water. Trolling just above or below the thermocline is a technique that can be quite successful, as the fish tend to hang out just below the thermocline. Go with the usual trolling lures, such as spinners and Flatfish, spoons and Wedding Bands.

In late September, the fishing picks up again. As the fish are getting ready for winter, they tend to chase after bigger food items, such as leeches and nymphs. Fly anglers will find these patterns produce, as do attractor patterns like Carey Specials and Doc Spratleys.

Fishing regulations include using a single barbless hook and no bait. Anglers cannot keep more than two fish a day and the lake is closed to fishing from December 1 to April 30.

Area Indicator

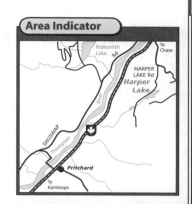

Harper Lake			
Fish Stocking Data			
Year	Species	Number	Life Stage
2011	Rainbow Trout	4,000	Yearling
2010	Rainbow Trout	4,000	Yearling
2009	Rainbow Trout	4,000	Yearling

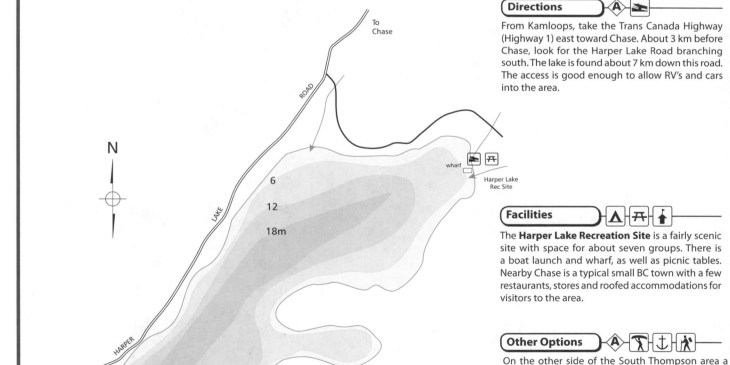

Directions

From Kamloops, take the Trans Canada Highway (Highway 1) east toward Chase. About 3 km before Chase, look for the Harper Lake Road branching south. The lake is found about 7 km down this road. The access is good enough to allow RV's and cars into the area.

Facilities

The **Harper Lake Recreation Site** is a fairly scenic site with space for about seven groups. There is a boat launch and wharf, as well as picnic tables. Nearby Chase is a typical small BC town with a few restaurants, stores and roofed accommodations for visitors to the area.

Other Options

On the other side of the South Thompson area a bunch of great fishing lakes. The closest of these is **Niskonlith Lake**, which is a great place to fish for rainbow to 1 kg (2 lbs) and kokanee to about half that. The lake is prone to the summer doldrums and, being a slightly larger lake, is a good trolling lake.

200m   0   200m   400m   600m
— Scale —

Location: North of Harrison Hot Springs
Elevation: 11 m (36 ft)
Surface Area: 21,780 ha (53,820 ac)
Max Depth: 279 m (915 ft)
Mean Depth: 150 m (492 ft)
Way Point: 49°32' N, 121°49' W

www.backroadmapbooks.com

Harrison Lake

Fishing

Harrison is a big lake, the biggest lake in Southwestern BC, seeming more like an ocean fjord at times with its stunning scenery and rugged shoreline. There are some isolated coves with pretty beaches, rocky islands and towering cliffs with waterfalls cascading down their sides.

The lake is over 55 km long and averages about 1.5 km wide. It is also very deep. Because the lake is so big, it can be tough to track down fish. Yes, there are plenty of big cutthroat, Dolly Varden, rainbow, kokanee and whitefish in the lake, but with 28,000 hectares to hide out in, they can be elusive. Local guides are a valuable addition.

The lake is best known for its cutthroat that can get to 40 cm (16 in). Because the lake is at such a low elevation, it can be fished year-round, even in the dead of winter. Salmon spawn in rivers and creeks around Harrison Lake and the flowing water washes many of the eggs back down the streams and into the lake. Cutthroats gather around these feeder streams and gorge themselves on salmon eggs. Using a single egg or casting small spinners and brass spoons can be very productive during this time.

However, winter storms and cold weather tend to keep pressure down until spring, when those salmon eggs begin hatching and the tiny fry begin moving downstream towards the ocean. Once again the cutthroat gather around these rivers, this time feasting on the fry. Working a gold or silver bodied minnow pattern or spoon, trolled or cast around the rivers and along the shore can work really well. Work in about four to eight feet of water, which is where most of the fry are found. This continues through to June.

In summer, the cutthroat feed on stickleback, which congregate around underwater points, sunken trees, pilings and anything that offers a little big of cover. Troll or cast around these and other structural elements.

Due to limited accessibility for bigger boats, most of the activity occurs at the south end. The best locations to fish near the south end of the lake are at the mouth of Cascade Bay, Celia Cove, around the drop-off of Green Point or along the shores north of the Harrison River outflow. Trolling along the shoreline in quite bays is most effective and will help keep you out of those notorious winds. People with small boats need to be extra cautious, especially during the middle of the day when the winds tend to kick up.

Directions

Getting to the big lake is as simple as getting to Harrison Hot Springs. From Highway 1, follow Highway 9 north to Agassiz. Continue west a short jaunt to the Hot Spring Road, which branches north from Highway 7. This road leads almost directly to a boat launch and marina at the east end of Esplanade Avenue. There are also launches at Green Point in Sasquatch Provincial Park on the southeast end of the lake or Twenty Mile Bay Recreation Site further north on the west side.

Facilities

There are a number of recreation sites on the shores of the lake including **Hale Creek** and **Twenty Mile Bay** on the west side as well as **Rainbow Falls, Cascade Peninsula, Bear Creek or Cogburn Beach** on the east side. These sites vary from drive-in access to hike or boat access only sites. Long Island Bay offers a few remote tenting sites too. See the Backroad Mapbook for Vancouver, Coast and Mountains for more details on the recreational opportunities abounding the lake.

For a little more luxury, the resort town of Harrison Hot Springs at the south end is world famous. The most popular stop is the resort and of course those relaxing mineral springs.

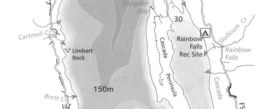

Location: Southwest of Harrison Hot Springs
Stream Length: 18 km (11 mi)
Geographic: 121° 56′ 00″W, 49°15′ 00″N

Harrison River

Fishing

For such a short river, the Harrison is quite popular and offers surprisingly good fishing. But what it lacks in length it makes up for in volume. It is the de facto continuation of the Lillooet River, which flows into Harrison Lake's north end. There is a small but thriving guiding industry for catch and release fishing for White Sturgeon, but the river is best known for its salmon and its cutthroat.

Because the river drains Harrison Lake, it isn't as subject to blowout as many of the other rivers in region since the debris has a chance to settle in the lake.

Chinook begin migrating into the Harrison River as early as June. These early season fish swim up the Harrison River, through Harrison Lake and into the Lillooet River. They are best fished from a boat using spoons like a Kitimat, Koho or Ironhead work well because they can be cast long distances. Spinners like Vibrax or a T-Spoon work okay too, but you will probably need to add some weight. If there is enough current, you can just leave the lure out in the water doing its thing. If the current is not strong enough, or you have too much weight on the line, the lure will just lie on the bottom.

Sockeye salmon enter the Harrison River, destined for Morris Creek and the Weaver Creek Spawning Channel. Since these tributaries are so short and have a low flow in the summer, the fish tend to hang out in the Harrison from July until they are ready to spawn in late September. They are followed by the famous Harrison Chinook, huge beasts that average 9 kg (20 lbs). These fish have white flesh and, while not noted for their eating, are much loved for their sheer brute size and strength. These are followed by Coho, chum and every odd-numbered year, 20 million pink salmon.

The Harrison is also a great cutthroat fishery, both sea-run and resident. Cutthroat love to feed on salmon eggs in the fall and salmon fry in the spring before run-off. If you chose gear to imitate these two foods, chances are you will meet with success. The cutthroat here can get to 4.5 kg (9 lbs) for the sea run variety. Fly anglers can work around the mouths of the feeder creeks and rivers (especially the Chehalis and Weaver Creek) with an egg sucking leech or a streamer pattern. Cutthroat are fairly nomadic. One day the fishing is excellent, the next, nothing.

Steelhead fishing can be decent in January and February using roe, lures or wool. They are present year round but rarely hold very long and are easily spooked in the clear water.

Directions

The Harrison is only about 8 km (5 miles) long, draining Harrison Lake into the Fraser River. To get here, take the Lougheed Highway (Highway 7) east of Mission to the Harrison River Bridge. Watch for the signs to Kilby Provincial Park, located just over the bridge. There is a boat launch here, as well as at Harrison Hot Springs, although there are some rough sections on the upper river.

Facilities

There is a boat launch and camping facilities at **Kilby Provincial Park**. Nearby Harrison Hot Springs features another boat launch, hotels and the chance to soak in the world famous springs. There are hatchery facilities on the Chehalis River and at Weaver Creek.

Harrison River			
Fish Stocking Data			
Year	Species	Number	Life Stage
2011	Cutthroat Trout	4,875	Smolt

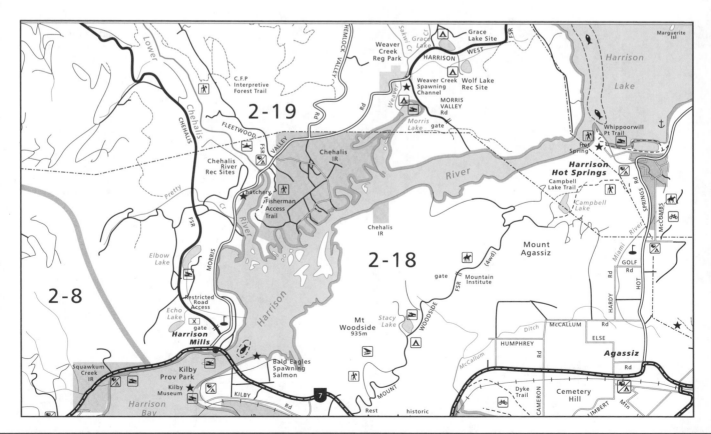

Location: 60 km (37 mi) east of Merritt
Elevation: 1,414 m (4,639 ft)
Surface Area: 108 ha (267 ac)
Max Depth: 12 m (39.4 ft)
Mean Depth: 5.4 m (17.7 ft)
Way Point: 49° 59' 23.0" N, 120° 2' 39.9" W

www.backroadmapbooks.com

Hatheume Lake

Area Indicator

Hatheume Lake			
Fish Stocking Data			
Year	Species	Number	Life Stage
2010	Rainbow Trout	2,000	Fingerling/Yearling
2009	Rainbow Trout	2,000	Fingerling/Yearling

Fishing

Hatheume Lake is managed as a trophy fly-fishing lake and is one of a number of great fishing lakes west of Kelowna in the Pennask Lake area. Found about halfway between Kelowna and Merritt off the Okanagan Connector, it is a resort lake that also features a fine recreation site for visitors.

As a quality fishery, the lake consistently produces rainbow in the 1.5–2 kg (3–4 lb) range and frequently trout are pulled out of here to 4.5 kg (10 lbs) and bigger.

Set fairly high up in elevation, the lake does not see spring as early here as lower elevation lakes. Often times, the lake is not ice-free by May 1, which is the first day of the year that you can fish the lake. This also sets back the time-table of insect hatches.

Beginning after the ice leaves in mid-May, a series of good spring chironomid hatches occur until early June. Brown and black pupae patterns sunk to the bottom and retrieved very slowly is the best way to fish the hatch. There are plenty of birds in the area, including swallows. The swallows feed on hatching chironomids and if you see a lot of avian activity, chances are, the fish will follow.

In late June to early July, a sedge hatch makes dry fly fishing a real pleasure. Damselfly, dragonfly and mayfly patterns work with varying success over the spring and into the fall. Leech and dragonfly patterns work later in the year.

The water in the lake is tannin stained, but marl shoals ring the lake, sloping gradually to deeper water. The lake has some nice shoals particularly at the northwest and southeast ends of the lake. The inflow creek at the southeast end of the lake and the outflow at the north end of the lake are two very inviting locations to fish. Another good place to fish is around the edges of a sunken island in the middle of the lake. The big fish seem to like holding around here.

In addition to the winter closure, there is a one trout daily limit, an ice-fishing ban, a bait ban, a barbless hook restriction and an engine size restriction. All these regulations have been put in place to help manage this quality fishery.

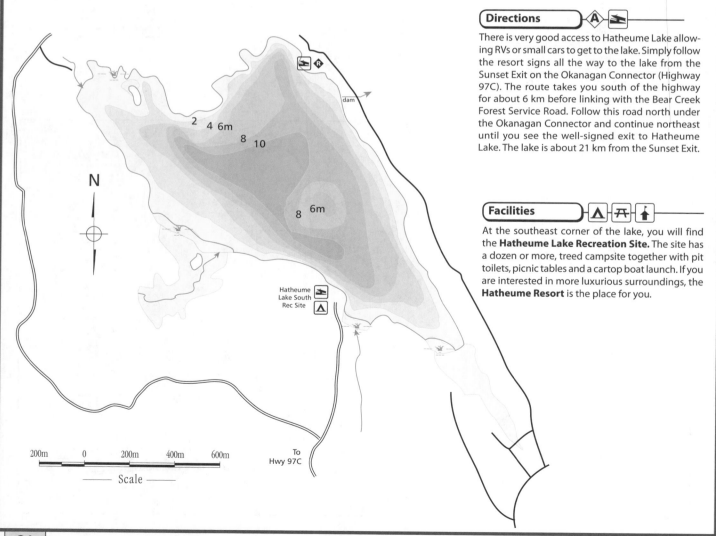

Directions

There is very good access to Hatheume Lake allowing RVs or small cars to get to the lake. Simply follow the resort signs all the way to the lake from the Sunset Exit on the Okanagan Connector (Highway 97C). The route takes you south of the highway for about 6 km before linking with the Bear Creek Forest Service Road. Follow this road north under the Okanagan Connector and continue northeast until you see the well-signed exit to Hatheume Lake. The lake is about 21 km from the Sunset Exit.

Facilities

At the southeast corner of the lake, you will find the **Hatheume Lake Recreation Site.** The site has a dozen or more, treed campsite together with pit toilets, picnic tables and a cartop boat launch. If you are interested in more luxurious surroundings, the **Hatheume Resort** is the place for you.

www.backroadmapbooks.com

Location: 30 km (18.6 mi) northeast of Kamloops
Elevation: 944 m (3,097 ft)
Surface Area: 222 ha (549 ac)
Max Depth: 24.3 m (79.7 ft)
Mean Depth: 11 m (36 ft)
Way Point: 50° 49' 52" N, 120° 3' 24" W

Heffley Lake

Fishing

Located along the road up to Sun Peaks Resort, Heffley Lake is a pretty cottage lake that also has a couple resorts and a well developed recreation site for visitors to enjoy. The lake is 7.2 km (4.5 miles) long and up to 30 metres (100 feet) deep in places. The size of the lake helps keep the fishing active throughout the year, even on those lovely warm summer evenings.

Because of the good access, Heffley Lake receives heavy fishing pressure. However, it still offers some reasonable fishing for rainbow trout in the 1–1.5 kg (2–3 lb) range.

Although trolling is the most popular method here, fly-fishing should not be ruled out. Fly anglers should try the shoals at the west end of the lake during the spring damselfly, chironomid or mayfly hatch. This is because there are some excellent weed beds great for insects and hiding rainbow. At the east end of the lake, you will find the inlet creek and the spawning channel. You can do well fishing near the deep pocket northeast of the small island. Also, the numerous bays and shallow areas on the main body of water offer many choice locations to cast a fly.

Fly patterns of choice are a damselfly or dragonfly nymph, shrimp imitations, Doc Spratley, chironomid papa and bloodworm, mayfly and leeches.

Spincasting a small lure (Flatfish, Mepps, Blue Fox or Kamlooper) around the drop offs or near the inflow and outflow creeks is productive as well.

The lake warms in the summer months forcing the fish to the depths of the lakes. Trolling with a Willow Leaf and worm, Flatfish or Apex then becomes the mainstay of the fishery until the lake water begins to cool in late September and into October. At that time, fly-fishing and spincasting the shoals and drop offs becomes productive again.

The open water season runs from the end of April to November. In the winter months, ice fishing with bait and a hook is effective as long as the ice is safe.

Area Indicator

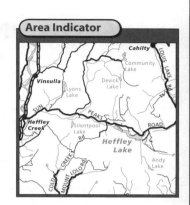

Directions

All types of vehicles easily access Heffley Lake because it is found right next to the paved Sun Peaks Road. To reach the lake, travel north from Kamloops on Highway 5 to the community of Heffley Creek. You can't miss the signage pointing the way to the Sun Peaks Ski Resort. Follow this road east for about 20 km (12 miles) and the first larger lake you pass on the south is your destination. For day trippers, there is a boat launch found near the northeast tip of the lake.

Facilities

The **Heffley Lake Recreation Site** is a very popular, RV friendly 19 unit site complete with a rustic boat launch. It is an enhanced site, which means there is a supervisor and fee to camp here from mid-May until mid-October. Heffley Lake also has two resorts and many private homes or cabins. The **Heffley Lake Fishing Resort** is on the south side of the lake and offers rustic cabins, lakeshore campsites and boat rentals. The **Hitch' N Rail Family Resort** also offers cozy lakeshore cabins, campsites and boat rentals. It also features a convenience store and restaurant.

Other Options

Just before reaching Heffley Lake you will pass by **Little Heffley Lake**. This 7 hectare lake is connected to the bigger lake and offers stocked rainbow that are usually smaller than in its neighbour.

Heffley Lake Fish Stocking Data			
Year	Species	Number	Life Stage
2011	Rainbow Trout	5,000	Yearling
2010	Rainbow Trout	5,000	Yearling
2009	Rainbow Trout	5,000	Yearling

To Kamloops

Little Heffley Lake

Kamloops IR

Heffley Cr

SUN

PERCH Rd

PEAKS

To Sun Peaks

ROAD

Heffley Lake Rec Site

N

200m 0 200m 400m 600m
— Scale —

Hoopatatkwa & Twin Lakes

Elevation: 1,393 m (4,570 ft)
Surface Area: 99 ha (245 ac)
Max Depth: 26.8 m (87.9 ft)
Mean Depth: 8.2 m (26.9 ft)
Way Point: 51° 11'38"N, 120° 28'21"W

Elevation: 1,458 m (4,783 ft)
Surface Area: 9.77 ha (24 ac)
Max Depth: 16.7 m (55 ft)
Mean Depth: 6.9 m (22.6 ft)
Way Point: 51° 12' 2"N, 120° 29' 21"W

Area Indicator

Twin Lake

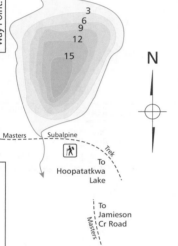

Hoopatakwa Lake

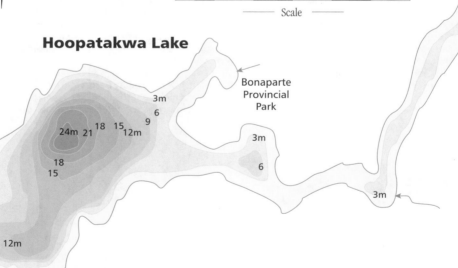

Fishing

Hoopatatkwa Lake (try saying that one five times fast) and Twin Lake are found in the north end of Bonaparte Plateau Provincial Park. They can only be accessed by air or along undeveloped and unmarked hiking trails.

The limited access has kept the quality of fishery high and both lakes offer good fishing for rainbow trout to 2kg (4 lbs) by fly-fishing, bait fishing or spincasting.

Hoopatatkwa Lake has a deep hole right in the middle of the lake. Also, some inviting drop offs are located at the south and north end of the main waterbody. A good shoal area extends to the east and west of the deep hole. However, the narrow bay to the east of the main body is not worth fishing as it is very shallow.

Twin Lake is a much smaller, shallower pothole lake. There are drop offs along the entire shores of the lake. It is possible to fish Twin from shore but a float tube will definitely improve success.

For dry fly fishers, getting to the lakes in late June or early July will reward you with a good sedge hatch. Damselfly, mayfly nymph and chironomid pupae patterns also work depending on the hatch. Just before dusk is a particularly good time to fish here.

In the summer, the fish retreat to the deepest parts of the lakes. Fishing slows in the summer months but that does not rule out using a sinking line with a nymph pattern or Doc Spratley fished deep. Also, bait fishing into the depths of the lake at that time of year can be effective.

By the early fall, the hatches are back into full swing and fishing the shoals and drop offs is effective again.

Directions

There is no road access into the lakes so you will have to make a long hike from the 65 km marker on the Jamieson Creek Road or fly in. To find the trailhead to the Masters Subalpine Trek is no easy task either. Take the Westsyde Road north of Kamloops until you reach the Jamieson Creek Forest Service Road. Head north on the Jamieson Creek Road avoiding the temptation to veer off the main road on one of the many, many logging roads leading from the main road. By the time you reach the trailhead after 65 km of gravel road you probably won't mind stretching your legs with a good walk.

Facilities

There is a resort at the Hoopatatkwa Lake that will fly you into the lake and provide float tubes and boats so that you don't have to carry all your gear in. For the do-it-yourselfer, there are some undeveloped camping areas around the lake. There are no facilities at Twin Lake, but again, there are some places where you could pitch a tent.

Hoover Lake

Location: 10.5 km (6.5 mi) north of Mission
Elevation: 420 m (1,378 ft)
Surface Area: 13 ha (32 ac)
Max Depth: 26 m (85 ft)
Mean Depth: 7 m (23 ft)
Way Point: 49° 15' 39.9" N, 122° 19' 41.5" W

Fishing

Hoover Lake is seldom visited, but is a good fishing lake and worth trying if you're in the area.

One of the reasons the lake is not visited as frequently as other lakes in the area is because of the 3.7 km (2.3 mile) hike to the lake. While people are willing to hike for many kilometres to visit scenic mountain lakes, Hoover Lake is not that. The lake is pretty enough, but it is set in a thick, dark forest, surrounded by shaggy hills.

The lake is a good size for float tubes; not too big as to be windy, but big enough that a tube is definitely an asset in getting around. Shoreline fishing is difficult, as the bush crowds the lake and the shoreline is filled with sunken logs, debris and weeds. If you don't have a tube, there are a few spots along the western shoreline that can be fished from shore.

The lake has a number of islands, shoals and underwater structure, which makes it a great lake for fishing. It offers good fishing for rainbow and cutthroat that average 20–30 cm (8–12 in) in size but can grow to 1.5 kg (3.0 lbs).

The low elevation lake can be fished as early as April. It remains good until late May when the waters begin to warm and the fish retreat to the deeper water. By the fall (October to November), fishing begins to pick up again.

Trolling a lake troll or a lure tipped with a worm around the perimeter of the lakes is perhaps the most productive fishing method, but do not rule out fly-fishing or casting small lures closer to shore. As always, fly anglers are best to match the hatch, while small spinners like Mepps or Panther Martin rarely disappoint. There are also two deeper pockets of water north of the large island. During the summer months, you should focus towards the drop-offs in those areas using a nymph or chironomid imitation on a sinking line.

Directions

Hoover Lake is found east of Steve Lake and north of the Mission landfill. From Mission, head northwest along the Dewdney Trunk Road heading towards Stave Falls. About 2.5 km before Stave Falls, you will see a gated road on the right. If you drive past the Mission landfill on the left you have gone too far.

From the Dewdney Trunk Road, an old road leads steadily uphill towards Hoover Lake for the first 3 km or so. The last 800 metres is on a trail, which descends 60 m (296 ft) to the lake. In total, the hike is 3.7 km (2.3 miles), gaining 300 m (984 ft) in elevation.

Facilities

There is a small camping area at the south end of the lake where the trail meets with the shoreline. Other than a few fire rings and an outhouse there is no other amenities at the rustic campsite.

The trail continues along the west side of the lake on a boardwalk over a marshy area to three other lakeshore campsites. Those campsites are little more than openings in the trees. They are found on the point south of the large island.

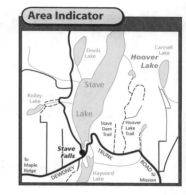

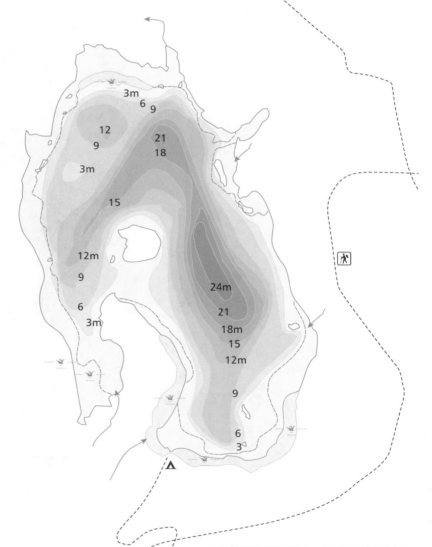

Other Options

There are several lakes near Hoover Lake, which do not involve the same hike as Hoover Lake, ranging from the mammoth **Stave Lake**, which is best trolled, to small lakes like **Hatzic or Rolley Lake**. Stave Lake and Rolley Lake are written up elsewhere in this book.

Horseshoe & Nanton Lakes

© Mussio Ventures Ltd.

Nanton Lake

Elevation: 168 m (551 ft)
Surface Area: 123 ha (304 ac)
Max Depth: 28 m (91 ft)
Mean Depth: 10 m (33 ft)
Way Point: 49° 54' 55" N, 124° 19' 27" W

Horseshoe Lake

Elevation: 164 m (538 ft)
Surface Area: 418 ha (1,033 ac)
Max Depth: 62 m (203 ft)
Mean Depth: 25 m (82 ft)
Way Point: 49° 54' 5" N, 124° 17' 9" W

Area Indicator

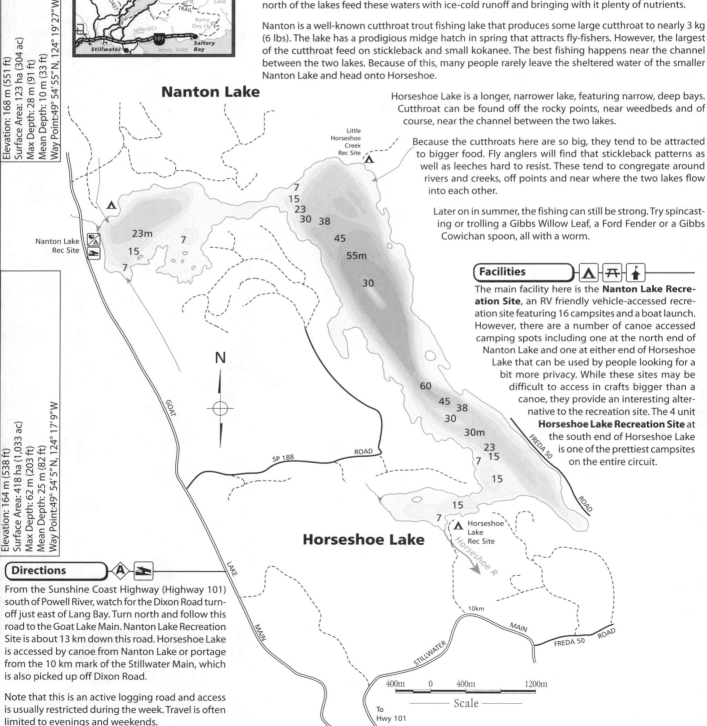

Fishing

While there are two names here, this really is one waterbody, connected by a rather broad channel. The two lakes are part of the Power Lake Canoe Circuit and see a fair bit of canoe traffic. However, like all the lakes on the circuit, there is a logging road that connects up to the lake where you will find a recreation site complete with a boat launch on Nanton Lake.

Even though these two are really one lake, the channel and the fact that the boat launch is on Nanton, gives Horseshoe Lake a feeling of remoteness that you don't find elsewhere on the circuit.

The lakes in this area are famous for their cutthroat fishery. The glacier of the rugged Coast Mountains north of the lakes feed these waters with ice-cold runoff and bringing with it plenty of nutrients.

Nanton is a well-known cutthroat trout fishing lake that produces some large cutthroat to nearly 3 kg (6 lbs). The lake has a prodigious midge hatch in spring that attracts fly-fishers. However, the largest of the cutthroat feed on stickleback and small kokanee. The best fishing happens near the channel between the two lakes. Because of this, many people rarely leave the sheltered water of the smaller Nanton Lake and head onto Horseshoe.

Horseshoe Lake is a longer, narrower lake, featuring narrow, deep bays. Cutthroat can be found off the rocky points, near weedbeds and of course, near the channel between the two lakes.

Because the cutthroats here are so big, they tend to be attracted to bigger food. Fly anglers will find that stickleback patterns as well as leeches hard to resist. These tend to congregate around rivers and creeks, off points and near where the two lakes flow into each other.

Later on in summer, the fishing can still be strong. Try spincasting or trolling a Gibbs Willow Leaf, a Ford Fender or a Gibbs Cowichan spoon, all with a worm.

Facilities

The main facility here is the **Nanton Lake Recreation Site**, an RV friendly vehicle-accessed recreation site featuring 16 campsites and a boat launch. However, there are a number of canoe accessed camping spots including one at the north end of Nanton Lake and one at either end of Horseshoe Lake that can be used by people looking for a bit more privacy. While these sites may be difficult to access in crafts bigger than a canoe, they provide an interesting alternative to the recreation site. The 4 unit **Horseshoe Lake Recreation Site** at the south end of Horseshoe Lake is one of the prettiest campsites on the entire circuit.

Directions

From the Sunshine Coast Highway (Highway 101) south of Powell River, watch for the Dixon Road turn-off just east of Lang Bay. Turn north and follow this road to the Goat Lake Main. Nanton Lake Recreation Site is about 13 km down this road. Horseshoe Lake is accessed by canoe from Nanton Lake or portage from the 10 km mark of the Stillwater Main, which is also picked up off Dixon Road.

Note that this is an active logging road and access is usually restricted during the week. Travel is often limited to evenings and weekends.

Hosli Lake

Location: 24 km (15 mi) southwest of Kamloops
Elevation: 1,179 m (3,868 ft)
Maximum Depth: 13.7 m (43 ft)
Way Point: 50° 31′ 30″ N, 120° 8′ 44″ W

Fishing

Hosli Lake is a small lake found south of Kamloops that produces some surprisingly large rainbow for such a small lake. It is also just off the beaten path to Roche Lake Provincial Park that many anglers overlook this lake.

Hosli is stocked annually with 2,500 All Female Triploid rainbow by the Freshwater Fisheries Society of BC. These fish are genetically incapable of reproducing and pour all the energy that they might have otherwise used on reproduction into getting nice and big for you to catch. As a result, every once in a while, you can hook into a 2.5 kg (5 lb) trout that will run for the deeps and give you a fight that will have you longing for more. The average fish in here are generally less than 1 kg (2 lbs).

The lake is a perfect interior plateau lake. Surrounded by trees, the wind does not whip up on the lake, making it a great place to fish in a small boat or float tube. There are sandy shoals, a small island, weed beds and quick drop offs.

The lake has lots of food for the trout to feed on, from Gammarus shrimp to chironomids to a rather impressive caddis hatch. Of these, the most common food is the shrimp.

The caddis hatch can happen any time from mid-June to mid-July, depending on the weather. This is one of the best times to fish the lakes and a traditional Elk Hair Caddis can generate a lot of action.

There is a nice place to fish in the shallows between the island and the shore. While the fish do not generally move into this area during the day (as it is too shallow and unprotected), in the evening it becomes a prime feeding ground.

Trolling a leech along the drop off is another popular method of fishing the lake. There is no boat launch, but it's possible to hand launch a small boat or use a float tube. Shore fishing is difficult, but spincasters will find a couple places to cast from.

The lake can be moody, though and it is possible to spend a day here without a strike. The weather seems to have an effect and when a cool, low pressure front moves in, things can slow down.

The lake is managed as a trophy fishing lake. There is a bait ban, a single barbless hook restriction and a daily catch limit of two. There is also no fishing from December 1 to April 30.

Directions

As the crow flies, Hosli Lake is 24 km southwest of Kamloops on the backroads north of Roche Lake Provincial Park. The best access is from the Roche Lake Road south of Kamloops. From the Trans-Canada Highway junction, travel south on Highway 5A for about 22 km. Turn east onto Roche Lake Road, which you will follow for about 9 km to the Bleeker Forest Service Road. This rough, but usually 2wd accessible road takes you past Bleeker Lake, Black Lake and then Hosli Lake.

The lake can also be accessed via 4wd roads from the north. For either direction, a truck, a GPS with the BC Backroad GPS Maps and a copy of the Backroad Mapbook for the Thompson Okanagan is highly recommended.

Facilities

There is rustic camping with space for about half a dozen groups on the lake. There is no boat launch, but it is possible to hand launch a cartopper. More formal camping is found at nearby **Roche Lake Provincial Park**.

Hosli Lake			
Fish Stocking Data			
Year	Species	Number	Life Stage
2008	Rainbow Trout	2,500	Fry
2007	Rainbow Trout	2,500	Fry
2006	Rainbow Trout	2,500	Fry

Area Indicator

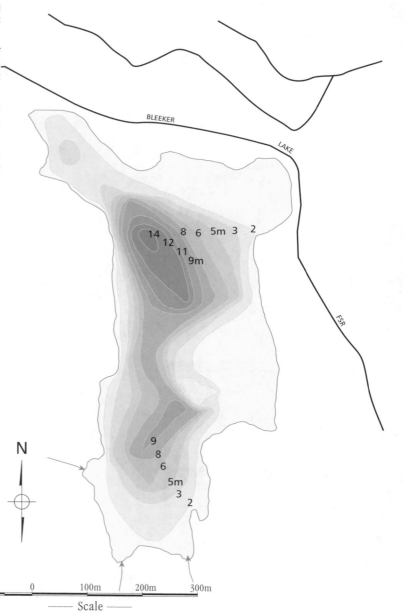

N

100m 0 100m 200m 300m

— Scale —

Hyas, Hadlow & Pemberton Lks

Hyas Lake

Elevation: 1,234 m (4,049 ft)
Surface Area: 64 ha (158 ac)
Max Depth: 21.9 m (71.9 ft)
Mean Depth: 8.2 m (26.9 ft)
Way Point: 50° 47' 52.4" N, 119° 58' 2.6" W

Hadlow Lake

Elevation: 1,241 m (4,072 ft)
Surface Area: 7 ha (17 ac)
Max Depth: 5.5 m (18 ft)
Way Point: 50° 48' 10" N, 119° 58' 46" W

Pemberton Lake

Elevation: 1,228 m (4,029 ft)
Surface Area: 14 ha (35 ac)
Max Depth: 14 m (45.9 ft)
Mean Depth: 6 m (19.8 ft)
Way Point: 50° 46' 51" N, 119° 57' 33" W

Area Indicator

Fishing

This trio of small mountain lakes is accessed by the Hyas Lake Road. While the lakes are small, they offer good fishing and are often busy, despite the rough access.

Although most of the fishing is focused around Hyas Lake, the fishing here tends to be slow. The rainbow average 0.5–1 kg (1–2 lbs) although there has been the very occasional rainbow to 4 kg (8 lbs). Since Hyas Lake has deep clear water, trolling is the primary fishing method. In particular, try trolling a leech pattern or a lake troll along the prominent drop offs for best success.

For the fly angler, the lake has a steep shoreline on the east and west sides and nice shoals near the north and south ends of the lake. The lake offers some very rewarding insect hatches. Leech, damselfly nymph, chironomid pupae, sedge or dragonfly nymph patterns are your best bet.

Fishing tails off somewhat in the summer months but the lake is a deep, high elevation lake and even in August remains reasonably cool.

Not so at Hadlow Lake, a tiny lake to the northwest. The shallow lake gets quite warm during the summer effectively shutting down the fishery. It is also prone to winterkill during long, cold winters.

Hadlow contains rainbow that can reach 1 kg (2-3 lbs) but are generally pan size. The lake is best fished by casting a lure and worm (Deadly Dick, Blue Fox or Panther Martin) or by fly-fishing with a damselfly or sedge imitation. The sedge hatch in the spring is the best time to fly-fish.

Pemberton Lake provides fairly good fishing for rainbow that can reach 1.5 kg (3 lbs). The lake has extensive weedbeds that line the lake offering good insect and aquatic vertebrae rearing grounds that the fish often forage. The lake is best fly-fished using a damselfly or dragonfly nymph cast near the weeds. Shrimp imitations and leech patterns also work well.

Some fishermen troll the lake using a lake troll (Willow Leaf and worm) but the depth and size of the lake requires careful maneuvering. Trolling a small lure or spinner (Flatfish, Blue Fox, Deadly Dick or Mepps) or a fly (leech or Doc Spratley) can also be productive.

It is best to fish the lake beginning in mid May until early July and again in late September to late October as the summer months are highly unproductive. Pemberton is subject to drawdown during the summer for irrigation purposes and the water warms significantly at that time of year.

All three lakes are closed from December 1 to April 30 or during the ice-fishing season.

Directions

To reach the lakes, travel 5 km (3 miles) north of Kamloops on Highway 5. Watch for the Paul Lake Road, heading east. You will pass Paul Lake and about 5 km past Pinanten Lake, you will come to the Hyas Lake Road, heading north. Follow that rough road to its end and you will reach Pemberton and Hyas Lakes. Hadlow Lake involves a hike from the north end of Hyas Lake.

Facilities

There are recreation sites at Hyas and Pemberton Lakes along with a good trail system. The **Hyas Lake South Recreation Site** offers 4 campsites, a rustic boat launch and wharf, while **Pemberton Lake Recreation Site** also has room for about four campers and a cartop boat launch. The rustic **Hyas Lake Resort** and private cabins are also found on Hyas Lake.

Hadlow Lake

2 5
3m

Hyas Lake

N

3m
6
9

9
12m

12
15
18

21m
18
15
12m

9
6
3m

Hyas Lake
South Rec Site

P

Hyas
Shaw
Trails

3
6 9
12m   3

Pemberton Lake
Rec Site

Pemberton Lake

Hyas Lake Fish Stocking Data			
Year	Species	Number	Life Stage
2008	Rainbow Trout	2,500	Fry
2007	Rainbow Trout	2,500	Fry
2006	Rainbow Trout	2,500	Fall Fry

Pemberton Lake Fish Stocking Data			
Year	Species	Number	Life Stage
2004	Rainbow Trout	1,000	Yearling

200m   0   200m   400m   600m
— Scale —

www.backroadmapbooks.com

Location: 24 km (15 mi) north of Port Moody
Stream Length: 27 km (17 mi)
Geographic: 122° 53' 00" W, 49° 28' 00" N

Indian River

Fishing

The Indian River is a beautiful, clear river that flows into the north end of the Indian Arm. It is a quiet destination that seems to be made for fly-fishing. Historically, it has been a difficult river to access and, with a major washout shutting the road down for at least the next few years (the Stawamus-Indian Road is now gated at the start of the road), getting to the Indian River from the Squamish side is now next to impossible.

The river is still accessible from the south, by boat up the Indian Arm. And, since only the first 8 km (5.2 miles) of the river are salmon bearing, this is the preferred method of getting to the river anyway.

While the river has a fair run of chum, insignificant runs of Coho, Chinook and mere rumours of steelhead and sockeye, the river is best known for its pink fishing.

The pink return in good numbers on odd numbered years (2009, 2011). While pink are second last in the salmon popularity contest, there is a growing sub-culture of anglers who have taken to fishing for pink on the fly.

Pink are the least popular salmon for eating and they lack the scrappiness of Coho, the fast and furious action of sockeye, or the sheer size and brute strength of Chinook. However, they are fairly aggressive biters, making them a good salmon to learn to fly-fish with.

The average sized pink weighs 2–2.5 kg (4–5 lbs), so you will want to use light gear–a five or six weight rod is great. Just about any wet fly will work well for pink, although they seem to have an affinity for pink. Pink streamers, pink Woolly Buggers …as long as the hook isn't too big, you should have no trouble catching one of these fish. Try using a #4 or #6, stripping fairly quickly, pausing a moment between strips to tempt the fish.

Spincasters will also sometimes fish pink. Again, there is no real secret. Try working Gibbs Crocodiles and Dick Nites with splashes of pink or red.

Later in the fall, in October and November, chum enter the system. The fishing is equally as good but you will need heavier gear to land one of these big salmon that can reach 9 kg (20 lbs). Wool is probably the most common lure for fishing for chum, but fly-fishers can try working Woolly Buggers and leech patterns. Green and purple tend to be the best colours.

The river is also home to rainbow and cutthroat trout and Dolly Varden. However, these fish are rarely targeted by anglers.

Directions

The Indian River is only accessible by boat, at the north end of Indian Arm. The closest boat launch is at Cates Park in North Vancouver. It is easily accessed off the Dollarton Highway, which is the first exit off the Trans Canada after crossing the Second Narrows Bridge. Follow the Dollarton for about 5 km (3 miles) to the park on your right.

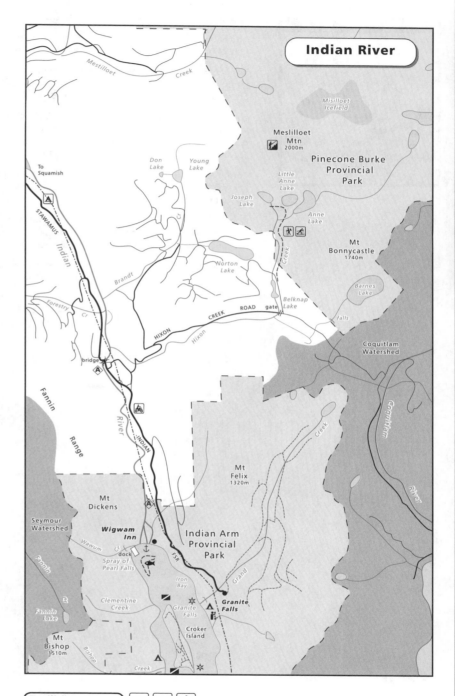

Facilities

The lower section of the Indian River is within **Indian Arm Provincial Park**, a wilderness park that protects much of Indian Arm. There is no camping at the river itself, but there are some informal camping spots available nearby. The closest boat-accessible campsite is at Granite Falls, on the east side of Indian Arm. There is also camping on the north and south sides of Bishop Creek and on North Twin Island.

The dock at the end of Indian Arm is private and owned by the Tsleil-Waututh Nation. Contact them at 604-929-3454 regarding access.

Location: 12 km (7.2 miles) north of Powell River
Elevation: 106 m (348 ft)
Surface Area: 349 ha (862 ac)
Max Depth: 45 m (147 ft)
Mean Depth: 22 m (72 ft)
Way Point: 49° 56' 24" N, 124° 29' 36" W

www.backroadmapbooks.com

Inland Lake

Area Indicator

Fishing

Also known as Loon Lake, Inland Lake is the feature attraction in Inland Lake Provincial Park. It is a popular destination for hikers, campers and anglers and is known for its 13 km (8 mile) wheelchair accessible trail circling the lake.

Inland Lake is one of the great cutthroat fishing lakes located in the Powell River area. The lakes here are famous for their cutthroat fishery, with trophy size trout commonly pulled out of these waters. The glacier of the rugged Coast Mountains north of the lakes feed these waters with ice-cold runoff, bringing with it plenty of nutrients.

There is no boat launch at the 5.5 km (3.9 mile) long lake, but it is a short portage to the water carrying a canoe, a cartopper or a float tube. The lake can get quite windy and caution is needed, especially in a float tube. There is a portage trail to (or from) the lake from Powell Lake, a distance of 2 km (1.2 miles). While this is not a common approach to the lake, it is an interesting side trip for canoeists on the Powell Lake Chain.

Cutthroats up to 3 kg (6 lbs) have been pulled out of the lake, which also holds rainbow trout to 1.5 kg (3 lbs), kokanee and the occasional Coho. The best time to fish for cutthroat is from April to June and then again in August and September.

One of the mainstays of fishing here is trolling Cowichan spoons behind a small boat. Spincasters should work brass-coloured spinners and rainbow coloured Krocodile spoons. Fly anglers should focus their efforts around inflowing streams. Try working a chironomid, a purple leech or Powell River Stickleback near the drop-off in these areas.

The rainbow and kokanee are best caught trolling Willow Leafs or Ford Fenders with a Wedding Band or Dick Nite lure and some bait.

There is a 10 hp motor limit on Inland Lake, which is also closed to fishing from November 1 to March 31. Also note the single barbless hook restriction and the fact that no cutthroat over 40 cm (15.5 in) can be retained.

Directions

From Haslam Lake Road in Powell River, head up a short but steep hill. Turn left onto the gravel road and follow that for 5 km (3 miles). Turn north onto Haywire Bay/Inland Lake Road and follow that for another 9 km (5.6 miles) to reach south end of the lake. The road to the lake is occasionally closed mid-week due to logging, so it's best to contact a local fishing store before heading out.

Facilities

Inland Lake Provincial Park has excellent camping, hiking, boating and swimming opportunities. There are 22 vehicle accessible campsites in the main camping area available on a first-come, first-serve basis, as well as a cartop boat launch. The campsite is open year round with full services from mid-May to mid-September. The two cabins at the main site are not open to the public, but there are three cabins spaced out around the lake for use by disabled people. Visitors will also find six fishing piers scattered around the lake, as well as eight picnic areas/rest areas along the wheelchair accessible trail that circles the lake. Those looking for a little more seclusion will find three nice walk-in campsites on Anthony Island.

People with disabilities are able to reserve the log cabins between April and October by calling Tourism Powell River at (604)485-4701.

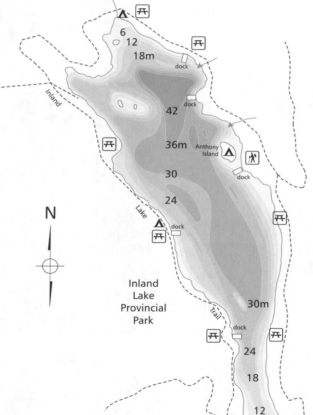

N

6
12
18m
dock
dock
42
36m   Anthony Island
30
24
Inland
Lake
Provincial
Park
Trail
30m
24
18
12
6
dock
Inland
Lake
Campsite

200m 0 200m   600m   1000m
Scale

INLAND   LAKE   ROAD

To
Hwy 101

92

Isobel Lake

Location: 15 km (9.3 mi) north of Kamloops
Elevation: 1,005 m (3,297 ft)
Surface Area: 24 ha (59 ac)
Max Depth: 9.5 m (31.2 ft)
Mean Depth: 3 m (9.8 ft)
Way Point: 50° 50' 38.1" N, 120° 24' 20.2" W

Fishing

Isobel Lake is an ideal lake for young anglers, eager to develop their skills. The lake is annually stocked with catchable sized rainbow that offers kids the perfect opportunity to get hooked on fishing.

Catchable rainbow are notoriously ignorant of the ways of fishing and will quite gladly chase after anything that even remotely looks like food or at least sparkles prettily. After being caught once or twice, the fish usually become a little more wary, but for the first few weeks after stocking, fishing is fast and furious for pan size rainbow. After about a month, the fishing does slow down after the fish that are most desperate to get caught have been.

As of 2008, Isobel is the first lake in the region with age restrictions, meaning only kids under the age of 16 and seniors with a valid BC Seniors Card. The lake is also open to people with a BC Disabled Card.

At 14 hectares (36 acres), Isobel Lake is small compared to other lakes in the region. An island by one bay of the lake and adjacent marshy wetlands allow anglers to explore and interact with the environment in ways not always possible at other lakes. The kids will enjoy cruising through the shallow channel that cut through the marsh at the end of the bay. The parents will enjoy seeing the excitement on their children's faces when they hook into these active trout. Eating their catch with the family will invoke a sense of pride for the young anglers. For families that don't have access to a boat, plans are currently underway to install a fishing dock on Isobel Lake.

When the fishing slows down, the family can take a relaxing walk around the lake on a well maintained interpretative trail. A kiosk with picnic tables on the trail is a great spot to stop for lunch.

For fly-fishers, an underwater point a couple hundred metres away from the boat launch, is a good place to start searching for fish. Anchor down where the point borders deeper water and try the usual assortment of chironomids or nymphs. Popular techniques for fishing Isobel Lake include a slowly trolled black leech, dragonfly nymph or Doc Spratley.

Trollers and spincasters should work the edges with spinners, spoons or a small Flatfish. Flatfish and other lures also attract the attention of trout, while a small live earthworm dangled beneath a slip bobber will be difficult for trout to ignore.

Ice fishing during the winter months is also popular here.

Directions

From downtown Kamloops, cross the Overlander Bridge and follow Fortune Drive to Eighth Street. Head north to Batchelor Drive and follow this road through the residential development to the gravel road and the entrance to Lac Du Bois Provincial Park. Follow Lac Du Bois Road for about 15 km (9 miles) to the McQueen Lake Interpretive Centre. Head east from the main road for 4 km and follow the signs to Isobel Lake.

Facilities

The **Isobel Lake Recreation Site** offers 4 campsites and a rustic is boat launch for cartop boats or canoes to get out on the lake. Part of the Isobel Lake Interpretive Forest, there is an extensive cross-country skiing trail system as well as motorized trails in the area to explore.

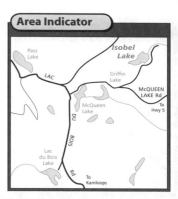

Isobel Lake Fish Stocking Data			
Year	Species	Number	Life Stage
2010	Rainbow Trout	2,000	Catchable
2009	Rainbow Trout	3,000	Catchable

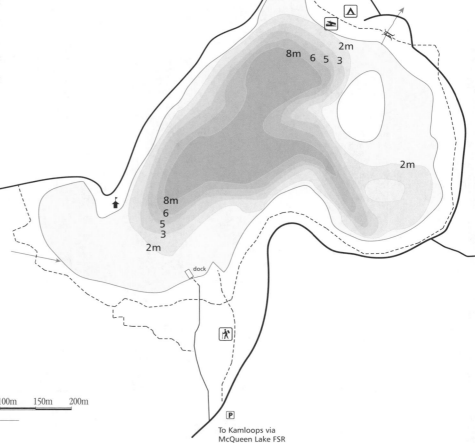

© Mussio Ventures Ltd.

Location: 10 km (6.2 mi) northeast of Pemberton
Elevation: 412 m (1,352 ft)
Surface Area: 9 ha (22 ac)
Max Depth: 6 m (19 ft)
Mean Depth: 2 m (6 ft)
Way Point: 50° 20' 19" N, 122° 45' 34" W

Ivey Lake

Area Indicator

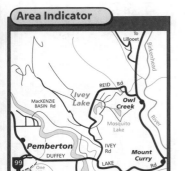

Ivey Lake
Fish Stocking Data

Year	Species	Number	Life Stage
2010	Rainbow Trout	250	Yearling
2009	Rainbow Trout	250	Yearling

Fishing

Nestled in the tall coastal cedars beneath the mountains that surround the Pemberton Valley, Ivey Lake is one of Region 2's trophy fly-fishing lakes. The small lake lies right on the divide between the coast and interior and as a result, is one of the most nutrient rich lakes in the area.

The lake has been stocked annually by the Freshwater Fisheries Society of BC with yearling all female sterile rainbow trout since 2005. These trout grow fast and big. To make sure the trout get big and can be enjoyed by all, there are several angling regulations on the lake; catch and release, artificial fly only, bait ban, single barbless hook and a winter closure from December 1 to March 31.

Late April to early May offers great chironomid fishing, try burgundy, red or black larvae imitations. Later in the spring, the black ant hatch is a fly-fishers dream for those who time this hatch correctly. They usually hatch on the first day over 27°C in May or June.

Ivey Lake is quite productive, with good damsel and dragonfly populations. In the early season, try a gomphus dragon fly on a full sink line with a long leader. As the temperature warms in June and July keep your eye on the hatches with action starting to move towards the deeper sections or down the west edge of the lake. Try a mayfly or halfback pattern at this time.

The shallow nature of the lake leads to warmer water temperatures and often a slower fishery. If fishing in mid-summer, it is best to try late evenings. If you do hook into a fish, play it quickly and release it gently to avoid stress, ensuring the continued success of this enhanced fishery.

In September and October fishing picks up again as water temperatures start to cool down. Try fishing around the docks where fish return to shallow water when the impulse to feed before winter returns. In the fall, bump a leech in black, burgundy, olive, or brown near the bottom. Trolling a searching pattern like a Doc Spratley in red or black is also effective.

A float tube, pontoon boat or a small portable boat works best as there is virtually no shoreline access. In fact, if visiting Ivey for the first time, watch that first step into the lake. What appears to be the bottom isn't. The real bottom is about 0.9 m (3 ft) below the surface of the muck and the smell you will stir up is one you won't soon forget. Those that are limited to shore fishing can access the lake at the northeast end of the lake and follow the channel to deeper water. If you do get out on the water, the best fishing is along the edges of the docks on the west side, down to the south end.

Ivey Lake is moody and has been known to humble more than a few anglers–but if you happen to be there when the fishing is on, you will create memories for life.

Directions

Take the Sea to Sky Highway (Highway 99) to Mt. Currie and then follow the road to D'Arcy north for 4 km. Turn left up Reid Road and then left again at the first intersection and park at the end. It is a short walk down a steep trail from the end of this public road. All other Ivey Lake access is private property.

Facilities

Surrounded by private property, there are no public facilities on the lake. There is camping at nearby **Owl Creek Recreation Site** on the road to D'Arcy.

Jacko Lake

Location: 7 km (4 mi) south of Kamloops
Elevation: 891 m (2,923 ft)
Surface Area: 47 ha (116 ac)
Max Depth: 24.8 m (81.4 ft)
Mean Depth: 10.9 m (35.8 ft)
Way Point: 50° 36' 40.3" N, 120° 25' 10.3" W

Fishing

Jacko Lake is one of the closest lakes to Kamloops, found just south of town. It is also one of the lowest elevation lakes in the area. As a result it is usually ice-free by the first week of April, making it a great early season lake.

Like most low elevation lakes, the water here becomes uncomfortably warm in the heart of summer and the trout become lethargic and not interested in feeding. Even if you were to snag a trout at this time, it wouldn't put up much of a fight.

In spring and fall; however, the lake offers great fishing for fish up to 3.5 kg (7 lbs). Back in the 1980s, there were a number of fish pulled out of the lake to 9.5 kg (20 lbs), but that hasn't happened for nearly a quarter century (at least not to our knowledge).

The lake is best fished from a float tube or a small boat. In early spring, fly anglers will find chironomids, bloodworms, micro-leeches and damsel nymphs with a strike indicator are most productive. A good place to start is the shallows in the southeast corner, near the outlet, or along the west and north shores.

As spring progresses, try fishing the drop offs with larger flies and fast sinking lines. In the evenings, fishing along the shoals with a variety of nymphs or leeches can produce some cruisers. Try a small Black Spratley or Woolly Bugger.

The fish tend to be pickier in the fall and you will probably throw most everything you have at the lake, trying to figure out what works. Some patterns that have been known to work are green shrimp (especially around the weeds) and water boatmen. Depending on the mood of the fish, these can produce well. Or you might wind up catching a whole lot of nothing.

Spincasters can fish from a float tube or from the shore and seem to have better success in the early summer and fall. A simple bait and bobber set-up can work wonders.

Trolling is also productive using small spinners and spoons.

Area Indicator

Jacko Lake Fish Stocking Data			
Year	Species	Number	Life Stage
2011	Rainbow Trout	6,500	Yearling
2010	Rainbow Trout	13,500	Fingerling/Yearling
2009	Rainbow Trout	10,032	Fingerling/Yearling

Directions

Jacko Lake is found just south of Kamloops along the Lac Le Jeune Road. From Kamloops, head west on the Trans Canada Highway to Hillside Drive and follow the signs south towards Lac Le Jeune and Logan Lake. About 5 km from the exit, you will pass through a culvert tunnel. The turn-off to Jacko Lake is immediately (and we mean immediately) after exiting the tunnel to your left. Follow this gravel road for 2 km to the lake.

Facilities

Jacko Lake is located on private land, but the landowners do allow people to fish here. However, there is no overnight camping and, while you should treat every lake with respect, leaving it in as good or better condition as you found it, here it is doubly important. Make sure you take your garbage with you. There are fences in the area. Please do not trespass.

Kamloops is only about 15 minutes away, where you will find all manner of accommodations, restaurants and other facilities. The nearest provincial park with a campground is Lac Le Jeune, about 20 minutes south of Jacko Lake.

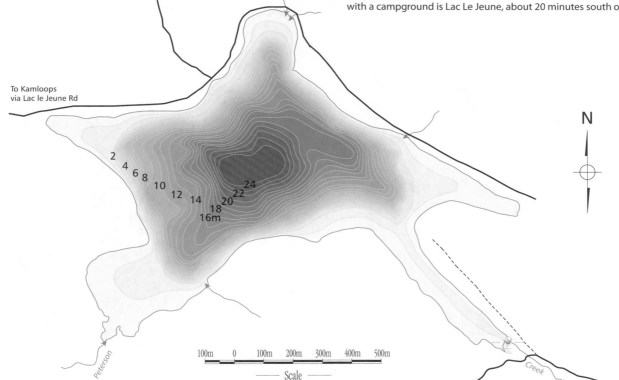

To Kamloops
via Lac le Jeune Rd

N

Peterson

Creek

100m 0 100m 200m 300m 400m 500m

— Scale —

Location: 39 km (24 mi) north of Chase
Elevation: 1,067 m (3,600 ft)
Surface Area: 362 ha (895 ac)
Max Depth: 59 m (193 ft)
Mean Depth: 17 m (57 ft)
Way Point: 51° 10' 9" N, 119° 44' 48" W

www.backroadmapbooks.com

Johnson Lake

Area Indicator

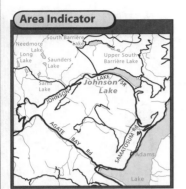

Johnson Lake Fish Stocking Data			
Year	Species	Number	Life Stage
2010	Rainbow Trout	5,000	Fry
2009	Rainbow Trout	5,000	Fry

Fishing

Johnson Lake is considered the Caribbean of the North for its clear waters that turn turquoise due to the limestone in the area. It is a high elevation lake where the water stays cool and the fishing stays hot through the summer.

The lake is about 5 km (3 miles) long, curving gently around Samatosum Mountain, and almost 60 metres (200 feet) deep. At the east end you will find white marl shoals. While the rest of the lake features fairly fast drop offs.

The shoals at the east end are where you will find the majority of insect hatches and, when a hatch is on, the rainbow come to feed. There are chironomid hatches early on, followed by mayflies, dragonflies and damselflies. The mayfly hatch and the travelling sedge hatch (usually sometime from mid-June to mid-July) can provide some of the best action all year.

During the hatches, the trout can be quite selective, especially when more than one insect is hatching. Figuring out what is on the menu for that day can be challenging.

However, the most plentiful and most common food is shrimp. The rainbow in the lake have a bright red flesh from the shrimp, which makes them a particularly popular fish to eat. They can also reach 2 kg (5 lbs) on occasion.

Another good area to try is the spawning channel located between Little Johnson and Johnson Lakes. It has a fish ladder to help the young fry return to the big lake and springs to life in May and June.

Spincasters can troll a variety of Flatfish, lake trolls with worms and spinners and spoons. However, the fish here are not easily fooled by gear, meaning that the cunning fly angler will usually have more luck than someone trolling a spoon. Larger fish especially are extremely wary of flashy objects that move in a straight line.

Even trolling flies can prove challenging and if it isn't working, stop and cast. Depending on what you are casting, work a slow retrieve, pausing frequently. Because the lake is so deep and so clear, the trout will often hold quite deep–down 15 metres (50 feet) or so. Getting a fly down that deep takes a lot of patience.

Some popular flies here include nymphs, chironomids, mayflies, caddis, leeches and shrimp. A bead head Woolly Bugger is a great pattern to test.

Directions

Access to the lake is via good gravel road, suitable for cars and RV's. From the west, follow Highway 5 north of Kamloops for about 60 km to the Agate Bay Road turnoff. Follow this paved road for 22 km to Minova Road, which branches north. This gravel road climbs quickly to the plateau and links to Johnson Lake Forest Service Road. It is about 16 km to the lake (follow the resort signs).

From the south, you will need to get to Adams Lake from the Squilax-Anglemont Road outside of Chase on the Trans-Canada Highway. At the end of pavement in Adams Lake, it is another 19 km to the Agate Bay Road turnoff. Follow this road out of the valley to the Minova Road junction and the route described above.

Facilities

The **Johnson Lake Resort** is found just off the west tip of the lake. It offers cabins and campsites, a boat launch and rentals along with a store for last minute supplies. On the opposite end of the lake, the **Johnson Lake East Recreation Site** provides six campsites and a boat launch. The access is good enough to allow small RV's and trailers.

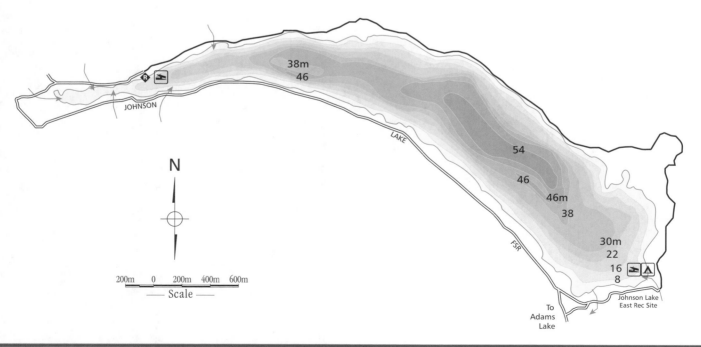

Jones (Wahleach) Lake

Location: 21 km (69 ft) southwest of Hope
Elevation: 640 m (2,099 ft)
Surface Area: 460 ha (1,137 ac)
Maximum Depth: 29 m (95 ft)
Mean Depth: 13.4 m (44 ft)
Way Point: 49° 13' 44" N, 121° 36' 43" W

Fishing

Jones Lake, also known as Wahleach Lake, is a BC Hydro Impoundment found in the Cascade Mountains at the east end of the Fraser Valley. Set behind Mount Cheam, it is a beautiful lake and surprisingly remote for being on the fringes of the most heavily populated area in the province.

The lake provides excellent sportfishing for coastal cutthroat trout, rainbow trout and kokanee. By far, the most popular fishery on the lake is for the cutthroat trout, which can attain sizes in excess of 60 cm (24 in) and 2.5 kg (5.5 lbs). Several years ago, the Ministry of Environment started a project to restore the recreational fishery. It consisted of a BC Hydro funded fertilization project to produce plankton to support kokanee stocked in the lake by the Freshwater Fisheries Society of BC. The society also stocks 3,000 sterile coastal cutthroat trout to control the stickleback population, which competes with kokanee for plankton. These fish feed prolifically on stickleback, allowing them to grow much larger than normal. The rainbow trout and kokanee average between 20–25 cm (8–10 in) and provide plenty of action.

There is no seasonal angling closure on Jones; but, because of its high elevation, it is usually not accessible between December and March due to deep snow. The best angling is from mid-May to mid-July and then again from September to the end of October.

Bobber or float fishing from shore with worms, casting or trolling small minnow imitations such as Krocodiles or fly-fishing with Muddler Minnows, leeches, or Woolly Buggers are all productive ways to fool the cutthroat. Rainbow trout are best taken on small black, green, brown or chrome chironomids during the months of May and June. The kokanee are most easily caught while trolling a Wedding Band and a worm.

Prior to this reservoir being formed, it was logged and then flooded; therefore the bottom is covered with woody debris and cut-off tree stumps. This provides excellent cover for the fish and their prey, but also creates a lot of hook ups (bring extra gear). The best angling for trout is within 50 m (164 ft) of the shoreline whereas the best bet for kokanee is at the mid-water zone farther out in the lake.

Check the regulations for gear restrictions.

Directions

To get to Jones Lake, take the Laidlaw/Jones Lake exit off of the Trans Canada Highway (Highway 1) about 15 km (9.3 mi) east of Bridal Falls near Chilliwack. Follow the exit for 0.5 km (0.3 mi) over Jones Creek, turn right onto Jones Lake Forest Service Road and follow this steep and rough road for about 11 km (7 mi) to the lake. A truck is recommended due to the rough nature of the road.

Facilities

The **Jones Lake Recreation Site** consists of two BC Hydro campgrounds sites on the north shore of the lake. There are a total of 50 sites, including designated wheelchair accessible sites, pit toilets, picnic tables and a boat launch. Several rustic campsites can also be found around the lake.

Boaters should note that the water levels can fluctuate dramatically over the course of the season. In addition to underwater hazards, launching of boats over 4 m (13 ft) can be an adventure.

Jones (Wahleach) Lake Fish Stocking Data			
Year	Species	Number	Life Stage
2009	Cutthroat Trout	1,007	Yearling
2007	Cutthroat Trout	2,002	Yearling
2006	Cutthroat Trout	3,000	Yearling

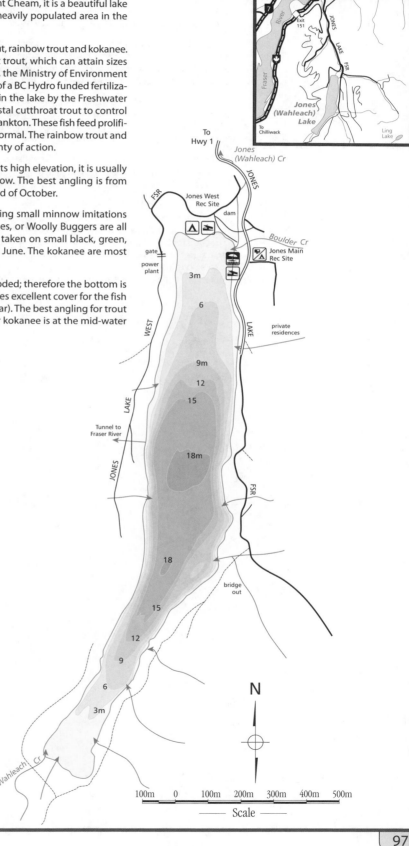

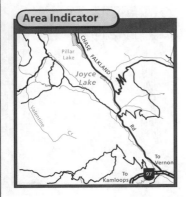

Location: 10 km (6.2 mi) north of Falkland
Elevation: 826 m (2,710 ft)
Surface Area: 6.4 ha (15.8 ac)
Max Depth: 7.5 m (24.6 ft)
Mean Depth: 2.3 m (7.5 ft)
Way Point: 50° 34' 7.9" N, 119° 36' 50.9" W

www.backroadmapbooks.com

Joyce Lake

Area Indicator

Fishing

Also known as Green Lake, Joyce is a tiny lake located near the popular Pillar Lake north of Falkland. The lake, little more than a pothole alongside the Chase Falkland Road is often passed over by anglers heading for Pillar, but those people are missing out on some surprisingly good fishing.

The lake is stocked with roughly 4,500 rainbow trout each year. Most of the fish stocked are Pennask Lake rainbow, which are well known for their insect diet, strong runs and acrobatic leaps. Every year, 500 of the stocked fish are triploid trout, rainbow that grow bigger than usual because they do not reproduce. These triploids have been stocked in the lake since 2002 and offer a pleasant surprise when caught.

Joyce Lake is an easy lake to fish from shore. However, it is not a great trolling lake because, with a maximum depth of 14 feet, it is too shallow. The bottom of the lake is also marred by old stumps. Those who want to troll should to stick to lures like small, unweighted Flatfish and shallow runners that will not hook up the stumps or the lake bottom. Better yet, cast spinners and small lures with lightweight spinning gear from the boat.

Fly-fishing or the good old worm-and-bobber fishing is popular at this lake. Chironomids are hard to beat, especially in the early spring. If you're on a boat, look for signs of moving fish and anchor close by. Try #12 or #14 black and reds or chromies beneath a strike indicator, with the fly hanging 30–45 cm (12–18 in) above the bottom.

The lake offers good ice fishing, especially in early December, once the ice is thick enough. Rainbow tend to become unenergetic later on in the winter, as the oxygen levels in the lake decrease, but early in the season they are still feisty. A simple spool of line and bait hooks sized 6–10, baited with deli shrimp, worms, Powerbait, or even cheese is all that is needed for ice fishing. Oh and a hole or ten. The vibrations from drilling a hole in the ice can scare the fish. Try drilling a series of holes over water anywhere from 1–3 m (3–9 feet), then going back to the first hole. Drop your baited hook so it is just off the bottom (a weight to get it down and a float to keep at the right depth will help). Some ice anglers like to lie on the ice and watch. If you haven't had any bites within about 15 minutes, move on to the next hole.

Directions

Found off Highway 97 about halfway between Kamloops and Vernon, the turnoff for this lake is at Falkland. Follow the Chase-Falkland Road north for about 10 km to the lake.

Facilities

The **Joyce Lake Recreation Site** is a small open site with space for four groups and a decent cartop boat launch. The good road access makes this a popular site.

Other Options

Pillar Lake, located just north of Joyce Lake, is the most popular rainbow lake in the Falkland area. Pillar Lake offers steep drop offs and deep holes ideal for trolling. For fly-fishers, chironomids produce in the early season with damselfly and dragonfly imitations performing best toward the summer months. Most fly anglers target the shoals at the north end of the lake.

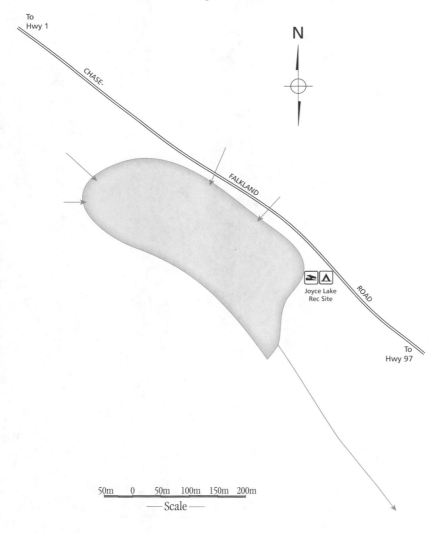

Joyce Lake			
Fish Stocking Data			
Year	Species	Number	Life Stage
2011	Rainbow Trout	4,000	Yearling
2011	Rainbow Trout	500	Catchable
2010	Rainbow Trout	4,500	Catchable
2009	Rainbow Trout	4,500	Catchable

www.backroadmapbooks.com

Kamloops Lake

Location: West of Kamloops
Elevation: 343 m (1,125 ft)
Surface Area: 5,585 ha (13,800 ac)
Max Depth: 150 m (495 ft)
Mean Depth: 74.1 m (243 ft)
Way Point: 50°44′00″N, 120°39′00″W

Fishing

Kamloops Lake is a huge, valley bottom lake that stretches from the city of Kamloops in the east to the community of Savona at its east. The lake is 1.6 km (1 mile) wide, 29 km (18 miles) long, and up to 152 m (521 feet) deep. The north and west shores of the lake are mostly steep sided, with only a few level areas near creek deltas and around the inlet and outlet of the Thompson River, which flows through the lake. Lake levels rise naturally as much as 10 metres (30 feet) from high season in June to low season.

Because the Thompson River drains the warm Shuswap Lakes, Kamloops Lake is also quite warm in summer. The lake is seldom iced over so it is possible to fish year round.

Despite the close proximity to Kamloops, the lake receives little fishing pressure. That is because the fishing is tough unless you know where to go. With some luck, it is possible to catch rainbow to 1 kg (2 lbs), Dolly Varden to 2 kg (4 lbs) and some small kokanee. The lake is usually fished from early spring to late fall. Trolling is the mainstay of the fishery although fly-fishing and spincasting at the river estuaries and at the outflow can be effective.

If you are fishing the kokanee, try a Willow Leaf and worm trolled near the surface (3–9 m/10-30 ft deep) on a very slow troll. Trolling in an "S" manner slows the lure even further while enticing the fish to bite because of the speed fluctuation of the lure.

Rainbow also take lake trolls as wells as a variety of plugs and lures such as the Kamlooper, Rapala, Flatfish or Apex. Dollies can be fished effectively at the river estuaries using a bait ball. Trolling with a Flatfish or a Krocodile lure between 10 and 30 m (30–90 feet) is also effective.

Fly-fishing is not common on big lakes like Kamloops, but some people have been known to try trolling a leech, Muddler Minnow or bucktail. Focus around the mouths of creeks.

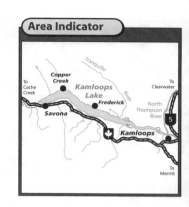

Area Indicator

Directions

The Trans Canada Highway (Highway 1) runs along the south shore of the lake providing access to the southwest shore of the lake. The northern shores of the lake are less accessible with few direct access points. There are boat launches at Savona and Kamloops.

Facilities

Full facilities are provided along Highway 1. There are three provincial parks that preserve portions of the shoreline but only the **Steelhead Provincial Park** provides facilities of interest for anglers. It is found at the southwestern end of the lake near Savona and offers camping and picnicking facilities as well as a wharf and boat launch. **Painted Bluffs Provincial Park**, on the northern shores of the lake near Cooper Creek, is an interesting stop to view the series of Indian Pictographs but does not have any facilities.

Day trippers will find another launching site and picnic area on the south shore near Savona. The city of Kamloops to the east provides all the amenities you could imagine including river access to the lake.

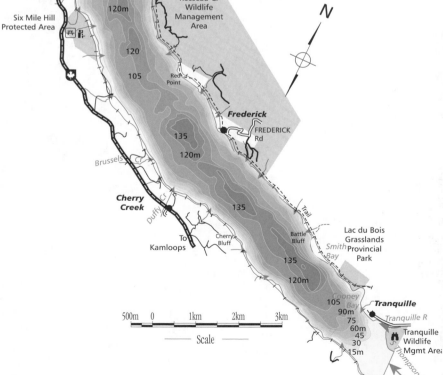

Location: 15 km (9 mi) south of Merritt
Elevation: 1,111 m (3,645 ft)
Surface Area: 8 ha (20 ac)
Max Depth: 9.5 m (31.2 ft)
Mean Depth: 5.2 m (17.1 ft)
Way Point: 49° 58' 41.6" N, 120° 41' 39.8" W

www.backroadmapbooks.com

Kane Lakes

Lower Kane Lake

Area Indicator

Kane #1 Lake			
Fish Stocking Data			
Year	Species	Number	Life Stage
2010	Rainbow Trout	2,000	Yearling
2009	Rainbow Trout	2,000	Yearling

Kane #2 Lake			
Fish Stocking Data			
Year	Species	Number	Life Stage
2010	Rainbow Trout	2,000	Yearling
2009	Rainbow Trout	2,000	Yearling

Fishing

There are a bunch of lakes in the Kane Valley, most of them offering great fishing. Most of the lakes in the area have names like "Upper" and "Lower" and "Upper Second" but you will also find one called "Chicken Ranch" here, too, just to mix it up.

All the lakes in the Kane Lakes, from Lower Kane to Chicken Ranch, have rainbow and brook trout. Chicken Ranch and the Upper Kane Lakes are both stocked with rainbow, while Lower Kane is stocked with Blackwater triploids, which feed on the illegally stocked red-sided shiners. The tiny shiners form vast schools that can eat the lake clean if not controlled; Blackwater trout love eating the shiner, and a balance is struck. As a happy coincidence, a healthy diet of red shiners causes the trout to plump up. While it doesn't happen every day, catches to 4 kg (8 lbs) are not unheard of.

Lower Kane and Upper Kane are closed until May 1. As a general rule, you should be able to fish here for a week or two before spring turnover. While rainbow are usually targeted during this time, it is the lake's population of brook trout that are most active. Brookies are much bolder and probably much hungrier during these first few weeks than they are at other times of the year. The combination of the top layer of water still being cool with life starting to return to the edges of the lake added to the fact that the fish have just spent the last six months under a protective sheet of ice all add up to good fishing.

Even in early spring, the lakes have a prodigious amount of shrimp, and casting a scud pattern is a good bet for success. While the fish are bolder than normal, you will improve your chances by not moving around too much when fishing. Fish interpret movement (quite rightly) as a possible predator and will head for the safety of the deep water if spooked.

After the water has turned over and begun to warm up, there are a number of hatches, starting with a variety of chironomids and moving on to dragonflies and damselflies. In the morning and early evening, the fish will rise to dry flies, especially during the hatches. At other times, fishing a nymph pattern can be magic.

Too often, though, people find the lakes have a stubborn reluctance to give up their fish.

Because the lakes are so food-rich, finding fish can sometimes be a challenge. With hundreds of thousands of rising chironomid, for instance, how do you make yours stand out? Sometimes fishing different is your best approach, although people have thrown their tackle box at the lake and only had marginal success.

The lakes are at a reasonably high elevation and as a result the fishing tends to stay fairly strong through the summer.

Directions

The Kane Valley Lakes are found off the Coquihalla Connector about 17 km southeast of Merritt. Follow the Kane Valley Road, which is a good gravel road, as it cuts through open ranchland. The first of the lakes–Chicken Ranch– is found on your left after about 3 km, while Lower Kane is about 9 km down the road.

Facilities

The **Kane Lake Recreation Site** is a very popular site found at the south end of the Lower Kane Lake. The enhanced site has room for eight units along with a boat launch and old wharf. There is a fee to camp here from early May until mid-October. The other lakes in the series all have cartop boat launch access points where people have been known to set up camp. While in the valley, be sure to explore the impressive **Kane Valley Cross-Country Ski Trails**.

Upper Kane Lake

Elevation: 1,111 m (3,645 ft)
Surface Area: 9 ha (22 ac)
Max Depth: 10.7 m (35.1 ft)
Mean Depth: 5.5 m (18 ft)
Way Point: 49° 58' 47" N, 120° 41' 18" W

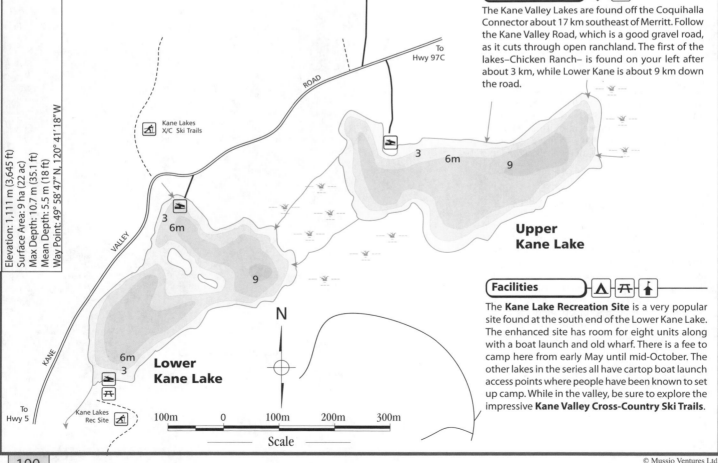

Kawkawa Lake

Location: 2 km (1 mi) northeast of Hope
Elevation: 60 m (196 ft)
Surface Area: 77 ha (190 ft)
Max Depth: 14 m (46 ft)
Mean Depth: 11 m (36 ft)
Way Point: 49° 23' 14" N, 121° 24' 4" W

Fishing

Kawkawa Lake is home to one of the best kokanee fisheries in the area. The lake also holds coastal cutthroat, Coho and even smallmouth bass. Wildlife enthusiasts will find freshwater crayfish, painted turtles, numerous bird species including loons, Canada geese, mallards, redtail hawks and bald eagles, as well as black bears and deer. About one half of this lake's shoreline is residential with the remainder steeply forested hillsides and rock slides.

Kokanee are the most plentiful and sought after fish in Kawkawa. These silver bullets ranging from 25–40 cm (10–16 in) are great fighters. Not to be outdone, there are decent numbers of cutthroat that can get up to 50 cm (20 in). There are five small, spring-fed tributaries that feed into the east shoreline which provide the natural spawning needed to sustain all of these fisheries.

The fishing is usually excellent right from the March 1st opening. The kokanee and Coho start off small, but will quickly attain sizes up to 35–40 cm (14–16 in) by June. When fishing in the early season, try using small flies, black, brown, or green chironomids on a floating line or trolling black Doc Spratley flies. Another productive early season method is to troll Wedding Bands with a worm or a Dick Nite trailer. Finally, don't pass on the opportunity to fish just off the bottom by jigging or by using a bobber with krill, worms or salmon eggs as bait. This method is by far the most productive from May to mid-August with the best place to fish usually in Rock Slide Bay located along the north shoreline. Trolling deep with lead lines and Wedding Bands or Dick Nite spoons can also be very effective.

The uniqueness of the kokanee fishery is that it lasts right into mid-summer with some of the best angling from June to August–a perfect time to take the whole family fishing. Both bait fishing and deep trolling are more productive as the lake water temperature climbs.

There has also been a recent report of a 3 kg (6.5 lb) smallmouth bass being pulled out of the lake. These fish are active year round and a good alternative when the other species are not biting.

The angling season runs from March 1 to November 30. There is a seasonal closure on Kawkawa Lake from December 1 to February 28.

Directions

Found just east of Hope this is a popular retreat for locals in the summer. The lake is easily located by following the park signs. From the Hope exit (Exit 170) on the Trans Canada Highway (Highway 1), turn right at the old Hope Princeton Highway and then left at 6th Street (at the Chevron Station). Approximately 1.2 km along 6th Street turn right on the Kawkawa Lake Road and follow the signs to the park.

Alternatively, follow the park signs from the Coquihalla Highway (Highway 5) further east. Watch for the Kawkawa Lake/Peers Creek exit and head south, back towards the town of Hope for about 2.5 km (1.5 mi).

Area Indicator

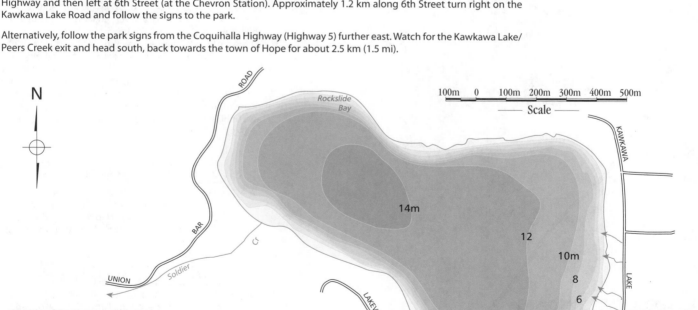

Facilities

Kawkawa Lake Park is a former provincial park offering picnicking facilities, a concrete boat launch, small dock and a sandy beach in the bay area on the south shoreline. For campers, the private campground to the east offers full services including boat launch facilities. Hotels, restaurants and a good tackle shop are available in downtown Hope.

Location: 7 km (4 mi) south of Clinton
Elevation: 902 m (2,959 ft)
Surface Area: 23.1 ha (57 ac)
Maximum Depth: 9 m (29 ft)
Mean Depth: 4.8 m (15 ft)
Way Point: 51° 2′ 4.9″ N, 121° 32′ 55.4″ W

www.backroadmapbooks.com

Kersey (6 Mile) Lake

Area Indicator

Fishing

South of Clinton, alongside Highway 97 is a series of pothole lakes known collectively as the Alkali Lakes.

One of these lakes–sometimes known as Kersey or Six Mile Lake–is unique because it is one of the few lakes in the region that is stocked with eastern brook trout. The lake is also stocked with rainbow trout.

Kersey or Alkali or Six Mile Lake is a fairly shallow, pothole lake. The lake warms in the summer months severely affecting fishing success. But that's okay, because the lake is best known for its winter, not summer fishing.

The lake is a mid elevation lake, and ice-off here is in late April. After the lake turns over, the trout begin to bite on small lures, like a Deadly Dick or Wedding Band or green Flatfish, usually tipped with a worm. If you have a float tube or small craft, you can cast from the deep waters into the shallow and retrieve across the drop-off. Fishing a traditional bobber and worm can also work well.

Those who want to troll should to stick to lures like small, unweighted Flatfish or Kwikfish and shallow runners that will not hook up the stumps or lake bottom.

Fly anglers will find some small hatches, but will have the most luck fishing attractor patterns like Doc Spratleys.

In the fall the fishing picks up again. Fishing an attractor type pattern like a red, black or yellow Doc Spratley or Woolly Bugger can yield unbelievable results. Colourful micro-leech patterns are also popular, as the brook trout really seem to like leeches. Spincasting at this time can be productive, too.

However, it is in the winter that this lake is most popular. Eastern brook trout are a much hardier species than rainbow. When the water gets cold and the oxygen levels start to drop, rainbow trout start to become lethargic. While they can still put up a good fight early in the season, later in winter, they become sluggish and no fun to catch. Brook trout, on the other hand, remain sprightly throughout the ice on season, offering some challenging hard water fishing.

Because the water is cool throughout the lake, and because they don't have to worry about predation from above due to the layer of ice on the lake, the fish move to the shallows where the food is. They can sometimes be found in as little as 1 metre (3 feet) of water, but generally are found between 2 and 4 metres (6–12 feet) beneath the ice. The noise from the ice auger can scare the fish away for a while, so it is usually best to drill a series of holes at a variety of depths first and then go back and start fishing. Most people use a simple bait and bobber setup, usually with a little sinker on the end to help get the hook down faster.

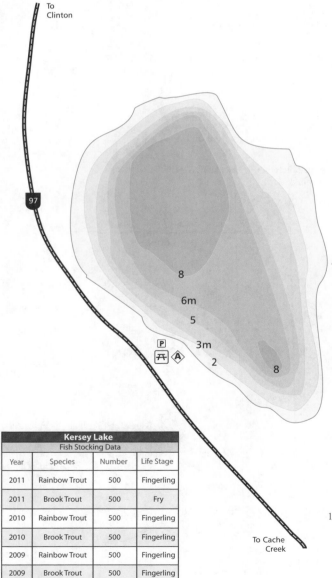

Directions

Kersey Lake is a pothole lake located in the heart of cattle country. To reach the lake, drive north of Cache Creek on the Cariboo Highway (Highway 97). The lake is right next to the highway south of Clinton.

Facilities

Although a park is proposed here, nothing has been formalized. There is a small roadside pull out and a place to launch a canoe or float tube.

100m   0   100m   200m   300m
— Scale —

| Kersey Lake | | | |
| Fish Stocking Data | | | |
Year	Species	Number	Life Stage
2011	Rainbow Trout	500	Fingerling
2011	Brook Trout	500	Fry
2010	Rainbow Trout	500	Fingerling
2010	Brook Trout	500	Fingerling
2009	Rainbow Trout	500	Fingerling
2009	Brook Trout	500	Fingerling

Klein Lake

Location: 4.5 km (2.8 mi) southeast of Earls Cove
Elevation: 142 m (466 ft)
Surface Area: 14 ha (35 ac)
Max Depth: 42 m (138 ft)
Mean Depth: 12 m (39 ft)
Way Point: 49° 43′ 47″ N, 123° 58′ 8″ W

Fishing

Klein Lake is a beautiful lake and an excellent place for swimming and canoeing as well as fishing. It is found at the north end of the Sechelt Peninsula near Earl's Cove and holds stocked cutthroat trout.

Klein is sometimes called Killarney Lake and less frequently Egmont Lake. For such a small lake, the lake is surprisingly deep, with a hole in the middle of the lake reaching 42 m (137 ft) deep. The depth keeps the water from getting too warm during the summer, although in July and August you will have better success in the cool of the evening than the heat of the day as the noise of swimmers and boaters tends to spook the fish. The best fishing happens in April to early July and then again in September.

Fishing from shore is difficult at the lake, so it is best to bring a boat or a float tube. In fact, the lake is a perfect lake for belly boating, sheltered, but not too small, with lots of coves and points that offer places for the fish to hide. Although small boats are allowed on the lake, there is no boat launch and the lake is electric motor only.

While there are cutthroats pulled out of here to 2 kg (4 lbs), you will more likely catch find them to about 1 kg (2 lbs). Trolling a Woolly Bugger can produce well here, as do purple leeches, but when the fish are rising, dry fly-fishing is the way to go.

For folks without a boat or float tube, there are two wheelchair accessible fishing piers that get you out farther onto the lake and give you casting space.

Area Indicator

Directions

Klein Lake is at the northern end of the Sechelt Peninsula on the Sunshine Coast, southeast of Earl's Cove. To get to the lake, turn east off the Sunshine Coast Highway (Highway 101) just before Earl's Cove and follow the Egmont Road to the west end of North Lake, to the North Lake Forest Service Road. Turn right (south) onto the road, then right again onto the Klein Lake Road at the south end of North Lake. Klein Lake will be on your right.

Facilities

The **Klein Lake Recreation Site** sits on the shores of beautiful Klein Lake. It is an improved site and one of two recreation sites on the Sunshine Coast that is managed with fees. There are 23 camping units here, tucked away in the trees and well spread out, so campers have a degree of privacy. There is a day-use picnic area and toilets. For anglers there are two fishing piers on the lake.

Other Options

Keeping straight on Egmont Road past **North Lake** will bring you to **Waugh Lake**, a bigger lake that holds stocked cutthroat trout. North Lake also holds a few cutthroat trout, but is not noted for its fishing.

On the other side of Highway 101 lay the much larger **Ruby** and **Sakinaw Lakes**. These lakes hold cutthroat trout and kokanee. Ruby Lake is one of the warmest lakes in BC in the summer, which is great for swimming, but not so much for fishing. However, in spring and fall the fishing is pretty good. Sakinaw Lake is the largest lake on the Sechelt Peninsula and is known as the best kokanee lake on the Sunshine Coast.

Klein Lake			
Fish Stocking Data			
Year	Species	Number	Life Stage
2005	Cutthroat Trout	500	Fall Catchable

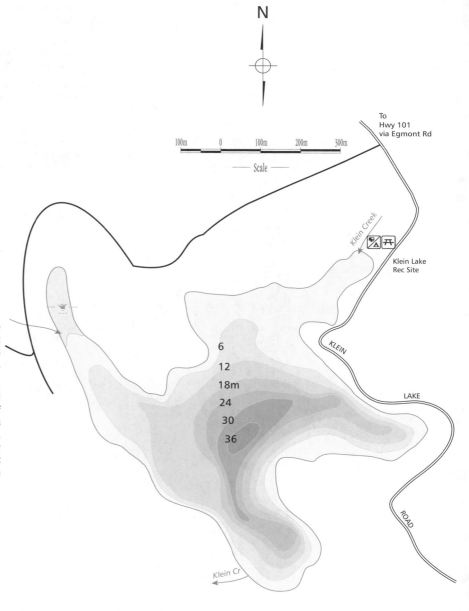

N

100m 0 100m 200m 300m
Scale

To Hwy 101 via Egmont Rd

Klein Creek

Klein Lake Rec Site

6
12
18m
24
30
36

KLEIN   LAKE   ROAD

Klein Cr

Location: 23 km (14 mi) south of Barrière
Elevation: 1,149 m (3,770 ft)
Surface Area: 103 ha (255 ac)
Max Depth: 24.1 m (79.01 ft)
Mean Depth: 9.5 m (31.2 ft)
Way Point: 50° 57′ 59″ N, 120° 7′ 4″ W

www.backroadmapbooks.com

Knouff (Sullivan) Lake

Area Indicator

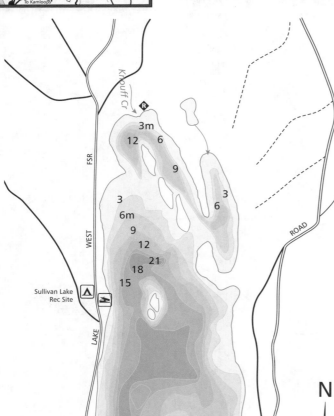

Fishing

While this lake is best known as Knouff Lake, it was officially renamed Sullivan Lake after the family that owned property on the lake for many year.

Knouff Lake is connected to nearby Little Knouff Lake by way of a creek. Rainbow trout spawn in this channel and so the trout population here is now self-sustaining, although it was stocked until 2003 with rainbow trout.

Knouff is a clear water lake with a gravel bottom and extensive areas of shoal. There are four islands in the lake, all with ample shoals and weedbeds. Just south of the islands in the eastern half of the lake are several sunken islands covered with weeds.

Knouff Lake offers good fishing for rainbow trout from May to October by trolling or fly-fishing. The lake is an excellent fly-fishing lake, with rainbow averaging 1–3 kg (2–6 lb), with 4–7 kg (8 to 16 lb) fish not uncommon. In fact, the North American record of 7.8 kg (17.25 lbs) for a rainbow trout caught on a dry fly was caught at Knouff Lake.

For fly-fishermen, try casting a fly near one of the many shoals or sunken islands that are easily spotted through the clear water. Also, match one of the sedge, mayfly damselfly or chironomid hatches. The flies of choice at the lake are the Knouff Lake Special, leech patterns, damselfly patterns, shrimp patterns, mayfly nymph, dragonfly patterns, sedge patterns and the Doc Spratley. In particular, the late evening sedge hatch can be a dynamite time to fish.

In the fall, a black or purple leech pattern can be killer. Damsel and dragonfly nymphs are also popular patterns, as the fish are bulking up for the ice on season.

Trollers use a Willow Leaf or Ford Fender with a worm. Trolling a froggy, silver & black or gold Flatfish is also effective.

North of Big Knouff Lake is Little Knouff Lake. This lake is very shallow, having a maximum depth of around 5 meters (15 feet). Under normal water levels Little Knouff is barren due to winterkill. In years with high spring runoff, trout from Knouff Lake enter Little Knouff via the spawning channel. Anglers might want to try fishing here these years.

Directions

To find the lake, head north on Highway 5 from Kamloops. Take the Sun Peaks Road exit heading east to the Knouff Lake Road heading north. This good logging road leads to the south end of Knouff Lake. RV's and large trailers can access the lake from this access route.

An alternative, steeper route is to drive north on Highway 5 past the Sun Peaks Road and take a right on the Vinsulla-Knouff Lake Road. Stay on the main road for 12 km and you will reach Knouff Lake.

Facilities

The **Sullivan Lake West Recreation Site** is actually made up of two sites on Knouff Lake. The bigger site offers 3 campsites, while the other single site is just past the boat launch on the west side of the road away from the lake. There is also a day use parking area at the boat launch. The busy site charges a fee to camp here on weekends…or at least used to.

The **Knouff Lake Resort** offers several rustic cabins, as well as serviced camping sites for RVs and more quaint tenting pads. A convenience store and boat rentals are also at the resort, which is open year round.

100m 0 100m 200m 300m
—Scale—

© Mussio Ventures Ltd.

Lac Le Jeune

Location: 21 km (13 mi) south of Kamloops
Elevation: 1,276 m (4,186 ft)
Surface Area: 198 ha (489 ac)
Max Depth: 27.7 m (90.9 ft)
Way Point: 50° 28' 50" N, 120° 28' 11" W

Fishing

Found on a plateau covered with lodgepole pine, Lac Le Jeune is a classic Kamloops area lake. The lake is a great place for anglers to spend a few hours or a few days enjoying nature. Moose, deer and bears are regular visitors to the shoreline, while loons and otters chase the fish within.

Lac Le Jeune is one of the first lakes used by fly-fishing's bold and brash pioneers. Early 20th Century Interior fly-fishers were captivated by the potential of the lake's crystal clear water, expansive marl shoals and delicate weed beds. It was originally called Fish Lake until it was re-named Lac Le Jeune in 1928.

Today, the lake is stocked annually with 15,000 Pennask rainbow trout yearlings. The world-class Kamloops trout are known for their strength and acrobatic ability. They jump high and run hard when hooked. Lac Le Jeune trout average 0.5–1 kg (1–2 lbs) but fish up to 2.5 kg (5 lbs) are hooked each season.

Lac Le Jeune is a classic fly-fishing lake. Abundant hatches of mayflies, caddis flies and sedges allow anglers to fish for trout on the surface with dry flies. Few activities are as exciting as watching trout rise to a sedge imitation skittering along the surface. The water is gin clear during most of the year, giving anglers the visibility to cast to fish as they see them. Of course, this means that the fish can see, too, so expect the trout to be skittish when the water is still. This makes fishing here more challenging, but fly-fishers love a good challenge.

Much of the dry fly action takes place from mid-June to early July. Timing is everything as hatches can be short-lived and often happen without warning. The marl shoals at the lake's west end and the drop offs that run perpendicular to the north shore are popular. While its reputation as a challenging, premier fly-fishing lake is well deserved–it was a practice lake during the 1993 World Fly-Fishing Championships held in Kamloops–Lac Le Jeune has a family friendly side as well. A 73 metre (240 foot) wheelchair accessible fishing wharf has been built at Lac Le Jeune Provincial Park, giving people who do not have a boat the opportunity to fish. A classic worm and bobber setup or assortment of small spinners should do the trick. The water off the wharf is not deep, so heavy gear will inevitably snag in the weeds. However, lightweight lures cast from ultra light rods and reels will work.

Note there is a 20 km per hour speed restriction on the lake.

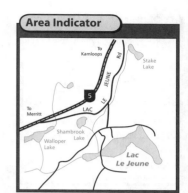

Area Indicator

Lac le Jeune Fish Stocking Data			
Year	Species	Number	Life Stage
2011	Rainbow Trout	15,000	Yearling
2010	Rainbow Trout	15,000	Yearling
2008	Rainbow Trout	15,000	Yearling

Directions

The lake, which is only 25 minutes south of Kamloops, is easily accessed via the Coquihalla Highway and Lac Le Jeune Road. These roads are paved and unaffected by weather. From Kamloops, take exit 223 and drive 26 km to the turnoff for the provincial park and Lac Le Jeune Lodge.

From Merritt, take exit 336 to the park entrance.

Facilities

The **Lac Le Jeune Provincial Park** rests on the north side of the lake and offers a full-service, 144 unit campsite, a paved boat launch, fishing wharf and day-use area with beach. The park is open to camping from mid-May to the end of September and reservations through www.discovercamping.com are recommended. A popular resort with boat rentals, a conference centre and a convenience store is also found the lake.

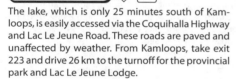

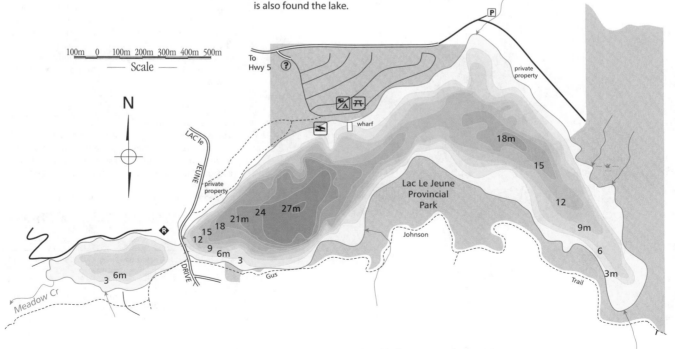

© Mussio Ventures Ltd.

Location: Coquitlam
Elevation: 35 m (115 ft)
Surface Area: 5 ha (12 ac)
Max Depth: 8 m (26 ft)
Mean Depth: 4 m (13 ft)
Way Point: 49° 17' 12.1" N, 122° 47' 20.1" W

www.backroadmapbooks.com

Lafarge Lake

Area Indicator

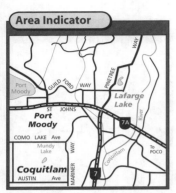

Fishing

Lafarge Lake is also known as the Coquitlam Pit. It used to be a large gravel pit operated by Lafarge Canada but has now been damned to make an urban fishing hole. The lake is located in the heart of Coquitlam in Town Centre Park and provides convenient access and fast fishing, making it a perfect lake for people just learning to fish.

The best fishing months are March to June and September to December. During spring and fall, Lafarge Lake is aggressively stocked (usually ten times a year) with between a hundred and a thousand catchable rainbow from the Fraser Valley Trout Hatchery.

Fishing can either be done from shore or in a float tube. Lafarge Lake is circled by a trail with virtually no surrounding vegetation or trees so shore access is easy. The bottom drops off quickly along the northern shore and fishing can be excellent at times.

As in other catch and keep lakes in the Lower Mainland, the stocked rainbow trout are easily caught on artificial or natural bait, especially just after they are stocked. The fish are usually fished out within a season and finding anything bigger than a pan-sized trout is nearly unheard of.

Because the fish are so indiscriminate, fishing gear can be as simple or as complex as you want it to be. A simple worm on a hook, dangled below a bobber, or possibly with a sliding weight to anchor the bait to the bottom usually works just as effectively as fly-fishing and trying to match the current hatch. Dew worm, deli shrimp or single eggs are commonly used bait.

Casting and slowly retrieving a small spoon can work well, too. Give your lure time to sink down to near the lake bottom before retrieving. Pausing for a moment or two while retrieving can help entice the fish to bite.

Common carp also inhabit in Lafarge Lake. The most common method of fishing for carp is to chum the water with sweet corn in water between 2 and 5 metres (5–15 ft), stringing some corn on a size 4–8 hook and then hiding it with the rest of the corn. Carp are light feeders so keep your eyes on your rod tip and don't get discouraged if you don't get a hit for a while; carp fishing, more than most, is a waiting game. Carp have soft mouths, so if you get a bite, don't pull too hard, but get ready for them to run for the hills when you snag them; best to loosen your drag slightly.

Directions

Lafarge Lake is located at Town Centre Park in Coquitlam, between Pinetree Way and Pipeline Road. The best access is via Pinetree Way, which heads north from the intersection of the Barnett Highway and Lougheed Highway in Coquitlam. The lake is about 1.4 km (0.9 miles) from the intersection. Several parking lots are available around the lake. The entire shoreline can be accessed by a walking trail.

Facilities

Town Centre Park offers washrooms, a walking trail and a nearby playground in the park. In the spring of 2008, a new fishing pier was built. There are no camping facilities nearby, but there are plenty of hotels, restaurants, gas stations and other amenities you would expect to find near an urban lake.

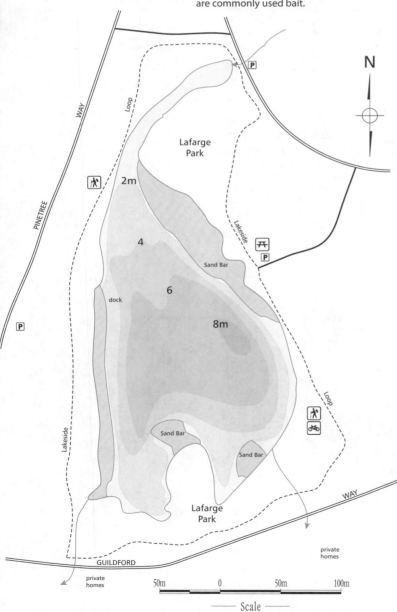

Lafarge Lake			
Fish Stocking Data			
Year	Species	Number	Life Stage
2011	Rainbow Trout	7,179	Catchable
2010	Rainbow Trout	12,138	Catchable
2009	Rainbow Trout	13,417	Catchable

© Mussio Ventures Ltd.

Lake Errock (Squakum Lake)

Location: 31 km (19 mi) east of Mission
Elevation: 20 m (66 ft)
Surface Area: 26 ha (64 ft)
Max Depth: 8 m (26 ft)
Mean Depth: 4 m (13 ft)
Way Point: 49° 13' 41" N, 122° 0' 37" W

Fishing

Lake Errock is a small, 26-hectare lake next to the Lougheed Highway west of Harrison Mills and is more of a recreation lake than a fishing lake. While it is not a private lake, much of the lakeshore is privately owned and access is difficult.

The lake has small cutthroat and rainbow best caught in the early spring or late fall. This is because the lake is small, relatively shallow (maximum 8 m/26 ft) and at only 30 m (98 ft) in elevation. Therefore, the water warms in the summer months making fishing very slow at that time of year.

Because of the warm water, there are more coarse fish than trout in the lake. The coarse fish include catfish and bullheads.

Private residences and extensive shallows surrounding the southern and western shoreline restrict shore fishing. The best drop-offs are off the eastern shoreline but access is difficult due to the steep shoreline and more private residences.

Having a boat or a tube is a real advantage. Focus along the eastern shoreline where the water drops off rapidly to 8 m (26 ft).

Area Indicator

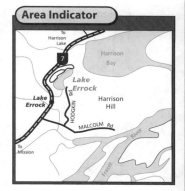

Directions

Lake Errock is the small, 26 hectare lake next the Lougheed Highway west of Harrison Mills. To reach the north end of the lake, take the Harrison Bay Road off the Lougheed Highway. After crossing the railroad tracks about 400 m from the Lougheed Highway hang a right on Squakam Road. That road leads along the western shores of Lake Errock providing three access points to the lake.

To reach the south end of the lake, take the Malcolm Road exit off the Lougheed Highway south of the little community of Lake Errock. About 900 m from the Lougheed Highway, take a left on Hodgkins Road and that road leads to the south end of the lake.

In both directions, a car can access the lake.

Please note that private property restricts access to the shoreline and there is limited parking in the area. Please do not trespass on private property.

Facilities

There are no camping facilities at Lake Errock. On the west side, there are two locations where you can launch a small boat or canoe. There is no real day-use area along the shoreline as most of the shoreline is private property.

Albert Jess Park, at the south end of the lake, is a grassy area with a beach and dock. It is a private park not available for use by the general public.

Other Options

To the northeast of Lake Errock are **Echo** and **Elbow Lakes**. Both lakes are accessed off the Chehalis Forest Service Road and offer good fishing for small rainbow and cutthroat. Elbow Lake is described in greater detail elsewhere in this book.

Lake Errock is separated from **Harrison Bay** by a small strip of land. This is a popular fishing area for people accessing the Fraser River, as well as the Harrison River and Harrison Lake. Try trolling the bay area with small crocs or small fry patterns. The Harrison River has good numbers of Cutthroat trout and whitefish through out the river, as well as salmon and steelhead that show up annually.

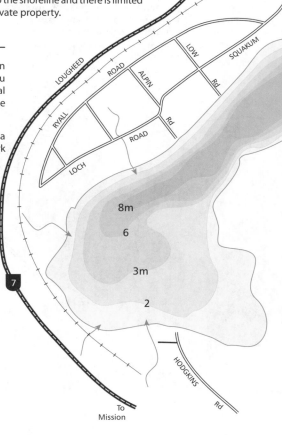

To Agassiz

To Mission

Lake Errock			
Fish Stocking Data			
Year	Species	Number	Life Stage
2008	Rainbow Trout	400	Spring Catchable
2007	Rainbow Trout	375	Fall Catchable
2007	Rainbow Trout	400	Spring Catchable

100m 0 100m 200m 300m 400m 500m

— Scale —

Location: 4 km (2.5 mi) north of Hope
Elevation: 162 m (531 ft)
Surface Area: 17 ha (42 ac)
Max Depth: 12 m (39 ft)
Mean Depth: 8 m (26 ft)
Way Point: 49° 24' 39.1" N, 121° 26' 49.2" W

www.backroadmapbooks.com

Lake of the Woods (Schkam)

Fishing

Schkam Lake is better known as Lake of the Woods and is conveniently located beside the Trans Canada Highway at the entrance to the scenic Fraser Canyon, just north of Hope. The lake is easily accessed and as a result sees heavy fishing pressure. It is a crater type lake framed with a heavily forested shoreline on the west side, a small private resort on the north end, a unique rock slide with car-size boulders on the south end and a rest area on the east side.

The Freshwater Fisheries Society of BC annually stocks 1,500 catchable-size rainbow trout in the lake and reports of fish over 1 kg (2 lbs) are not uncommon. During the summer months, if the fish are not cooperating, you can enjoy a refreshing swim in the pretty, but cool lake.

Schkam Lake can easily be fished from shore or from belly boats, pontoon boats, canoes, or small car toppers. Anglers are reminded that there is an electric motor only restriction on this waterbody.

The rainbow in this lake can be taken by several different methods depending on the time of year. During winter and early spring, angling on or near the bottom or bobber fishing near the surface with salmon eggs, Powerbait, krill or worms will produce plenty of action.

In late spring, try trolling or casting Wedding Bands with a worm trailer, small leech imitations, frog-style Flatfish, or small Willow Leaf trolls near the shoreline. During the summer months, fishing usually tails off except just before dark when a small Tom Thumb or mosquito fly on floating fly line can be very effective.

Directions

Lake of the Woods is easily accessible, located alongside the Trans Canada Highway (Highway 1) about 90 minutes from Vancouver. Follow the highway north through the town of Hope and you will see the lake on the left just as you enter the Fraser Canyon.

Lake of the Woods			
Fish Stocking Data			
Year	Species	Number	Life Stage
2008	Rainbow Trout	550	Spring Catchable
2007	Rainbow Trout	550	Spring Catchable
2006	Rainbow Trout	550	Catchable

Other Options

Across the Fraser near Hope is **Kawkawa Lake**, one of the best fishing spots for kokanee in the area. The lake also features good fishing for cutthroat and there are rumours of bass being found in the lake as well. Most people who fish the lake are looking for kokanee. Alternatively, Hope is also a popular place to access the **Fraser River**. Bar fishing or bottom bouncing from the large gravel bars found alongside the river below the Fraser Canyon can produce a fish of a lifetime. Most anglers in the Hope area are targeting Chinook, but all five species of salmon are available along with cutthroat and even resident rainbow.

Facilities

Public access is via the rest area/parking lot located between the lake and the highway. Small boats or canoes can be launched from this site, although it is somewhat steep. A small private resort is located on the north end of the lake. Other motel and campground accommodation can be found in Hope just five minutes south of the lake.

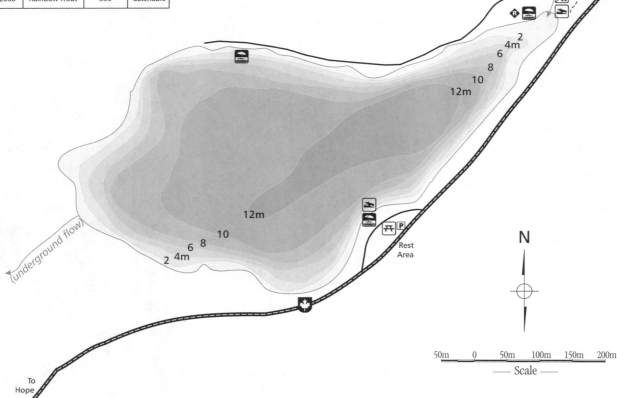

© Mussio Ventures Ltd.

Levette Lake

Location: 11 km (6.8 mi) north of Squamish
Elevation: 403 m (1,322 ft)
Surface Area: 15 ha (37 ac)
Max Depth: 30 m (98 ft)
Mean Depth: 10 m (33 ft)
Way Point: 49° 49′ 54.8″ N, 123° 11′ 18.5″

Fishing

Levette Lake is set beneath the rugged snow capped peaks of the Tantalus Range, making the scenery truly spectacular. A number of impressive looking private cabins line the lake, adding to the beauty.

There is a trail that circles the lake offering access for shore fishermen. However, the heavy vegetation restricts casting in most places, but there are a few open areas. Better yet, it is well advised to bring a float tube, canoe or small electric motor boat to the lake. No powerboats are allowed on the lake.

The fish can be greedy, striking anything you offer, especially in early spring. If they are being more discerning in their tastes, try trolling a leech pattern (not too slowly) on a type III sinking line near the bottom. Anglers have reported having lots of luck not near the edges, not where you would expect, but right in the middle of the lake, near the underwater point. Other places to try include around the islands towards the southwest end of the lake or off the rock bluffs on the north end of the lake.

Since the water at Levette Lake is fairly clear, you can see the drop-offs fairly easily. Make sure, if you are shore casting, that your bobber, fly or lure is getting beyond the drop-off. Working a chironomid pattern just off the shoals early in the season can be very effective. Early in the hatch, try a bloodworm closer to bottom for rainbow. During the warmer months it is better to work around the deeper hole near the north side of the lake.

The rainbow trout here are generally small with a 30 cm (12 in) fish being on the large size. There are also conflicting rumours that the fish are affected by a white worm infestation.

Directions

To reach the lake, head north of Squamish on the Sea to Sky Highway to the Squamish Valley Road turnoff. This paved road will bring you over a railroad track and then across the Cheakamus River Bridge. Turn right at the Paradise Valley Road junction and follow this road to the long straight stretch. Halfway along the straight stretch, a side road heads west and is marked "Evans Lake". The road is found across from the Outdoor Recreation School. Follow this road steeply uphill keeping right at all junctions. The first part of the road is partially paved (on the hills) but after passing Evans Lake Demonstration Road, the road becomes rough, steep and narrow. At 3.5 km, you will reach the public access area to Levette Lake.

A truck is highly recommended as the last section to the lake features a steep climb that might be too much for cars with poor traction.

Facilities

A day-use area is found at the public access to the lake. There is a rustic boat launch and an outhouse but not much else.

Other Options

En route to Levette, you will pass **Evans Lake**. Unfortunately, the rainbow are infested with white worms and are not worth catching. Beyond Levette, an old, gated road heads north to **Hut Lake**. The long trek deters most from venturing in. On last report, there were numerous small rainbow for the taking.

Area Indicator

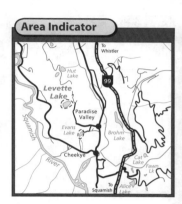

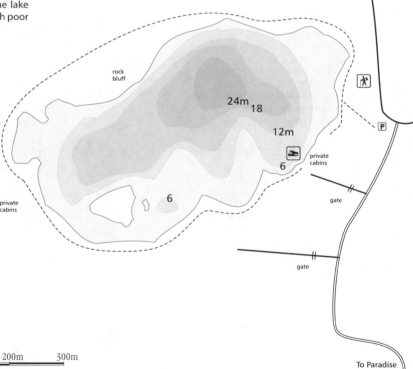

N

100m   0   100m   200m   300m

— Scale —

Location: Manning Provincial Park
Elevation: 1,250 m (4,101 ft)
Surface Area: 52 ha (128 ac)
Max Depth: 8 m (26 ft)
Mean Depth: 3 m (10 ft)
Way Point: 49° 2' 55" N, 120° 50' 31" W

Lightning Lake

Area Indicator

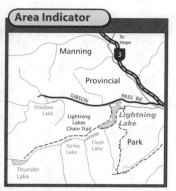

Fishing

Lightning Lake is the hub of Manning Provincial Park. The pretty lake is where much of the recreational activity happens. The largest campground in the park is found here and many of the most popular trails in the park start from here.

As you might expect, the lake also sees the heaviest fishing pressure in the park. However, the fishing remains strong during the ice-free season; partially because the high elevation lake is only ice-free starting in mid-June or early July and extending over to October. The rest of the year, the trail is covered with snow and the lake is iced over.

The lake contains many small cutthroat and rainbow caught by fly-fishing or spincasting. For fly-fishermen, a caddisfly hatch occurs in early July and a mayfly hatch occurs in the later part of June. During the rest of the year, a good trout fly like a Royal Coachman or Grizzly King, Doc Spratley, Carey Special or nymph pattern are good searching patterns.

Most small lures with some bait will produce. In fact, because the fish are usually so hungry, a simple worm and bobber set up is usually a good choice. If that isn't enticing the fish to bite, try a Wedding Band with a worm or a small silver or brass coloured spoon.

During the heat of the day, the lake is a popular swimming destination. The noise produced by people swimming can scare the fish; try working well away from the swimming area, or better yet, focus your efforts early or late in the day, before the beach gets too active. This is usually the best time to fish anyway, as the larger rainbow are more likely to be actively feeding.

The shallow lake is subject to winterkill during harsh winters. As a result catching a fish over the 30 cm (12 in) size is a rare occasion indeed.

Directions

Lightning Lake is the hub of Manning Provincial Park. The lake is easily accessed off the end of the Gibson Pass Road. To find that road from the Crowsnest Highway (Highway 3), watch for signs pointing to the Manning Park Lodge area. The paved road heading south is the Gibson Pass Road. Simply follow the signs from there.

Facilities

Lightning Lake is the main camping area in **E. C Manning Provincial Park.** Visitors will find a total of 143 units crammed into a forested area next to the lake along with a day-use area with picnic facilities and a boat launch for non-powered (motor or electric) boats. Camping is usually available from late May to mid-October depending on snow. Reservations are possible through wwww. discovercamping.com. The **Lightning Lake Loop** circles the lake offering several good shore fishing opportunities. The loop trail is 9 km (2.5 hours) long.

Other Options

Within the park, there are a number of sub-alpine lakes, which provide fast action for small rainbow (average 20–25 cm/8–10 in). The success really depends on the access with the more remote lakes providing the better fishing. All the lakes in the park are best fished beginning in the early summer through to the fall given that the ice is not out until late June. The closest lakes to Lightning are the other lakes in the Lightning Lake Chain, including **Flash, Strike** and **Thunder Lakes**. See our write-up on Flash and Thunder earlier in this book.

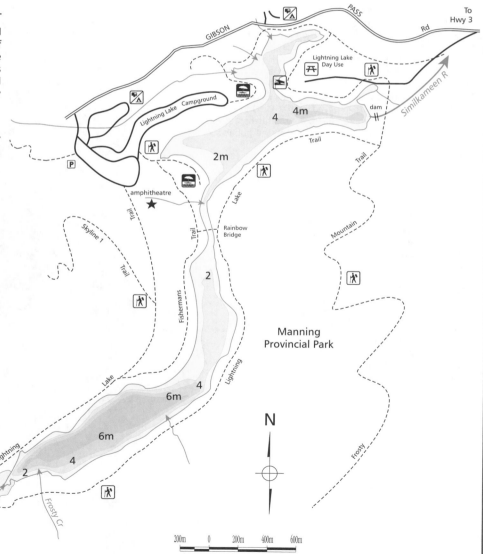

Lindeman Lake

Location: 25 km (15.5 mi) east of Chilliwack
Elevation: 817 m (2,680 ft)
Surface Area: 12 ha (29 ac)
Max Depth: 20 m (65 ft)
Mean Depth: 8 m (26 ft)
Way Point: 49° 6' 55" N, 121° 27' 25" W

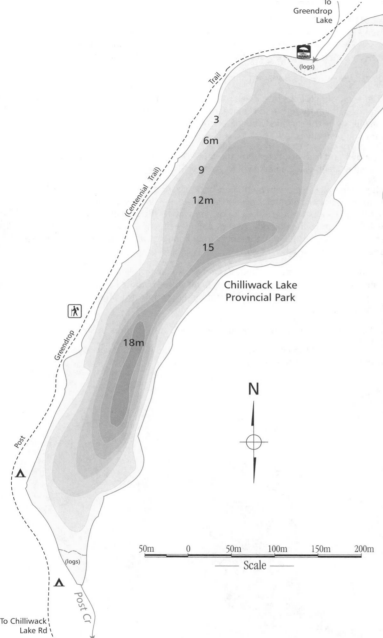

Chilliwack Lake
Provincial Park

Area Indicator

Fishing

Located in the mountains north of Chilliwack Lake, this lake is only accessible by foot, via a steep trail that will take less than an hour to hike for most reasonably fit hikers. It's a grunt up to the lake, but it is worth it, as this is one of the most beautiful lakes you will have the pleasure of fishing. The water is rich blue-green colour and surprisingly clear. You can often see fish at a distance of 10 meters (30 feet).

While some folks claim this lake is devoid of fish, it simply isn't true. It can be sometimes extremely tough to find them, yes, but they are there: brook, cutthroat and rainbow trout, which can get to 40 cm (14 inches).

The lake is extremely moody; one day the trout will be all but throwing themselves out of the water at you, the next day the place is a ghost town. This more than anything has kept this lake from becoming more popular with anglers. It is an extremely popular hiking destination, but few anglers are willing to haul their gear up to the lake when there is a good chance that the fish will simply ignore anything and everything thrown at them for no real reason other than they can't be bothered.

This is surprising since fish in most high elevation lakes are usually more than willing to hit anything you throw at them. But this lake does have a longer ice-free season than most sub-alpine lakes. The fishing can start as early as March, although the trail isn't usually snow free for another month or two. The fishing continues relatively unabated into November.

The most consistent action comes from fishing along the drop offs with a Doc Spratley on a fast-sinking line. You can fish from shore, but if you can manage hauling a float tube up to the lake, you will probably have much more success. In the fall, try working a leech or nymph pattern.

Spincasters have reported good success using small silver spinners, but the fish can be quite fickle, so bring along a selection of lures and be prepared for anything. Bait fishermen can do very well by using worms or a single egg cast from shore with a bobber.

Directions

Take the Vedder Road exit off the Trans Canada at Chilliwack and follow this road south. You will pass through Sardis and soon come to the Chilliwack River Bridge. Before the bridge, take a left on the Chilliwack River Road and drive all the way to Chilliwack Lake along the river.

As you near Chilliwack Lake, there is a short gravel side road that leads north to the former Post Creek Recreation Site. Here you will find the trailhead for the 3.4 km (2.1 mile) return hike to Lindeman Lake. The trail begins by rising sharply from the Chilliwack River Valley before reaching Lindeman Lake. Greendrop Lake is an additional 3.5 km one way to the north.

Facilities

Lindeman Lake is located in **Chilliwack Lake Provincial Park.** There is a rustic camping site and even a pit toilet at the southwest end of the lake. It is possible to hike to the lake and back in a day, allowing you the option to spend the night at the old recreation site or at Chilliwack Lake.

Location: Chase
Elevation: 347 m (1,138 ft)
Surface Area: 1,813 ha (4,480 ac)
Max Depth: 59.4 m (194.9 ft)
Mean Depth: 14.3 m (46.9 ft)
Way Point: 50° 51' 15" N, 119° 37' 57" W

Little Shuswap Lake

Area Indicator

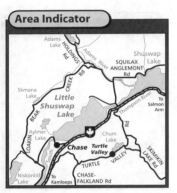

Fishing

Little Shuswap Lake fronts the town of Chase and is seen from the Trans Canada Highway as you are driving east towards Sorrento and Salmon Arm. It is a pretty lake set in the South Thompson Valley. In fact, the lake is formed by a dam on the South Thompson River. Unlike most of the good fishing lakes in this region, Little Shuswap is a bona fide low elevation lake, but because it is a big, deep lake, fish can still be found in the summer.

Like the big lake, Little Shuswap Lake offers reasonable fishing for rainbows to 5 kg (10 lbs) primarily by trolling.

In the late spring (May and June), fishing is at its best given the fact that the rainbow are actively feeding near the surface on salmon fry before the salmon fry return to the ocean. To take advantage of the feed, it is best to troll a silver bucktail or silver spoon quickly on the surface. Often times, the salmon fry hold up in small bays and fly-fishing or spincasting in these areas is very effective.

By the summertime, the rainbows and lake trout creep to the depths as the water warms. It is best to troll with a downrigger at 10–25 metres (30–90 feet) using a Rapala plug, Apex or Flatfish.

In October to November, the fishing picks up again by trolling bucktails, Apex or a plug near the surface. Trolling quickly in an erratic pattern might get you a nice rainbow and lake trout. If you are lucky, you may be able to hook one of the big Chinook salmon that pass through the lake on the way to the spawning grounds. Flashers and hoochies and big spoons will also work for the Chinook. As they are not actively feeding, the best way to get a bite is to aggravate them. The bigger and uglier the lure, the better your chances with Chinook. As always, watch the regulations for openings and closures on the lake.

There is a small population of kokanee as well as some Dolly Varden. For kokanee, the best fishing begins in July and extends into August. The fish are easily caught using a Wedding Band with a maggot or a worm trolled dead slow near the surface. If you catch one kokanee, chances are, you have found a school of kokanee so it is best to troll over the same area continuously for best results.

Spincasters and fly anglers should focus their effort at the outflow to the South Thompson River.

Please note that the northeastern end of the lake is closed to fishing. And while there are prodigious returns of salmon that pass through this lake, it is closed to salmon fishing year round.

Directions

The southwest end of the lake is easily accessed by driving into Chase and heading for the water. There is a public boat launch at the park. The northeast end is reached by taking the Squilax-Anglemont Road over the Shuswap River and then heading west on the Little Shuswap Road.

Facilities

The **Little Shuswap Park**, at the southwest end of the lake in Chase, offers a boat launch, beach and picnic site. There is private camping along the lake as well as numerous private residences. The **Quaaout Lodge** is also on the lake and is a first class facility for those looking to pamper themselves.

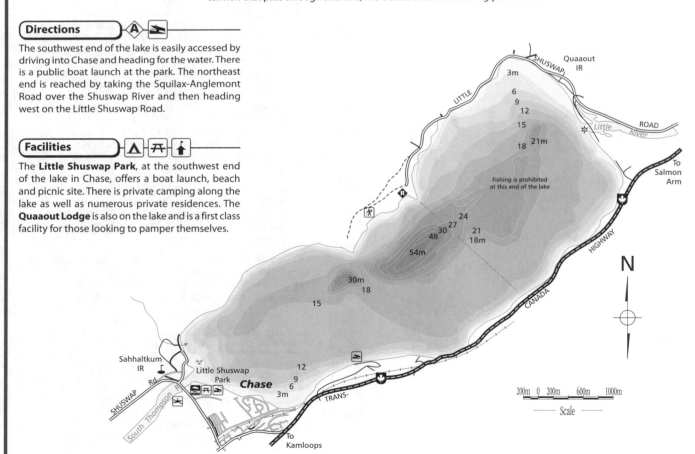

Lodgepole Lake

Location: 20 km (12 mi) south of Kamloops
Elevation: 1,408 m (4,619 ft)
Surface Area: 7 ha (17 ac)
Max Depth: 9 m (29 ft)
Way Point: 50° 31' 1" N, 120° 31' 3" W

Fishing

Lodgepole Lake is one of the many good fishing lakes found in the Lac Le Jeune area. It is a high elevation lake and so fishing for rainbow trout does not begin until mid to late May. However, the high elevation means that the water stays cool and the summer fishery usually remains active.

The rainbow average 1 kg (2 lbs) here, but every once in a while someone will pull out a fish to 3 kg (6 lbs) that creates quite a buzz in the valley.

The lake is best fished from a float tube or a small boat. Fly-fishing is the mainstay of the lake, and in early spring, fly anglers will find chironomids, bloodworms, micro-leeches and damsel nymphs with a strike indicator are a good place to start.

Other patterns that work well here are dragonfly nymph and shrimp patterns. Fish the shrimp or scud patterns near the bottom on a fast sinking line whereas the nymph patterns are best cast towards the drop offs at the west and east ends of the lake. The shoal areas at the north and south end also look inviting.

Casting from the deeper water into the shallow water allows you to retrieve across the drop off. Hungry rainbow don't like to venture too far away from the relative safety of deeper water. So if you were to cast from shallow water into deep, you would be slowly be pulling your lure farther away from the rainbow's comfort zone, making it less and less likely that you'll get a strike. Casting along the edge of the drop off is a viable strategy, too.

Spincasting a small lure such as a Flatfish or Deadly Dick is productive. Again, cast along or across the drop offs from deep to shallow.

The lake is not very deep and there was a real problem with winterkill in the past. However, an aerator has been installed and so the problem has been reduced.

The aerator makes ice fishing here more difficult, as the ice doesn't get as thick. While ice fishing is certainly possible, hard water anglers need to be cautious when heading out onto the ice. As a general rule, ice needs to be at least 15 cm (6 inches) to bear body weight.

Please note that there is an electric motor only restriction on the lake.

Directions

Lodgepole Lake is found on the east side of the Coquihalla Highway east of the State-McConnell Recreation Area. Take the Lac Le Jeune Exit (Exit 336) and head north to State Lake. You will find the Chewhels Mountain Road leading west from the north end of State Lake. Follow that road under the Coquihalla Connector before climbing to the north end of Lodgepole Lake about 5 km later.

Facilities

Lodgepole Lake Recreation Site is a ten unit site on the west side of the lake used primarily by fishermen or visitors to the Chewhels Mountain Motorcycle Trails. A cartop boat launch allows fishing at the lake, while the wharf is a convenient addition. There is also a trail down the west shore of the lake for shore anglers to attempt to cast into deeper water.

Those looking for a peaceful experience with nature might think twice about visiting here as this is a popular dirt bike riding area.

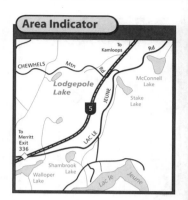

Area Indicator

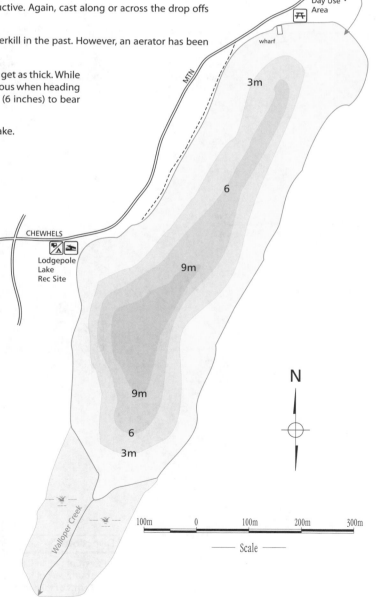

Lodgepole Lake			
Fish Stocking Data			
Year	Species	Number	Life Stage
2010	Rainbow Trout	3,000	Yearling
2009	Rainbow Trout	3,000	Yearling

Location: Logan Lake
Elevation: 1,098 m (3,602 ft)
Surface Area: 6 ha (15 ac)
Max Depth: 7.6 m (24.9 ft)
Way Point: 50° 29' 47.0" N, 120° 48' 24.7" W

Logan Lake

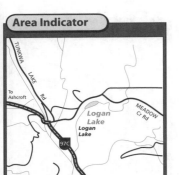

Area Indicator

Logan Lake			
Fish Stocking Data			
Year	Species	Number	Life Stage
2011	Rainbow Trout	3,000	Yearling
2010	Rainbow Trout	4,000	Yearling
2009	Rainbow Trout	4,000	Fingerling

Fishing

Logan Lake is a small lake located in the town of Logan Lake. It is a pretty lake that is used for fishing and swimming in the summer and playing hockey, skating and ice fishing in the winter.

The lake was originally a slough and has been transformed into a nice clear water lake with good fishing and rainbow trout as large a 7 kg (15 lbs). Although it has seen many improvements since its days as a slough, Logan Lake is still a work in project. Expect to see even more improvements and changes over the next few years.

Unfortunately, the lake suffers from heavy growth of milfoil that mats together in the summer. The shallow areas can get completely overrun by these plants, which make travel through the shallow areas difficult, and raise the temperature of the surrounding water to 20°C or more, making it unsuitable habitat for fish. Further, when the water level is down and the plants surface in the summer, the boat launch is unusable.

The lake is stocked multiple times a year with a mix of Fraser Valley and Blackwater rainbow trout. The Blackwater stocks help control the red-side shiners that were illegally introduced into the lake. The red-side shiners took a real liking to the lake, and were basically eating all the food until the Blackwaters were introduced. Now the piscivorous trout eat the shiners and because there's so many, the trout can get quite large.

Because the lake is so small, and the boat launch is so hard to access, the best way to fish the lake is from a tube or pontoon boat. Fly-fishers can try the usual fly patterns: a variety of chironomids (red, green), purple or black Woolly Buggers, scud patterns, etc. While spincasters can work their favourite trout gear: small spoons and spinners or a Wedding Band tipped with a worm.

There is a spawning channel on the lake to help with spawn bound trout. As the lake was formerly a slough, there is no creek flowing into or out of the lake that provides adequate spawning habitat.

Because of the milfoil, and because the lake is quite small, it can be difficult to fish with any success in the heat of summer. It is best fished in the spring, before the milfoil growth gets too out of control.

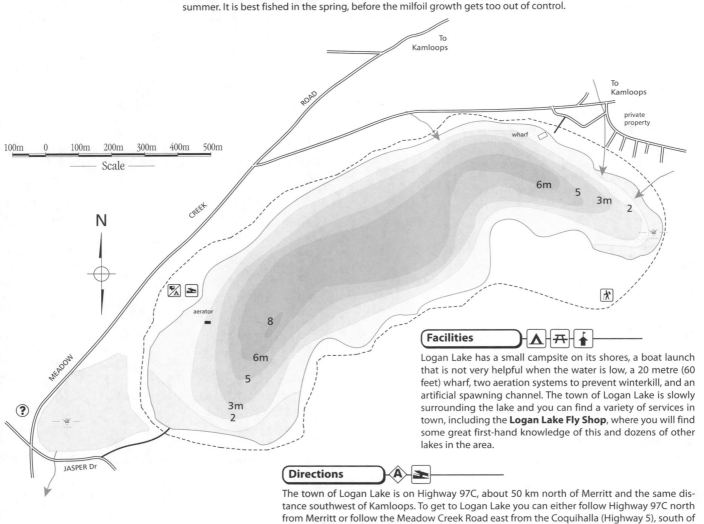

Facilities

Logan Lake has a small campsite on its shores, a boat launch that is not very helpful when the water is low, a 20 metre (60 feet) wharf, two aeration systems to prevent winterkill, and an artificial spawning channel. The town of Logan Lake is slowly surrounding the lake and you can find a variety of services in town, including the **Logan Lake Fly Shop**, where you will find some great first-hand knowledge of this and dozens of other lakes in the area.

Directions

The town of Logan Lake is on Highway 97C, about 50 km north of Merritt and the same distance southwest of Kamloops. To get to Logan Lake you can either follow Highway 97C north from Merritt or follow the Meadow Creek Road east from the Coquihalla (Highway 5), south of Kamloops. The lake is on the south side of Meadow Creek Road on the eastern edge of town.

Lookout Lake

www.backroadmapbooks.com

Location: 34.5 km (21.4 mi) north of Chilliwack
Elevation: 595 m (1,952 ft)
Surface Area: 11 ha (27 ac)
Max Depth: 20 m (65 ft)
Mean Depth: 8 m (26 ft)
Way Point:49° 29′ 53″ N, 121° 54′ 42″ W

Fishing

Lookout Lake is a fairly small lake located on the west side of Harrison Lake. Accessed by a rough 4wd road, many anglers pass on this one preferring instead to visit the easier to access lakes closer to the main road.

The mid elevation lake contains good numbers of rainbow and cutthroat in the 25–35 cm range. There are rumours of fish approaching 2.5 kg (5 lbs) but like most fishing stories, we are sure these fish have gotten bigger over time.

The lake has some rather inviting bays at the south end. These bays not only channel the fish, but they also have prominent shoals to test. They are a great place to fly-fishing a sinking line or spincasting a lure with bait.

The north end of the lake, where the outflow creek is, offers good fly-fishing and spincasting as well. In the summer months, it is best to try around the deeper hole towards the middle of the lake.

To best fish the lake, you should bring a canoe or float tube to the lake because the shoreline is cluttered with brush, marshy areas and logs. The western shoreline is particularly uninviting for shore fishermen whereas the eastern shoreline does have a prominent drop-off within casting distance from shore.

Area Indicator

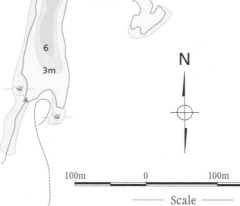

Directions

Getting to Lookout Lake is a difficult task and a copy of the Backroad Mapbook for the Vancouver, Coast and Mountains and a GPS with the BC Backroad GPS Maps is recommended. As is a high clearance 4wd vehicle. Better yet bring an ATV or be prepared to walk in.

From the Lougheed Highway (Highway 7) at Harrison Mills, follow the Morris Valley Road until it turns into the Harrison West Forest Service Road. This road is a good all season gravel road, which leads northward on the west side of Harrison Lake. Continue beyond the 24 km and the Harrison Lookout Trail markers until you come to the signed Mystery Creek Forest Service Road. Follow this road for a short distance before branching south on a narrow spur road. This rough road switchbacks up the hill to the height of land. After 2 km, you will come to a gravel parking lot overlooking the lake. It is possible to drive the final 50 metres down from the parking area to the lakeshore but it is probably not worth beating up your vehicle for the short walk it saves.

Last reports indicate the spur road leading south to Lookout Lake is gated.

Other Options

There is a number of good fishing lakes found along the west side of Harrison Lake. The closest lake is **Sunrise Lake**, also accessed off the Mystery Forest Service Road, which offers fair fishing for small cutthroat trout. It is described in more detail later in the book.

Lookout Lake			
Fish Stocking Data			
Year	Species	Number	Life Stage
2010	Rainbow Trout	500	Yearling
2009	Rainbow Trout	500	Yearling

Facilities

The single campsite at **Lookout Lake Recreation Site** is maintained by the Four Wheel Drive Association of BC. Needless to say, access is rough and best suited for tenters looking for a quiet location with decent fishing. There is no formal launching site, but is possible to hand launch smaller craft here. Bear in mind that most of the shoreline is less than inviting with a multitude of logs and brush to negotiate through.

The closest developed campsite is at Sunrise Lake to the south. Also maintained by the local 4wd club, the access into this lake is very rough.

To Mystery Cr FSR

Lookout Lk Cr

4wd only

18m

15

12

9m

6

3m

N

100m 0 100m 200m

Scale

Location: 29 km (18 mi) east of Clinton
Elevation: 825 m (2,707 ft)
Surface Area: 694 ha (1715 ac)
Max Depth: 64.9 m (212.9 ft)
Way Point: 51° 6' 44" N, 121° 14' 11" W

Area Indicator

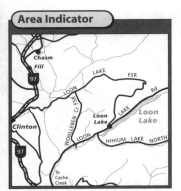

Fishing

Loon Lake is a unique body of water that is more than 13 kilometres long and less than 500 metres wide. Usually, things that look like this are called rivers but not Loon Lake. The steep valley walls that surround the lake constrain it into this long, narrow shape.

The lake is located between the Bonaparte Plateau, the Arrowstone Hills and the Thompson Plateau. It is a popular recreational lake with numerous homes, cabins, and resorts along its northwestern shore.

The lake is populated by large numbers of naturally reproducing rainbow trout. Spawning occurs in the numerous creeks that flow into Loon Lake, including Thunder Creek. The lake is deep–descending to about 20 metres (65 feet) at its deepest points–and clear with thin ribbons of shoals along the shoreline. Unfortunately, bulrushes and other shoreline vegetation make it difficult to fish the shallows. As a result, the lake is popular with trollers.

The long length of the lake and its deep water is ideal for trolling. No driving around in circles for hours here. Instead, it is possible to troll for a couple hours in one direction. Flatfish, spoons, small inline spinners such as Panther Martins and Mepps, and Ford Fenders tipped with a hook and worm work well. Proper selection of trolling depth is important, so boats equipped with electronic fish-finders have a distinct advantage. Use weights or a small downrigger help to consistently put your lures in front of the trout. The fish are not very big (averaging close to 0.5 kg/1 lb) so your presentation needs to be smaller.

Fly-fishing here is not impossible, just more challenging. It is worth the effort for those willing to target the shoals or drop offs. Good hatches of mayflies, chironomids and dragonflies, as well as freshwater shrimp and leeches, are available year-round. While you can find trout throughout the length of the lake, most anglers concentrate on the ends.

Note that a fishing closure is in effect all year off the mouth of Thunder Creek and within 500 metres of the outlet stream at the southwest end of the lake from December 1 to April 30. Signs mark the boundaries of the closed areas.

Facilities

There are at least five private resorts on the shores of the park. The provincial park that once graced the shores of the lake has now been permanently closed, and all facilities removed. That includes access to the boat launch that once provided access to the lake. Your best bet for both launching a boat and for accommodations is with one of the resorts.

However, if you would prefer to stay at a public park or recreation site, the nearest option is **Hihum Lake** along the road to the lake leaves the Loon Lake Road just before reaching Loon Lake.

Directions

Loon Lake is found nearly due north of Cache Creek. Cache Creek is found at the junction of Highway 1 and Highway 97, while the turnoff for the Loon Lake Road is about 32 km north on Highway 97 at 20 Mile House. Turn right and follow the Loon Lake Road northeast for about 17 km to reach the southwest end of the lake.

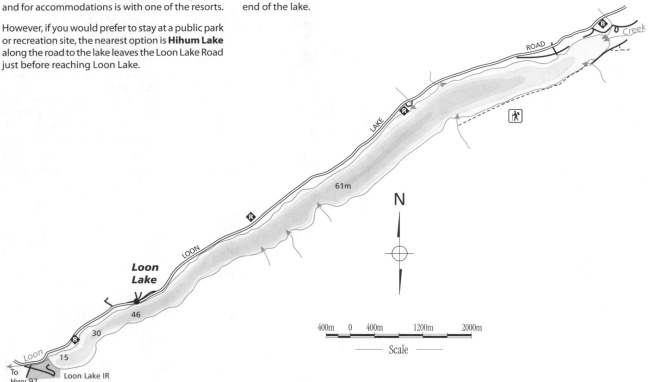

© Mussio Ventures Ltd.

www.backroadmapbooks.com

Lost Lake - Whistler Area

Location: 2 km (1.2 mi) north of Whistler Village
Elevation: 685 m (2,247 ft)
Surface Area: 16 ha (41 ac)
Maximum Depth: 23 m (75 ft)
Mean Depth: 8 m (26 ft)
Geographic: 50° 7' 43" N, 122° 56' 14" W

Fishing

Despite the name, Lost Lake is easy to find. In fact, during summer daytime hours, there is a bus drop-off while a free shuttle bus runs every 15 minutes from Whistler Village. The lake is stocked annually with catchable trout, which keeps the fish population high. And, since freshly stocked catchable-sized trout are notoriously easy to catch, the lake makes a great place to introduce new people to fishing.

Anglers will be rewarded with rainbow or bull trout to 1 kg (2 lb) that can be caught with lures, bait or flies. This lake is one of several in Whistler where you can plan on taking fish home for dinner. The fish aren't huge, but some up to 40 cm (16 in) have been caught. While there are some opportunities for shore fishing on this small lake, most anglers use canoes, pontoon boats or float tubes. Concentrate your efforts along the south, west and east shorelines, in small bays and around the docks and drop-offs.

If you are using spinning gear try casting a Roostertail, Dick Nite or other small spinner from shore or you can troll these same offerings around the lake to bring results. The main beach area is a good shore casting spot but it can be busy in the summer with swimmers and sunbathers. Evenings and early mornings are generally best.

Fly-fishing or trolling a fly can is also a very successful fishing method in Lost Lake. Known for a strong caddisfly hatch in early June, a caddisfly imitation can often bring success from June through August, with greater success at dusk. Right before sunset on August evenings, is a great time to cast flies to rising fish just off the beach. Successful flies include Woolly Buggers in green or brown, or occasionally red or yellow.

Use the hand-twist retrieve when fly-fishing with a wet line, varying speeds of retrieval until you hit the jackpot, a slow kick in a belly boat while maintaining line tension is often enough to get connected with one of the locals. Try "bumping" a leech, near the weed beds, giving an occasional hard twist during the hand-twist retrieve.

Dry fly-fishing in the evening can also be very rewarding when the alpenglow lights up the snowcapped peaks, framed with evergreen forests. A small Tom Thumb or Adams can end up testing your light gear to the limit.

Directions

Lost Lake is found just north of Whistler Village. From the Sea to Sky Highway (Highway 99), turn east onto Lorimer Road. Drive about 1.5 km (0.9 mi) along Lorimer to Lost Lake Road. Turn north (left) and proceed about 2 km (1.2 mi) to the parking lot. You can hand launch small craft from here, but it is about a 100 metre carry down to the lake.

Facilities

Lost Lake Park is a local park that offers a host of facilities and trails. There is a sandy beach abutting a grassy area on the edge of Lost Lake where you will find picnic tables, a concession in summer months and washrooms. There is also a designated dog beach along the east side, complete with a specially equipped doggy dock ramp. The swimming dock at the northeast end of the lake can be used for casting when the weather cools.

Lost Lake			
Fish Stocking Data			
Year	Species	Number	Life Stage
2010	Rainbow Trout	1,000	Catchable
2009	Rainbow Trout	1,000	Catchable

Area Indicator

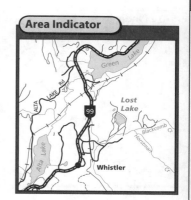

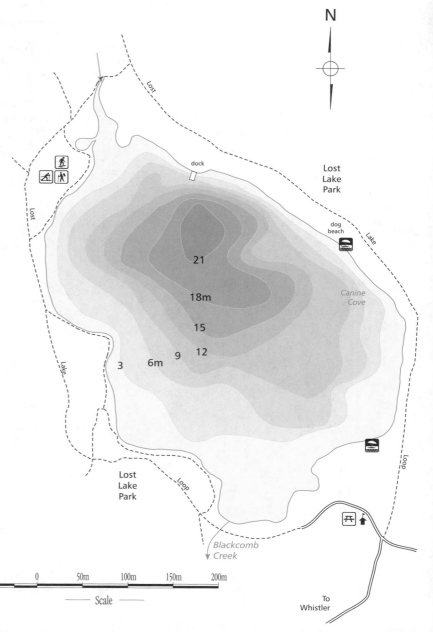

Scale
50m   0   50m   100m   150m   200m

© Mussio Ventures Ltd.

Location: 14 km (8.7 mi) northwest of Little Fort
Elevation: 1,229 m (4,032 ft)
Surface Area: 44 ha (110 ac)
Waypoint: 51° 29′ 35″ N, 120° 21′ 18″ W

Lynn Lake

Area Indicator

Fishing

The higher in elevation you go, the cooler the ambient air temperature, and as a result, the cooler the water. In the summertime warm water causes the trout to stop feeding actively and they lose their zip and vigour in low elevation lakes. Even if you do manage to snag a trout at this time, they'll put up very little fight. And warm water trout just don't taste as good, either.

The higher up into the mountains you go, though, the less and less a problem that becomes.

Lynn Lake isn't the highest elevation lake, but it isn't the lowest, either. The clear, shallow lake offers fair fishing for small stocked rainbow and brook trout that can reach 1.5–2 kg (3–4 lbs). The season begins in mid May, but slows down in mid-July.

Fortunately, there's only a couple or six weeks when the fishing slows down here, and by early September, fishing begins to improve and remains active until the lake freezes over in early November.

Trolling a lake troll (Willow Leaf and worm), Flatfish or attractor type fly such as a leech is the most productive fishing method.

Spincasters can have good success casting a Deadly Dick, Flatfish, Panther Martin or Blue Fox near the drop offs. Spincasters and fly fishers will also have good luck near the mouth of streams.

The lake has most of the hatches common to the region so try to match one of them for best success. Fly fishermen should try being here for the late June and early July caddis fly and mayfly hatches. During this time, there is some great dry fly fishing for rising trout. There is also a reliable chironomid hatch. Having a dip net along will allow you to quickly check what colour of chironomids are in the water. If you don't have a dip net, start with darker colours, and work through your box until you find something that works. A throat pump is a great help to check what the fish are actively feeding on.

While there are often chironomid hatches in the fall the fish are getting ready for the long, cold winter and are usually more interested in larger food. This is not to say that chironomid patterns won't work, but you will probably have more luck trolling a leech pattern or a dragonfly nymph.

Brook trout are known for offering good ice-fishing opportunities. Alas, the lake is closed to ice fishing.

Directions

Lynn Lake can be found by an access road that branches south off Highway 24. Take the Yellowhead Highway (Highway 5) north from Kamloops to Little Fort. Here, Highway 24–the so-called Fishing Highway–heads west into the high country of the Bonaparte Plateau. After travelling along the highway for 19 km a rough secondary road heads south to the lake. It is only a few hundred metres from the highway.

Highway 24 can also be accessed from Highway 97 in the west. If you are coming from this direction, the turnoff to Lynn Lake is 31.5 from Bridge Lake.

Facilities

There is a fishing camp at the lake, but no other facilities. It is possible to hand launch a cartopper. The nearest recreation site is across the highway at **Goose Lake**.

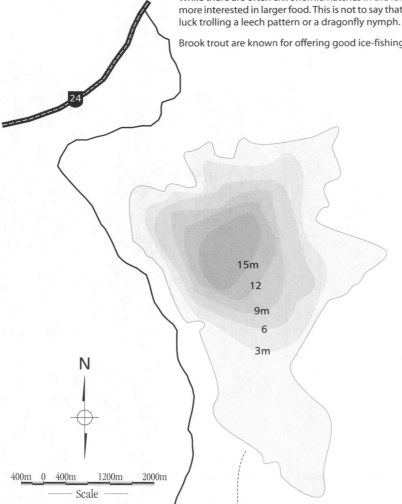

Lynn Lake			
Fish Stocking Data			
Year	Species	Number	Life Stage
2010	Brook Trout	1,000	Fingerling
2010	Rainbow Trout	3,045	Yearling
2009	Brook Trout	1,000	Fingerling
2009	Rainbow Trout	3,048	Yearling

www.backroadmapbooks.com

Machete Lake

Location: 26 km (16 mi) west of Little Fort
Elevation: 1,123 m (3,684 ft)
Surface Area: 440 ha (1,087 ac)
Max Depth: 10.6 m (34.8 ft)
Mean Depth: 6.2 m (20 ft)
Way Point: 51° 22′ 59″ N, 120° 34′ 37″ W

Fishing

Machete Lake is a resort lake found on the Bonaparte Plateau. Like most lakes on the plateau, Machete provides fair fishing for rainbow trout to 1kg (2 lbs) in size as well as small kokanee. The fishing begins shortly after ice-off in mid May and stays steady throughout the season all the way to early November when the lake freezes over. Summer doldrums are not a significant problem as the lake is fairly high in elevation and quite deep so the water stays cool throughout the year.

The preferred method of fishing is by trolling a lures or leech pattern within 3–5 m (10-15 ft) of the surface. Fly-fishermen should try an attractor type pattern such as a Doc Spratley or Woolly Bugger. Matching the chironomid, damselfly, dragonfly or mayfly hatches can also yield results. Focus your casting around the shoals and drop offs.

For the kokanee, slowly troll a Willow Leaf and worm, a pink Dick Nite or pink Flatfish. Troll very slowly in an S-pattern, and keep an eye out for any nibbles. Kokanee have very soft mouths. Setting the hook too hard can result in tearing the hook out of the fish's mouth, which is bad.

Kokanee are also very sensitive to water temperature, preferring to hang out in a narrow band of water that is about 10°C (50°F). This can make them frustrating to find. This layer of water is usually down around 3–6 m (10–20 feet), but having a fish finder will certainly improve your chances if not your success.

People who have become experts in trolling for kokanee often refuse to use a motor, as it's just too fast. They prefer to use oars instead, which gives them finer control over the speed of the lure. With oars, it is also possible to give a quick pull that causes the lure to speed up. Kokanee need to be enticed by a lure and if it is travelling in a straight line at a constant speed, it isn't very enticing. If the lure is weaving and wobbling, and every once in a while makes a burst like it is trying to get away, it can often trigger the predatory nature of the kokanee to strike.

Please note that the daily limit for kokanee is two and there is a single barbless hook restriction. The lake is closed to fishing from Jan 1-April 30.

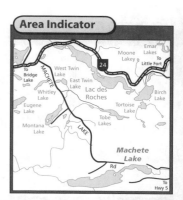

Area Indicator

Machete Lake Fish Stocking Data			
Year	Species	Number	Life Stage
2010	Kokanee	50,000	Fry
2010	Rainbow Trout	10,000	Yearling
2009	Kokanee	50,000	Yearling/Fry
2009	Rainbow Trout	15,000	Yearling

Directions

The easiest route into the lake is from the north off Highway 24. Highway 24 is also known as the Fishing Highway and it links 100 Mile House and Highway 97 with Little Fort and Highway 5.

The Machete Lake Road heads south about 4.5 km east of the Bridge Lake Store on Highway 24. Follow this road for about 14 km from the highway.

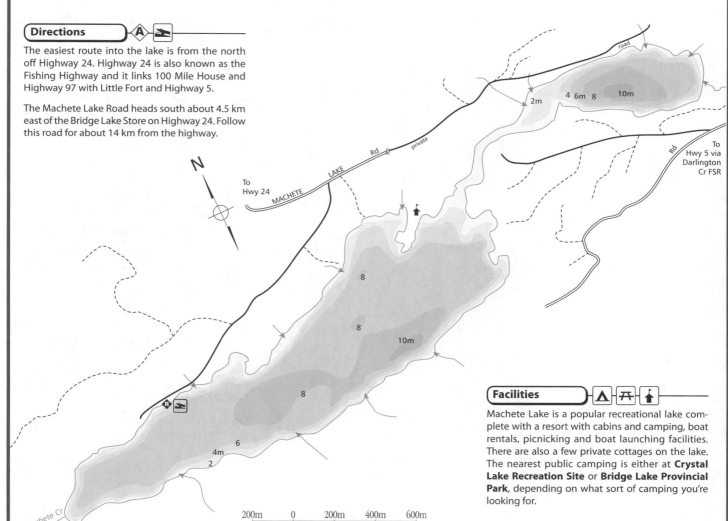

Facilities

Machete Lake is a popular recreational lake complete with a resort with cabins and camping, boat rentals, picnicking and boat launching facilities. There are also a few private cottages on the lake. The nearest public camping is either at **Crystal Lake Recreation Site** or **Bridge Lake Provincial Park**, depending on what sort of camping you're looking for.

Location: 34 km (21 mi) north of Merritt
Elevation: 955 m (3,133 ft)
Surface Area: 165 ha (408 ac)
Max Depth: 14 m (46 ft)
Mean Depth: 5.5 m (18 ft)
Way Point: 50° 23′ 7″ N, 120° 48′ 17″ W

Mamit Lake

Area Indicator

Fishing

Mamit is a large, shallow lake found right next to Highway 97C between Logan Lake and Merritt. Being a roadside lake there is pretty steady fishing throughout the year.

Mamit Lake offers fair fishing beginning in early May for rainbow trout reaching 2 kg (5 lbs) but usually averaging less then a pound. Most fishermen troll the lake with a lake troll and worm, Flatfish or Wedding Band. Trolling a Muddler Minnow, black leech or gomphus nymph is also productive. Fly-fishermen can also do well during the spring mayfly hatch, while attractor type patterns work throughout the spring or fall.

The lake has expansive shoals at the north and south end as well as two small islands near the south end of the lake. The shoals are easily seen, as the water is fairly clear. There is a moderately deep hole (8m) towards the northeastern end of the lake and the deepest area is found in the middle near the eastern shores.

Given the shallow depths of the lake, the fishing drops right off by mid July and the fish do not become active again until late September.

The lake also has a good population of ling cod, or burbot. Burbot would be a more popular catch, but regulations state they must be released. Unfortunately burbot don't provide the fight of a rainbow, and are best known as a good eating fish. Since you can't keep them…well, what's the point?

However, they do provide a nice distraction in the winter. Burbot love cold water, and they are most active when the lake is frozen. The rainbow in the lake are usually quite sluggish later in winter, but burbot still provide a good fight. And while finding them in summer is difficult as they tend to head for deep, cool water, they move into shallower water (less than 8 m/25 feet) after the lake is frozen. Burbot are usually found just off the bottom, so using a weight to get the hook down faster is common.

Burbot are piscivorous and tend to be attracted to smelly meat: cut herring, chicken liver and the like.

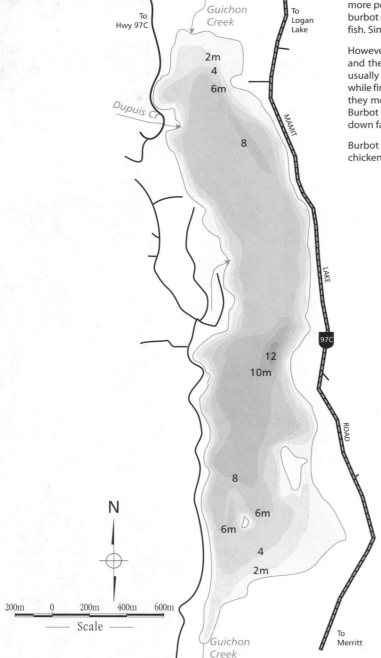

Directions

Mamit Lake is easily accessed by driving north on Highway 97C from Merritt or south from the town of Logan Lake. The highway, which is also called the Mamit Lake Road, is paved so an RV and car can easily reach the lake. It is the only large lake next to Highway 97C between Merritt and Logan Lake so you can't miss it.

Facilities

The only developed facility at the lake is a cartop boat launch. For people looking to stay in the area there are a half dozen or so recreation sites on lakes west of Mamit, including **LeRoy Lake, Antler Lake, Gypsum Lake, Dot Lake, Billy Lake, Tupper Lake** and **Roscoe Lake**. Better yet, why not stay in town and take advantage of the amenities there and the knowledgeable staff and the local tackle shops.

Other Options

West of Mamit is a series of small fishing lake that all offer good fishing and those ever popular recreation sites. Of these, the most popular is probably **Billy Lake**. The road into here is rough in places and a 4wd is required. It is possible to launch a cartop boat to help track down those large rainbow that can get up to 2 kg (4 lbs) here.

www.backroadmapbooks.com

Location: Squamish
Stream Length: 36.71 km (23 mi)
Geographic: 49° 43' 56.9" N, 123° 8' 53.7" W

Mamquam River

Fishing

The Mamquam is one of the biggest tributaries of the Squamish, flowing into the bigger river just above where the Squamish itself flows into Howe Sound. As part of the Cheakamus Recovery program, the Blind Channel is being reconnected to the Mamquam River. The Blind Channel was cut off from the rest of the Mamquam River back in 1921 when the Mamquam was diked.

The river holds all five species of salmon, as well as rainbow, cutthroat and bull trout. It is basically fishable year-round, with caveats. The river valley has been heavily logged and as a result is prone to blow out. When the water runs high, it runs dirty and is generally unfishable. If it rains, you are basically out of luck for three or four days until the water levels settle. You can save yourself the drive and check river levels at the Water Survey Canada website at www.scitech. pyr.ec.gc.ca/waterweb.

This penchant for running dirty includes spring freshet, which as a general rule starts in early May and ends in late June. Once the spring melt is over, the river is quite fishable. It is highly accessible, especially in its lower section, which is crossed by the Sea to Sky Highway and has dike trails running along much of its bank. The upper sections of the river can be accessed along the Mamquam Forest Service Road.

The Mamquam is a great fly-fishing river, broad, with lots of shoreline to access the river from. Spincasting can work here, too, but the river has a very rocky bottom and it is quite common to lose a fair bit of tackle in the stones. Bring lots of gear if you are spincasting here.

A set of waterfalls at the 6 km (3.6 mile) mark restricts salmon spawning or moving up to the upper river. While the upper reaches of the river still offer good trout fishing, salmon fishers will want to stay below the falls.

Speaking of trout, the Mamquam does offer some good nymph and dry fly-fishing. There are some good hatches of mayflies and caddis flies. Czech Nymphs, Hare's Ears and Elk Hair Caddis patterns work really well.

The river also has plenty of bull trout. The best time to catch bull trout is in winter, starting in October and continuing to May. Work streamers, popular flies and anything that imitates fry.

Directions

The Mamquam is an easy river to access. It is crossed by the Sea to Sky Highway (Highway 99) at the north end of Squamish. A popular spot to access the river is from the Squamish Valley Golf Course. Turn right on Mamquam Road, your first right after crossing the Mamquam River Bridge. From here, there are dike trails up and down the river. Alternatively, you can park the bridge crossing the river on Government Road and walk down to this popular hole.

South of town, the Mamquam Forest Service Road follows the river upstream. While you won't find salmon here, the upper river does offer good, usually secluded fishing for trout.

Facilities

The Mamquam flows through **Squamish**, where you will find hotels, restaurants, fishing retailers and other services. There are also private campgrounds in town if that is your preference. The nearest provincial park that offers camping is **Alice Lake,** which is found just north of Squamish.

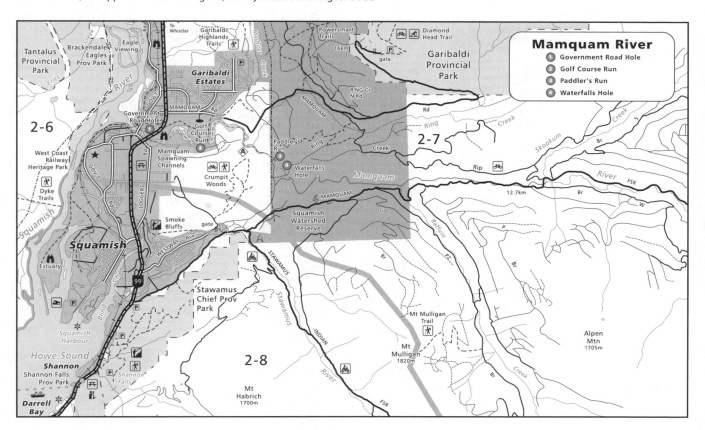

Location: 21 km (13 mi) north of Horseshoe Bay
Elevation: 478 m (1,568 ft)
Surface Area: 6 ha (15 ac)
Max Depth: 12 m (39 ft)
Mean Depth: 5 m (16 ft)
Way Point: 49° 33' 9" N, 123° 10' 34" W

www.backroadmapbooks.com

Marion Lake

Area Indicator

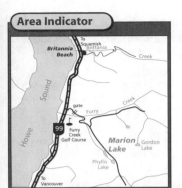

Fishing

Marion Lake is not a popular fishing destination. The lake is found at the end of a 6 km (3.6 mile) hike climbing nearly 500 metre (1,640 feet). Alas, the trail (actually a gated road) doesn't lead to a glorious alpine lake, nestled beneath towering peaks. It leads to a rather uninspiring little lake nestled beneath transmission lines.

That's two strikes against the lake. The big question is: how's the fishing?

Since the lake doesn't receive much pressure, the fishing is actually pretty good for small cutthroat. Not spectacular, but there are lakes that provide far less action. Of course, those lakes are usually accessible for far less effort and for most people, the trade-off between effort and angling here isn't worth it.

The lake is usually ice-free by early April and fishing is good in the spring and fall. In summer the fishing does slow, but if you can fish the two deep pockets on the lake–one towards the north end, one toward the south–you will have fairly good success. The lake is located beneath a ridge that keeps the sun off it starting in the late afternoon, which does help keep the water cooler and the fish rising.

While the lake has some fairly open areas around the shore, casting to the drop-off can be difficult. You can try shore fishing near the inflow creek at the south end of the lake, which is one of the most open areas around the lake. Bush-whacking to the southwest shore, which is steep and rocky, will get you within casting distance of the deep sections, but will probably prove more difficult than it is worth. A float tube is a valuable addition to fishing the lake.

Cutthroat can be voracious and like to eat. While they can sometimes be tempted to the surface to hit a dry fly, more often than not you will find them near the bottom. Spincasters can try working small spoons, or use a weight to anchor a baited hook (worm or Powerbait work best) near the bottom. Fly casters can try working their favourite attractor patterns, though black or maroon leeches do sometimes work. A good streamer here is the Grizzly Hackle Sculpin pattern that is regularly used in the East Kootenays for cutthroat and.

Directions

Marion Lake is a small lake found above the Furry Creek Golf Course. To reach the lake, head north on the Sea to Sky Highway (Highway 99) and watch for a gated logging road leading sharply uphill just past the golf course.

Park your vehicle and get ready for a pretty steep climb from the highway to the north end of Marion Lake along an old logging road up the Phyllis Creek drainage. You may wish to push a mountain bike uphill. While it won't save you much time on the trip to the lake, it will speed up the return trip to the highway.

Facilities

There are no developed facilities at the lake, but it is certainly possible to pitch a tent somewhere near the lake, or at the very least, up on the road. The nearest campsite is found along the highway at **Porteau Cove Provincial Park**. Here you will find a campsite with 44 vehicle-accessible and 16 walk-in sites. The park can be busy, but sites can be reserved ahead of time at www.discovercamping.ca.

To Hwy 99

Phyllis Cr

6m

4

2m

4

6m

8

10

12m

N

To Phyllis Lake

Phyllis Cr

50m   0   50m   100m   150m   200m

— Scale —

McConnell Lake

Location: 18 km (11.2 mi) south of Kamloops
Elevation: 1,285 m (4,216 ft)
Surface Area: 39 ha (96 ac)
Max Depth: 24.2 m (79.4 ft)
Mean Depth: 8.7 m (28.5 ft)
Way Point: 50° 31' 28.6" N, 120° 27' 30.1" W

Fishing

McConnell Lake is fairly good for rainbow trout that top 1.5 kg (3 lbs). The season extends from ice-off in early May all the way to ice-on in November. The summer doldrums do not set in because the lake is quite deep and high enough in elevation so that the water does not warm significantly in the heat of the summer.

The lake is effectively worked by trolling with a lake troll (Willow Leaf and worm) or a Flatfish being the most popular gear. Trolling a Leech or a Doc Spratley is also a good bet.

However, the lake has expansive shoals towards the north and east ends of the lake that makes it a fly angler's delight. Nice drop offs are found on both the west and east ends. Try casting a fly towards these areas using a Doc Spratley, Woolly Bugger or dragonfly nymph pattern. Chironomid, mayfly and sedge patterns are also worth a try when the hatch is on.

The water is very clear so you will be able to spot the drop offs and shoals. However, this means that the fish can also spot you. Fish hang around the drop offs because the deeper water offers a means of escape from predators. If you are too noisy or too obvious as you approach these areas, the fish will merely disappear into the depths of the lake. That makes fishing here challenging, which is just the way many fly anglers like it.

Clear water also means that insects hatch in deeper water. A common strategy in fishing clear lakes like this is to use a long leader with a dry line, especially when fishing bloodworm or chironomid patterns. Getting your fly down to the 5–7 metre (18–22 feet) level will improve your chances. Yes, casting with such a long leader is awkward, but with insects hatching as deep as 6 or 10 metres (20–35 feet), the long leader will help you get down to where the fish are.

As the shores of the lake are forested, it is well advised to use a float tube or boat to fish rather than trying to cast from shore.

Area Indicator

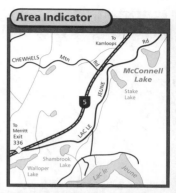

McConnell Lake			
Fish Stocking Data			
Year	Species	Number	Life Stage
2010	Rainbow Trout	5,000	Yearling
2009	Rainbow Trout	5,000	Yearling

Directions

McConnell Lake is easily accessed by taking the Lac Le Jeune Exit (Exit 336) on the Coquihalla Connector between Merritt and Kamloops. Head east on the Lac Le Jeune Road and after passing State Lake, you will see McConnell Lake on the right.

For a more scenic route, travel south on the Lac Le Jeune Road from the outskirts of Kamloops. McConnell is the first big lake heading south. The road is paved so all types of vehicles can reach the lake.

N

| 0 | 100m | 200m | 300m |

— Scale —

Facilities

McConnell Lake Provincial Park encompasses McConnell Lake. This day-use park offers a gravel boat launch for anglers, as well as a primitive hiking trail around the lake that shore anglers can use. There are no camping facilities, and there is only one picnic table on site.

For anglers looking to stay in the area, nearby **Lac Le Jeune Provincial Park** has 144 camping sites. That park is quite popular, and reservations are recommended, especially if heading there for the weekend.

To Kamloops

ROAD

LAC LE JEUNE

To Hwy 5
Exit 336

To Stake Lake

Sand Bar

McConnell Lake
Provincial Park

McConnell Lake
Provincial Park

Anderson Cr

dam

Sand Bar

2m
4
6
8m
10
12
14
16m
18
20
22
24m

Sand Bar

4m

Location: 12 km (7.5 mi) northwest of Chase
Elevation: 1,399 m (4,590 ft)
Max Depth: 15.2 m (49.9 ft)
Way Point: 50° 51' 17" N, 119° 50' 11" W

Area Indicator

Fishing

In July and August, low elevation lakes do not offer good fishing, but that's when a lake like McGillivray comes into its own. While there are several high elevation lakes in the region, none are as accessible as McGillivray Lake, which is just a short hop from bustling Sun Peaks Resort.

McGillivray Lake is a dark-water, tannic lake with lily pads that fringe its shorelines and shallow bays. The main body of the lake runs north to south, with two small islands at the south end. At just 91 hectares (224 acres), the lake is still small enough to make rowing possible but big enough to make a motor appreciated. There is a good boat launch.

Since rainbow trout are able to enter the lake via McGillivray Creek, which also provides a natural spawning ground, the lake is not stocked. The fish average 0.5–1 kg (1–2 lbs), but size can be cyclical depending on the success of the spawning season. For example, in a year that follows low natural recruitment, the size of the fish will be bigger, but there will be fewer of them. In a year when there are lots of fry entering the lake, there is more competition for food and the fish don't get as big.

Fly-fishers will find the usual stillwater tactics apply at this lake. Target the edges of weed beds when the sun is high as trout often cruise the shaded pockets beneath the lily pads. But don't fish in the weeds themselves because a trout can quickly tangle around the thick stalks of the pads. In late June and early July, McGillivray Lake is host to a prolific hatch of caddis flies.

This lake has expansive shoals, including one long shallow ridge that runs south and points like a finger toward the middle of the lake. Fish the shoulders of this underwater ridge.

Trollers should stay clear of the weeds as the deeper waters around the ridge are more productive. Instead, target the holes to the west of the islands at the south end of the lake.

Note there are fishing restrictions to be aware of.

Directions

From Kamloops, take Highway 5 north to the Sun Peaks Exit and drive 38 km to Sun Peaks Resort. Continue east for 6 km through residential neighbourhoods until you reach a gravel road. The development in the area can make the McGillivray Lake Forest Service Road difficult to find, but signs and directions are posted. Once on the gravel road, climb the hill and keep right when the main roads forks. A sign marks the left hand turn to the lake.

Alternately, the lake can be found from the south near Chase. Follow the Niskonlith Lake Road southwest past Niskonlith Lake to meet up with the McGillivray Lake Forest Service Road. This road climbs steeply to the lake and can be quite rough in sections.

Facilities

McGillivray Lake West Recreation Site offers three campsites at the south end along with a cartop boat launch, outhouses and picnic tables. Despite the mosquitoes and less than appealing shoreline, the site remains quite popular with the fishing crowd.

There are also a series of trails to explore in the area, while nearby **Sun Peaks Resort** is one of the fastest-growing, all-season resorts in southern BC. With a multitude of activities available at the resort, you can go mountain biking, horseback riding, golfing and alpine hiking all in one day.

To Sun Peaks FSR

LAKE

2m
3
5m
6
8m
9
111
12
13m

McGillivray Cr

McGillivray Lake West Rec Site

Moose Island

6
8
9m

Burnt Island

McGILLIVRAY

N

To Hwy 1 via Pemberton-Shuswap Rd

100m   0   100m   200m   300m
Scale

Meadow & Lost Horse Lakes

Meadow Lake

Elevation: 1,365 m (4,478 ft)
Surface Area: 10 ha (25 ac)
Max Depth: 10 m (32.8 ft)
Mean Depth: 3 m (10 ft)
Way Point: 51° 33' 49" N, 120° 24' 17"W

Fishing

The Nehalliston Plateau is littered with countless small lakes that all seem to produce trout. Some are small, shallow pothole lakes like Meadow Lake, while others are a bit deeper and offer more structure like Lost Horse Lake. Regardless of your pleasure, they all seem to hold fast growing trout.

Meadow Lake offers fair fishing for small rainbow that can reach 1.5–2 kg (3-4 lbs). The season begins in mid May, but the fishing drops off by mid July. Because it is a small, shallow lake, the water does warm up, and fishing slows in the summer. Fortunately, by early September, fishing begins to improve and remains active until the lake freezes over in early November. Trolling a lake troll, Flatfish or attractor type fly such as a leech is the most productive fishing method. Fly-fishermen and spincasters can work the drop off near the southeast end of the lake or the shoal at the north and west ends.

Nearby Lost Horse Lake is a much deeper lake than Meadow Lake, and so the water does not warm as much. If Meadow Lake is unresponsive, this lake is worth trying. It has good fishing for rainbow that reach 1 kg (2 lbs). There is a nice bay at the southeast end with expansive shallows for insect rearing. There are also some inviting shoals at the north end of the lake and productive drop offs on the eastern and western shores. Another bonus is the fact that the lake does not receive the same intense fishing pressure as other lakes in the area so you can expect some element of solitude when you arrive.

Area Indicator

Friendly Lake
Lost Horse Lake
Meadow Lake
Portage Lake
Randy Lake
Deer Lake
Nora Lake
Laurel Lake
Long Island (Janice) Lake
24
To Bridge Lake
To Little Fort
TAWEEL LK.

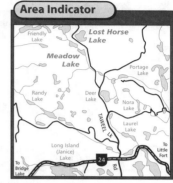

Both lakes fish somewhat similarly. The fishing season runs from early May at ice-off to November. Trollers do well with the usual lake trolls (Willow Leaf and worm) or with a Flatfish. Spincasters can have good success casting a Deadly Dick, Flatfish, Panther Martin or Blue Fox near the drop offs.

Fly-fishers should try being here for the late June and early July caddis fly and mayfly hatches. When there isn't an active hatch happening, say in fall, trolling a leech pattern can work quite well. Attractor type flies are also quite effective in the area. Bring a good variety of colours in sizes 8 and 10.

3m
6
9
12m
15
18
21m

TAWEEL LAKE ROAD

△ Lost Horse Lake Rec Site

Lost Horse Lake

Lost Horse Lake

Elevation: 1,373 m (4,505 ft)
Surface Area: 39 ha (96 ac)
Max Depth: 24 m (78.7 ft)
Mean Depth: 7 m (24 ft)
Way Point: 51° 34' 21.7" N, 120° 24' 15.4"W

Directions A

This pair of pothole lakes is just a sampling of the many lakes located west of Little Fort. To reach the lakes, follow Highway 24 west from Little Fort and continue on the highway until you reach the Taweel Lake Road. Head north on this road past Deer Lake and avoid the resort signs leading to Taweel around the 11 km mark. Continue north and the rough road will bring you right past Meadow and then Lost Horse Lake.

A 4wd truck, a GPS and a copy of the Backroad Mapbook for the Thompson Okanagan region is a definite advantage when exploring this prime fishing area.

N

TAWEEL LAKE ROAD

To Hwy 24

R

100m 0 100m 200m 300m
— Scale —

2m
3
5m 6
9m

Facilities △ 🅿 ♿

The **Meadow Lake Fishing Camp** offers rustic accommodation and a few amenities for fishermen using the lake. Further north, there is a user-maintained campsite at Lost Horse Lake with space for about five groups here. Launching small boats or tubes from roadside is certainly possible.

Meadow Lake

Location: 6 km (3.7 mi) northeast of Maple Ridge
Elevation: 245 m (804 ft)
Surface Area: 4 ha (10 ac)
Max Depth: 5 m (16 ft)
Way Point: 49° 16' 27.7" N, 122° 32' 22.8" W

www.backroadmapbooks.com

Mike Lake

Area Indicator

Mike Lake			
Fish Stocking Data			
Year	Species	Number	Life Stage
2011	Rainbow Trout	1,100	Catchable
2010	Rainbow Trout	1,650	Catchable
2009	Rainbow Trout	1,650	Catchable

Fishing

Mike Lake is a good little fishing hole found in Golden Ears Provincial Park. It is a shallow, intimate lake surrounded by marshy wetlands that is situated in a heavily timbered bowl on Maple Ridge.

People who haven't been to the lake recently will probably remember how fun it was to launch a tube or small boat here, sinking up to their knees in the mud…. Well, BC Parks has built a fishing dock, which not only allows for easier entry into the water, it allows people who don't have a tube or small boat to get out onto the water, too. With the addition of the dock, Mike Lake has become a great family fishing area, where parents can take their kids to cast off the dock.

The lake is stocked multiple times a year with a few hundred catchable size rainbow that are generally small. However, every once in a while the Freshwater Fisheries Society of BC will drop a bunch of brood stock in the lake that get to 2 kg (4 lbs) to mix things up.

The lake can be stupid busy at times, with dozens of float tubes out on the water and people fighting for space on the dock. However, the lake is a great escape for people who want to go fishing for a few hours after work.

Mike Lake has a muddy bottom and marshy shoreline and is a great chironomid lake. Hatches tend to be brown or green, but it is always best to take a sample to see what colour the day's hatch is. They can hatch as early as March here with bloodworms and later phases of chironomids, as well as small pheasant tail nymphs all working. Dragon nymphs also work well, as can a small green shrimp pattern. Later in the year, dry flies can be a lot of fun on this lake. Try working around the logs at the east end or the weeds on the northwest side.

Spincasters can try working bait or spinners. The best strategy, though, is to use a baited hook and simply let it rest on the bottom. Trolling a Flatfish near the bottom can also be effective.

Please note that there is a powerboat restriction at the lake.

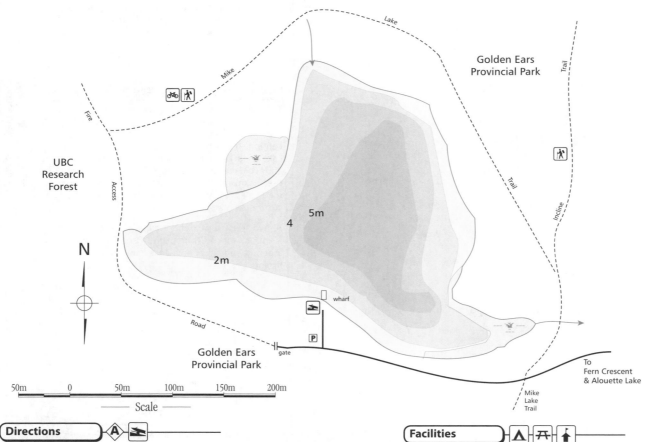

Directions

Mike Lake is located on the boundary of the UBC Research Forest, just inside Golden Ears Provincial Park. To find the lake from Vancouver, travel east on the Lougheed Highway (Highway 7) and you will see a sign pointing the way to the Golden Ears Provincial Park. The route takes you along Dewdney Trunk Road, to 132 Avenue and then finally along Fern Crescent. Fern Crescent follows the Alouette River and when you reach the park headquarters, take a quick left onto the gravel road. About 1.9 km later, you will find a parking lot. A 100 metre walk from the parking lot brings you to the lake.

Facilities

There is a wharf, day-use area and cartop boat launch at the lake. The **Mike Lake Trail** circles the lake, but the reedy nature of the shoreline limits shore casting possibilities. For camping, **Golden Ears Provincial Park** has three different camping areas, at Alouette, Gold Creek and North Beach with over 400 campsites and a separate day-use area and boat launch onto Alouette Lake.

Mill Lake

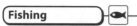

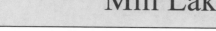

www.backroadmapbooks.com

Location: Abbotsford	
Elevation: 54 m (177 ft)	
Surface Area: 18 ha (44 ac)	
Max Depth: 11 m (36 ft)	
Mean Depth: 2 m (7 ft)	
Way Point: 49° 2′ 41.5″ N, 122° 18′ 42.6″ W	

Fishing 🐟

Mill Lake is an urban lake in the heart of Abbotsford next to the Seven Oaks Shopping Mall. Despite the lake's small size, it has a disproportionate number of large fish. Some people claimed to have pulled rainbow to 4.5 kg (10 lbs) out of here. Although that sounds suspiciously like one of those fishing stories, there are definitely some big fish here.

There is also a good variety of fish with rainbow trout, cutthroat, bullheads, crappies and largemouth bass all providing a bit of action. The lake is lined with weeds and lilies but it is possible to fish from shore by casting off the dock or from the beach in front of parking area. There is also a boardwalk on the east side that allows casting.

Anglers who have a float tube or boat can work the deeper parts of the lake as well as the shallow, weedy area that is found in the centre of the lake. Please note that you are limited to electric motors less then 2.5 horsepower.

For bass, which can get up to 3 kg (6 lbs), try working dark coloured plastics in the 4-6 inch range. In spring, the best place to fish is the drop-off just off the lily pads at the west end of the lake, while later in the year, you will have more luck fishing the shallow weeds in the centre of the lake.

Bass like to work under cover, which means that on hot summer days your best bet is to work the shady areas (weeds, docks, lily pads) or to wait for sunset, when the bass become bold and cruise from their places of cover in search of food. In fact, one of the more popular methods of fishing for bass here is working a white-coloured topwater lure on moonlit summer nights, just off the dock.

This urban lake is heavily stocked with rainbow. Due to the muddy bottom, anglers should use light gear (no weights). Earlier in the year, the lily pads on the west side are a good place to work. As the water warms the fish go deeper. At that time try working the middle section around the weeds. You should try fishing the shallows only at dusk when the fish move towards the shallow areas in search of food. Flies, small spinners and the classic bobber and bait work well for trout.

For something different, anglers can also go after crappies. These warm water fish like the marshy nature of the lake and hang around the weeds. They will take almost all types of bait, small spinners or small wet fly patterns. They are located in schools so once you catch one chances are you should hook many.

Area Indicator

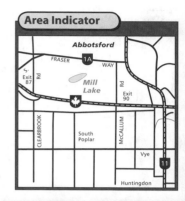

Mill Lake			
Fish Stocking Data			
Year	Species	Number	Life Stage
2011	Rainbow Trout	41,917	Fry
2011	Rainbow Trout	2,000	Catchable
2011	Rainbow Trout	165	Yearling
2011	Rainbow Trout	10,250	Mixed
2010	Rainbow Trout	4,151	Catchable
2010	Steelhead	2,100	Catchable
2009	Rainbow Trout	3,709	Yearling
2009	Cutthroat Trout	12,936	Adult

Directions 🅰

To reach the lake, take the McCallum Road exit (Exit 90) off Highway 1 and head north. Turn left on Marshall Road followed by a right on Ware Street and then a left on Bourquin Crescent. Once on Bourquin, you will soon see the Mill Lake Road leading to the left. The road brings you right to the north end of the lake where the main facilities are located.

Facilities 🏕 🪑 ⛲

Mill Lake Park, at the north end of the lake, provides a concrete boat launch, a floating dock, picnic tables, washrooms and walking trails around the lake.

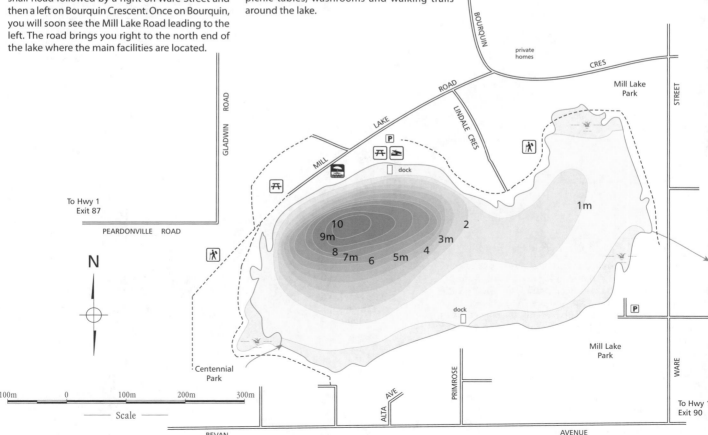

© Mussio Ventures Ltd.

Location: 30 km (18.6 mi) west of Seymour Arm
Elevation: 457 m (1,499 ft)
Surface Area: 203 ha (502 ac)
Max Depth: 55 m (180.4 ft)
Mean Depth: 34.6 m (113.5 ft)
Way Point: 51° 19' 27" N, 119° 20' 58" W

Momich Lake

Area Indicator

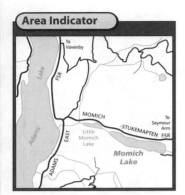

Fishing

Momich Lake is a gorgeous green coloured lake that does not get the fishing pressure such a scenic lake deserves. This is no doubt due to the long drive discourages day trippers. Unfortunately, a forest fire in 2009 damaged much of the surrounding area and it is unclear if this will affect the fishery.

Despite being so far from civilization in what seems like remote mountainous country, Momich Lake opens up fairly early in the season. The fishing does stay fairly steady throughout the ice-free season as the water is deep enough to ensure that it does not warm significantly in the summer months.

The big lake is best trolled for kokanee, rainbow trout and Dolly Varden. Unfortunately, there are a lot of coarse fish in the lake that are competing heavily with the sportfish. The trout do grow to 2 kg (5 lbs), but are somewhat difficult to catch due to the size and depth of the lake.

Trollers should work the northern and southern shores of the lake using a lake troll, a lure (Krocodile or Kamlooper) or searching pattern like a Doc Spratley. There are nice drop offs along the shoreline as well as small feeder streams.

Fly-fishers and spincasters should focus their efforts at the inflow and outflow of Momich River. These are also good areas to toss a bobber with bait setup. Small minnows can be deadly.

Kokanee seem to be doing well in the lake and can be caught with the usual lake troll set up. Remember to troll slowly and keep you gear at the level the fish are holding. A fish finder will help locate the fish.

Directions

The long drive into this lake is guaranteed to limit a lot of outdoorsmen from fishing the lake. The road to the lake, however, is very good so even a car or RV could conceivably reach the lake although it is certainly not recommended.

From Chase, head along the Trans Canada Highway for 5.5 km northeast to the Squilax-Anglemont Road. Follow this road north to Holdings Road, which turns into the Adams West Forest Service Road. At km 72, turn east on the Adams Lake East Road and follow this road to its junction with the Mowich-Stukemapten Forest Service Road. This road climbs out of the Adams Lake Valley and takes you past Little Momich Lake and then the main lake.

Other Options

If fishing is slow in Momich Lake you may wish to try **Little Momich Lake**. Since this lake is smaller than Momich Lake, fly-fishing and spincasting from a float tube or from shore are much more productive here. It is possible to canoe through the wetland connecting the two lakes.

Facilities

Momich Lakes Provincial Park is a large 1,648 hectare park that extends up the Momich River Valley from the shores of the Adams Lake encompassing three lakes; Little Momich Lake, Momich Lake and the Third Momich Lake. The **Momich River Campsite** is presently the only site open due to the fire in 2009. It offers 20 campsites and access to Adams Lake. Unfortunately, the **Momich Lake West Site Campsite,** a small two table site with rough road access, and the **Momich Lake East Campsite,** the nicer site with trailer access, a sandy beach and boat launch, are presently closed.

Be sure to enquire with BC Parks as to the status of the sites before venturing in.

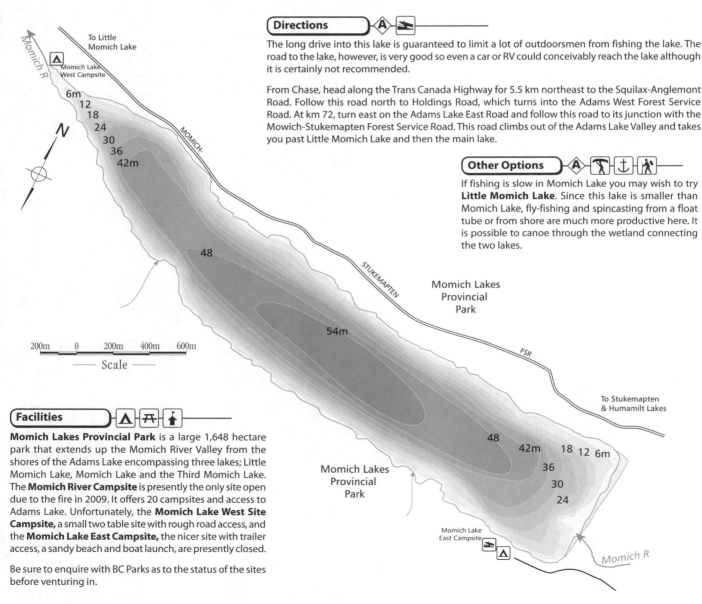

© Mussio Ventures Ltd.

Monte Lake

Location: 44 km (27.3 mi) east of Kamloops
Elevation: 690 m (2,264 ft)
Surface Area: 176 ha (435 ac)
Max Depth: 36.3 m (119.1 ft)
Mean Depth: 21.6 m (70.9 ft)
Way Point: 50° 30' 38" N, 119° 50' 17" W

Fishing

Found next to Highway 97 west of Westwold, Monte Lake is a pretty lake in a pretty valley. The lake is located just metres off the highway, so access is great, but the cars whizzing past do tend to kill the ambiance.

There are a handful of pullouts along the highway, as well as off of Mill Road, at the north end of the lake.

Monte Lake has not been known as a fishing destination lake in the past, but this is changing. Historically, it has offered slow fishing for rainbow trout to 2 kg (4 lbs). There are many course fish in the lake, which have been out competing the rainbow for the available food source.

But since 2004, the Freshwater Fisheries Society of BC has been stocking the lake with Blackwater rainbow. Blackwaters are a fish-eating species of rainbow, and love dining on the red-sided shiners that are found in the lake. One of the side benefits of dropping Blackwater rainbow into a lake overrun with shiners is you wind up with a lot of fat, happy trout. This makes anglers happy, too.

This has gone a long way to improving the habitat for the other fish. So much so that in 2007, the Society started stocking kokanee in the lake, too. Most people aren't fishing for kokanee here yet, but over the next few years, expect the quality of fishing to get better as these fish get bigger.

Kokanee are best caught by trolling a small Willow Leaf. Pink is usually a good colour to start out with. Troll in a slow, broad S-pattern, varying your speed and be ready for the soft tentative bite of a kokanee. Don't yank too hard, as kokanee have soft mouths and instead of setting the hook, you may just rip the hook right through the fish's mouth. A rubber snubber will help protect the kokanee.

Trout anglers will find the lake is well suited for trolling beginning in early May. Try a gang troll or a small lure such as a Panther Martin, Flatfish, Krocodile or Kamlooper. Trolling a leech, Muddler Minnow or Doc Spratley is also a good idea.

However, the lake is not known for being a great fly-fishing lake. Fly anglers should focus their effort around the outflow creek towards the south end of lake. The lake also has distinctive drop offs around its entire length which can be tested. There are few shoals to work, however.

Directions

Monte Lake is found right next to Highway 97 northwest of Westwold. The highway passes by the eastern shores of the lake so it would be hard to miss.

To reach Highway 97, drive north of Vernon or east of Kamloops on the Trans Canada.

Facilities

Monte Lake Provincial Park is on the eastern shores of the lake. There are no facilities at the park. For people hoping to spend the night, there is a private, full service campground right next to the park. There are also a couple boat launches on the lake.

Other Options

Biancotto Lake and **Paxton Lake** are two small lakes located east of Monte Lake. The lakes are found off the Paxton Valley Road and offer fly fishing and spincasting for small trout.

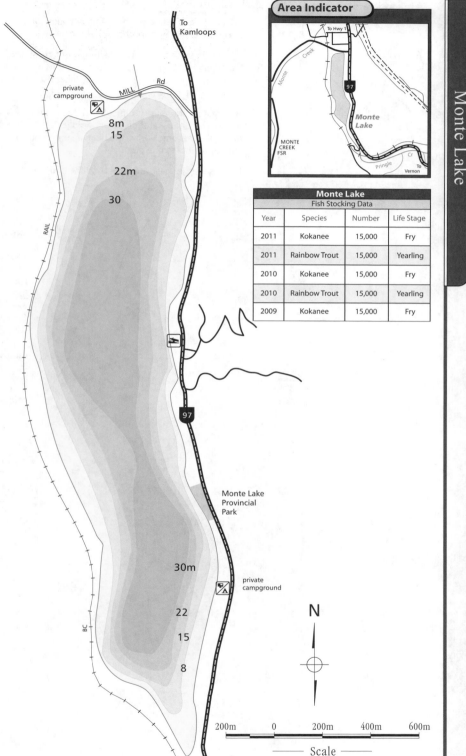

Area Indicator

Monte Lake			
Fish Stocking Data			
Year	Species	Number	Life Stage
2011	Kokanee	15,000	Fry
2011	Rainbow Trout	15,000	Yearling
2010	Kokanee	15,000	Fry
2010	Rainbow Trout	15,000	Yearling
2009	Kokanee	15,000	Fry

| Location: 22 km (13.6 mi) north of Mission |
| Elevation: 305 m (1001 ft) |
| Surface Area: 18 ha (44 ac) |
| Max Depth: 50 m (164 ft) |
| Mean Depth: 18 m (59 ft) |
| Way Point: 49° 20' 55.6" N, 122° 20' 0.7" W |

www.backroadmapbooks.com

Morgan Lake

Area Indicator

Fishing

Morgan Lake is found on the divide between Alouette Lake and Stave Lake. The north end of the lake is connected to Florence Lake by a short channel.

The lake has good fishing for eastern brook trout primarily because of the intensive regulations in place at the lake. The lake, until the early 1990s, was closed to fishing and now it is a catch & release, single barbless and fly-fishing only. Some trout reach 2 kg (4.5 lbs) in size so you have a chance at a beauty. In fact, the lake holds some of the biggest trout in the region.

The western shoreline is difficult fish due to an excessive amount of logs, marshy areas and brush. If you can find a place to cast, the water drops off rapidly. Packing in a float tube or canoe to cast towards shore is your best bet in the cooler seasons. During the heat of summer the fish retreat to the deep hole in the middle of the lake and are all but impossible to lure out.

There is a large shallow area around the island at the north end of the lake. In the spring, this area can be extremely productive.

Fly anglers will find a variety of good hatches. Dragonflies, damsels can produce a flurry of action, while lesser-known hatches such as the Callibaetis and alderfly rise in season. However, the fish are finicky and patience is needed on this lake.

The early season chironomid hatch can provide some great action. These chironomids are smaller than the ones you will find in Interior lakes and usually range in size from #14–20. The hatch usually starts just after ice off, which can be as early as the end of February or early March. In some years it lasts until late May. The trout like to feed on bloodworms (chironomid pupae) near the bottom, so you will have to get your presentation down deep. Chironomids are not a speedy creature when they are in the water, so the slower your retrieve the better. And because they are so small, the trout tend to sip them in, making detecting a strike difficult.

While the colour of the hatch can vary from day to day, common colours are brown, black and green.

Directions

Morgan Lake is found west of Stave Lake. From the Dewdney Truck Road at Stave Falls, look for the Florence Lake Forest Service Road heading north. That road will bring you past Devils Lake and Sayres Lake. After 16 km, you will reach the south end of Morgan Lake with the last part of the road being quite rough. The road parallels the shoreline of Morgan Lake where you will find several rough trails leading down to the water. An overgrown trail circles the lake providing access to shore fishing. It is also possible to camp at the northwest end of the lake near an old squatter's camp.

Facilities

There are no developed facilities at the lake. However, about halfway along the western shore of the lake is a clearing. It is possible to pitch a tent here (you have to hike a hundred feet or so into the spot) as well as hand launch a canoe or small boat. The nearest official campsite is all the way back down at south end of **Stave Lake**.

To Florence Lake

FSR

Foam Cr

LAKE

abandoned cabin

FLORENCE

6

10m

20

30m

40

45m

30m

20

10m

6

Foam Cr

N

100m   0   100m   200m   300m
— Scale —

To Dewdney Trunk Rd

www.backroadmapbooks.com

Morris Lake

Location: 7.5 km (4.7 mi) west of Harrison Hot Springs
Elevation: 15 m (49 ft)
Surface Area: 8 ha (20 ac)
Max Depth: 7 m (23 ft)
Mean Depth: 4 m (13 ft)
Way Point: 49° 18' 49.8" N, 121° 52' 27.2" W

Fishing

Morris Lake does not receive the same fishing pressure as other lakes off the Harrison West Forest Service Road because the road in is quite rough. In fact, there is no access directly to the lake anymore and you will have to walk in. The lake abuts a slough, which in turn connects to the Harrison River, so it is unique among lakes in this area in that salmon spawn through here.

Morris Lake offers a good cutthroat fishery for trout that can get to 50 cm (20 inches) as well as rainbow trout, some whitefish, catfish and Coho in season. Indeed, the lake is a dark and nutrient rich waterbody that produces some large fish.

Cutthroat love spawning salmon, or rather, they love the results of spawning salmon: eggs in fall and fry in spring. If you are planning on fishing here, that knowledge will help you plan your gear. Fly casters should work imitation salmon eggs in the fall and something that will fake fry in the spring, like a streamer or Muddler Minnow. The lake is home to a good population of stickleback, which is also popular cutthroat chow. Although there is a good chironomid hatch in spring and a small mayfly hatch, the cutthroat and rainbow prefer to eat bigger food, if possible.

Spincasters will find working a spoon that look like a salmon fry in the spring quite rewarding. However a simple bait and bobber set-up (worm or roe) can work wonders here, especially in fall.

There is no really good place to shore fish where the road meets up with the lake, but if you bring a pair of waders, or don't mind getting your feet wet it is a short walk through the water to access some great places to cast from. As you work your way towards the lake's outlet, there is a nice gravel bar and, if the fish aren't biting in the lake, you can work your way down Morris Creek and into the slough area.

Please note that there is a two trout limit and all fish under 30 cm must be thrown back. The lake is quite shallow so it warms in the summer months. Stick to the spring and fall for best results.

Area Indicator

Directions

At the south end of Morris Lake is the Weaver Creek Spawning Channels. You will drive by these, which are found 11 km from the Lougheed Highway (Highway 7) and Morris Valley Road junction. The first spur road heading south, which is about 1 km past the spawning channels, leads to the lake. You will have to walk the last few hundred feet to the lake.

Facilities

Although there is no forest service recreation site at the lake, lots of people camp at the northwest end of the lake. Where the road comes down to the lake, it is possible to launch a small car topper, but remember it is a bit of a carry from the end of the road. An open area on the western shore is a nice place to have a picnic or cast a line from shore.

Those looking to camp in the area will find several recreation sites to choose from. The **Chehalis River Recreation Site** to the southwest and the **Grace Lake Recreation Site** to the northeast are the closest. That is where the similarity ends; Chehalis is a large, often busy site, while Grace Lake is much smaller.

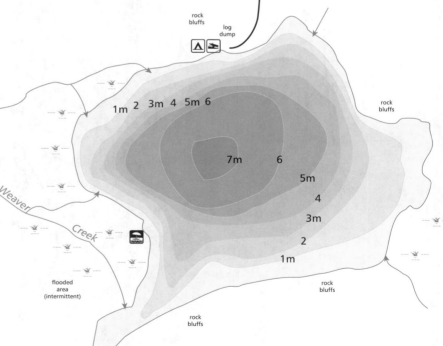

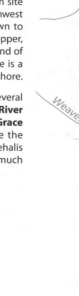

N

100m   0   100m   200m   300m

Scale

Location: 44 km (27 mi) northeast of Cache Creek
Elevation: 782 m (2,566 ft)
Surface Area: 29 ha (72 ac)
Max Depth: 13.7 m (44.9 ft)
Mean Depth: 9.4 m (31 ft)
Way Point: 51° 2' 13.7" N, 120° 53' 35.0" W

Mowich Lake

Area Indicator

N

100m 0 100m 200m 300m 400m 500m

— Scale —

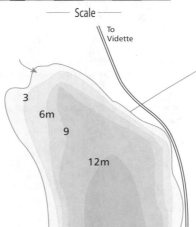

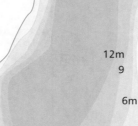

Fishing

Mowich Lake is the first in a series of lakes located in the Dead-man Valley. The lake has reasonably good fishing for rainbow and kokanee that reach 1 kg (2 lbs) in size. Nice fertile shoals are located near the north and south ends of the lake. Productive drop-offs are found around the entire lake.

Trollers should use a Willow Leaf and worm or maggot for both the rainbow and kokanee. Some of the smaller lures such as a Flatfish, Panther Martin or Deadly Dick also work for the rainbow. However, the lake is not that deep and so trolling is restricted to the 3–6 m (10–20 feet) level.

Pink lures such as a Spin-n-Glo and Dick Nite take kokanee. Kokanee are not as aggressive as rainbow. When trolling for kokanee, the trick is to keep your speed down, just fast enough to keep the lure fluttering gently behind the boat. People who have become experts in trolling for kokanee eschew motors in favour of paddles, which allow them to keep the speed down. It also allows them to take one hard stroke every once in a while. Kokanee will often follow a lure for long distances; a short burst of speed can fool them into thinking their prey is making a run for it and trigger a strike response.

Another common bit of wisdom when trolling for kokanee is to troll in an S-pattern. This randomizes the pattern the lure travels in, making it more appealing to the kokanee. Keep a close eye on your rod as kokanee often nibble rather than hitting hard like rainbow sometimes do.

Speaking of rainbow, fly fishers should focus their efforts around the shoals at the north end or the drop-offs around the rest of the lake. In the early season, working a chironomid or bloodworm pattern near the drop off along the shoals will work. As the season progresses, keep an eye out for other hatches.

When hatches overlap, it is sometimes difficult to determine what the fish are feeding on that day, or even in the last few hours; a throat pump can help immensely during these times. That is, if you can manage to catch a fish.

It is possible to fish from shore as the lake drops off rapidly but a float tube or boat is definitely a real benefit. The lake, given its elevation and depth, has a reasonably good fishery during the summer months.

Directions

At the east end of Kamloops Lake, the Trans Canada Highway crosses the Thompson River on a breath-taking bridge. Head north from the bridge and you will soon cross the Deadman River. The Deadman-Vidette Road leads directly north from the west side of the Deadman River Bridge. Stay on the main logging road avoiding any detours. The first lake you will reach is Mowich Lake, which will be on the west side of the road.

Facilities

There are no developed facilities here. Camping or launching at roadside is certainly possible but please avoid private property in the area.

Murtle Lake

Location: 226 km (140 miles) north of Kamloops
Elevation: 1,067 m (3,501 ft)
Surface Area: 7,630 ha (18,854 ac)
Max Depth: 333 m (1,092 ft)
Mean Depth: 107 m (351 ft)
Way Point: 52°9' N, 119°39' W

Fishing

Murtle Lake is a big lake, averaging 3 km (1.8 miles) wide and the north and west arms are about 20 km (12 miles) long. It is the sort of lake that was made for trolling, except for one small thing: there is no road access to the lake. Instead it is world famous for being the largest canoe-only lake in North America with over 100 km of shoreline to explore.

Because it is such a big lake, it is subject to strong winds and storms that roll in from down the mountain. It is a beautiful, but dangerous place and paddlers always have to be alert when on the lake. Never try and outrun a storm; find the nearest place to land and wait out the bad weather.

The calmest period of the day is usually early morning or late evening, and just by coincidence, these are usually the best times to go fishing.

Because of the long portage, the lake sees very little fishing pressure. This is great news. Some of the best fishing happens just out from where you launch your canoe. At the southeast end of the lake, separated from the main lake by a short channel, is the Murtle Lagoon. The lagoon is an almost self-contained area that offers anglers shelter from the wind and some good fishing. There is a second lagoon area, called Diamond Lagoon, where the Murtle River flows out of the lake. Some big rainbow are landed here annually.

Another place that offers great fishing is in the narrows around Fairyslipper Island, especially between the island and the point of land on the south shore.

For spincasters, the best strategy is to set up near one of the many streams that flow into the lake and work these areas using a small spinner or spoon. It is possible to fish from shore by wading out into the water or simply work the drop offs in the canoe. Try using a Krocodile or a Gibbs Croc.

It is still possible to troll from a canoe, although it can be awkward. If trolling, try a lake troll followed by a silver Flatfish or Kwikfish.

Fly fishers will have good luck using chironomids in spring and leeches in summer and fall, but as always, keep your eye out for any hatches that are occurring.

In summer, also keep an eye out for mountain pine beetle flights. These pesky creatures have all but devastated the interior pine forest. From mid-July to mid-August, they leave their tunnels to fly to new trees. Often, they don't make it, and fall instead in the lake. These are just one of many terrestrials that can provide lots of great dry fly fishing.

Area Indicator

Facilities

Murtle Lake is found in **Wells Gray Provincial Park.** There are 69 wilderness/canoe-in tenting sites around the lake, as well as a handful of hiking trails. There are no facilities at the trailhead other than the parking lot.

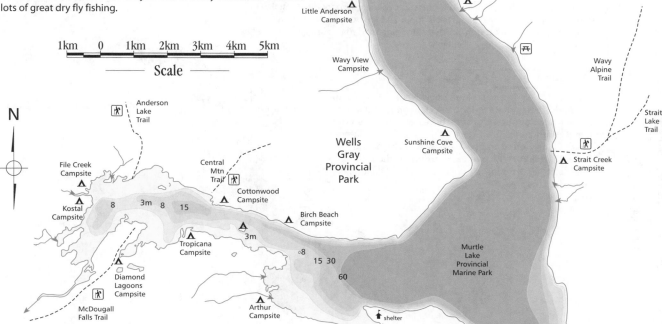

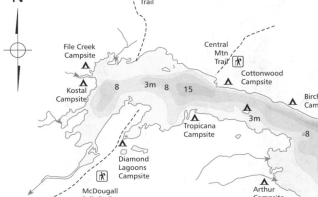

1km   0   1km   2km   3km   4km   5km

Scale

N

Directions

Murtle Lake is found in the eastern reaches of Wells Gray Provincial Park. To get to the lake, travel 226 km (140 miles) north of Kamloops along the Yellowhead Highway (Highway 5). At the town of Blue River, watch for the BC Provincial Park signs pointing the way to Murtle Lake. Turn west and follow the Blue Lake Road for 23 km (14 miles) to the parking lot to Murtle Lake. From here, it is a 2.5 km (1.5 mile) portage to the lake.

East Nahatlatch Lake

Elevation: 335.3 m (1,100 ft)
Surface Area: 152 ha (712 ac)
Max Depth: 61.6 m (202 ft)
Mean Depth: 31 m (102 ft)
Way Point: 49° 59' 54" N, 121° 44' 22" W

West Nahatlatch Lake

Elevation: 335.3 m (1,100 ft)
Surface Area: 143 ha (355 ac)
Max Depth: 28.9 m (95 ft)
Mean Depth: 11.6 m (38 ft)
Way Point: 49° 59' 54" N, 121° 44' 22" W

Area Indicator

Fishing

South of the Stein, east of Harrison and west of the Fraser is an area rarely travelled, hidden behind the seemingly impenetrable face of the Fraser Canyon. But most of the valleys have logging roads heading up them; rarely travelled, but they are there nonetheless.

An exception to this rule is the Nahatlatch Valley. The Nahatlatch River was discovered years ago by white-water kayakers and the area has become one of the more popular kayaking and rafting areas in the region.

Word is getting out to the broader recreation community about this beautiful area. It was recently declared a provincial park and anglers are discovering the good (not great, but good) fishing that the trio of lakes here offer.

The largest and furthest west of these lakes is Nahatlatch Lake. Lakes, actually, as there are two lakes separated by a short channel. Nahatlatch Lake West is much deeper and the water drops off rapidly, allowing the chance to shore fish. Nahatlatch Lake East has more expansive shallows. It is still possible to fish from shore but using a boat is a better idea.

The lake has fair to good fishing for rainbow, dollies and cutthroat in the 20–30 cm (8–12 in) range. The occasional fish grows to 1.5 kg (3 lbs).

The Nahatlatch River flows into the west end of the Nahatlatch Lake West. The lake is initially shallow near the inflow and then drops off quickly. At this location, fly-fishing and spincasting can be quite effective. Other prime holding areas include the many small feeder streams and the inflow and outflow on Nahatlatch Lake East. During spring, the channel separating the two lakes can be dynamite.

Trolling with a lake troll (Willow Leaf and worm) or wet fly (leech, Doc Spratley or green Carey Special) in the spring or fall are your best bets.

There is a single barbless hook restriction at these lakes.

Directions

Nahatlatch Lake is the furthest from the highway of the three lakes in the Nahatlatch River Valley. To reach the lake, drive to Boston Bar on the Trans-Canada Highway (Highway 1). Turn west at the main intersection in Boston Bar, at the sign indicating to North Bend. Continue over the bridge to the west side of the Fraser River and follow the Nahatlatch Forest Service Road and the Nahatlatch Provincial Park entrance. Follow the park directional signs. The Nahatlatch Lake Campsite is about 29.5 km from the North Bend School along a narrow, rough and active logging road that is usually busy Monday thru Friday. Drive carefully.

Facilities

Nahatlatch Lake is located in the new **Nahatlatch Provincial Park.** There are three former recreation sites that offer camping for about 16 groups between. The **Squakum Campground** is the biggest with 11 campsites; the **Salmon Beach Campground** offers two sites and a rustic boat launch, while the **Nahatlatch Lake Campground** is the first in the series offering 3 campsites. The rough access limits trailer access into the area.

East Nahatlatch Lake

West Nahatlatch Lake

Nahatlatch Lake Rec Site

To Hannah Lake

Salmon Beach Campground

Saquakum Campground

Squakum Cr

NAHATLATCH

Nahatlatch

400m 0 400m 1200m 2000m

— Scale —

© Mussio Ventures Ltd.

Nicola Lake

Location: 11 km (7 mi) east of Merritt
Elevation: 637 m (2,090 ft)
Max Depth: 57 m (187 ft)
Mean Depth: 23 m (77 ft)
Way Point: 50° 10' 33" N, 120° 30' 39" W

Fishing

Located a short drive north of Merritt on Highway 5A, Nicola Lake is a narrow, deep lake that was carved out by glaciers during the last ice age. The first settlers in the area settled around Nicola Lake, although now there are few people who live here year-round, mostly in Quilchena, about halfway along the lake. The lake stretches 22 km (13.6 miles) from the Nicola Dam at the lake's southwest end to its northeast end.

The lake is known more for its windsurfing, sailing, boating and swimming than for its fishing, but it does offer fair fishing for small kokanee to 0.5 kg (1 lb) and some rainbow trout to 2 kg (4 lbs) beginning in April and lasting into December. The lake receives fairly light fishing pressure when you think of how easy it is to access.

Trolling is the mainstay of the lake. Roostertails, Mepps, Flatfish, Wedding Bands, Lyman, Dick Nite, Kwikfish and Spin-n-Glo's all work for both the kokanee and rainbow.

The lake is a low elevation lake and the water can get quite warm in summer. When the water begins to warm in the summer months, the rainbow retreat to the depths. You can still catch the rainbow so long as you fish deep, usually in the 10–20 m (30-60 feet) level.

A Willow Leaf with bait (maggots or worm) trolled slowly during June to mid-July is the most effective for the kokanee. Keep the gear down at around 3–6 m (10–20 feet). Kokanee like water that is around 10°C (50°F) and tend to be found in a very narrow band of water. A depth finder will help locate them. Often, the two biggest mistakes made when trolling for kokanee are trolling too fast and trolling too shallow or too deep.

Water from the lake is used for irrigation, but because the lake is so big and deep, drawdown is not a major concern. However, because the lake is long and narrow, winds can get whipping up pretty good. The sailors and windsurfers who come here love the wind, but it can make fishing difficult.

In the winter, burbot fishing is good but the fish must be released. Burbot love cold water, and they are most active when the lake is frozen. Finding them in summer is difficult, but once the lake is frozen, they move into shallower water (less than 8 m/25 ft). Burbot are usually found just off the bottom, so using a weight to get the hook down faster is common. Burbot are piscivorous, and tend to be attracted to smelly meat: cut herring, chicken liver and the like.

Directions

Nicola Lake is found northeast of Merritt. The lake is set in a dry, open landscape where trees are a rarity. To reach the lake, head northeast on Highway 5A from Merritt. The main access is found at Monck Provincial Park. Simply follow the signs to the park.

Facilities

As a popular summer retreat, the lake has a variety of facilities lining the lake from private residences to campgrounds to boat launches. **Monck Provincial Park i**s found on the northern shores of Nicola Lake. It is a popular park, open from mid-May to the end of October and offers 120 campsites and a large day-use area with sandy beach and boat launch. Reservations are recommended through www.discovercamping.com.

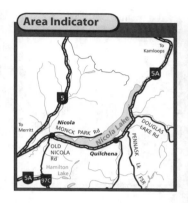

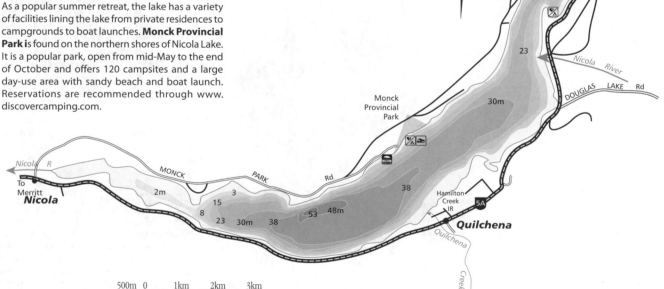

www.backroadmapbooks.com

Nicomen Lake

Location: Manning Park
Elevation: 1,791 m (5,876 ft)
Surface Area: 6 ha (15 ac)
Max Depth: 6 m (20 ft)
Mean Depth: 3 m (10 ft)
Way Point: 49° 13′ 30.8″ N, 120° 51′ 34.0″ W

Area Indicator

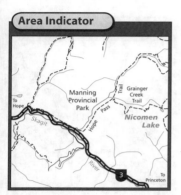

Fishing

Nicomen Lake is one of the hardest lakes to get to of any in this book. But it is also one of the prettiest to get to, especially via the Heather Trail.

More importantly, the lake offers fast and furious fishing for the hardy few willing to invest the time. You can hike to the lake in about ten hours, but since you've gone through all the trouble to get here, you will want to dedicate at least one day to fishing, making this a three day trip, minimum. Surprisingly, it can be quite busy here on summer weekends.

The lake is a high elevation lake, which means the lake isn't accessible, let alone ice free, until mid-June and often not until early July and the snow starts to fly again in early October. This means that the fish only have four ice-free months to prepare for winter and will indiscriminately take anything that even remotely looks like food. We've heard of people landing 60+ fish in a couple hours. As long as your gear is small enough, you can basically throw what you want at these fish.

While most of the fish are small (less than 30 cm/12 inches), a few do get up to 35 cm (14 inches). The bigger fish are found out past the drop offs, but are hard to catch because you will usually have a strike before it sinks deep enough. Seriously!

The lake is fairly brushy on one side, with a scree slope on the other, so shoreline fishing is limited. Since few carry a tube to the lake, you will have to make due.

Directions

There are a couple different ways to get to Nicomen Lake, all of them involving a fairly long walk.

The shortest but hardest access is from the north. To reach this trailhead, take the Crowsnest Highway (Highway 3) east through Manning Park towards Princeton. After crossing the Whipsaw Creek Bridge (about 38 km northeast of Eastgate), take the Whipsaw Creek Forest Service Road southwest until you reach the trailhead for the Hope Pass Trail. The route is overgrown in places and sometimes hard to follow (the sign pointing the way to Nicomen Lake is on the backside of a tree, for instance; watch for it over your shoulder just past Marmot City). If you don't get lost, the trail will bring you to Nicomen Lake in about five hours.

A much longer, but more beautiful approach is from the Blackwall Parking lot near the core of Manning Park. To get to the parking lot, watch for a flashing amber light just past the Manning Park Lodge. Turn left and follow the road to the parking area. From here it is a gorgeous 21 km (13 mile) one-way trip gaining 347 m (1,138 ft) along the Heather Trail. When the wildflowers are in bloom, this is one of the prettiest trails anywhere.

It is also possible to get to the lake along the Hope Pass Trail, but this is the most difficult access.

Facilities

Nicomen Lake rests along the northern boundary of **Manning Provincial Park**. The small lake is a popular backpacking destination. Even during mid-week, there will maybe be one or two other groups. If you are looking for a little more peace and tranquility, there are other rustic camping facilities along the Heather Trail at Buckhorn or Kickinghorse to the south. Further north, both Fido Camp and Marmot City are designated backcountry sites.

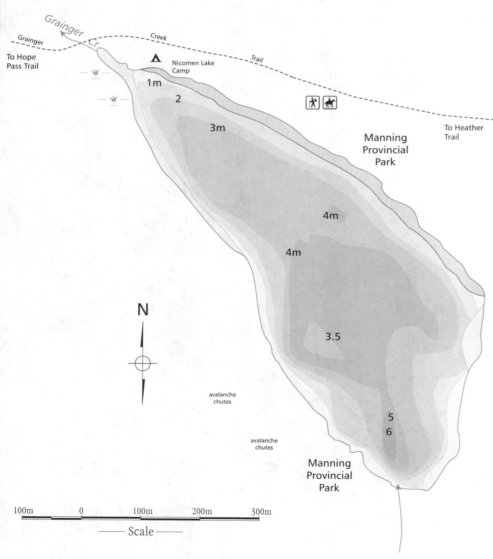

Niskonlith Lake

Location: 6 km (4 mi) southeast of Chase
Elevation: 518 m (1,699 ft)
Surface Area: 405 ha (1,001 ac)
Max Depth: 36.7 m (120.4 ft)
Mean Depth: 19 m (62.3 ft)
Way Point: 50° 46' 55" N, 119° 46' 18" W

Fishing

Located in the ranching country on the northwest side of the Thompson River, Niskonlith Lake is surrounded by fir and pine forests, interspersed with grassy meadows.

The lake is on the side of the Thompson opposite of the Trans Canada and the river serves as a natural barrier to keep the hordes from getting to the lake. As a result, the lake sees light fishing pressure, which in turn keeps the quality of fishing high for those people willing to make the trip.

The lake is a mid-sized lake, a mere puddle compared to nearby Adams Lake and Shuswap Lake, but larger than most of the small lakes that dot the nearby Shuswap Highlands.

Because of its size, the lake is mostly trolled by gear anglers, who use a variety of small spinners and spoons to catch the lake's rainbow trout, which can get up to 1 kg (2 lbs), or kokanee, which can get up to 0.5 kg (1 lb). A Wedding Band, Flatfish or small spinner works wonders with the rainbow, while a Willow Leaf with a maggot, trolling slowly in a broad S-curve pattern should do well for the kokanee.

The lake has large shoal areas at both the north and south ends of the lake. There is also an island near the northeast end of the lake. Fly anglers usually focus their energies around these locations.

In the spring, the shoals see a good chironomid hatch. Work a bloodworm pattern or a chironomid in the shoals near the drop off using a slow retrieve. As the year progresses, there are a variety of hatches, including mayflies, dragonflies and damselflies.

During the summer, the lake warms up and the fish retreat to the cooler waters. While they still can be taken by trolling, fly-fishing is not productive during these times.

In the fall, the fish begin to come into the shoals again, and working an attractor type pattern like a Doc Spratley or a Woolly Bugger can be productive.

There is a 10 hp engine power restriction on the lake.

Directions

Regardless of your approach to the lake, the access is along good gravel roads. From Kamloops, follow the Trans Canada Highway to Pritchard and cross the bridge over the South Thompson River to the Shuswap Road. Continue on this road northeast and within 7 km, the Niskonlith Lake Road heads north. Follow that road for a few kilometers and you will reach the south end of the lake.

From Chase, take the Shuswap Road past Little Shuswap Lake and across the South Thompson River. Soon you will be heading south and the Loakin-Bear Creek Road will appear as the first major intersection on the right. Follow this road and after a few switchbacks, you will be at the Niskonlith Lake Road junction. Take that road and within 2 km you will be at the north end of the lake.

Facilities

Niskonlith Lake Provincial Park is a small park located on the eastern shores of the lake with 29 campsites available on a first-come, first-served basis. Boaters will find a rustic launching area for small cartop boats. The lake is a popular destination for people who enjoy swimming, hiking, canoeing, kayaking, scuba diving and windsurfing. It is even a popular place for birdwatchers in the spring.

Area Indicator

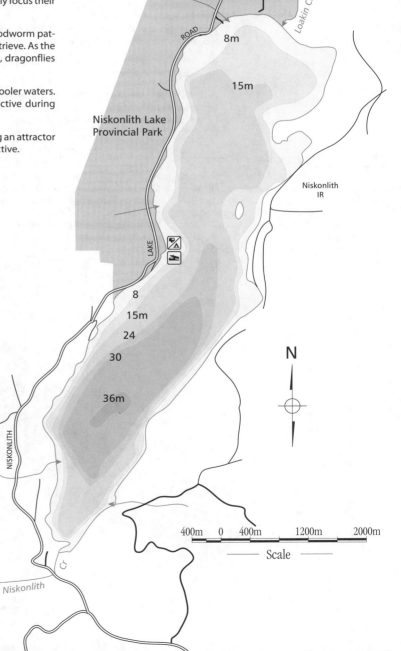

www.backroadmapbooks.com

North Barrière Lake

Location: 29 km (18 mi) south of Vavenby
Elevation: 641 m (2,103 ft)
Surface Area: 520 ha (1285 ac)
Max Depth: 53.9 m (176.8 ft)
Mean Depth: 34.7 m (113.8 ft)
Way Point: 51° 20' 9" N, 119° 50' 20" W

Area Indicator

Fishing

North Barrière Lake is a deep, cold lake, which does not receive a lot of fishing pressure. However, the lake contains a number of species, including Dolly Varden and bull trout (to 5 kg/11 lbs), rainbow trout (to 2 kg/4 lbs) and lake trout (to 4 kg/9 lbs). There are also some smaller brook trout, kokanee, whitefish and lingcod (burbot). Salmon also run through the lake.

Fishing is generally slow from ice-off in early May to when the lake freezes over in November. However, if you hit one of the dollies, rainbow or lake trout, the fish is likely to be big.

The preferred method of fishing is trolling. For the lake trout and dollies try a plug or spoon such as an Apex, Krocodile or large Flatfish. Earlier in the spring and late in the fall, you can fish near the surface in 3–6 m (10–20 ft) of water focusing on the steep drop off areas at the north and south ends of the lake. As the summer approaches, the fish move into the depths so drop your lure to the 9–27 m (30–90 ft) level.

Both the rainbow and the kokanee take a Willow Leaf and worm. Rainbows also strike small lures such as a wedding band, Flatfish or Mepps. Try trolling an attractor type fly for the rainbow like a leech or Doc Spratley.

Fly fishermen will be a little disappointed with this lake. They should focus their efforts at the outflow to the Barrière River located at the west end of the lake. The shallows at the east end also look fairly inviting. However, many simply work the estuary of Vermelin Creek. Chironomid pupae (bloodworms), mayfly nymphs or damselfly nymphs are recommended patterns depending on the local hatch.

While most of the Thompson Lakes that hold burbot are catch and release, North Barrière is an exception. Burbot are not a popular fish for catch and release fishing, but they are an extremely popular eating fish, for those in the know.

Burbot are long, eel-like fish that will never win any beauty contests. They are the only freshwater species of cod and when boiled and dipped in garlic butter they tastes almost exactly like lobster. Thus the nickname "poor man's lobster." Burbot are best fished through the ice since they go deep during the summer. Winter is also the best time to fish for lake trout, too.

Directions

North Barrière Lake is located to the west of Adams Lake and east of Barrière. Head north on Highway 5 from Kamloops to Barrière. Follow the paved Barrière Lakes Road east. Continue up the valley until you cross the Barrier River, where the North Barriere Lake Forest Service Road leads north to the lake. Follow the resort signs and you will soon pass the recreation site.

Facilities

At the mouth of Vermelin Creek the **North Barriere Lake Recreation Site** is a recently upgraded and renamed site. There are now 25 sites, a boat launch, nice beach and trails to explore. The popular family destination charges a fee from mid-May until mid-October. Also in the area is the **North Barriere Lake Resort.** It hosts seven rustic cabins together with 35 campsites, including some with hook-ups, a boat launch and boat rentals.

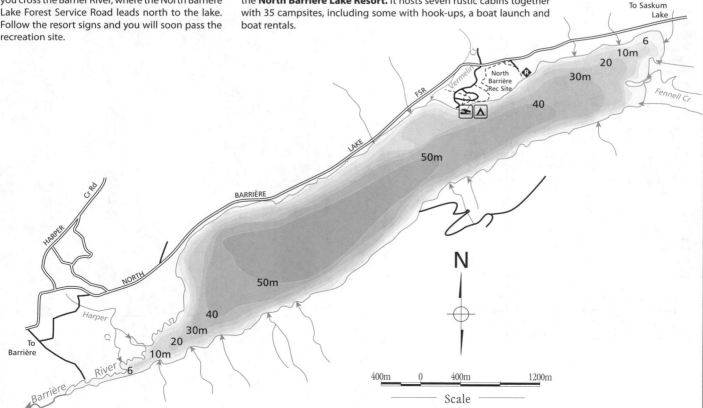

Location: 44 km (27 mi) southeast of Merritt

Paradise & Island Lakes

Fishing

Paradise Lake is a good family fishing lake as it has many small rainbow trout easily caught by fly-fishing or trolling. The odd rainbow grows to 2 kg (4-5 lbs).

The lake has dark, nutrient rich water ideal for insects and aquatic vertebrae. The lake is not that deep and has some nice shallows near the south end. As a result of the depth and the water warming in the summer, the summer doldrums hit the lake with a vengeance.

Trolling the lake in the spring and fall is common. The gear of choice is small lures, a Flatfish or a small lake troll. Trolling an attractor type pattern such as a leech or Doc Spratley should be also considered.

Fly anglers can do well casting a damselfly or dragonfly nymph near the shallows at the south end, especially during the fall, when the fish are more actively seeking out larger food.

In the early spring, fishing a chironomid or bloodworm pattern (a bloodworm is the pupal stage of a chironomid) is quite popular. The trick is to figure out what colour of chironomids are hatching that day. Most people start with dark colours (black, brown, etc), and work their way through their chironomid patterns until they get a hit. Having a net to scoop up a few samples or having a throat pump will help angler's get a bead on what the fish are eating at that moment in time.

Because the water is tannin-stained, working darker colour lures and patterns often tend to produce better. For gear anglers, black and gold spoons and dark coloured Flatfish can be productive. Lures with red and copper also seem to work well.

Area Indicator

Elevation: 1,500 m (4,921 ft)
Surface Area: 136 ha (39 ac)
Max Depth: 12 m (176.8 ft)
Mean Depth: 5.2 m (17 ft)
Way Point: 49° 54'59" N, 120° 16'35" W

Island Lake is found a few minutes to the northwest of Paradise. Although Island is smaller than Paradise, the lake remains cool during the summer and the fishing remains hot.

The lake usually offers up rainbow in the 0.5 kg (1 lb) range, but every once in a while, someone pulls a big fish out of here. Like 4.5 kg (10 lb) big.

It is rumours of big fish like this that makes this lake so popular, but its days on the water without a single catch that makes it so frustrating. Because the lake is so moody, most people give up on it, but the patient angler is usually rewarded, (although they might have to be very, very patient). Very rarely are they rewarded with a giant trout. If the lake is not producing, there are a bunch of other lakes within easy driving distance of Island that are less moody.

Elevation: 1,498 m (4,915 ft)
Surface Area: 46 ha (114 ac)
Max Depth: 7.9 m (25.9 ft)
Mean Depth: 4 m (13 ft)
Way Point: 49° 55'34" N, 120° 17'26" W

Island Lake

3

5m

5m

3

3

FSR

Island Lake Rec Site

LAKE

PARADISE

Paradise Lake Rec Site

Quilchena Cr

1m

4m

3   2

4m

N

Directions

Paradise and Island Lakes are two of 13 lakes located in an area north of the Elkhart Exit on the Okanagan Connector (Highway 97C). After exiting the highway, head north on the Elkhart Road and then Paradise Lake Road. Continue for about 8 km to the end of the pavement (past Elkhart and Bobs Lake) and turn right to access Paradise Lake or left to access Island Lake. Signs point to the various recreation sites and even the resort in the area.

Facilities

Paradise Lake Recreation Site is a small site with space for two groups and a cartop boat launch. Many prefer to stay at the **Paradise Lake Resort,** which offers camping and beautiful cabins for rent.

Island Lake Recreation Site offers space for eight groups with a cartop boat launch. Many of the trees have been removed due to the pine beetle resulting in a more open area. The access into the site is rough and not recommended for RVs or trailers.

To Hwy 97C

To Hwy 97C

Paradise Lake

100m   0   100m   200m   300m   400m   500m

— Scale —

Location: 24km (15mi) southwest of Kamloops
Elevation: 1,451 m (4,760 ft)
Surface Area: 50 ha (123.5 ac)
Max Depth: 29 m (95.1 ft)
Way Point: 50° 31' 34.1" N, 120° 39' 6.8" W

Paska Lake

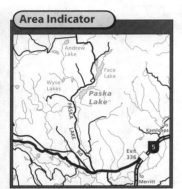

Area Indicator

Fishing

Paska is a small lake that is indicative of many of the lakes in the Kamloops area: small, angler-friendly and productive. The lake sees good hatches of chironomids, caddisflies, mayflies and dragonflies. Add in the big number of freshwater shrimp and you can see why the lake is prime for fly-fishing.

Unlike some of the better known lakes in the area, Paska is not known for producing big fish. Instead, it has lots and lots of small fish, just begging to be caught. However, catches to 1 kg (2 lbs) do occur and are nothing to sneeze at.

The lake is a great family fishing lake, as the fish can usually be caught on most anything. For fly fishers wishing to hone their techniques, this is the perfect lake to practice on. Lots of fish means fast action for anglers, and, because the lake isn't ice free until later in the spring, the fish here are usually more than willing to strike at anything and everything offered.

One of the techniques that can be practiced here is using a chironomid pattern under a strike indicator. This allows the chironomid to hover just off the bottom near the drop off, where the fish cruise into for a quick bite before retreating. The strike indicator not only keeps the chironomid at a set height off the bottom (usually a few inches to a few feet works best), it also, as the name implies, let's the angler know when there is a strike. A variation of this technique, best used when the water is still, is to use a full floating line, allowing the leader to sink down to the right level.

Green is usually the magic colours for flies here, working some standard patterns like damsels and scuds and attractor patterns like Woolly Buggers, Carey Specials, halfbacks and Doc Spratleys. However, sometimes the fish have a thing for reds, too.

Trollers are more successful than fly fishers on hot summer days when fish go for deeper water and the spring's intense hatches of insects have flown. Flatfish, Panther Martin spinners and Dick Nite spoons are all effective on this lake.

The temperature at this high elevation lake usually stays cool enough throughout the heat of summer, which means fishing is decent all season long. In fact, the rainbow trout in these waters are hard fighters when the water is cool. Ice typically comes off Paska Lake in mid-May and fishing continues through until late October.

The lake is not stocked on a regular basis as there is natural recruitment from two small creek systems.

Facilities

The popular **Paska Lake Recreation Site** has been upgraded to allow space for about 50 groups. The semi-open site is RV friendly and charges a fee to camp here from mid-May until mid-October. Anglers can launch small trailered boats here.

Directions

Paska Lake is found off the Meadow Creek Road that links Logan Lake to the Coquihalla Highway (Highway 5). Look for the road about 8 km from Exit 336 on the Coquihalla Highway (Hwy 5). The lake is found another 8.8 km or so up the good gravel Paska Lake Road.

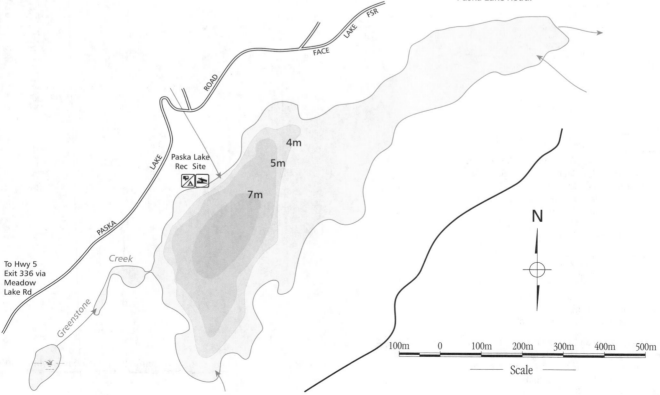

www.backroadmapbooks.com

Pass Lake

Location: 17 km (10 mi) north of Kamloops
Elevation: 961 m (3,153 ft)
Surface Area: 28 ha (69 ac)
Max Depth: 12.8 m (42 ft)
Mean Depth: 7.3 m (24 ft)
Way Point: 50° 50' 29.6" N, 120° 28' 30.5" W

Fishing

The small lake is managed as a trophy trout lake and as a result produces big trout for such a small lake. Many locals in the Kamloops area would pick this as their favourite fly-fishing lake in the region. While Pass Lake is a moody lake, often unwilling to offer up its inhabitants, chances are the fish you find are going to be big. Six 6 kg (12 lb) fish are not out of the question.

Okay, so that's an exception, but the lake is known for its big, wily fish. Even on a good day, don't expect to catch more than a few fish.

The lake is ringed with shoals, and the clear water makes it easy to spot fish in the shallows. Try working on either side of the boat launch or along the northeast shore. The biggest fish are often caught at the northwest end of the lake near the Agricultural Research station.

The small lake offers up a veritable smorgasbord for the local inhabitants, with shrimp and leeches, dragonflies, water boatmen and midges. Preferred flies are black/red and maroon and green leeches and basic black chironomid patterns, with or without a bead head. Earlier in the year, bloodworm patterns work, while Mikaluk sedges are a popular choice during caddis hatches. Using an Elk Hair Caddis or the traditional Tom Thumb can produce well at that time, too.

When fishing in water over 6 metres (20 feet) deep, a chironomid on a fast sinking line can be extremely productive. Chironomid are not the fastest insects in the lake, especially when they're emerging. The fish are suspicious of unnatural movements, so use a slow retrieve. When the trout hit they hit hard, so be prepared, lest you lose your rod.

Spincasters will find it harder to capture the big fish. Most of the bigger fish have been caught at least a couple times before and have become extremely wary of things that don't look exactly like food. Some suggested hardware that might work include Flatfish, Kamloops spoons, a Wedding Band or a Dick Night. Trolling is typically effective, but again, the biggest fish tend to be leery of unnatural behavior, and most food doesn't move in straight lines. Troll slowly, change directions frequently, and vary your speed; a short pause followed by a quick tug is sometimes all that is needed to trigger the predatory instincts of the fish.

Even so, patience is a virtue here. Catching a couple fish in an evening's fishing is fast and furious for this lake.

Area Indicator

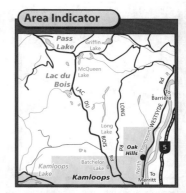

Directions [A]

From downtown Kamloops, cross the Overlander Bridge and follow Fortune Drive to Eighth Street. Head north to Batchelor Drive and follow this road through the residential development to the gravel road and the entrance to Lac Du Bois Provincial Park. Follow Lac Du Bois Road for about 15 km (9 miles) to the McQueen Lake Interpretive Centre. Head west from the main road for about 3 km to find Pass Lake.

Facilities

The **Pass Lake Recreation Site** is a scenic treed site found at the southeast end of the lake. There is space for about 13 camping units here as well as a boat launch.

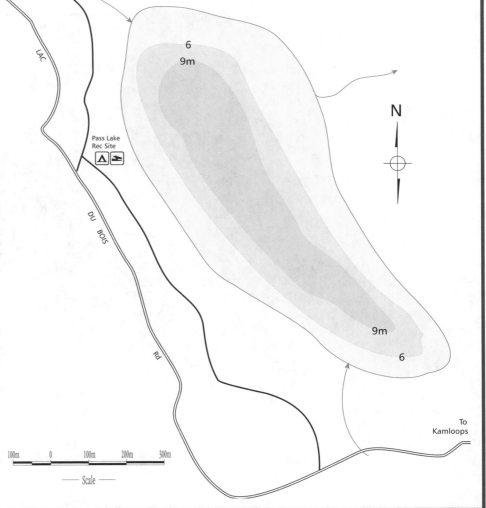

Pass Lake			
Fish Stocking Data			
Year	Species	Number	Life Stage
2011	Rainbow Trout	3,000	Yearling
2010	Rainbow Trout	3,000	Yearling
2009	Rainbow Trout	4,000	Yearling

100m 0 100m 200m 300m

— Scale —

Location: 23 km (14.3 mi) east of Kamloops
Elevation: 769 m (2,523 ft)
Surface Area: 390 ha (964 ac)
Max Depth: 73 m (239.5 ft)
Mean Depth: 29 m (95 ft)
Way Point: 50° 44' 26" N, 120° 6' 49" W

www.backroadmapbooks.com

Paul Lake

Area Indicator

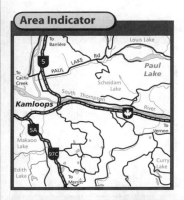

Paul Lake			
Fish Stocking Data			
Year	Species	Number	Life Stage
2011	Rainbow Trout	45,000	Yearling
2010	Rainbow Trout	55,038	Yearling
2009	Rainbow Trout	55,066	Yearling

Fishing

Paul Lake is steeped in fly-fishing history. It was the home base of Bill Nation, the renowned fishing guide who stocked area lakes with trout in the 1920s and 1930s. Paul Lake was one of his favourites. He served clientele from around world, many of which came because of this lake's reputation for big, tough trout.

Today, Nation's Resort on Paul Lake is gone. Homes, cabins and Paul Lake Provincial Park now dot its shores. But the fishing is still good and worth a visit any time of the year. While ice fishing is particularly good during the early part of the winter, the best fishing of the open water period occurs as soon as the ice comes off the lake.

Paul Lake is a top-notch fly-fishing lake. It is a big lake with several deep holes. The expansive marl and mud shoals and weedbeds provide ideal conditions for productive insect hatches.

There is an entire subculture of fly-fishers who do nothing but fish chironomid patterns and this lake offers some prodigious hatches of chironomids. You will need a box full of a various colours and sizes of these little critters, which are the first and last hatches to occur on the lake. It is preferred to use a floating line with a leader long enough to get down to just about the bottom. The retrieve needs to be dead-slow. But when the water is too deep, or the weather is rough, using a full sinking line and a strike indicator will work, too.

However, it is the early hatches of mayflies in mid-May and early June that bring many anglers to Paul Lake each spring. The shoals in front of the condominium development at the lake's west end can see intense fishing action during these mayfly emergences. Shoals are also found at the lake's east end and north shore, just off the provincial park beach. In addition to mayflies, the lake sees prolific hatches of and damselflies. Troll a damselfly nymph pattern slowly behind your boat across the weedbeds in front of the park.

Dry fly-fishing can also be spectacular here on early summer evenings.

The lake is stocked heavily with rainbow trout. Many are Blackwater trout, which are piscivorous by nature and stocked to control illegally introduced populations of red-sided shiners. Flies, lures and spoons that mimic the swim or look of small shiners will often capture the attention of these big fish. Other good patterns include bead head Hares Ears, Adams, and shrimp patterns.

If you're not into fly-fishing don't fret, trolling lake trolls or lures like a Flatfish or Krocodile can work as well. Spincasting with a bait and bobber or small spinners can also be effective.

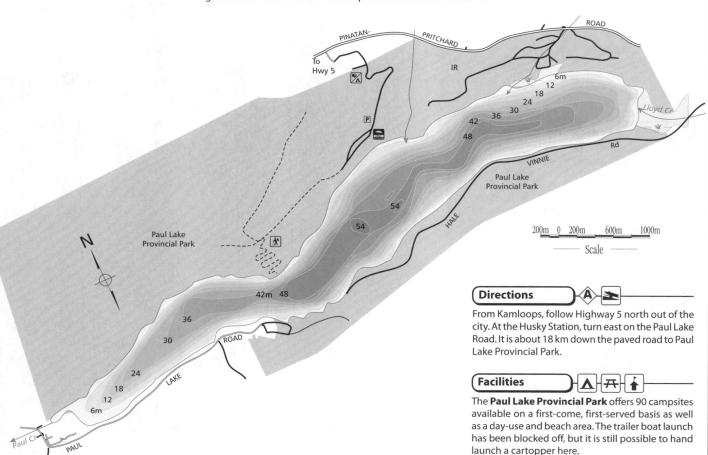

Directions

From Kamloops, follow Highway 5 north out of the city. At the Husky Station, turn east on the Paul Lake Road. It is about 18 km down the paved road to Paul Lake Provincial Park.

Facilities

The **Paul Lake Provincial Park** offers 90 campsites available on a first-come, first-served basis as well as a day-use and beach area. The trailer boat launch has been blocked off, but it is still possible to hand launch a cartopper here.

www.backroadmapbooks.com

Pavilion Lake

Location: 29 km (18 mi) north of Lillooet
Elevation: 805 m (2,641 ft)
Surface Area: 262 ha (647 ac)
Max Depth: 56.1 m (184 ft)
Mean Depth: 25.3 m. (83 ft)
Way Point: 50° 51' 47" N, 121° 44' 11" W

Fishing

Pavilion Lake is a gorgeous little piece of water along Highway 99 that has recently become a bit of a phenomenon internationally. The lake is part of Marble Canyon Provincial Park, and in the last few years has been studied by students from local schools, from the University of British Columbia and scientists from NASA.

What interest does an organization dedicated to Space Exploration have in a tiny lake that sits in the southern interior of BC? Microbes.

Pavilion Lake is a deep lake, more than 60 m (200 ft) at its deepest. Scientists have discovered unique structures called microbialites that they claim could be as old as 11,000 years.

How does this affect anglers on the lake? In a couple ways. In 2008 scientists and astronauts took a submarine down to the floor of the lake; research trips like this may happen again in the future, and access to the lake might be impacted during these study times.

Secondly, because these structures are so unique and so fragile, anglers are asked not to use downrigger gear or anchors in the lake.

With those concerns aside, Pavilion is a great fishing lake. Not as fast as some, but usually consistent throughout the year. The setting makes up for the slow stretches.

Pavilion Lake has fair fishing for rainbow to 1.5 kg (3 lbs) primarily by trolling a lake troll with a Wedding Band and worm. A Hotshot or Flatfish can often trick the bigger guys.

The water is crystal clear, and usually doesn't turn over because the lake is so deep. It is a high elevation lake that fishes well through the ice-free season, with the fish concentrated in the shallows during spring and fall. During the heart of summer, the fish move into the deeper water and anglers should follow suit.

There are some open areas along the northeastern shore, and spincasters will have fair to good luck casting a variety of spoons and spinners, or even a bobber and worm.

Fly anglers will find the lake has a good amount of shoal area, scattered around the lake. There is no one area where the shoal is concentrated, so the fishing is spread out around the lake. There is a great damselfly hatch, a fairly good mayfly hatch and the occasional chironomid hatch. At other times of the year, try casting an attractor type fly near one of the creek estuaries or at the outflow at the northwest end of the lake.

Area Indicator

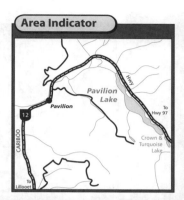

Pavilion Lake			
Fish Stocking Data			
Year	Species	Number	Life Stage
2011	Rainbow Trout	40,000	Yearling
2010	Rainbow Trout	40,000	Yearling
2009	Rainbow Trout	40,000	Yearling

Directions

Pavilion Lake is located east of the tiny First Nations community of Pavilion on Highway 99. Take Highway 99 north from Lillooet winding along the east banks of the Fraser River until you reach Pavilion. Continue along the highway from Pavilion until you reach the northwest end of Pavilion Lake.

Alternatively, drive north of Cache Creek on Highway 97 until you reach the junction with Highway 99. Turn left and follow the highway until you reach the lake.

Facilities

At the southeast end of the lake is the **Marble Canyon Provincial Park**. There are a total of 30 campsites available on a first-come, first-served basis. Picnicking, swimming, fishing and hiking are the primary attractions to the park. Anglers can also stay at **Sky Blue Waters Resort**, which features seven rustic cabins, RV campsites and a picnic area. Boat and canoe rentals are also available.

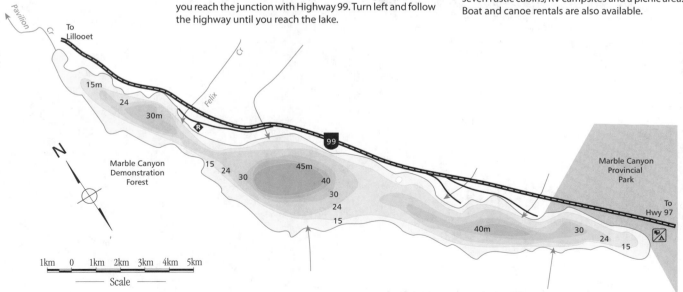

Pennask Lake

Elevation: 1,426 m (4,678 ft)
Surface Area: 959 ha (2,370 ac)
Max Depth: 50 m(164 ft)
Mean Depth: 21 m (69 ft)
Way Point: 50° 0'5" N, 120° 7'44"W

Area Indicator

Jackson Lake			
Fish Stocking Data			
Year	Species	Number	Life Stage
2010	Rainbow Trout	2,000	Fry

Pennask Lake
No Record of Stocking

Jackson Lake

Elevation: 1,438 m (4,718 ft)
Surface Area: 38 ha (94 ac)
Max Depth: 15.8 m (51.8 ft)
Mean Depth: 4.3 m (14.1 ft)
Way Point: 50° 1'28" N, 120° 6'11"W

Fishing

You may never have fished Pennask Lake, but there's a good chance you've caught a fish from here. One of the biggest rainbow trout hatcheries in the province is located here and these fish are taken to lakes across the province.

Pennask is a large lake with a fly-fishing only restriction. It produces consistently for rainbows in the 0.5–1 kg (1–2 lb) range. The lake is said to have the largest run of spawning, wild rainbow in the country, if not the world. As a result the fish don't get very big. Despite the fast action, the lake only receives moderate fishing pressure because of difficult access and fly only regulations.

The most consistent fly patterns seem to be shrimp or mayfly imitations or a #12 black Doc Spratley. However, since the fish are plentiful, just about any fly in your tackle box works making this a good training lake.

Nearby Jackson Lake offers good fishing for rainbow trout to 2 kg (4 lbs). However, they average under a pound. The small lake has a distinct hole near the western most bay. As summer approaches, the fish tend to hang out around the deep hole off the western most bay so you can try sinking a line into the depths. Nice shoal areas are found at the northeast as well as at the south end of the lake. These are the areas to focus on in the spring and fall. Try casting a lure with bait (Deadly Dick, Panther Martin, Flatfish or Mepps) or casting a fly (caddisfly, leech or dragonfly pattern).

For both lakes, fishing remains active all the way from ice off in early May to when the lake freezes over in November. The high elevation helps maintain a summer fishery. In the spring and fall, focus on the shoals and drop-offs. As summer approaches try deeper or wait until dusk to catch a cruising trout looking for an easy meal near the shallows.

Directions

To reach the lake, leave the Okanagan Connector (Highway 97C) at the Sunset Exit. Follow the road east for about 6 km where the Bear Creek Forest Service Road branches north. Follow this road under the Connector and look for the road leading north to the Pennask Lake Provincial Park. It is found about 13.5 km from the exit. Unfortunately, the access road into the lake is very rough and a 4wd vehicle with a lot of patience is recommended.

Jackson Lake is best reached by taking a boat from the north end of Pennask Lake. It is about a kilometre walk or portage. A trail system also leads to the lake from the north. A copy of the Backroad Mapbook for the Thompson Okanagan is recommended when exploring remote lakes like that.

Facilities

Pennask Lake Provincial Park is a difficult to access park on the southeast shore of the lake. There are about 25 rustic, user maintained campsites, a few boat access sites and even a day-use area and rough boat launch. Please pack out what you pack in and go prepared for a wilderness camping experience.

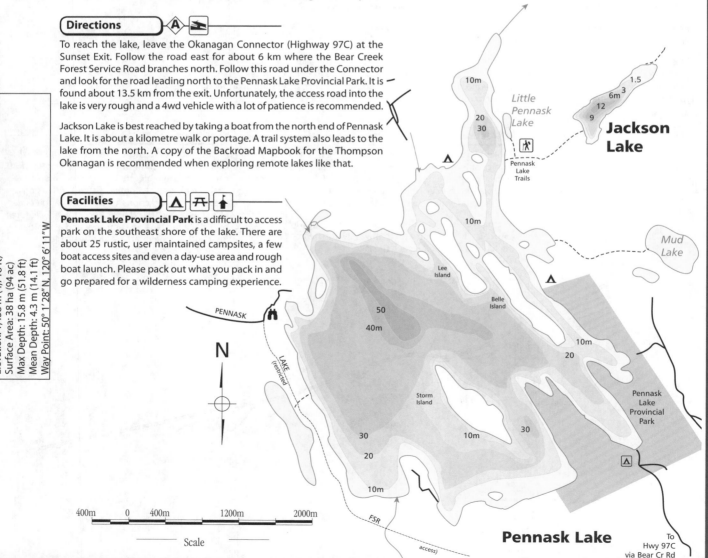

N

| 400m | 0 | 400m | 1200m | 2000m |

Scale

© Mussio Ventures Ltd.

Peter Hope Lake

Location: 39 km (24 mi) northeast of Merritt
Elevation: 1,095 m (3,593 ft)
Surface Area: 116 ha (287 ac)
Max Depth: 33 m (108 ft)
Mean Depth: 12 m (39 ft)
Way Point: 50° 17′ 38″ N, 120° 18′ 59″ W

Fishing

Peter Hope Lake is a man-made lake, dammed in the 1930s for irrigation purposes. In 1942, the lake was stocked with rainbow and has been a consistent producer of large Kamloops trout ever since.

The lake has deep, clear water surrounded by extensive marl flats ideal for insect life. The shoreline is reed covered and there are two submerged islands with deep channels between them. Can the terrain be any better for fly-fishing?

The lake is rumoured to have some very large Kamloops trout exceeding 20 pounds. These may or may not exist, but trout are regularly caught in 2 kg (4 lb) range. If you get one in the 3 kg (6–7lbs) range you will have bragging rights for the weekend.

Beginning after ice off in early May, the rainbow are seen cruising the extensive flats so you should focus on the fringe area between the flats and the deep water. Chironomid pupae work all season on a sinking line retrieved slowly from the depths. Because the water here is so clear, vegetation will grow down to about 6 metres (20 feet), bringing along with it a variety of aquatic insects, especially the aforementioned chironomids. Anglers in Peter Hope Lake tend to use long leaders, in the 5–7 metre (18–22 foot) range. For anglers who have cut their teeth fishing rivers, this long leader will seem awkward and ungainly. However, it seems to improve success, especially when fishing a chironomid or bloodworm.

Mayfly, dragonfly nymphs and damselfly nymphs produce beginning in June. Caddisfly patterns are also productive in late June-early July. At this time, fishing at dusk can be excellent.

In the summer months, the fish retreat to the depths. Weighted dragonfly nymphs or bloodworm patterns on a fast sinking line cast along the drop-off at the edge of the shoals is very productive. By mid-September to late October, the fish begin cruising the flats again and you should move back to the fringes.

To help maintain the fishery, the lake is closed for ice fishing, has a bait ban, requires a single barbless hook and has a daily limit of two rainbow.

Directions

Peter Hope Lake is found northeast of Nicola Lake in cattle country. To reach the lake, begin on Highway 5A from either Kamloops or Merritt. 3 km south of Stump Lake, or 10 km from the north end of Nicola Lake, you will find the Peter Hope Road leading east. Drive east on the road and stay on the main road all the way to the north end of the lake. It is about 8 km from the highway to the recreation site.

Facilities

The **Peter Hope Recreation site** is found in a partially treed area at the north end of the lake. It has room for 24 groups and a cartop boat launch. This is an enhanced site, meaning there is fee to camp here from May 1st to mid-October.

The old lodge has since been turned into a time share venture. If you like fishing here, why not buy in?

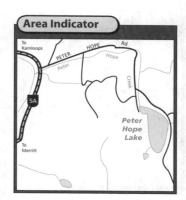

Area Indicator

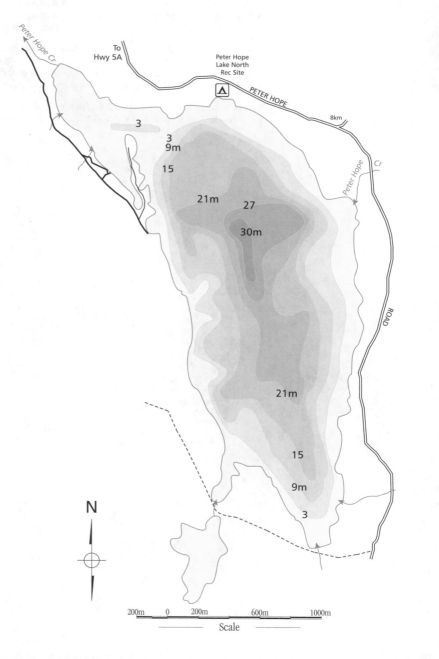

Peter Hope Lake			
Fish Stocking Data			
Year	Species	Number	Life Stage
2011	Rainbow Trout	30,000	Yearling
2010	Rainbow Trout	29,928	Yearling
2009	Rainbow Trout	12,045	Yearling

| | Location: 26 km (16 mi) east of Chilliwack
Elevation: 1,357 m (4,452 ft)
Surface Area: 18 ha (44 ac)
Max Depth: 34 m (111 ft)
Mean Depth: 13 m (43 ft)
Way Point: 49° 3' 50.0" N, 121° 37' 43.0" W |

www.backroadmapbooks.com

Pierce Lake

Area Indicator

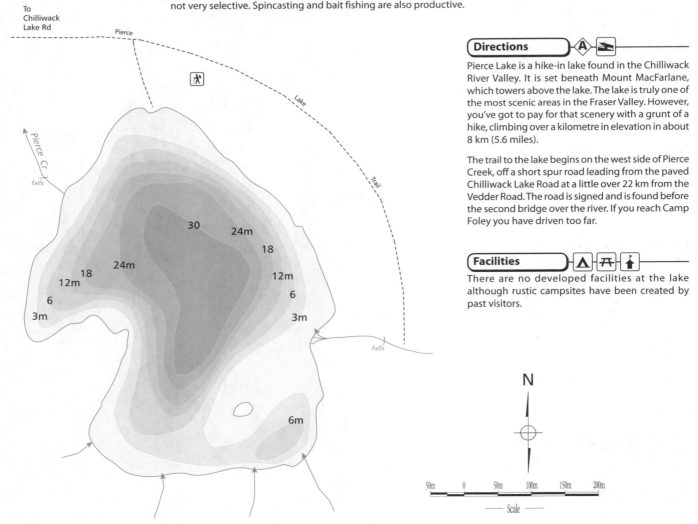

Fishing

First the good news. Pierce Lake is considered an excellent fly-fishing lake for rainbow trout that (some claim) grow to 50 cm (20 in) in size.

Now the bad news. To get to the lake, you have to climb more than 1 km up across an 8 km (5.6 mile) trail that will tax the fittest of hikers.

However, the lake itself is probably one of the prettiest lakes you will ever have the good fortune to fish in; an azure lake set beneath some dramatic peaks. While the lake isn't above treeline, it is close to it and there are very few trees around the lake's rocky shores.

The high elevation lake offers a late season fishery, beginning in June and running until October. The trout are generally small in size (in reality a trout over 25 cm/10 in here is considered big) and there are even Dolly Varden here…a rarity for a mountain lake. Unfortunately both are not found in great numbers.

A float tube is a very good option if you want to sample the deeper waters. Most people are unwilling to go to the effort of hauling a tube, choosing instead to fish from shore. Although the shoreline is open, the often still water makes it difficult to fish from shore because anglers approaching the edge of the lake often spook the fish. If you have made the trek up to the lake, don't go stomping up to the edge of the water and scare all the fish away.

The lake is set in a depression. Take a few minutes to observe the lake from the top of the low ridge that surrounds the lake, watching for trout working the edge of the lake. Trout often hold in the same spot for a long time and then dart at unsuspecting prey. If you do see fish in the shallow, approach cautiously and cast from as far back as you feel comfortable. If you spook the fish into deep water, you're going to have to work much harder to catch them.

Most of the usual trout fly patterns (Doc Spratleys, Adams, Elk Hair Caddis, etc.) work at Pierce Lake because the fish are not very selective. Spincasting and bait fishing are also productive.

Directions

Pierce Lake is a hike-in lake found in the Chilliwack River Valley. It is set beneath Mount MacFarlane, which towers above the lake. The lake is truly one of the most scenic areas in the Fraser Valley. However, you've got to pay for that scenery with a grunt of a hike, climbing over a kilometre in elevation in about 8 km (5.6 miles).

The trail to the lake begins on the west side of Pierce Creek, off a short spur road leading from the paved Chilliwack Lake Road at a little over 22 km from the Vedder Road. The road is signed and is found before the second bridge over the river. If you reach Camp Foley you have driven too far.

Facilities

There are no developed facilities at the lake although rustic campsites have been created by past visitors.

© Mussio Ventures Ltd.

Pillar Lake

www.backroadmapbooks.com

Location: 52 km (32 mi) east of Kamloops
Elevation: 889 m (2,917 ft)
Surface Area: 41 ha (101 ac)
Max Depth: 16 m (52.5 ft)
Mean Depth: 10.2 m (33.5 ft)
Way Point: 50° 35' 42" N, 119° 38' 29" W

Fishing

Pillar Lake is found north of the town of Falkland and is a favourite with local anglers. This popular family fishing lake may not be very big, but it has an excellent sport fishery that is not too heavily fished.

Trout in this lake can reach up to 1 kg (2 lbs). Although they are rarely larger than this, they are known to be extremely active. The lake, which is stocked each year by the Freshwater Fisheries Society of BC, received 11,000 Pennask rainbow trout in 2006.

Pillar Lake offers steep drop offs and deep holes ideal for trolling. For fly-fishers, chironomids produce in the early season with damselfly and dragonfly imitations performing best toward the summer months. Most fly-anglers target the shoals at the north end of the lake.

Chironomid imitations are best fished close to the bottom of shoals or near drop off areas. A floating line and enough of a leader to get down to just above the bottom is one of the most popular techniques. Usually, just allowing the wind to blow your line around is more than enough movement.

When the pupae are ascending, the fish begin to feed voraciously. A typical chironomid emergence sees thousands of these tiny insects rising to the surface and trout eat them like popcorn. The major hatches tend to occur between 10 am and 3 pm.

Many people start to retrieve too soon, not allowing the fly enough time to sink down to the right depths and then retrieve too fast. You are trying to imitate a chironomid, which aren't the fastest swimmers in the pond, so to speak. During this time, you want to retrieve very slowly using a hand-twist method. If it takes you less than 10 minutes to retrieve a 20 metre (60 foot) cast, you're moving to fast.

The lake is not all about fly-fishing. It is possible to troll small lures and spinners, or cast with spinning gear from a boat or from shore to catch the feisty rainbow.

The lake is closed to ice fishing in the winter and has a motor-size restriction of no larger than 10 hp during the open water season. By first day of the season (May 1), the lake is usually ice-free. The lake does get warm during the summer, impacting fishing through late July and most of August. By September, the fishing is usually on the upswing, just in time for another chironomid hatch.

Directions

From Kamloops, follow the Trans Canada Highway east to Highway 97. Head south on this quieter highway and drive for about 45 km to Falkland. At Chase-Falkland Road, turn north and drive for 12 km to Pillar Lake. The road is paved for most of the way.

Facilities

While there is a provincial park near Pillar Lake, it is a day-use park set aside to protect the stone pillar that the lake is named for. It is a 15 minute walk to view the pillar and the trail is the only facility in the park. There is a public day-use cartop boat launch is located near the south end of the lake. The nearest public camping is at **Chase Creek Recreation Site**, a five unit campsite set in the forest alongside Chase Creek, just off the Chase-Falkland Road.

Pillar Lake Fish Stocking Data			
Year	Species	Number	Life Stage
2011	Rainbow Trout	11,000	Yearling
2010	Rainbow Trout	11,000	Yearling
2009	Rainbow Trout	11,000	Yearling

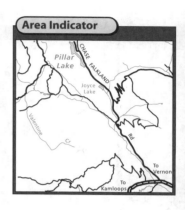

Area Indicator

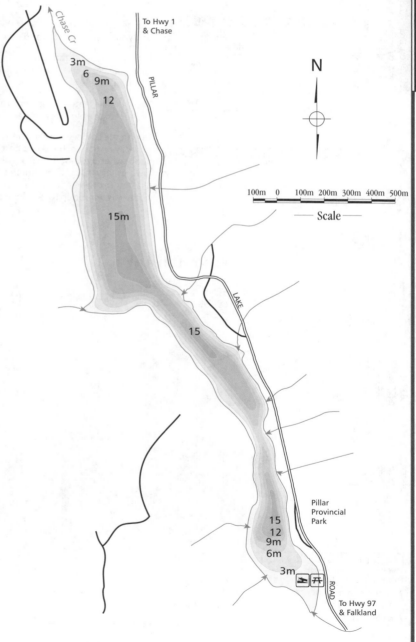

Pinantan & Little Pinantan Lakes

Pinantan Lake

Area Indicator

Elevation: 863 m (2,831 ft)
Surface Area: 68 ha (168 ac)
Max Depth: 18.5 m (60.7 ft)
Mean Depth: 10.6 m (34.8 ft)
Way Point: 50° 43' 22" N, 120° 1' 18" W

Pinantan Lake Fish Stocking Data			
Year	Species	Number	Life Stage
2011	Rainbow Trout	4,000	Yearling
2010	Rainbow Trout	4,000	Yearling
2009	Rainbow Trout	4,000	Yearling

Little Pinantan Lake
No Record of Stocking

Little Pinantan Lake

Elevation: 864 m (2,835 ft)
Surface Area: 10 ha (25 ac)
Max Depth: 12 m (39.4 ft)
Mean Depth: 6.6 m (21.7 ft)
Way Point: 50° 43' 33" N, 120° 0' 39" W

Fishing

Pinantan Lake is one of the region's best family fishing lakes. Not only is it easy to access, but there are plenty of trout and various places to find them to make a day on the water pure fun.

Natural spawning allows these trout to reproduce naturally, which normally results in tiny fish. But not so in Pinantan Lake. The abundance of insects and aquatic invertebrates provide enough food to support big populations of trout. With lots of trout up to 0.75 kg (1.5 lbs) and several reports of 1.5–2 kg (3–4 lb) trophies, even serious anglers will be interested in this lake.

Another explanation for such large fish could be the population of red-sided shiners. The Freshwater Fisheries Society of BC stocks Pinantan Lake with fish eating Blackwater rainbow trout to help control the small minnows that were illegally introduced decades ago. The shiners are a good source of nutrition for the Blackwater trout, and as a result, they tend to grow quite large.

Fly-fishers should take their cues from the abundant hatches of chironomids, mayflies, caddis flies, damselflies and dragonflies as imitations should prove successful. Cast towards the shoals and drop offs at the lake's edges or around the islands.

The deep hole in the middle of the lake is popular with trollers. Use Flatfish, inline spinners, lake trolls or try small silver spoons and Rapalas to lure one of the trout.

Little Pinantan is attached to the larger lake by way of a channel. It is a much smaller and quieter lake, but still offers great fishing. Because it is smaller, the lake does tend to suffer from the summer doldrums sooner.

The little lake features good drop offs all the way around, but two of the best places to fish are near the channel to the big lake and near the inflow of Paul Creek.

During the cold season, Pinantan Lake is popular with ice-fishermen. Bring your auger and lawn chair for a day on the ice. The lake is best fished earlier in the season, as soon as the ice is hard. Later in winter rainbow tend to slow down as the oxygen level in the water drops. The best ice fishing is in the shallows, usually in less than 4 metres (12 feet) of water. Because the noise of the ice auger can scare fish, it is best to drill a series of holes at the start of the day and then return to the first hole to start fishing. If a hole is unproductive for more than 15 minutes, move on to the next.

Directions

From Kamloops, head north on the Yellowhead Highway (Highway 5). Turn right at Paul Lake Road (look for the Husky Station on the right) and drive for 20 to 30 minutes down this paved road to the small residential community of Pinantan Lake. You will pass Paul Lake Provincial Park along the way.

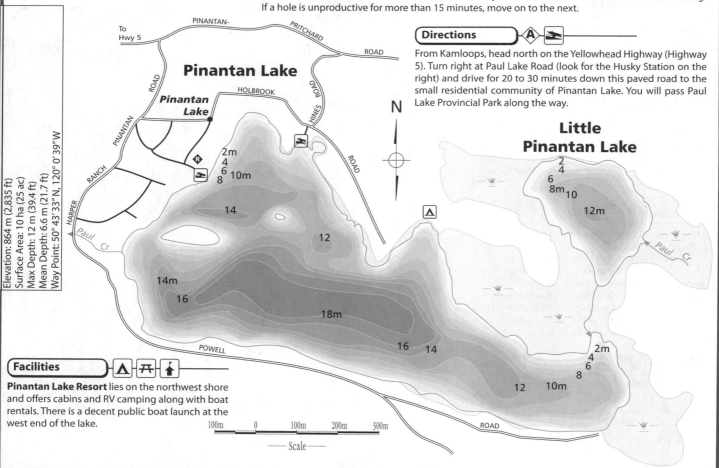

Facilities

Pinantan Lake Resort lies on the northwest shore and offers cabins and RV camping along with boat rentals. There is a decent public boat launch at the west end of the lake.

Pitt Lake

Location: 16 km (10 mi) north of Maple Ridge
Elevation: 3 m (10 ft)
Surface Area: 5382 ha (13298 ac)
Mean Depth: 46 m (151 ft)
Max Depth: 142.6 m (468 ft)
Way Point: 49°25'00"N, 122°32'00"W

Fishing

Pitt Lake is one of the biggest lakes in the area, stretching 24 kilometres back into the Coastal ranges. The south end of the lake is found in the Fraser Valley floodplains, but you don't have to go very far back to be surrounded by some of the most rugged, mostly untouched scenery that the Lower Mainland has to offer.

The lake can get quite windy. Add that to the many large, shallow sandbars and floating debris and you have a lake that needs to be treated with respect. Boaters need to follow the navigational aids at the south end of the lake to avoid the shallows.

The lake holds rainbow and cutthroat trout, as well as sturgeon and Dolly Varden. Steelhead and salmon pass through the lake on their way to the Pitt River spawning grounds, one of the last great returns in the Lower Mainland.

The lake is known for it's year round fishing, starting in early spring, when you can find plenty of fish working the creek mouths and shorelines using a fly. Brighter presentations help, since the waters are often murky in the early spring. During this time, salmon fry make their way down the lake on the way to the ocean, providing food for the trout and dollies that reach 2.5 kg (5 lbs). One of the best places to work is just up from Grant Narrows, where the big fish lie in wait for the fry to get caught up in the shifting tide. Fishing this area at slack time, especially at the crack of dawn, can be some of the most productive early spring fishing around.

Also in spring (April–May), sea-run cutthroat cruise to the north end of the lake looking for salmon fry. Try fly-fishing a silver minnow imitation, bait fishing or casting a small silver lure to land one of these prized fish. But remember to use only single barbless hooks and release all wild trout and char at the head of the lake.

The tidal lake can be productive in summer. Fly anglers will note a prominent hatch of mayflies that can lead to some fast action for anglers, while in fall, the fish's main diet is stickleback; using a green Woolly Bugger can work, but a stickleback imitation is your best bet.

Trolling can be extremely productive as well, using a downrigger in the deeper sections to find dollies. The stickleback like to hang around structure, which draws the big fish, so working around pilings, fallen trees and underwater points will be quite productive, as will bays and around the mouths of feeder creeks.

Directions

To get to Pitt Lake, take the Lougheed Highway over the Pitt River Bridge. Turn north on Harris Road, where a large sign points to Pitt Lake and Grant Narrows Regional Park. Turn right on McNeil Road, then left on 132nd Avenue and left again at Neaves Road. Neaves turns to Rennie. Follow the road to the end.

Facilities

Most people getting on to Pitt Lake launch at **Grant Narrows Regional Park**. There are also canoe rentals here. Those looking to camp will find a variety of rustic campsites along the shores of the lake. The dock at the north end is used by anglers wishing to fish the river.

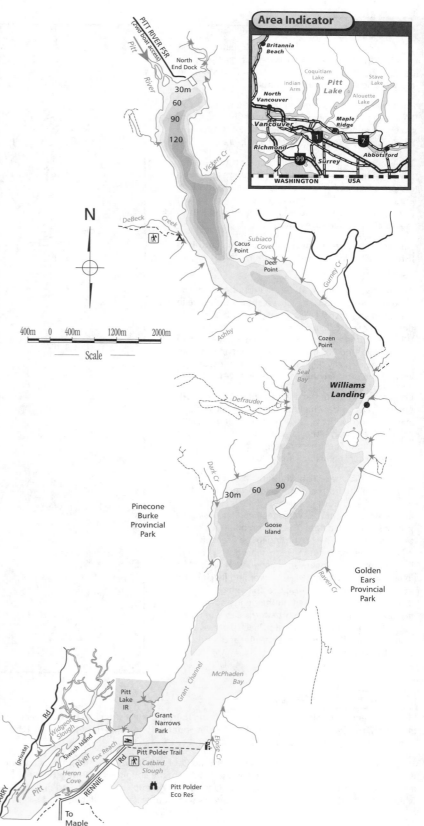

Area Indicator

Location: North of Port Coquitlam
Stream Length: 74 km (46 mi)
Geographic: 122°38'00"W, 49°34'00"N

Pitt River

Fishing

The Pitt River, by some accounts, is the greatest fishing river in North America. Not the lower Pitt, but the Upper Pitt that is. This wild, braided stream offers stunning scenery and endless holes to sample.

The river sees strong runs of Coho, sockeye and steelhead and small but growing returns of Chinook. There is a native population of rainbow trout and sea run and resident populations of cutthroat and bull trout.

The year starts off with a steelhead return, which actually begins in December and carries through to the end of April. Steelhead are one of the most prized sportfish around–aggressive, strong and big, getting up to 9 kg (20 lbs). All the steelhead on the Pitt are wild, which means catch and release only.

Just as the steelhead runs tapers off, the cutthroat fishing really picks up, with sea-run cutthroat returning to the river.

Around the end of July until the end of August, the sockeye return. This is the largest strain of sockeye in the world, averaging 4–5 kg (8–10 lbs) with some getting up to 7 kg (15 lbs). When they hit the Pitt, they are still fresh–chrome coloured and full of fight. The run size averages around 100,000 fish and how many you can catch in a day really depends on your stamina, as they willingly hit most anything you toss at them.

Coho returns start at the end of September and continue into December. This is the largest run of wild Coho in the province, with over 20,000 fish returning annually. As with the sockeye, they arrive in the Pitt still bright and full of fight. The fish average 4–6 kg (8–12 lbs), with some monsters breaking 9 kg (20 lbs).

In addition to these fish, the Pitt has lots of trout. Rainbow and cutthroat can be found in the system year round. Bull trout can get up to 7 kg (15 lbs) and are sometimes confused with steelhead because they put up such a good fight. The sea run bull trout spend ten months in the river, returning to the ocean in early may for two months. In the early season, egg sucking leech patterns and Squamish poachers work well, while in late spring and summer, start working leech or fry patterns. When the sockeye are spawning, all three 'trout' species of trout feed on their eggs, so work an egg pattern, although leech patterns can work well, too. In fall and winter, minnow and leech patterns work well, while dry flies that imitate mayflies and caddis are a real treat for the rainbow.

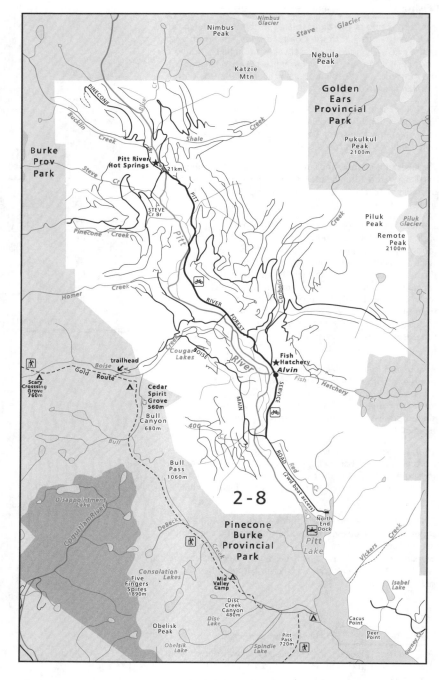

Directions

The Pitt River can only be accessed by water or air. There is a short stretch of river connecting Pitt Lake to the Fraser River known as the lower Pitt, but this is not what most people are referring to when they talk about the Pitt River.

To get to the Upper Pitt, you will need to get onto Pitt Lake. The most common boat launch is at Grant Narrows Regional Park. Follow the signs from the Lougheed Highway (Highway 7) after crossing over the Pitt River Bridge. It is a long boat ride up to the north end of the lake where there is a dock that can be used by anglers on foot or smart enough to bring a bike.

Facilities

This is a wilderness area and bears are a real concern to those spending time in the area. There is random camping wherever you can pitch a tent, but most people who fish here stay at the **Pitt River Lodge**, www.pittriverlodge.com. A popular side trip is the **Pitt River Hot Springs** found well up the valley. The Vancouver Coast and Mountains Backroad Mapbook describes access into this spectacular site in detail.

www.backroadmapbooks.com

Location: Manning Park
Elevation: 1,741 m (5,712 ft)
Surface Area: 6 ha (15 ac)
Max Depth: 16 m (52 ft)
Mean Depth: 7 m (23 ft)
Way Point: 49° 5′ 19.4″ N, 120° 57′ 16.2″ W

REGION 2

Poland Lake

Poland Lake

Fishing

Poland Lake is a high elevation lake found well off the beaten track in Manning Provincial Park. Getting to the lake involves a fair bit of effort, but you will be rewarded with fast fishing for the lake's small rainbow.

The lake isn't ice-free until mid-June at the earliest. As a result, the fish that inhabit the lake are usually voracious eaters, hitting most anything you're willing to throw at them. Of course, the rainbow don't usually get much bigger than 20 cm (8 inches), but there are lots of them.

The pothole lake has expansive shallows ringing the shoreline. Although this might make casting to the drop off difficult, fly-fishing these shallows can be great. Because the lake remains cool during the summer, you are more likely to find fish cruising the shallows, especially during the early morning or late evening, when the sun isn't shining directly on the lake. And because the ice-off season is so short, the trout feast on whatever they can find in the lake. For the first few weeks after ice-off especially, you will find them cruising the shallows, where the sun warms the bottom of the lake and new food is most plentiful.

However, the fish can be easily spooked by too much movement on the shores of the lake. While the lake is not above treeline, there are some fairly open areas around the lake's shoreline.

This is a beautiful fly-fishing lake and can be fished from the shore or, when the trout are to be found around the drop-off, from a float tube if you're willing to pack one in. The fish will hit most anything you throw at them. Try casting a good trout fly like a Royal Coachman or Grizzly King in the early morning or late in the evening when the fish are rising. A Doc Spratley, Carey Special or nymph pattern are also good choices, as long as the fly isn't too big.

Try working the east side of the lake, where there is a more pronounced drop-off or the northwest corner of the lake, where a number of feeder streams flow into the lake. Watch out for marshy areas. For spincasters, most small lures with some bait will produce.

By early October, the snow is usually starting to fly, making accessing the lake uncomfortably cold and wet.

Directions

Poland Lake is a remote trail accessed lake found in Manning Provincial Park. The best way to reach the lake is to take the 8 km (2.5–3 hour) trail from the gate at Strawberry Flats near the Gibson Pass Ski Area. The trailhead is found past the Manning Park Lodge and Lightning Lake Campsite. Although you gain 435 m (1,427 ft) along the way, the trail remains quite popular because of its relatively easy terrain compared to other parts of the park. The trail is open to mountain bikers and horses as well. A bike is great, especially for the return trip.

A second, more difficult route, to reach the lake is to start at Allison Pass and climb to Poland Lake. This hike is 9 km (3-4 hours) one-way from Allison Pass to the lake. You follow the unmaintained Memaloose Trail through the Memaloose Creek drainage.

Facilities

There is a spot to pitch a tent at the north end of the lake. The shoreline is rather marshy here and mosquitoes can be a problem.

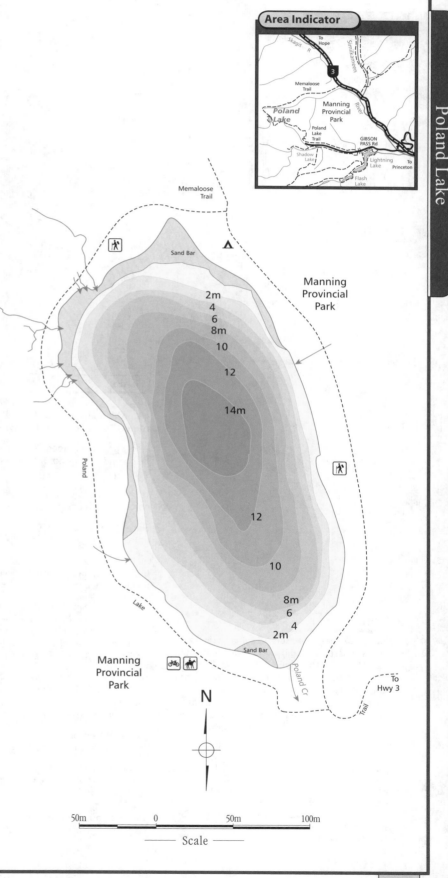

Memaloose Trail

Sand Bar

Manning Provincial Park

2m
4
6
8m
10
12
14m

Poland

12

10

8m
6
4
2m

Sand Bar

Manning Provincial Park

Poland Cr

To Hwy 3

Lake

Trail

N

50m 0 50m 100m

Scale

Location: 70 km (43 mi) north of Cache Creek
Elevation: 1,018 m (3,340 ft)
Surface Area: 57 ha (141 ac)
Max Depth: 31 m (101.7 ft)
Mean Depth: 7.2 m (23.6 ft)
Way Point: 51° 22' 27" N, 121° 2' 18" W

www.backroadmapbooks.com

Pressy Lake

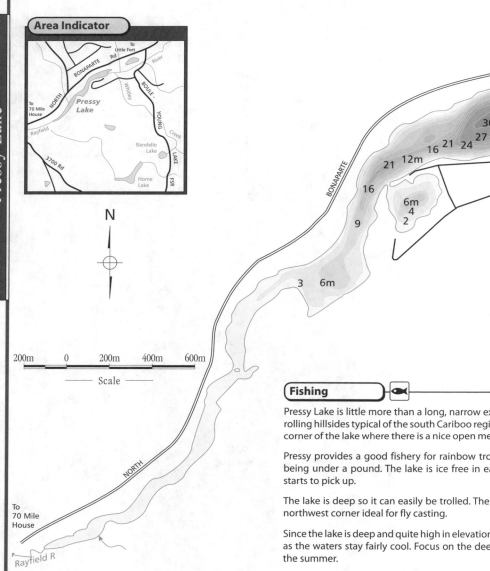

Area Indicator

N

200m   0   200m   400m   600m
Scale

Fishing

Pressy Lake is little more than a long, narrow expansion of the Rayfield River. It is found in the rolling hillsides typical of the south Cariboo region. The lake is tree lined except at the northeast corner of the lake where there is a nice open meadow and wetland extending out into the lake.

Pressy provides a good fishery for rainbow trout to 1 kg (2 lbs) in size with the average fish being under a pound. The lake is ice free in early May and after the turn over, fishing really starts to pick up.

The lake is deep so it can easily be trolled. There are also some nice shoals particularly at the northwest corner ideal for fly casting.

Since the lake is deep and quite high in elevation, the summer doldrums are not a great concern as the waters stay fairly cool. Focus on the deeper parts of the lake or wait until dusk during the summer.

In late September, the fishing picks up and can be very good as the fish actively feed in preparation for the winter months.

A boat with a small motor (must be less than 10hp) or a float tube is a definite advantage. If trolling, try a lake troll followed by a silver Flatfish, Kwikfish, or a Wedding Band and small piece of bait. Also try trolling black/silver speckled Flatfish or Kwikfish, a Dick Nite spoon, or a Luhr Jensen brass needlefish. If desired, a lake troll can accompany these lures. Regardless of the lure, work around the perimeter of the lake.

There are some places along the shoreline where it is possible to cast spinning lures from. Trout can be tempted from shore while casting spoons, such as the Krocodile from Luhr Jensen or the Gibbs Croc or by simply still fishing bait under a bobber or off the bottom. Spinners, such as a Mepps or Gibbs black/orange dot, tipped with a piece of worm are other good casting options.

Fly-fishers have plenty of opportunities to match the hatch and connect with some nice trout. The hatches common to the region are present here.

Fly anglers will find the usual assortment of hatches here, starting with a chironomid hatch in late May, and followed by mayflies, damselflies and caddis flies. Dry fly-fishing during these latter hatches can be very productive and exciting. In the summer, the hatches tail off, and trolling usually produces the best result. Using an attractor pattern like a leech or a Doc Spratley can work in summer and into fall.

Directions

Pressy Lake lies in the south Cariboo region and is best accessed by heading north from Clinton to 70 Mile House on Highway 97. Take the Green Lake Road and then the North Bonaparte Road northeast from 70 Mile House. Pressy Lake is located right next to the good logging road after you pass Tin Cup Lake and the Eagan Bonaparte Forest Service Road. The road is a good gravel road and is suitable for cars and RV's.

Facilities

Pressy Lake Recreation Site is a small campsite located on the northeast end of the lake. There is space for three vehicles at the site. The sites are large enough to accommodate a small RV. There is a boat launch at the site, too.

www.backroadmapbooks.com

Red Lake

Location: 44 km (27 mi) east of Cache Creek
Elevation: 950 m (3,117 ft)
Surface Area: 109 ha (269 ac)
Max Depth: 10 m (34 ft)
Mean Depth: 5.7 m (18.7 ft)
Way Point: 50° 53′ 34″ N, 120° 47′ 27″ W

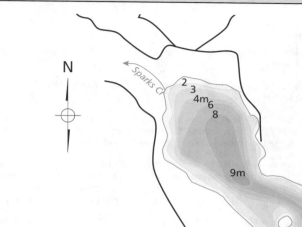

Red Lake Fish Stocking Data			
Year	Species	Number	Life Stage
2011	Brook Trout	28,000	Fry
2011	Rainbow Trout	11,000	Fingerling
2010	Brook Trout	39,494	Fingerling
2010	Rainbow Trout	13,654	Fingerling
2009	Brook Trout	32,630	Fingerling
2009	Rainbow Trout	9,000	Fingerling

Area Indicator

Fishing

Red Lake has a fairly good population of brook trout to 1 kg (2 lbs). These sometimes elusive fish are best fished during the fall or during ice fishing season.

There are not many lakes that hold brook trout or speckled trout as some people call them. Brook trout are one of the prettiest fish there is, and while they are not as spirited of fighters as rainbow, they are still tenacious and rarely give up on a fight.

The brook trout is actually a char, and prefers to stay deep, making short strong runs, as opposed to the aerial acrobatics of a rainbow. They are a hardier species and can withstand greater extremes in temperature and lower levels of oxygen that would kill off rainbow trout. This is good, because Red Lake is prone to winterkill.

The lake is stocked multiple times a year. In 2008, for instance, there were 45,000 triploid brook trout stocked in the lake. Red Lake is also stocked with rainbow trout. These stocked fish are non-reproducing triploid that have a tendency to get big fast, as they put all their energy into growing. While the lake is very productive, the lake is fairly shallow, and winterkill can knock back the fishery, especially the rainbow fishery.

Spincasting and trolling small lures such as a Deadly Dick and worm is the most effective manner to fish the brook trout. Flies simply are not well received by the brook trout except in the fall when the fish congregate in the shallows for spawning. At that time, casting a large attractor type pattern near the weeds and shallows can produce very well.

Fly-fishermen wishing to fish the lake in the spring should try a shrimp pattern. Use a sinking line and drop the fly to near the bottom.

Spincasting and trolling are effective in the spring and to a limited degree in the summer. That is because the waters warm significantly in the summer and the fishing falls off.

Late September to October is definitely the best time to fish. However, ice fishing using bait (worm, corn or maggot) and a hook is rewarding, as brook trout remain much more active in winter than rainbow.

There is an engine power restriction of 10hp at the lake.

Directions

Red Lake is found via series of confusing backroads and a copy of the Backroad Mapbook for the Thompson Okanagan region and a GPS is a definite asset in finding the lake.

From the Trans Canada Highway, follow the Deadman-Vidette Road north to Criss Creek. The Johnson/Criss Creek Forest Road branches east and loops and twists over to the Cooper Creek Road via the Seven Lakes Road. Take the Cooper Creek Road north and Red Lake will appear on the west side of the road.

Other Options

Around the Red Lake area is a series of tiny mountain lakes (**Sparks Lake, Moutray Lake, Cayuse Lake and Wadley Lake**). Each of these lakes can offer decent fly-fishing and spincasting if the fish at Red Lake are not cooperating.

Facilities

The lake has a cartop boat launch together with a rustic undeveloped camping area. The nearest established campsites are at Saul Lake, east of Red Lake, or back to Savona and Steelhead Provincial Park.

Scale
200m 0 200m 400m 600m

Location: 14 km (9 mi) west of Clearwater
Elevation: 1,384 m (4,541 ft)
Surface Area: 48 ha (119 ac)
Max Depth: 12 m (39 ft)
Way Point: 51° 43' 20.5" N, 120° 12' 23.4" W

www.backroadmapbooks.com

Reflector Lake

Area Indicator

Fishing

Reflector Lake is a small, shallow lake northwest of the town of Clearwater. The lake holds fair numbers of rainbow to 2 kg (4 lbs) that average much smaller than that.

The southeast and northwest ends of Reflector Lake are extremely shallow at less than 3 m (10 feet) deep. These areas are great areas for insect and aquatic invertebrate growth.

Ice-off at the lake is usually by end of April. Early in the year, the water is still quite cold and the rainbow trout are much more willing to venture into the shallows. It is often possible to shore fish for trout at this time. However, most people usually wait until the lake has turned over, which usually happens by mid-May.

For fly-fishers, the fishing starts shortly after turnover when the first chironomids start hatching. For many fly anglers, taking a trout on a chironomid pattern is a thing of beauty. Many anglers use a sinking line with a strike detector to get the chironomid pattern down to within about a metre (three feet) off the bottom and then slowly work the pattern around. Some even allow the movement of the wind and the waves to push the chironomid around.

Following the chironomid hatch are mayflies, damselflies, caddisflies and dragonflies. Dry fly fishing can be quite exciting during this time using a Tom Thumb or Elk Hair Caddis. The fringe areas between the deep hole and the shallows are good areas to test.

Trolling a lake troll, Flatfish, attractor type fly (leech, Muddler Minnow or Doc Spratley) or small lure produces so long as you troll around the center of the lake near the drop offs. You will need to keep your gear near the surface to avoid weed hang-ups, because nothing ruins a good troll faster than a chunk of weed stuck to your lure.

Given the shallow nature of the lake, fishing falls right off in early July and does not pick up until late September. October is a good time to visit the lake as the fish are actively feeding in preparation for the ice over in mid November. There is often some form of chironomid hatch in the fall, but most fly-fishers choose to work a leech pattern or other attractor pattern like a Carey Special. These patterns are bigger than a chironomid and the fish are usually looking for bigger food sources in fall. Dragon or damselfly nymph patterns can also work later in the year.

Check with the locals before heading out in the spring to see whether winterkill severely affected the fish stock.

Directions

Reflector Lake is located northwest of Clearwater. To find the lake from Highway 5, turn north on the Clearwater Village Road, then immediately left onto the Old Highway 5. After 1.2 km turn right onto Camp 2 Road and follow this road east to the Road 5 junction. Road 5 leads to the north end of Reflector Lake, about 12 km later.

To reach the south end of Reflector Lake, take the Road 3 heading north about 3.5 km past the Road 5 junction.

Facilities

The **Reflector Lake East Recreation Site** is the main access point to the lake. Visitors will find room for about three camping groups along with a cartop boat launch. There is also an informal campsite and launching area on the south side of the lake.

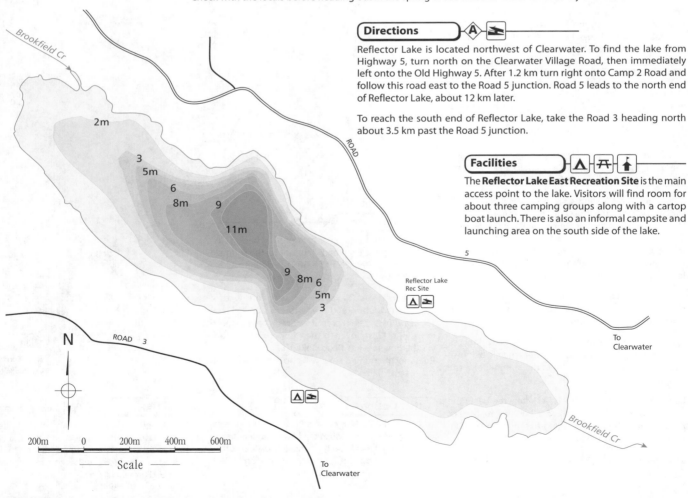

Rice Lake

Location: 6 km (3.7 mi) northeast of North Vancouver
Elevation: 201 m (659 ft)
Max Depth: 5 m (16 ft)
Way Point: 49° 21′ 24.0″ N, 123° 0′ 49.2″ W

Fishing

Rice Lake is located in the Seymour Demonstration Forest in North Vancouver at the foot of the North Shore Mountains. The man-made lake was once a reservoir to serve drinking water for North Vancouver residents. Today, it is a small, picturesque lake that is maintained as a family fishing lake, perfect for bringing young children to learn how to fish. Surrounded by nature, it is easy to forget you are but a stone's throw from a large metropolitan area.

Not only is the lake easy to access, it offers a myriad of other recreational opportunities as well. From the public parking lot in the Seymour Conservation Reserve, the lake is a five minute walk on a good trail. There is a floating dock at the southeast corner of the lake, which affords good access to the lake.

The lake is stocked multiple times a year with catchable sized rainbow that are usually between 25–30 cm (10–12 inches) in size. This is part of the reason the lake is such a great place to take kids fishing for the first time. Stocked catchable sized rainbow are notoriously easy to catch, which means that the action is fast and furious, especially during the first few weeks after stocking.

You can fish from the dock or shore, as boats–including belly boats–are not allowed. While the lake can be fished in a variety of ways, bait fishing is generally the most successful and is simple to learn. A worm, cocktail shrimp, marshmallow or other artificial bait such as Powerbait (pink is the preferred color), fished under a float or suspended off the bottom is a tried and true method. Of course other methods of angling will also work and it is always worth bringing a variety of tackle on any fishing outing just in case the fish are not keen on your initial offering. Bring along an assortment of spoons, spinners and even flies, which can be fished using a float.

During the spring and again in the fall, water temperatures allow for fishing all day however, during the summer months, the lake gets quite warm. At this time, try fishing in the mornings or evenings when the fish are most active.

Directions

If travelling north from Vancouver on Highway 1, cross the Ironworkers Memorial Bridge and take Exit 22 north towards Capilano College/Lillooet Road. Drive past Capilano College and follow the signs into the Seymour Conservation Reserve. It is 4 km (2.5 miles) along a gravel road to the Rice Lake gate checkpoint. At the north end of Lillooet Road you will find parking.

Facilities

Rice Lake is a day-use area only in the **Seymour Demonstration Forest**. There are washrooms, picnic tables and a covered gazebo near the lake. There is a fishing dock at the southeast corner of the lake designed specifically for disabled anglers, but is often used by able-bodied anglers as well. Rice Lake sits near both Lynn Canyon and Lynn Valley Parks. From the lake it is possible to hike into both parks, or deeper into the demonstration forest.

Rice Lake			
Fish Stocking Data			
Year	Species	Number	Life Stage
2011	Rainbow Trout	5,049	Catchable
2010	Rainbow Trout	11,181	Catchable
2009	Rainbow Trout	10,228	Catchable

Area Indicator

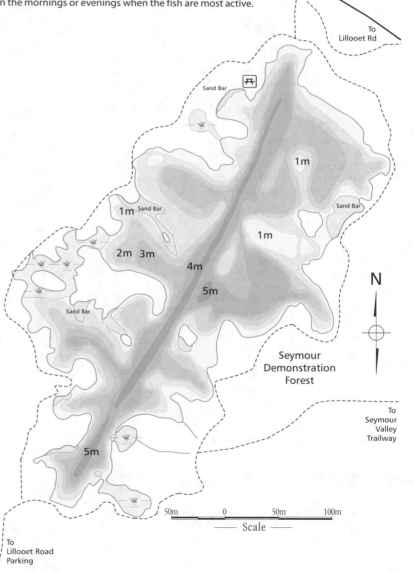

Seymour Demonstration Forest

To Lillooet Rd

To Seymour Valley Trailway

To Lillooet Road Parking

50m   0   50m   100m
— Scale —

Roche Lake Group

John Frank Lake

Elevation: 1,145 m (3,757 ft)
Surface Area: 24 ha (59 ac)
Max Depth: 4.5 m (14.8 ft)
Mean Depth: 1.7 m (5.6 ft)
Way Point: 50° 28' 10" N, 120° 8' 5" W

Frisken Lake

Elevation: 1,153 m (3,783 ft)
Surface Area: 29 ha (72 ac)
Max Depth: 9 m (29 ft)
Way Point: 50° 27' 42" N, 120° 8' 33" W

Area Indicator

Fishing

There are seven world-class stocked rainbow trout lakes in Roche Lake Provincial Park. Roche Lake itself is one of the best known fishing lakes in the region and is a popular destination as it usually produces consistently. It is managed as a trophy lake, meaning there are single barbless gear restrictions and electric motors only are allowed on part of the lake. The lake is closed from December 1 to April 30 and there is a two trout daily limit.

Because the lake is larger than the other lakes, it is not well suited for belly boats, although they can be used on the lake. A small boat will help you get around quicker, but if you don't mind kicking a couple kilometres to get to the far end of the lake, or if you plan on sticking close to the campsite, then by all means, use a float tube.

The lake is highly productive and full of nutrients, ideal for insects to proliferate. As a result, there are abundant chironomids, sedges, damselflies, mayflies, dragonflies, water boatman, as well as freshwater shrimp and leeches. All this food means that the fish eat well, and can get to 2.5 kg (5 lbs). However, all that food also means that there is less chance of them picking your offering out of the crowd. Thus the fish can be notoriously hard to land. And most of the bigger fish have usually been caught at least once or twice, making them a bit shy around lures. And, just to stack one more thing against the angler, the water is quite clear, meaning the fish spook easily.

The lake has some huge shoals and expansive weed beds. There are a number of islands, as well as a number of bays, making this a perfect lake for the fly-fisherman.

The most common way for spincasters to fish the lake is trolling using a Wedding Band or Flatfish. Fly anglers can also troll the lake using a leech pattern or a Woolly Bugger. If the big fish aren't biting, try trolling slower and more randomly. The food these fish eat rarely swims in straight lines back and forth across the lake. Try swinging from side to side and pausing for a moment, then make a short quick movement. This works best when paddling or kicking, not with an engine.

Fly anglers have a better chance of catching a veteran than a gear angler does. The big fish tend to lurk just off the drop offs, coming in to nab an easy meal before flitting back to the depths. Casting along the edge of the drop offs near structure can work well. Fishing at dusk, when the big fish are willing to come out under cover of semi-dark to feed on the insects in the shoals is also a good strategy.

The lake has a good chironomid hatch that starts fairly early each spring. Sinking a chironomid pattern to the depths of the lake, then slowly retrieving it is very effective. The trouble is that there are so many variations of chironomids, finding something that the fish are currently feeding on can be difficult. Starting with a #12–#16 black, olive or brown pattern is always safe, but if those aren't working, you're going to have to start exploring. If you do managed to catch one, having a pump to check what they're feeding on will be most helpful.

There is a damselfly hatch in late May and early June. It is not as big as it used to be, but it can still be very productive. A pale green imitation is the fly of choice. Shrimp patterns can be successful in June and again in October.

In July and August, the summer doldrums hit and your best bet is to troll deep with a Willow Leaf and a worm or with a nymph or leech pattern. The fishing picks up again in late September, offering anglers a couple of months of good fishing; the lake is noted for being a good late season lake.

Frisken Lake is a shallow lake south of Roche and is susceptible to winterkill; check with the fishery biologist or some locals before heading out in early spring. If the fish do survive, they can get up to 2.5 kg (5 lbs); by first year fall they are usually around 1 kg (2 lbs). The lake has some great hatches, starting with chironomids in late May, followed by caddisflies, damselflies, mayflies and dragonflies. Like Roche, the lake is prone to the summer doldrums.

John Frank Lake is another shallow lake subject to both winterkill and summer drawdown. But the fish grow rapidly in the lake. The lake has tea-coloured waters and lots of lily pads. In the early spring or late fall, try working around these areas for best success.

Tulip Lake holds a good population of stocked brook trout, which can get to 1 kg (2 lbs). Spincasting and trolling small lures such as a Deadly Dick and a worm is usually quite effective. Fly-fishing on this and the other brook trout lakes just isn't as effective, except in the fall when the fish spawn. There is an aerator to counteract winterkill.

The rest of the lakes in the group, including Ernest, Bulman, Bog and Horseshoe, are all fine fishing lakes in their own rights. Ernest and Bulman are stocked with rainbow trout, Bog Lake is stocked with brook trout and the other two lakes are stocked with both species of fish.

Directions

Roche Lake Provincial Park is found southwest of Kamloops. From the Trans Canada junction, travel south on Highway 5A for 22 km. Turn east onto Roche Lake Road, which leads directly to the park after about 9 km. Roche Lake is about 11 km in. Beyond Roche, the roads get progressively worse and a 4wd vehicle is an asset.

Facilities

Roche Lake Provincial Park hosts a trio of campsites available on a first-come, first-served basis. Roche Lake North (8 sites), Roche Lake West (21 sites), and Horseshoe Lake (4 sites) all offer rough boat launches suitable for small boats. Frisken Lake also features a cartop boat launch.

For those who prefer their backcountry with a bit of style, the **Roche Lake Resort** is a full service resort next to Roche Lake. There is a swimming pool, Jacuzzi and private cabins, as well as boat rentals, fly-fishing lessons and guiding services.

John Frank Lake			
Fish Stocking Data			
Year	Species	Number	Life Stage
2010	Rainbow Trout	3,000	Fry
2009	Rainbow Trout	3,000	Fry

Frisken Lake			
Fish Stocking Data			
Year	Species	Number	Life Stage
2010	Rainbow Trout	8,000	Fingerling
2009	Rainbow Trout	8,000	Yearling

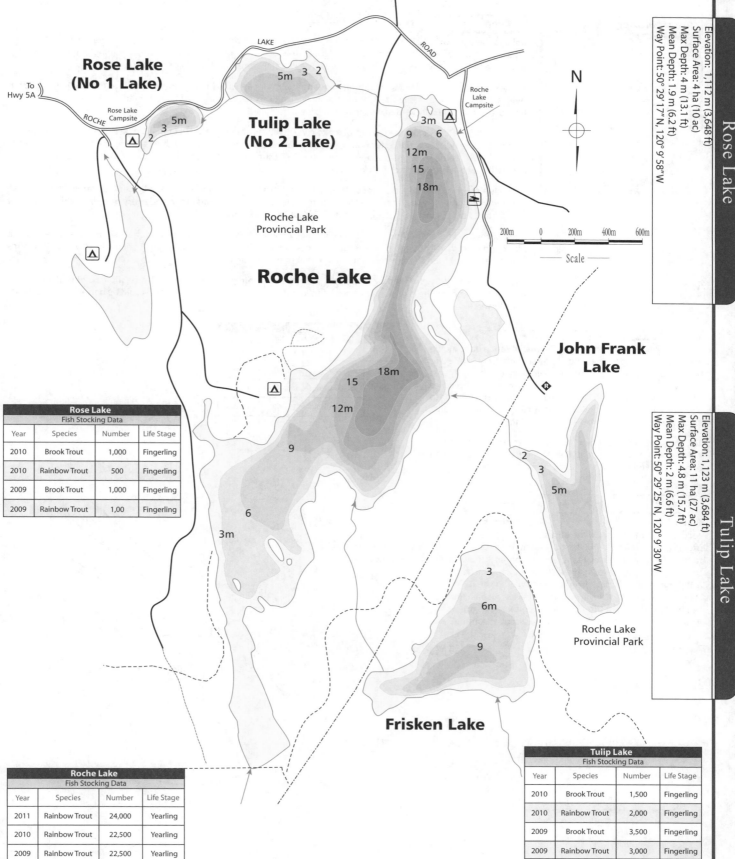

www.backroadmapbooks.com

Roche Lake Group

Roche Lake
Elevation: 1,145 m (3,757 ft)
Surface Area: 132 ha (326 ac)
Max Depth: 21.3 m (69.9 ft)
Mean Depth: 8.1 m (26.6 ft)
Way Point: 50° 28' 33" N, 120° 8' 58" W

Rose Lake

Elevation: 1,112 m (3,648 ft)
Surface Area: 4 ha (10 ac)
Max Depth: 4 m (13.1 ft)
Mean Depth: 1.9 m (6.2 ft)
Way Point: 50° 29' 17" N, 120° 9' 58" W

Tulip Lake

Elevation: 1,123 m (3,684 ft)
Surface Area: 11 ha (27 ac)
Max Depth: 4.8 m (15.7 ft)
Mean Depth: 2 m (6.6 ft)
Way Point: 50° 29' 25" N, 120° 9' 30" W

Rose Lake
(No 1 Lake)

To Hwy 5A

Rose Lake Campsite

Tulip Lake
(No 2 Lake)

Roche Lake Campsite

Roche Lake Provincial Park

Roche Lake

John Frank Lake

N

| 200m | 0 | 200m | 400m | 600m |

Scale

Roche Lake Provincial Park

Frisken Lake

Rose Lake			
Fish Stocking Data			
Year	Species	Number	Life Stage
2010	Brook Trout	1,000	Fingerling
2010	Rainbow Trout	500	Fingerling
2009	Brook Trout	1,000	Fingerling
2009	Rainbow Trout	1,00	Fingerling

Roche Lake			
Fish Stocking Data			
Year	Species	Number	Life Stage
2011	Rainbow Trout	24,000	Yearling
2010	Rainbow Trout	22,500	Yearling
2009	Rainbow Trout	22,500	Yearling

Tulip Lake			
Fish Stocking Data			
Year	Species	Number	Life Stage
2010	Brook Trout	1,500	Fingerling
2010	Rainbow Trout	2,000	Fingerling
2009	Brook Trout	3,500	Fingerling
2009	Rainbow Trout	3,000	Fingerling

Location: 15 km (9 mi) northwest of Mission
Elevation: 222 m (728 ft)
Surface Area: 23 ha (56.8 ac)
Maximum Depth: 19 m (62.3 ft)
Mean Depth: 8.8 m (28.9 ft)
Way Point: 49° 14' 43" N, 122° 23' 13" W

www.backroadmapbooks.com

Rolley Lake

Area Indicator

Fishing

Rolley Lake was named after James and Fanny Rolley, who were one of the first homesteaders here back in 1888. The area around the lake has been logged (for a decade or two in the early 1900s, the lake was a holding pond for short logs that were fed from the lake to a mill 5 km away by a wooden flume), but the forest has grown back nicely.

The lake itself has been stocked, although not continually, since 1942, with rainbow trout. Since the 1990s, the lake has been stocked with catchable sized rainbow, usually five or six times annually. In addition to stocked rainbow, the lake has cutthroat trout Dolly Varden, kokanee and brown bullhead.

Because of this, Rolley Lake is a perfect place to take the kids fishing for the first time. Stocked catchable are famously ignorant in the ways of artificial lures and Powerbait and don't understand why there are J-shaped worms just sort of hanging there in the water, just asking to be eaten…. Freshly stocked catchables will chase just about anything once and, because the lake is a catch and keep lake, once is about the only chance they get.

Rolley is a much bigger lake than most of the other catch and keep lakes around the Lower Mainland. While the lake sees heavy fishing pressure, there is a fair bit of room for the fish to spread out in and every once in a while a rainbow will get to 35 cm (14 inches) or so, but most are about 25 cm (10 inches).

Most of the traditional methods of fishing work fine here. Fly anglers will kick around the lake in a float tube trolling black and olive Woolly Buggers (size 8 usually works well), spincasters can troll a small Willow Leaf with bait (worms work fine), or fish from shore with a bobber and bait or bottom rig and bait.

The lake is completely encircled by trails and there are three fishing docks on the northwest shores of the lake. Here the water is the deepest. The lake is small enough for float tubes, but a canoe or small boat would be better. No powerboats are allowed.

Directions

Rolley Lake is found in Rolley Lake Provincial Park, a park known for its lush forest dominated by large second growth trees. To reach the lake, take the Lougheed Highway (Highway 7) east past Maple Ridge. Turn right onto 287 Street, which becomes Wilson Street and ends at Dewdney Trunk Road. Turn right onto Dewdney and watch for Bell Road about 2 km (1.2 miles) along. If you reach Stave Lake, you've gone too far.

Turn left onto Bell Road and follow that route for 2.3 km (1.3 miles) north. Near the end of Bell Avenue, turn on to a signed gravel road and 600 metres later you are at the lake.

Facilities

Rolley Lake Provincial Park offers 64 campsites set in the tall, second growth timber on the east side of the lake. The campground is open from April 1st through mid-October and has toilets, wood, running water, a sani-station and showers. On the west side of the lake is a gravel boat launch, which requires a 100 metre (328 ft) pack from the roadway to use it. There is also a picnic area and beach on the west side. The park receives heavy use throughout the year given its proximity to the Fraser Valley and reservations through www.discovercamping.com are recommended.

Rolley Lake			
Fish Stocking Data			
Year	Species	Number	Life Stage
2011	Rainbow Trout	3,301	Catchable
2010	Rainbow Trout	3,850	Catchable
2009	Rainbow Trout	3,909	Catchable

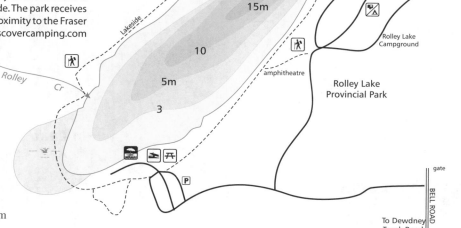

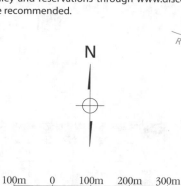

100m   0   100m   200m   300m

Scale

© Mussio Ventures Ltd.

Ruby Lake

Location: 3 km (1.9 mi) south of Earls Cove
Elevation: 24 m (78 ft)
Surface Area: 466 ha (1152 ac)
Maximum Depth: 112 m (367 ft)
Mean Depth: 52 m (171 ft)
Marie Plavetic: Waypoint:49° 43' 22" N, 123° 59' 20" W

Fishing

Like many of the lakes on the Sunshine Coast, Ruby Lake is a good cutthroat lake. And, like nearby Sakinaw Lake, Ruby also supports a good population of kokanee.

The lake is best known, however, for its warm water and in the summer, there are plenty of boats, swimmers and other noise to spook the fish. That and the warm water make fishing in the summer almost a complete write-off.

Cutthroats are voracious and will eat most anything they can: insects, leeches, stickleback and kokanee fry. All of which are present in this lake. What you should fish depends on when you go. Kokanee spawn in the fall into Ruby Creek. Like Sockeye, they turn a brilliant red; there is a viewing area on the creek for people who want to watch them spawn. While the bay at the mouth of Ruby Creek is closed to fishing to protect spawning cutthroat and kokanee, working just outside this area with an egg pattern (or, for spincasters, actual eggs) can prove to be productive. In spring, working a fry pattern in this area can work well.

Generally speaking, cutthroats are piscivorous, or fish eaters. While smaller cutthroat may feed on insects, the bigger fish favour the bigger food. Why waste all that energy to eat a whole bunch of hatching insects when you could eat just one stickleback and get the same nutritional value? You can try working a larger chironomid pattern during the spring hatches, but most people find a black Woolly Bugger (not too big though) works really well. In the fall, the fish tend to eat a lot of leeches. Black, purple maroon and tan all work well. While there are other things that will work, leeches tend to be the favoured pattern. Top water fishing can sometimes be productive, but more often than not you will want to be fishing on a sinking line and a slow retrieve or troll.

Spincasters will have good luck using small spinners, Kwikfish or Flatfish. Fishing Powerbait off the bottom can work well, too.

The cutthroat can get up to 1.5 kg (3 lbs), but are generally much smaller. There is a two fish limit for wild cutthroat, none over 40 cm (16 inches).

Directions

Ruby Lake is quite easy to find. From the Langdale Ferry Terminal, take Highway 101 almost all the way to Earl's Cove. The lake will be on your left hand side. Watch for the turn-off to Dan Bocsh Regional Park near the south end of the lake. This is the best place to access the lake from.

Facilities

Dan Bosch Regional Park has a sandy swimming beach, picnic tables and a short trail along the shores of the lake. There is no boat launch here, but it is possible to hand launch a boat or float tube.

Nearby **Ruby Lake Resort** rents canoes. The resort also provides accommodations in the form of cottages and traditional Canadian Outpost Tents. If you like camping a little more rustic, the nearest recreation site is at Klein Lake. While the lake is just across Highway 101 and up the hill, driving to the lake takes a little longer as you must drive almost all the way to Earl's Cove; turn right onto the Egmont Road, then right again onto the North Lake Road. Stay right to get to the **Klein Lake Recreation Site.**

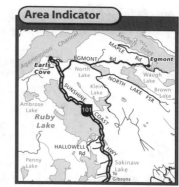

Area Indicator

Scale
200m 0 200m 600m 1000m

Location: 64 km (40 mi) northeast of Merritt
Elevation: 929 m (3,047 ft)
Surface Area: 123 ha (304 ac)
Max Depth: 11.9 m (39 ft)
Mean Depth: 5.8 m (19 ft)
Way Point: 50° 16' 9.1" N, 120° 0' 13.9" W

Salmon Lake

Area Indicator

Salmon Lake Fish Stocking Data			
Year	Species	Number	Life Stage
2011	Rainbow Trout	5,000	Yearling
2010	Rainbow Trout	5,000	Yearling

Fishing

Don't believe the name: there are no salmon in Salmon Lake, not even the landlocked variety. Salmon Lake is located on Douglas Lake Ranch property, but unlike most of the other lakes on the ranch, this lake is open to the public for fishing. The ranch even maintains a resort at the lake.

Salmon Lake is a popular fly-fishing destination, which holds good numbers of rainbow trout–nicknamed Ranch Rainbows–that average 1 kg (2–3 lbs), with the largest fish caught and released here at 2.5 kg (5.5 lbs).

The lake is choc-a-block with food for the rainbow, including leeches, shrimp, chironomids, damselflies, dragonflies, water boatmen and caddisflies. It is a perfect fly-fishing lake, which is good, because the lake is regulated as an artificial fly only lake using a single barbless fly. There is no ice fishing.

Most fly-fishers cast towards the weed beds that line the west side of the lake using a damselfly (green), shrimp or chironomid pattern. Trolling a leech pattern is also effective. In 2007, the "fly of the year" at Salmon Lake was a cinnamon and brown leech.

Other popular patterns here are Rabbit Strip Black Leeches and burgundy Woolly Buggers tied on number 6 to 8 hooks, black and brown chironomids and red bloodworms (chironomid pupae) tied on number 12 hooks, green and yellow shrimp, brown boatmen and red, green and yellow Carey Specials on size 8 to 10 hooks. Green damselflies and dragonflies on size 6 to 10 hooks can also work wonders.

The lake is perfect for belly or pontoon boats, but small rowboats and other cartoppers are welcome here, too. There is a charge to launch your boat or you can rent a rowboat and electric motors on-site.

For people who have little fly-fishing experience, Douglas Lake Ranch can provide licensed guides and even offers three-day "fly-fishing school" for people to learn the art of fly-fishing.

The lake is quite shallow and awfully silty so it warms significantly in the summer prompting an algae bloom and poor fishing. If that doesn't discourage you from fishing in the summer months, try a dry fly or try trolling a slow sinking line. Either way, the fly will remain near the surface and the algae will not affect your presentation as much.

Directions

Salmon Lake is easily accessed on the Douglas Lake Road. To reach the road, simply drive on Highway 5A from Merritt to the beginning of the Douglas Lake Road near the north end of Nicola Lake. The Douglas Lake Road is a good, all weather access road. About half way to Westwold on Highway 97 and the end of the Douglas Lake Road, the road passes by the north shore of the lake. It is hard to miss as there is a resort on the lake.

Facilities

The **Salmon Lake Resort** is part of the Douglas Lake Ranch and offers lakeside cottages and camping. A convenience store, outdoor heated pool and boat launch help you enjoy the resort. They even maintain a fly shop at the resort stocked with dozens of patterns.

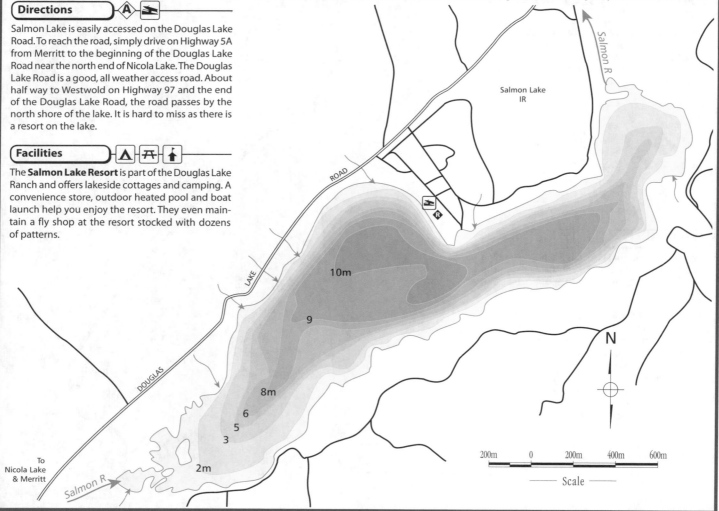

www.backroadmapbooks.com

Salsbury Lake

Location: 22 km (13.6 mi) north of Mission
Elevation: 431 m (1,414 ft)
Surface Area: 79 ha (195 ac)
Max Depth: 19 m (62 ft)
Mean Depth: 8 m (26 ft)
Way Point: 49° 21' 51.4" N, 122° 13' 14" W

Fishing

Salsbury Lake is one of a series of lakes located east of Stave Lake. The last few kilometres in to the lake are a little tricky to navigate.

Scenically, the lake is fairly unremarkable, but it offers pretty good fishing for small rainbow and kokanee, which don't usually get much bigger than 30 cm (12 inches). However, the lake does occasionally surprise with a bigger trout, although usually not that much bigger. The rainbow are stocked on a somewhat sporadic schedule by the Freshwater Fisheries Society of BC.

The lake has extensive shallows around most of the lake. The northeast corner of the lake drops off rapidly and has three inflow creeks. It is at that location that shore fishing is the best. The rest of the shoreline is tough to fish since there are numerous logs, lots of brush and expansive shallows.

In the summer months, try near the north end where the deepest pocket of water is found. The fish tend to retreat there as the waters warm. Another option is past the rocky island near the boat launch. There is a deep hole here that seems to hold fish.

For spincasters, the rainbow will take to a variety of small spinners and spoons. Some people have reported that a Willow Leaf with a red and green Wedding Band and dew worm works well.

For fly anglers, the early season chironomid hatch can provide some great action. These chironomids are smaller than the ones you will find in interior lakes and usually range in size from #14 to #20. The hatch usually starts just after ice off, which is usually end of February or early March and lasts until late May. The trout like to feed on nymph chironomids near the bottom, so you will have to get your presentation down deep. Chironomids are not a speedy creature when they are in the water, so the slower your retrieve the better. And because they are so small, the trout tend to sip them in, making detecting a strike difficult. While the colour of the hatch can vary from day to day, common colours are brown, black and green.

The lake is susceptible to strong winds so canoeists and those using float tubes should be wary.

Directions

Salsbury Lake is found in a heavily logged valley off the Lost Lake Forest Service Road. Although it is possible to access the lake with a car throughout the summer months, a truck is strongly recommended.

To access the lake, travel east of Hatzic Lake on the Lougheed Highway (Highway 7) and turn on to Sylvester Road heading north. Follow Sylvester Road to its end where it becomes the Lost Creek Forest Service Road. The road leads past Davis Lake and soon reaches Salsbury Lake at just over the 11 km mark.

Facilities

The former Salsbury Recreation Site is comprised of two locations. At the southeast end, there is a pull-out off the main road which overlooks the lake. It is possible for a couple of parties to camp at that location. It is a gentle 75 metre hike down to the lakeshore where there is a small gravel beach that some people choose to camp at. The better spot to camp is at the northwest end of the lake where there are several lakeshore campsites and a gravel boat launch.

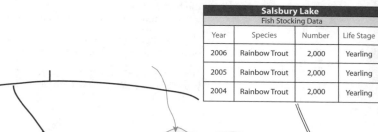

Salsbury Lake Fish Stocking Data			
Year	Species	Number	Life Stage
2006	Rainbow Trout	2,000	Yearling
2005	Rainbow Trout	2,000	Yearling
2004	Rainbow Trout	2,000	Yearling

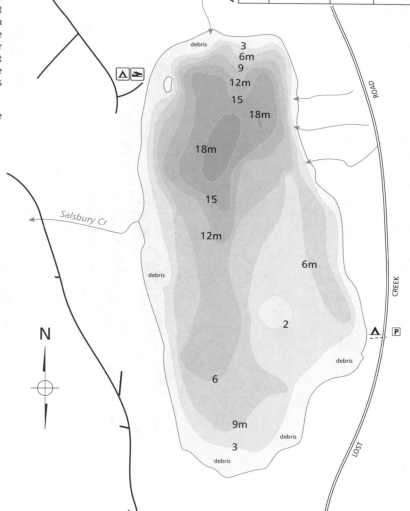

© Mussio Ventures Ltd.

Location: 6 km (3.7 mi) northwest of Port Moody
Elevation: 47 m (154 ft)
Surface Area: 45 ha (111 ac)
Max Depth: 33 m (108 ft)
Mean Depth: 18 m (59 ft)
Way Point: 49° 19' 11.2" N, 122° 53' 24.2" W

www.backroadmapbooks.com

Sasamat Lake

Area Indicator

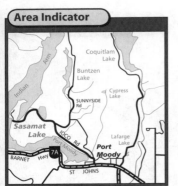

Fishing

Sasamat Lake is better known for its great beach and picnic facilities than for its fishing. But it is a pretty spot and, while the trout don't get very big, they are plentiful and seem to like getting caught. The lake is surrounded by gentle hiking trails that provide access for anglers. At the south end of the lake, there is a floating bridge that spans the narrow outflow of the lake and is a popular angling spot.

In spring and fall, Sasamat Lake is a great place to fish. The lake is stocked multiple times a year with catchable-sized rainbow trout. As these fish have never seen a hook before, they are suckers for most anything you can throw at them… at least for the first few weeks after they are stocked. As a result, this is a great place to teach kids how to fish, as you don't need special gear to find fish.

There are some fish each year that avoid getting caught for a season or two and can get to 45 cm (18 inches). By and large, though, the average size here is 25–30 cm (10–12 inches).

There are many fishing techniques that can be used here. Since the fish are usually indiscriminate, no one technique works best. You can spin, float fish, bottom fish, jig, drift fish or fly-fish. For kids, the simplest presentations are often the best. A simple bobber and worm set up can result in multiple hits over the course of a short time. In addition to worms, popular baits include Powerbait, roe or single Jensen eggs.

The floating bridge is the most popular fishing spot, but if it is too crowded, you can usually find a patch of shoreline open enough to cast. The western shoreline drops off faster than the east, offering the better fishing.

The lake does get fairly deep and if you want to fish the deepest holes (a good idea during the busy summer months), you will need a canoe or float tube. From May to September, only electric motors are allowed on the lake.

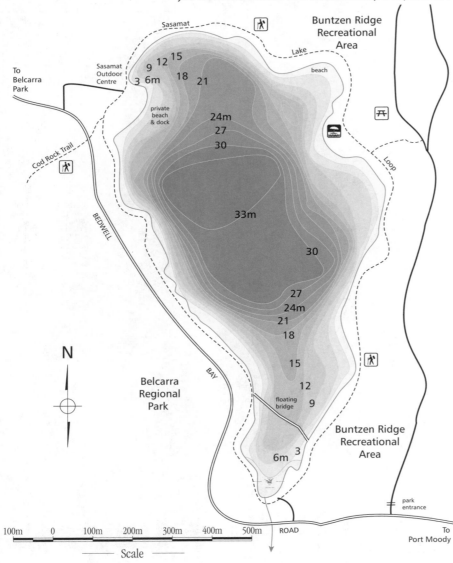

Directions

Sasamat Lake is located on the Bedwell Bay Road within Belcarra Regional Park north of Port Moody. It is easily accessed by car.

To find the lake, drive on the Lougheed Highway (Highway 7) through Port Moody. Head north on Ioco Road, which is a major road junction that follows the northern shores of Port Moody. The road turns into First Avenue at the 1600 block. Head north on First Avenue and then take a left at the fork in the road, onto Bedwell Bay Road. Follow the road to the south end of Sasamat Lake. In summer, finding a place to park can be a challenge.

Facilities

Belcarra Regional Park is a popular retreat for city folks. Sasamat Lake forms the hub of the park and is best known for the **White Pine Beach** area at the northeast end of the lake. It has a large parking area together with a large sandy beach, concessions stand and washroom facilities. The **Sasamat Lake Loop Trail** circles the lake and crosses the floating bridge at the south end. At the northwest end of lake is the **Sasamat Outdoor Centre**, which is accessed by the Bedwell Bay Road.

Sasamat Lake			
Fish Stocking Data			
Year	Species	Number	Life Stage
2011	Rainbow Trout	3,790	Catchable
2010	Rainbow Trout	3,875	Catchable
2009	Rainbow Trout	3,850	Yearling

© Mussio Ventures Ltd.

Saskum Lake

www.backroadmapbooks.com

Location: 18 km (11 mi) south of Vavenby
Elevation: 852 m (2,795 ft)
Surface Area: 115 ha (284 ac)
Max Depth: 33 m (108 ft)
Mean Depth: 18 m (59 ft)
Way Point: 51° 24' 35" N, 119° 41' 47" W

Fishing

Saskum Lake has a combination of rainbow trout, lake trout, whitefish and kokanee. The rainbow and lakers can reach 2 kg (4–5 lbs) in size, but tend to average less than a pound. The kokanee are up to 1 kg (2 lbs) but are usually quite small.

Fishing is generally slow from ice-off in early May to when the lake freezes over in November. The preferred method of fishing is trolling.

Saskum Lake is upstream from North Barriere Lake, which also holds lake trout. These lakes are two of a handful of lakes in the area that hold lakers. Lake trout are not a common fish in the area and as a result, go relatively unnoticed by most anglers. It doesn't help that lake trout (which are actually a char, go figure) tend to spend most of the ice-free season down at the bottom of the lake, far below where most anglers focus their efforts.

In early spring, lake trout can be found near the surface of the lake feeding on smaller fish. By summer, though, they have moved to the depths of the lake and can only be found with the aid of a downrigger or with a very deep jig. In the fall the lake trout move closer to the surface again to spawn and in winter, they can offer quite a fun ice-fishing experience.

Both the rainbow and the kokanee take a Willow Leaf with a Wedding Band and worm. Rainbow also strike small lures such as a Flatfish or Mepps. Trout also take well to an attractor type fly like a leech or Doc Spratley when trolled. Kokanee seem to have a thing for the colour pink, including flies. When trolling for kokanee, troll slowly, in a broad, looping S-pattern. While rainbow are willing to hit a faster moving lure, kokanee will ignore it if it moves to fast. Instead, they are attracted to random moving lures that dart and weave.

Fly-fishermen will be a little disappointed with this lake. They should focus their efforts at the outflow and inflow to the Barriere River located at the south and north ends of the lake.

Directions

Saskum Lake is located to the west of Adams Lake and east of Little Fort. Head north on Highway 5 from Kamloops to Barriere. Follow the paved Barriere Lakes Road east. Continue up the valley until you cross the Barrier River, where the North Barriere Lake Forest Service Road leads north. The road will soon lead along the northern shores of North Barriere Lake. After leaving that lake, cross the Barriere River Bridge and take the next major road heading north. The main haul logging road, called the Saskum Lake Forest Service Road, will take you to the south end of Saskum Lake.

Facilities

Saskum Lake Recreation Site offers a boat launch and a nice sandy beach. There are 11 campsites at the somewhat remote site making it a good destination for those looking for a nice place to fish, canoe or camp.

Other Options

There are not many lakes in the Saskum Lake area. The closest lake is **Jeep Lake,** a tiny pothole about a kilometre east that holds a small population of rainbow trout. It is approached up a different drainage, though and getting there requires a bit of a drive. Better to keep heading back along the North Barriere Lake Forest Service Road to **North Barriere Lake,** which is described elsewhere in this book.

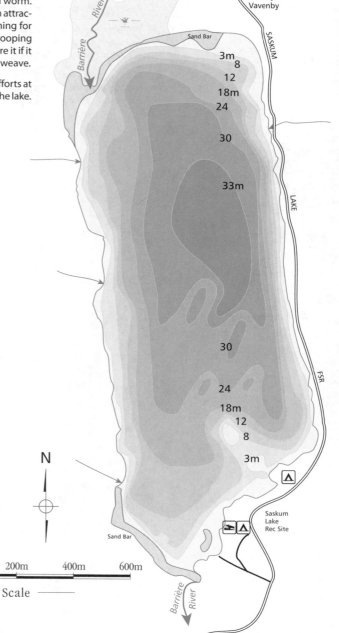

Area Indicator

To Hwy 5 & Vavenby

Saskum Lake

Sand Bar

3m
8
12
18m
24
30
33m
30
24
18m
12
8
3m

Sand Bar

Saskum Lake Rec Site

N

200m   0   200m   400m   600m
Scale

Location: 30 km (18.6 mi) northwest of Kamloops
Elevation: 1,469 m (4,820 ft)
Max Depth: 7.8 m (25.6 ft)
Mean Depth: 2.6 m (8.5 ft)
Way Point: 50° 54' 56.3" N, 120° 38' 28.4" W

www.backroadmapbooks.com

Saul Lake

Area Indicator

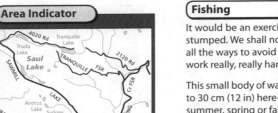

Fishing

It would be an exercise in pure folly to call any lake a sure-fire producer of fish, a place where anglers are never stumped. We shall not engage in such foolishness, because we know that there are anglers out there who know all the ways to avoid catching fish. But we are sorely tempted. Saul Lake is one of those lakes where you have to work really, really hard to not catch a fish.

This small body of water on the Tranquille Plateau is bursting with rainbow trout. Not big ones – "big" trout are up to 30 cm (12 in) here–but there are lots of them and they are easy to catch. It doesn't matter whether it is winter, summer, spring or fall. If you have been having a run of bad luck fishing some of the more moody lakes and just want to remember what it feels like to have a fish on, then Saul Lake is the place to go.

The nature of this sport fishery makes Saul Lake a good place to go with children, especially first-timers who crave their first catch. It will be easy to thrill five-year-olds at Saul Lake because a successful day on the water is virtually a guarantee.

Ultralight tackle, such as small rods and reels with lines in the four to six-pound test range as well as small hooks between number 12 and 14, are best on this lake. While the regulations do not require it, pinch down the barbs of your hooks. Since you will have a great deal of catching and releasing to do, barbless hooks will make the job easier and make the fish happier.

There is no real secret to catching fish here. Spincasters, trollers and fly casters will all fair reasonably well. For the younger generation, a simple baited worm, suspended under a bobber will perform fantastically. And there is something magical the first time that bobber starts to wobble and then disappears under the water…

This is a great place for people who are learning to fly-fish to come, too. Discovering the patience of a hand-twist retrieve on a chironomid pattern, learning the magic of topwater fishing…heck, even just learning to cast the darn thing. It's also a great place to learn how to release a fish properly.

Directions

From downtown Kamloops, cross the Overlander Bridge and follow Fortune Drive to Eighth Street. Head north to Bachelor Drive and follow this road through the residential development to the gravel road and the entrance to Lac Du Bois Provincial Park. Follow Lac Du Bois Road until it leaves the park and continues northwest into the Tranquille Plateau on what is now called the Sawmill Lake Forest Service Road. Saul Lake is on the right-hand side of the gravel road, about 15 km past Pass Lake, which in turn is about 5 km past the boundary of Lac Du Bois Provincial Park.

Facilities

The **Saul Lake Recreation Site** is maintained by the Kamloops Indian Band. The site offers four campsites, with no camping fees and a rustic launch for cartopper boats. If the site is full, there are a few other recreation sites within a half hour drive. The area is also a popular snowmobile area and countless trails are found around the lake.

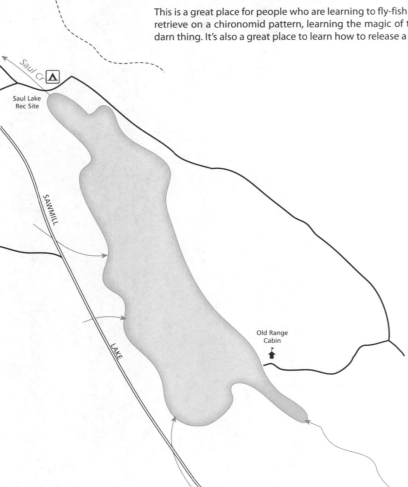

Old Range Cabin

N

100m 0 100m 200m 300m 400m 500m

— Scale —

To Kamloops

Sayres Lake

Location: 17 km (10.6 mi) north of Mission
Elevation: 192 m (630 ft)
Surface Area: 78 ha (193 ac)
Max Depth: 84 m (276 ft)
Mean Depth: 47 m (154 ft)
Way Point: 49° 19' 16.7" N, 122° 19' 33.4" W

Fishing

Located on the west side of Stave Lake, Sayres Lake is not as popular as many of the surrounding lakes because it can be temperamental. However, it is one of a small number of lakes in the Lower Mainland that offers brook trout. There are also rainbow trout, both of which can get to 30 cm (12 inches).

The lake is surrounded by steep terrain except at the south end of the lake. Despite its relatively low elevation, the lake opens up a little later than some of the other valley lakes.

Up until a few years ago, the BC Correction Agency operated a net pen hatchery program, where rainbow fry were held in (and frequently escaped from) pens in the lake. Unfortunately, the program has since been discontinued and the fishing has suffered.

Which is not to say that the fishing here is terrible, just a lot slower than it used to be. And the lake can be moody, sometimes extremely reluctant to offer up its fish. Add it all up and you have a lake that many people are willing to overlook. If they're going to the trouble to come out here there are other, more consistent lakes in the area.

But for people who like a challenge, this can be a good lake to fish. It is also one of the few lakes in the Lower Mainland that holds brook trout. Brook trout are a cautious fish and quite hard to catch. They are often extremely suspicious of anything that doesn't look just right. Fly anglers usually have the edge here, but a natural looking retrieve is often the most important thing. Spincasters can have good success working ultra-light gear, especially when the water is slightly murky.

Float tubes can be used effectively since the lake is fairly sheltered. Cast or troll towards the centre of the pothole lake where it is deepest. Shore fishermen should stick to the south end of the lake as the water drops off rapidly in that location. If all else fails, try off the dock.

There is a bait ban in effect at the lake. Also, a catch limit and a single barbless hook restriction have been implemented in hopes of improving the fishery. As always, check the regulations before heading out.

Area Indicator

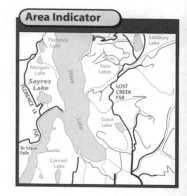

Directions

Sayres Lake is found between Alouette Lake and Stave Lake and is accessed by the Florence Lake Forest Service Road. To access the lake, drive along the Dewdney Truck Road from the Lougheed Highway to Stave Falls at the south end of Stave Lake. Florence Lake Road branches north and will bring you past Devils Lake. At around 11 km (6.7 miles), you will come to a service road heading off to the right. This road is usually gated within 100 metres of the main road so you are looking at an 800 metres walk uphill to the south end of Sayres Lake. With some care, a car can be used to reach the parking area near the gate.

There is also a trail beginning at the 12.7 km mark along the Florence Lake Forest Service Road. However, it is not well developed so packing in a canoe to the lake is a real adventure.

Facilities

At the south end of the lake, you will find a wharf and rough cartop boat launch. There is space to pitch a tent here, but no formal camping facilities.

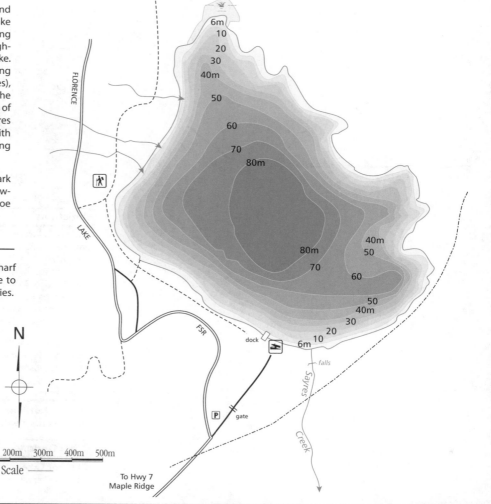

100m 0 100m 200m 300m 400m 500m
— Scale —

N

To Hwy 7
Maple Ridge

Location: 70 km (43 mi) southwest of Clearwater
Elevation: 1,228 m (4,029 ft)
Surface Area: 29 ha (72 ac)
Max Depth: 17 m (55.8 ft)
Mean Depth: 5.7 m (18.7 ft)
Way Point: 51° 14' 37.8" N, 120° 45' 38.8" W

www.backroadmapbooks.com

Scot Lake

Area Indicator

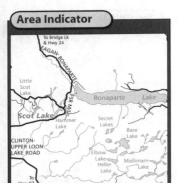

Fishing

Scot Lake is a good fishing lake for rainbow in the 1 kg (1-2 lb) range. Expansive shoals are located at the inflow creek at the southwest end of the lake and at the outflow area at the northeast end of the lake. The lake gets to about 50 feet deep with two distinct potholes, one towards the northeast end of the lake and one near the middle of the lake.

The ice comes off the lake in early May and for a few weeks, the trout cruise the shallows of the lake looking for food. This can be a highly productive time for shoreline anglers, as they don't have to cast into deep water to have success.

As the water begins to warm, the fish retreat to the edge of the drop off. At this time, the lake is usually fished using a lake troll, Flatfish or small lure. Because the rainbow trout are hanging out around the edge of the drop off, trolling around the drop off, cutting back and forth from shallow water to deeper water will be the most productive.

Fly-fishermen should focus their efforts around the shoals at the southwest and northeast ends of the lake. Early in the year, chironomids make an appearance here and offer fly anglers their first insect hatch, followed by mayflies, damsel and dragonflies and caddisflies. The later hatches offer some good topwater fishing, especially during the late spring evenings when the water is calm and the trout are rising.

By summer, the fishing slows down with the best time to fish in the early morning or in the late evening. Trolling deep in one of the two potholes or use a sinking line and fly-fishing a shrimp or nymph pattern into the depths are your best chance. By late fall, the chironomids start hatching again and the fishing picks up. While it is possible to fish chironomids in the fall, the fish seem to favour larger patterns, like leeches in black, maroon and brown and dragon and damselfly nymphs. As the cooler weather sets in, the fish begin bulking up for the upcoming winter and one leech is worth a few hundred chironomids to the trout.

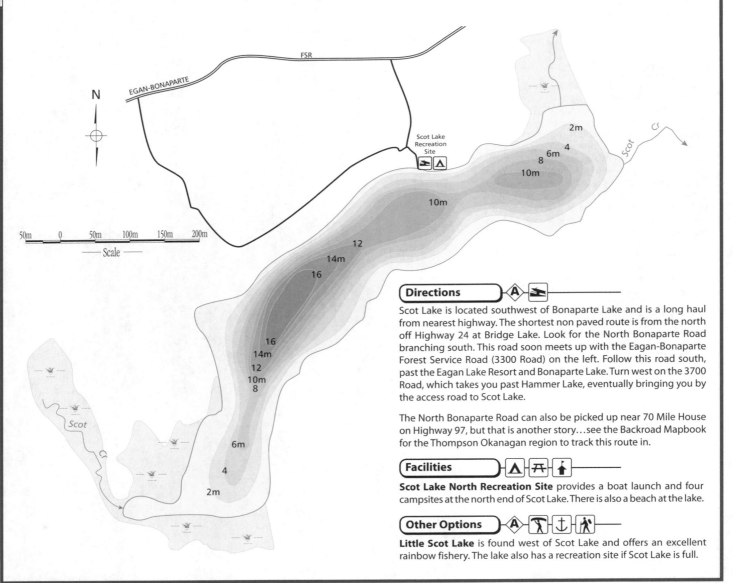

Directions

Scot Lake is located southwest of Bonaparte Lake and is a long haul from nearest highway. The shortest non paved route is from the north off Highway 24 at Bridge Lake. Look for the North Bonaparte Road branching south. This road soon meets up with the Eagan-Bonaparte Forest Service Road (3300 Road) on the left. Follow this road south, past the Eagan Lake Resort and Bonaparte Lake. Turn west on the 3700 Road, which takes you past Hammer Lake, eventually bringing you by the access road to Scot Lake.

The North Bonaparte Road can also be picked up near 70 Mile House on Highway 97, but that is another story…see the Backroad Mapbook for the Thompson Okanagan region to track this route in.

Facilities

Scot Lake North Recreation Site provides a boat launch and four campsites at the north end of Scot Lake. There is also a beach at the lake.

Other Options

Little Scot Lake is found west of Scot Lake and offers an excellent rainbow fishery. The lake also has a recreation site if Scot Lake is full.

www.backroadmapbooks.com

Scuitto Lake

Location: 18 km (11 mi) southwest of Kamloops
Elevation: 1,047 m (3,435 ft)
Surface Area: 94 ha (232 ac)
Max Depth: 8 m (27 ft)
Way Point: 50° 32' 58.1" N, 120° 8' 11.9" W

Fishing

Fans of Scuitto Lake will tell you that this is one of the most productive fly-fishing lakes in the Kamloops Area lakes. That's a pretty bold claim for a patch of water that as unappealing as it is. The water is tea-coloured and there is algae permanently growing on the lake, giving the whole place a rather slimy sort of appearance. In summer, the lake is subject to drawdown, which does nothing to enhance the appearance.

And it's true that in the heart of summer, the fishing is pretty poor, but for the rest of the year, the lake offers some great fishing.

The nutrient rich waters of the lake provide the perfect breeding ground for all manner of insects, which in turn feed the rainbow here. Trout are regularly caught in the 2 kg (4-5 lbs) range and have been known to reach 5 kg (11 lbs).

The lake is quite shallow and has a large island in the middle, which is surrounded by inviting shoals. The area north of the island is the deepest part of the lake.

Given the depth, the lake is tough to troll unless you are fishing for "weed trout". Trolling a leech or dragonfly nymph on a full sinking line can produce well. Trolling works better when there is no hatch on, especially in fall.

The four main patterns to use on the lake are: chironomid, leech, shrimp and caddis. Chironomids, micro-leeches, shrimp and caddis pupa are usually fished on a dry line with a long leader. But the best fishing happens from mid-June to early July, when the caddis hatch is on. The hatch is huge. Casting an Elk Hair Caddis or a Tom Thumb near the weed beds and shorelines can offer some extremely fun fishing.

Spincasters and trollers need to use light gear and small lures or spinners. The shallow nature of the lake makes it difficult to cast from shore, but those with a float tube or similar can effectively work the deep pockets. Favourites like the Panther Martin or Mepps Black Fury can work. But as always, check locally for the current hot lure.

Access to Scuitto Lake is through private property, be sure to get permission before fishing the lake. Also be careful as wind can play havoc on boaters.

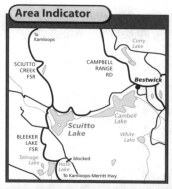

Area Indicator

Scuitto Lake			
Fish Stocking Data			
Year	Species	Number	Life Stage
2011	Rainbow Trout	4,000	Yearling
2010	Rainbow Trout	4,000	Yearling
2009	Rainbow Trout	4,000	Yearling

Directions

Scuitto Lake is located southwest of the tiny community of Bestwick in the heart of rangeland. The lake is best reached by taking the Barnhartvale Road from the Trans Canada Highway east of Kamloops. Continue past the community of Barnhartvale to the Robins-Campbell Range Road, which leads south to Bestwick. Look for the Scuitto Lake Forest Service Road branching west. The lake is about 12 km along this rough, but generally good logging road.

Facilities

There are no developed facilities at the lake. However, there is a lot of open area in which to access the lake, especially at the north and northeast end of the lake. Camping is offered at nearby **Campbell Lake Recreation Site**. Many who stay here explore both lakes on the same weekend. They are both good alternatives early in the year, although Campbell is a better lake to troll.

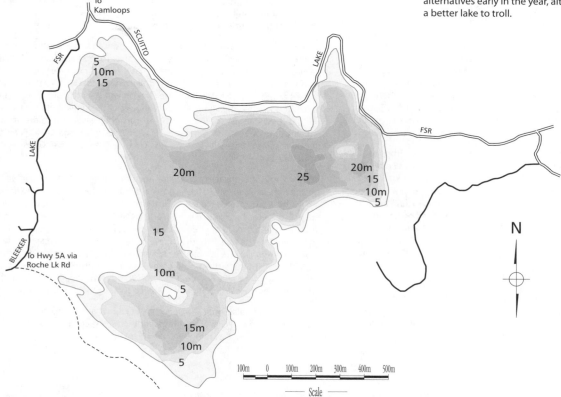

Location: North of Salmon Arm
Elevation: 347 m (1,139 ft)
Surface Area: 31,000 ha (123,520 ac)
Max Depth: 161 m (528 ft)
Mean Depth: 62 m (203 ft)
Way Point: 50° 56′ 00″ N, 119° 17′ 00″ W

Shuswap Lake

Area Indicator

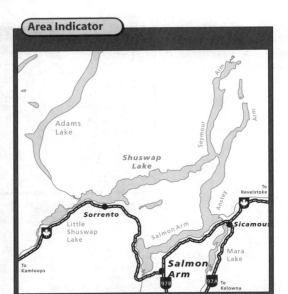

Directions

The Trans-Canada Highway skirts the southern shore of Shuswap Lake between Chase and Sicamous providing easy access to the Main Arm and Salmon Arm of the big lake. From the highway notable roads include the Squilax-Anglemont Road that access the North Shore region, and the Blind Bay and Eagle Bay Roads that access the South Shore region of the Main Arm. Sunnybrae-Canoe Point Road is another popular access point on the Salmon Arm. Of course, marinas and boat launches are found in most communities including Sorrento, Blind Bay, Salmon Arm and Sicamous.

Facilities

Shuswap lake area is very popular for both year round and seasonal residents and is home to countless tourist destinations including resorts, campgrounds, provincial and marine parks and of course the houseboats. One of the best places to begin exploring Shuswap Lake is at Sicamous, the Houseboat Capital of Canada. Marinas and watercraft rentals are located here. The other notable communities including Sorrento, Blind Bay, Salmon Arm and Canoe also have marinas and boat launches to get out on the lake from.

For camping enthusiasts, there are a few BC Park campsites to explore. The busiest and most developed is **Shuswap Lake Provincial Park** near Scotch Creek on the north shore. If features 260 campsites, a large beach and picnic area and paved boat launch. Much smaller, but no less popular, is **Herald Provincial Park** with 119 campsites and large day-use area with a paved boat launch. A lot more remote is the **Silver Beach Provincial Park** at the head of Seymour Arm. Accessed by a long, gravel road or by boat, the former gold rush town of Ogden City now offers 30 campsites and a nice picnic area.

However, the pride and joy of Shuswap Lake has to be the impressive **Shuswap Lake Marine Provincial Park** system. With 26 sites scattered around the shoreline, boaters will find plenty of places to spend the day or night. Please remember these are wilderness sites and please pack out what in.

Fishing

Named after the Shuswap Indians an Interior Salish tribe, Shuswap Lake is one of the most popular destination lakes in British Columbia. With over 1,400 km of shoreline, it is also one of the biggest. The large lake is home to numerous residences, summer cabins, resorts and campgrounds as well as an impressive marine park system spread available around the more remote stretches of the lake. Shuswap Lake also has the largest houseboat fleet in Canada, and one of the largest in the world, offering a fabulous way to vacation with family and friends.

The big lake is made up of several large arms that converge at Cinnemousun Narrows, northeast of Sicamous to give it its distinct addled H shape. The Main Arm runs east-west between the Adams River and the Narrows with notable communities of Sorrento, Blind Bay and the North Shore providing good access. Seymour Arm continues north from the Narrows and accesses many remote marine parks as well as the small community of Seymour Arm. Running parallel to the east is Anstey Arm. This is the smallest arm providing access to an even more remote section of the lake with several marine parks to visit. Finally there is Salmon Arm, which makes up the southern reaches of the big lake between the towns of Salmon Arm and Sicamous.

The big lake has several inflow streams into each arm but only one outlet, Little River, which flows from the Main Arm into Little Shuswap Lake and the South Thompson River. Shuswap Lake is a very clear lake that is considered relatively oligotrophic or low in nutrients and plant life. Countering this lack of productivity are the hundreds of thousands of sockeye salmon that run through the western tip of the lake on their long trek to their spawning grounds in the Adams River and other inlet streams every fall. Although there is no fishery for the salmon, they attract rainbow and lake trout who feast on the eggs in fall and the fry in spring.

Anglers will find excellent fishing for a number of fish species including rainbow trout, kokanee, lake trout, burbot and whitefish. The most popular catch is rainbow, which are the famed Kamloops strain that are noted for their acrobatic performance when hooked. Although not the biggest, rarely getting over 2 kg (5 lbs) in size, they are especially playful if caught on light gear or trolling flies. These trout average around 50 cm (24 in) in length or just over 1 kg (2 lbs) in weight and can be caught by bucktailing or using lures, spoons or plugs that imitate minnows or salmon fry. Look for areas with some weeds to attract the baitfish that bigger fish feast on.

Earlier in the year in May and June, both rainbow and lake trout can be found closer to the surface. The rainbow chase after rolled muddlers or bucktails trolled near the surface in. Alternatively an Apex Trout Killer with green or red in it or a black and silver Rapala trolled in the top 3 m (10 ft) can land a nice sized fish. As the lake heats up the fish will start to hold deep so more weight is needed. By summer a downrigger or heavy weights are essential to get deep enough for the trout. Most turn their attention to the kokanee at this time of year using gang trolls with Wedding Rings or similar. Other popular lures on the lake include small Matrix Blue Fox, silver Gypsy spoons and blue Lyman plugs.

Known hot spots are across from Copper Island at Reedman Point or McBride Point. Fish 20-25 m (60-80 ft) off shore and look for the shallow ledge at Reedman and work towards Blind Bay. Further east, between Ross Creek and Fraser Bay also seems to produce well. Work in the 10–15 m (35–50 ft) depth first thing in the morning or later in the evening. If you are fishing up one of the quieter arms, the river mouths can be quite productive, especially in the fall using anything that resembles the spawning salmon eggs (roe, egg/flesh pattern flies, etc.). Finally the mouth of the Adams and Little River at the extreme western tip of the lake is a great location when it is open. Try using anything that imitates the salmon fry as they make their way out to the Thompson.

Anglers should also note the special regulations and licenses on Shuswap Lake. There are conservation stamps required to keep lake (trout) char over 60 cm (24 in) as well as rainbow over 50 cm (20 in).

www.backroadmapbooks.com

Shuswap Lake

Location: North of Salmon Arm
Elevation: 347 m (1,139 ft)
Surface Area: 31,000 ha (123,520 ac)
Max Depth: 161 m (528 ft)
Mean Depth: 62 m (203 ft)
Way Point: 50° 56′ 00″ N, 119° 17′ 00″ W

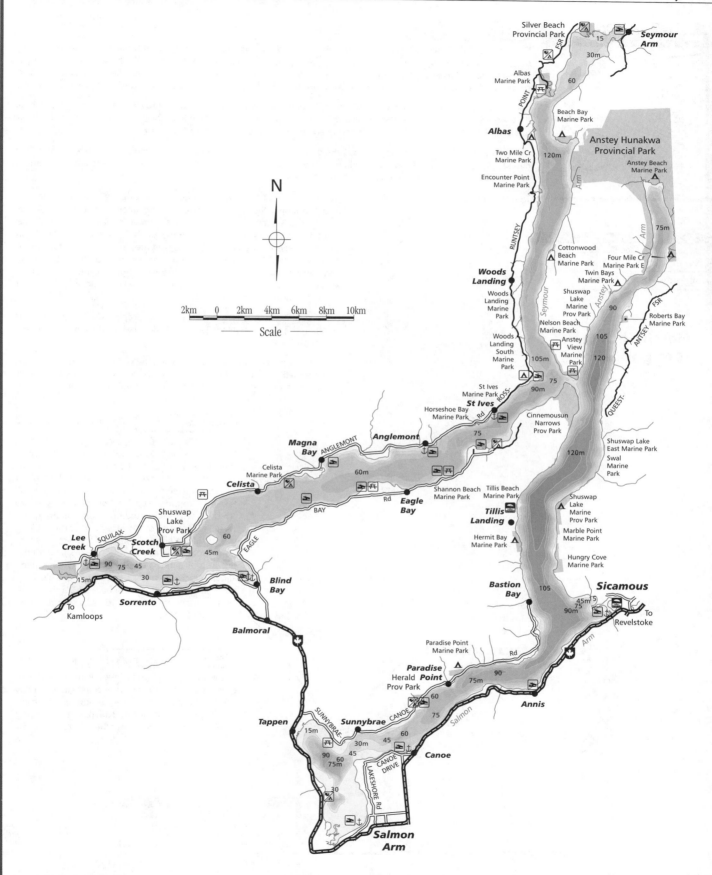

N

2km 0 2km 4km 6km 8km 10km
— Scale —

Silver Beach
Provincial Park
15
30m
Seymour
Arm

Albas
Marine Park
60

Beach Bay
Marine Park

Anstey Hunakwa
Provincial Park

Albas
120m

Anstey Beach
Marine Park

Two Mile Cr
Marine Park

Encounter Point
Marine Park

Woods
Landing

Cottonwood
Beach
Marine Park

Four Mile Cr
Marine Park E

Twin Bays
Marine Park

75m

Woods
Landing
Marine
Park

Shuswap
Lake
Marine
Prov Park

Roberts Bay
Marine Park

90

Nelson Beach
Marine Park

Woods
Landing
South
Marine
Park

Anstey
View
Marine
Park

105

120

105m

75
St Ives
Marine Park

90m

St Ives

Horseshoe Bay
Marine Park

Cinnemousun
Narrows
Prov Park

Shuswap Lake
East Marine Park

Magna
Bay

Anglemont

75

Swal
Marine
Park

Celista
Marine Park

60m

120m

Shuswap
Lake
Marine
Prov Park

Celista

Shannon Beach
Marine Park

Tillis Beach
Marine Park

Eagle
Bay

Tillis
Landing

Marble Point
Marine Park

Lee
Creek

Shuswap
Lake
Prov Park

Scotch
Creek

60

45m

Hermit Bay
Marine Park

Hungry Cove
Marine Park

90 75 45

30

15m

Blind
Bay

Bastion
Bay

105

Sicamous

45m
90m

To
Kamloops

Sorrento

To
Revelstoke

Balmoral

Paradise Point
Marine Park

Paradise
Point

90

Herald
Prov Park

75m

Annis

Tappen

60

75

15m

Sunnybrae

30m

Canoe

90 60
75m

45

60

45

30

Salmon
Arm

Location: 9 km (5.6 mi) north of Whistler
Elevation: 926 m (3038 ft)
Surface Area: 10 ha (25 ac)
Max Depth: 11 m (36 ft)
Mean Depth: 4 m (13 ft)
Way Point: 50° 12' 26.5" N, 122° 57' 32.4" W

www.backroadmapbooks.com

Showh Lakes

Area Indicator

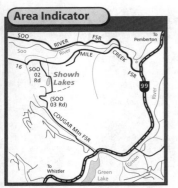

Fishing

South and North Showh Lakes are located high on Cougar Mountain and offer spectacular views out over the valleys on either side of the ridge. While both lakes have been stocked in the past, only North Showh–known locally as Cougar Lake–is stocked these days; a program that resumed in the fall of 2008 after many years. The lakes do have a self-sustaining population of rainbow and so the Freshwater Fisheries Society of BC is stocking North Showh with cutthroat.

Designated fly-fishing only and found on a rough logging road with sections that need a 4wd vehicle, you would think they would be an isolated retreat. Think again. The secret is out. The restrictions, which also include single barbless hooks and catch and release only, are working and word is there are some big trout here.

North Showh or Cougar Lake is regarded as the better of the two, being more nutrient productive with resultant larger rainbow to 1.5 kg (3 lb). The south shoreline is usually productive, while the weed beds on the east side are foraging grounds for the fish and a favourite searching area for fishers.

The two lakes are typical high-elevation lakes, where summer arrives late and fall comes early. The lakes offer the unique option of fishing the transition area between the treeline and alpine. Ice-off usually occurs by mid-June and the following few weeks are always a good opportunity to catch some hungry fish. Trolling flies works well in this lake; the ever popular Doc Spratley or Carey Special are old favourites. In late June and July, try a light green damsel larvae to hook into a feisty rainbow. Keep the tension on that line from the moment your fly strikes the water, as the fish are aggressive and have to take advantage of a very short feeding season to survive.

Other common flies to use are gnats and chironomids, which represent an emerging invertebrate while a simple deer hair Tom Thumb represents almost anything else.

These lakes make a great alternative when the summer doldrums roll into the other Whistler lakes. They are found high enough to offer cooler water temperatures and more active fish during the heat of the summer.

North Showh Lake			
Fish Stocking Data			
Year	Species	Number	Life Stage
2010	Cutthroat Trout	1,000	Catchable

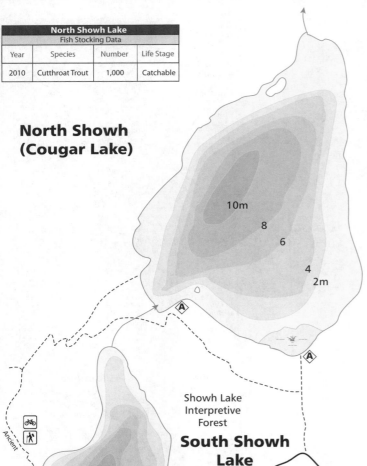

North Showh (Cougar Lake)

10m
8
6
4
2m

Showh Lake Interpretive Forest

South Showh Lake

12
12
10m
8
6
4m
2

To Hwy 99

50m   0   50m   100m   150m   200m

— Scale —

N

Directions

To get to this pair of lakes, take 16 Mile Road, which leaves the Sea to Sky Highway (Highway 99) just past the end of Green Lake. The rough, sometimes 4wd logging road will take you to South Showh Lake if you take the left fork. From here, a walking trail will take you around the back of South Showh and into North Showh. Taking the right fork will bring you within 400 metres of the other end of the walking trail, which is not well signed. However, this section of road is extremely rough. A small float tube put-in is situated at the North Showh shoreline allowing access without disturbing the banks. A few minutes walk from the back of South Showh along the gravel trail takes you to a second put-in option for float tubes.

Facilities

There are no camping facilities at the lakes. However, if you like to do a couple of activities in a day combine fishing with a hike through the spectacular, old growth forest located nearby. Take your bug repellant because sometimes the fish aren't the only things biting.

South Showh Lake			
Fish Stocking Data			
Year	Species	Number	Life Stage
2010	Cutthroat Trout	250	Catchable
2009	Cutthroat Trout	200	Catchable

Six Mile (Pat) Lake

Location: 25 km (15.5 mi) west of Kamloops
Elevation: 600 m (1,968 ft)
Surface Area: 10 ha (23 ac)
Max Depth: 8 m (26 ft)
Mean Depth: 2.7 m (8.8 ft)
Way Point: 51° 1′ 25″ N, 121° 32′ 46″ W

Fishing

For many years, Six Mile Lake was the place to be on April 1st, which is the first day of fishing after winter closure for many of the Interior's fly-fishing lakes.

A low elevation grassland lake, Six Mile was always one of the first lakes to become ice-free. Also known as Pat Lake, anglers flocked there in big numbers, creating an annual fishing ritual that many looked forward to. However, low water levels over several consecutive years led to devastating winter fish kills and high pH levels made angling difficult as trout endured uncomfortable conditions. As a result, Six Mile Lake faded from many anglers' minds.

Today, the lake is back in prime condition. A watershed enhancement project was established by the provincial Ministry of Environment, Ducks Unlimited, local fish and game clubs and local water users. This project has created a stable inflow of water that has reduced the pH to normal levels and restored water to many of the lake's shoals.

Continued annual stocking of 3,000 Pennask rainbow trout by the Freshwater Fisheries Society of BC means the lake has a healthy population of trout. Expect to catch fish up to 2 kg (4 lbs).

Six Mile Lake is not very big. Most of the fishing takes place in the bays at each end of the lake. The usual fly-fishing patterns, particularly small chironomids in the early season and shrimp year-round, are very effective. The clear water demands skill from anglers. With so much natural feed to choose from and such water clarity, trout are able to pick over a pattern's details. Using a long leader on a floating line in this lake can be very effective. The long leader allows the fly to sink down to near the bottom where the fish are feeding and keeps the thicker fly line out of sight of the suspicious fish.

Trollers may find it hard to fish due to the number of anchored fly casters to weave around. But, once the early season passes, the lake does get quieter. Fly anglers can troll leeches, dragonfly nymph patterns or shrimp.

The lake is not a fly-fishing only lake, though it might seem that way in early spring. But gear anglers can fish the lake, too. It is a small lake and trolling is not the easiest thing to do, but dragging a Flatfish and spinners around edges of the deep hole near the south end of the lake can be effective. Spincasters can set up near the edge of the hole and retrieve across the drop off.

Six Mile Lake is closed to fishing from December 1 to March 31.

Area Indicator

Six Mile Lake Fish Stocking Data			
Year	Species	Number	Life Stage
2008	Rainbow Trout	3,000	Yearling
2008	Rainbow Trout	500	Spring Catchable
2007	Rainbow Trout	4,500	Yearling
2007	Rainbow Trout	860	Spring Catchable
2006	Rainbow Trout	3,000	Yearling

Facilities

There are no services at the lake or overnight camping as the lake is surrounded by private land. The nearest place to camp is just west of Savona, at Steelhead Provincial Park.

Directions

From Kamloops, take the Trans Canada Highway west toward Savona. At the entrance to Six Mile Ranch, now known as the Tobiano residential and golf course development, turn south and go up the narrow frontage road. This was once a paved route to Ashcroft. The pavement is now broken up, but the road is still passable during the angling season. The lake is found 3 km from the highway.

Location: Southeast of Hope
Stream Length: 57 km (35 mi)
Geographic: 121° 10' 1"W, 49° 7' 4" N

Skagit River

Fishing

Anglers who are passionate about fishing the Skagit call it the prettiest trout stream in North America. This is pretty high accolades for a continent full of beautiful trout streams. However, resting about 2.5 hours east of Vancouver, the Skagit is definitely one of the best trout rivers in the province.

The river is managed as catch and release only and has a bait ban. While it is not a fly-fishing only river, it certainly feels like one and it is one of the most popular fly-fishing destinations from Vancouver. The river is closed to fishing from November 1 to June 30. In the four months that these waters are open, though, it offers some of the best dry fly-fishing in the province for rainbow that can on occasion get to 50 cm (20 inches).

The river is divided into two sections: The upper and lower Skagit. The upper section is accessed from the Sumallo Grove Day Use Area along the Crowsnest Highway. From here, an angler's trail follows the river downstream. Because this section of the river is only accessible by foot, it sees far less action than the lower section and the farther you walk, the better the chances you will have the river all to yourself. It is this remote section that angler's are talking about when they get that dreamy, far-away look in their eyes.

The lower Skagit is accessible from the Silver Skagit Road and there are nine parking areas/picnic sites along the road from which you can access the river. This section is much more popular because of the road access.

The biggest hatch on the river is the Western Green Drake, but there are also good hatches of caddis flies and stoneflies. Fishing terrestrials like grasshoppers can work extremely well, too. Some of the most popular dry flies are the Adams, Parachute Adams, Humpies, Royal Wulff and Elk Hair Caddis.

Nymph fishing is best during the long, hot days of August when the fish hold in deeper, cooler pockets of water. Try a Hare's ear, Prince Nymph or a Green Drake Nymph, in sizes #8–12. There are plenty of mosquitoes about, too. You can try working a mosquito imitation, but it is better to just bring along lots of repellant.

In fall, the rainbow begin heading back towards the deep water of Ross Lake and so the lower portion is your best bet.

The river also holds some large Dolly Varden. These are best fished with streamer patterns or Woolly Buggers.

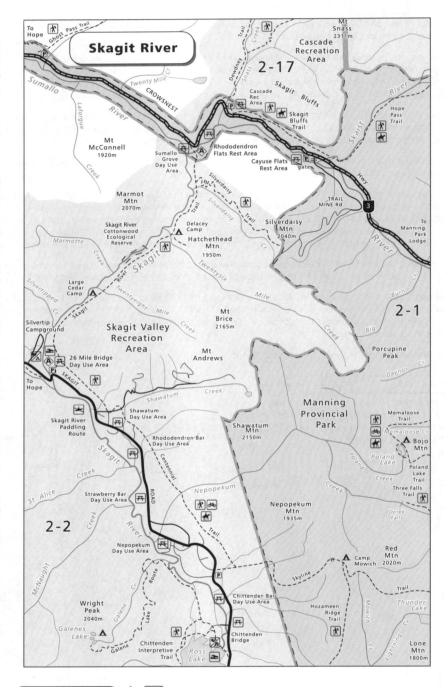

Facilities

In addition to Sumallo Grove, Rhododendron Flats and Cayuse Flats are other day use areas in the upper reaches of the river that offer washroom facilities and picnic tables. The lower reaches also offer many day use areas (see above) as well as camping at Silvertip and Ross Lake. All are part of the **Skagit Valley Provincial Park**. In between the two sections is the **Skagit River Trail**. There are a few rustic backcountry campsites along the trail.

Directions

Sumallo Grove is found along the Crowsnest Highway east of Hope, near Manning Park. Watch for the day use parking area about 14 km (8.7 miles) past Sunshine Valley. The river is accessed by trail from here.

Getting to the lower section involves taking the Silver Skagit Road exit (Exit 168) off the Trans Canada, just west of Hope. Follow the road for about 42 km (26 miles) to the 26 Mile Bridge Day Use Area of Skagit Valley Provincial Park. As you make your way southeast, watch for a variety of day-use and parking areas which provide access to the river including Shawatum, Rhododendron Bar, Strawberry Bar, etc.

Skookum & Snohoosh Lakes

Skookum Lake

Elevation: 867 m (2,844 ft)
Surface Area: 19 ha (47 ac)
Max Depth: 8.8 m (29 ft)
Mean Depth: 4.5 m (15 ft)
Way Point: 51° 6' 35.6"N, 120° 52' 48.7"W

Snohoosh Lake

Elevation: 827 m (2,713 ft)
Surface Area: 91 ha (225 ac)
Max Depth: 25.9 m (85 ft)
Mean Depth: 13.9 m (45.6 ft)
Way Point: 51° 4' 35"N, 120° 52' 35"W

Fishing

These lakes are found in the heart of the Dead-man Valley. Despite a series of decent fishing lakes and fine recreation sites, this dramatic, dry valley does not see the crowd's common to other areas of the region.

Skookum Lake is a shallow lake with some nice shoals at the southeast end and at the north end. The lake drops off rapidly particularly at the east and west ends of the lake. Nearby Snohoosh Lake is a long, narrow lake that offers similar fishing. Both lakes offer rainbow and kokanee that can reach 1 kg (2 lbs) in size.

Fishing is best beginning in mid-May after the lake has turned over and before mid-July. By the summer, the fish are very inactive as the water has warmed because of the shallow depths. Even if you were able to get a bite, the fish are lethargic and provide little fight in summer. It is not until late September that the fishing picks up again.

Trolling is tough on Skookum because of the shallow depths but it is possible to troll small lake trolls, fly or small lure near the surface. On the other hand, Snohoosh is a popular trolling lake. For the kokanee and rainbow, try a Willow Leaf and worm or maggot. A pink lure such as a Dick Nite or pink Flatfish also works for the kokanee. The rainbow also take to small lures.

Fly-fishermen should focus their efforts around the shoals and the nice drop offs. Most of the insect hatches common to the region (chironomids, mayflies, damsel and dragon flies, etc) are also found at the lakes. Try matching one of the many hatches.

Using a float tube or boat and casting towards shore will improve the chances of success. In the summer months, it is possible to shore fish because the water level tends to drop.

Directions

To reach the lakes, take the Deadman-Vidette Road leading north from the Trans Canada Highway just west of the impressive Deadman River Bridge. The road follows the Deadman River for what appears like an eternity until you reach Skookum Lake. The road is quite rough in places, which limits larger units from wanting to venture in.

Facilities

Snohoosh Lake North Recreation Site is found at the north end of the lake and offers a boat launch and a couple campsites. Shore casting from the campsite is a possibility in the summer months when the lake is at its lowest water level. A private campground is also located at the south end of Snohoosh.

There used to be a recreation site on Skookum, but it is no longer. People still camp and launch from the large grassy area next to the lake.

To Vidette

Snohoosh Lake Rec Site

To Vidette

DEADMAN-

Skookum Lake

To Hwy 1

N

200m 0 200m 600m 1000m
Scale

Snohoosh Lake

VIDETTE

ROAD

Deadman R

To Hwy 1

Area Indicator

Location: 19 km (11.8 mi) west of Hope
Elevation: 1,258 m (4,127 ft)
Surface Area: 26 ha (64 ac)
Max Depth: 47 m (154 ft)
Mean Depth: 22 m (72 ft)
Way Point: 49° 24' 36.5" N, 121° 42' 26.1" W

www.backroadmapbooks.com

Slollicum Lake

Fishing

Slollicum Lake is found in a beautiful sub-alpine valley to the east of Harrison Lake. People who have spent lots of time visiting lakes in the region proclaim this as one of the nicest, if not the nicest lake to visit in the Lower Mainland. At the north end of the lake is an expansive alpine meadow worth the hike. Rugged cliffs and talus slopes surround the south end of the lake.

The high elevation lake provides an excellent summer fishery, as the water remains cool through August.

If you're looking for a trophy trout, look elsewhere. As with most small alpine or sub-alpine lakes, the fish here are small. If you do go, expect fast fishing for small rainbows that average 25–30 cm (10–12 in).

Because the lake is such a high elevation lake, it often isn't accessible until mid-June, and even later in years with lots of snow. Be prepared to have to turn around if you go up too early in the year. Better to wait until at least early July to go to the lake. By then the trail should be free of snow and the lake free of ice.

Because the lake is a hike-in lake, you'll have to carry any gear you want with you. And since you gain nearly a kilometre in elevation, chances are, you'll want as little gear as possible. If you decide to haul a float tube with you, you will probably have better luck than people stuck on shore, but the fish are pretty easy to catch either way. If you're stuck onshore, there is a nice ledge right off the northern shore near the meadow. Use a bobber with a worm or a single egg or try fly-fishing.

Because the lake has a short ice-off season, the fish are quite voracious. There is no real secret to catching the fish here, other than getting a hook in front of them. Small spoons, spinners and a variety of fly patterns will all work. As long as it looks vaguely edible and isn't too big, the fish will try and eat it.

Area Indicator

Directions

To reach the lake involves some route finding and so it is well advised to bring along a copy of the Backroad Mapbook for Vancouver, Coast & Mountains.

From Harrison Hot Springs, follow Lillooet Avenue east, eventually curving left and on to Rockwell Drive. Follow Rockwell Drive along the eastern shore of the lake to the entrance to Sasquatch Provincial Park.

Just inside of the park, turn left onto the Harrison-East Forest Service Road. Follow this road for 4.8 km (3 miles), then turn right onto the rough Slollicum Forest Service Road. Follow the branch road on foot or by 4wd for about 800 metres to a fork in the road. People with modified 4wd trucks can get past this point, but this is about as far as most vehicles can make it.

From here, you're looking at a 13.5 km (8.3 mile) return hike, gaining 924 metres (3,031 ft) in elevation. Take the branch road on the left. The route is flagged up a talus slope to hook up with a logging road. Turn left. Where the road forks, stay right, and follow an ever-fainter trail to the lake.

Facilities

There are no developed facilities at the lake. However, the beautiful meadow at the south end is ideal for camping

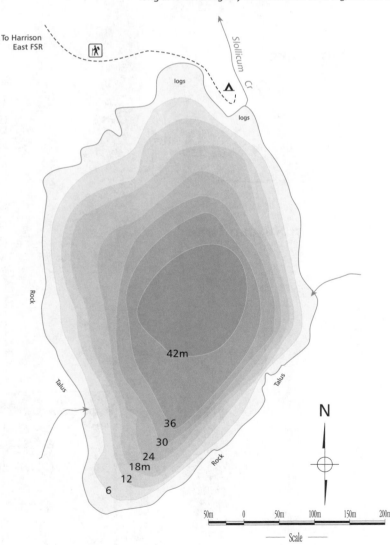

www.backroadmapbooks.com

South Alouette River

Location: North of Maple Ridge
Stream Length: 31.63 km (19.7 mi)
Geographic: 49° 14′ 22″ N, 122° 34′ 56″ W

Fishing

The story of the Alouette plays like a tragedy, one that is familiar to many people across the province. The river was originally called the Lillooet River and the lake Lillooet Lake, but in 1915, the name was changed to Alouette. Ten years later, construction was approved on a dam on the Alouette with no provisions for fish to bypass, no minimum downstream flow and no flood control measures. Two years later, seven species of fish were either mostly or completely wiped out of the river. Sockeye, which spawned in the lake and higher, were the first to go, followed by Chinook and pink.

In the early 1990s, the Alouette River Management Society was formed. One of the goals was to try and bring life back to the dying river. Part of that included the negotiation of a minimum flow level above the two cubic feet per second the DFO had managed to get in 1971. By 1996, the average flow was increased to 92 cubic feet per second. And in July 2007, after an eighty-year absence, sockeye salmon returned to the Alouette.

All this is to say that the Alouette is a river in recovery, but it's doing much better, thank you. The river is about 45 minutes from downtown Vancouver and flows out of Alouette Lake in Golden Ears Provincial Park to the Fraser.

The river has steelhead, cutthroat, Dolly Varden, chum, pink, Coho, Chinook and the aforementioned sockeye, almost all of which are enhanced by the Allco Hatchery. It is catch and release for Dolly Varden, chum and pink.

The river is closed to fishing around the Correctional Facility and is closed above 216th Street from May 1–June 30.

When the river re-opens in July, chum fry are present in the river. Cutthroat trout like to feed on them and anglers will have good luck using something that imitates the fry. For fly casters, Muddler Minnows and streamer patterns work well, while spincasters can work small spoons and spinners. In places, a simple bobber and worm set-up can be just as effective.

There is no retention for chum which begin returning in September, but once again, the cutthroat fishing picks up as they begin to feed on floating eggs. An egg sucking leech pattern works great for fly fishers, while spincasters can work a single egg on a hook.

The Coho return in October. Currently anglers are allowed to retain one hatchery Coho per day until December 31, but check the regulations before heading out.

In December, steelhead enter the system. These are usually taken on the fly or float fishing.

Directions

The South Alouette flows south out of Alouette Lake, then west to the Pitt River, joining up with the North Alouette—which flows out of the UBC Research forest. The bottom section of the river is diked and easily accessed from a variety of dike trails that follow the river for many kilometres. One of the easiest places to access the lower river is to head north from the Lougheed Highway on Harris Road to the bridge.

Facilities

There is camping in Golden Ears Provincial Park and all variety of services in Maple Ridge and Pitt Meadows, which the river flows through. **The Trans Canada Trail** skirts part of the south shore of the river and there is a good dike trail system throughout.

South Alouette River			
Fish Stocking Data			
Year	Species	Number	Life Stage
2011	Cutthroat Trout	8,761	Smolt
2011	Steelhead	31,141	Smolt

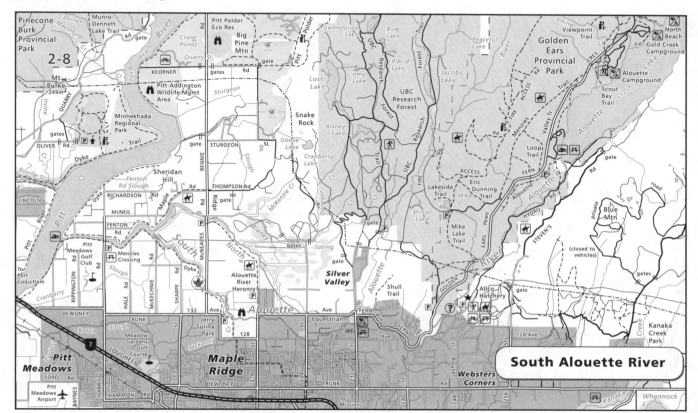

South Alouette River

Location: East of Kamloops
Stream Length: 63.1 km (39.2 mi)
Geographic: 50°39' N, 119°52' W

South Thompson River

Fishing

While the Thompson River is known for its phenomenal steelhead fishing (world's greatest steelhead river, many would argue), that basically ends at Kamloops Lake. Most of the steelhead spawn up the Nicola, Bonaparte and Deadman Rivers and while there are some steelhead that do come up this way, the South Thompson is better known for its rainbow and Dolly Varden fishing.

The South Thompson flows westward from Shuswap Lake, through the town of Chase before joining forces with the North Thompson at Kamloops to become simply the Thompson River.

The South Thompson moves at a fair clip, without the same rapid/pool sort of structure you will find on other rivers. Instead, the grade is fairly continuous, flowing over a rocky bottom. The river is a popular river for drift fishing.

The river does get good runs of salmon. Chinook, Coho, chum, pink and sockeye are all found in the South Thompson. In fact, the famous Adams run of sockeye passes this way on their way to their spawning beds. However, the river is closed to salmon fishing year-round, except for a summer opening for Chinook.

During this time, people tend to bottom bounce for Chinook using Spin-N-Glos or coloured wool. And while there are some nice sized Chinook caught here, the fish can get pretty bruised and beaten up as they make their way up river, especially during low water.

However, during the salmon spawn, the river's gigantic rainbow trout, which can get to 4.5 kg (10 lbs) and Dolly Varden feed on dislodged salmon eggs. Fishing can be fast and furious for these species, especially in the upper reaches of the river.

The river is usually accessed from the north side, along the Shuswap Road. While the last few kilometres of the river are mostly through the Kamloops Indian Reserve (and is sometimes closed; check with the local shops for access updates), there is great access to the river from the north side.

The best fishing is from January to March for the big trout and Dolly Varden. Because the current is relentless, you will need some weight on your line to get down low. Some people use a Bouncing Betty Rig using worms and salted roe.

Other lures that seem to produce well are silver and black Apex and brown Flatfish.

Directions

The South Thompson River flows from Chase to Kamloops. The Trans Canada Highway follows its south bank its entire length, but most anglers prefer to access the river from the more sedate north side, especially since so much of the south side of the river is private land. One of the most popular places to access the river is at Pritchard, where you will find a bridge over the river and a provincial park.

Facilities

Pritchard Provincial Park is a popular place to access the river. However, it is a day use park, with no overnight camping. There are some places to camp in the area, including **Niskonlith Lakes Provincial Park**, just north of the river near Chase and a whole mess of recreation sites and private campsites within 20 km or so of the river. Both Chase and Kamloops provide accommodation and full services including local tackle shops to pick up last minute supplies.

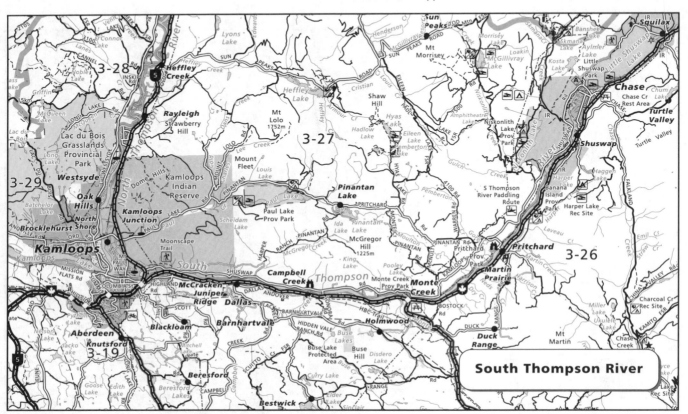

South Thompson River

www.backroadmapbooks.com

Location: Squamish
Stream Length: 89 km (55 mi)
Geographic: 123°23′00″W, 50°6′00″N

REGION 2

Squamish River

Squamish River

Fishing

Arguably the prettiest river in BC, the Squamish is also known for its wildlife. There is a small elk population in the area, lots of grizzly and black bears when the salmon are spawning and during the winter, the area is home to the greatest population of bald eagles in the country.

The bears and eagles come here for the salmon, as do hundreds of anglers each year. The best fishing happens upstream of the Ashlu/Squamish confluence or downstream from the Cheakamus confluence. The middle section is broad and meandering with a sandy bottom, poor fishing and limited access. The most popular spot is around the Cheakamus.

The river is especially popular with fly-fishers, who love the wide-open casting. Anglers seeking solace will want to head for the upper Squamish, where they will find resident Dolly Varden and bull trout. During spring and summer they feed on juvenile fish, while in the autumn they feed on salmon eggs and salmon carcasses. In the spring, streamer patterns will work well, while in fall, the ever-popular egg-sucking leech is a good choice.

But most people who fish the river in autumn are here for the salmon. The Squamish features a good run of Chinook, Coho, chum and during odd years, a strong run of pink. The best month for Chinook is September, while Coho peak a few weeks later.

Pink are aggressive biters, making them a good salmon for people learning the sport. They are also the most plentiful of all salmon found on the Squamish, with people pulling out dozens of pink in a day. The average sized pink weighs 2–2.5 kg (4–5 lbs) and fly-fishing is popular. These fish seem to have an affinity for the colour pink. Pink streamers, pink Woolly Buggers… as long as the hook isn't too big, you should have no trouble catching one of these fish.

Chum are another popular catch later in the year with the run peaking in late October. These fish can be caught by bottom bouncing, using lures or spinners or even fly-fishing. Wool is probably the most common lure for chum, but fly-fishers can try working green or purple Woolly Buggers and leech patterns.

There are also cutthroat trout and rainbow trout in the river and a late run of winter steelhead, which peaks in April. By early May the river is usually too high and murky to fish effectively, so the steelhead season is very short. It should also be noted that the river swells quickly after rains and should be avoided at those times.

Directions

The Squamish River drains into Howe Sound at Squamish and can be accessed from a variety of roads and trails in the town. However, the fishing south of Brackendale is poor so it is best to fish from the diked trails between here and the mouth of the Cheakamus.

To access the upper reaches of the Squamish, take the Squamish Valley Road off the Sea to Sky (Highway 99) across from Alice Lake Provincial Park. Follow this road north across the Cheakamus where the road splits. Stay left along the Squamish Valley Road, which is paved until about the Ashlu Confluence.

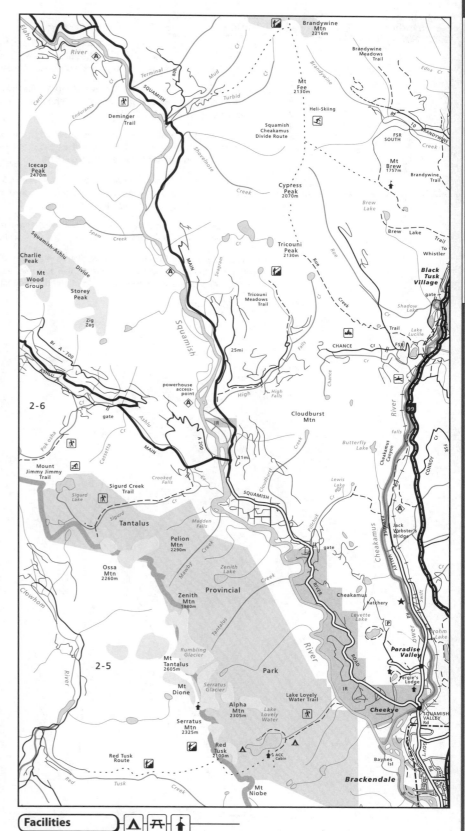

Facilities

There are some rustic camping sites up the Squamish Valley, mostly undeveloped save for the Hideaway Recreation Site, which is currently closed indefinitely. Nearby **Alice Lake Provincial Park** provides developed camping, while there are all manner of services in Squamish.

Location: 8 km (5 mi) southwest of Harrison Hot Springs
Elevation: 783 m (2,569 ft)
Surface Area: 3 ha (7 ac)
Max Depth: 9 m (30 ft)
Mean Depth: 5 m (16 ft)
Way Point: 49° 15' 58.8" N, 121° 52' 25.7" W

Stacey Lake

Stacey Lake

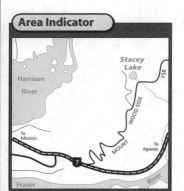

Area Indicator

Fishing

Located on the top of Mount Woodside west of Agassiz, this lake features some spectacular views. The pristine lake is very small–less than 2.8 hectares. Even though the lake is surrounded by dense forest, there is a walking trail around the entire lake, providing reasonably good access for shoreline fishing.

There is no natural production at Stacey Lake so the Freshwater Fisheries Society of BC stocks the lake several times a year to ensure that adventurous anglers will be rewarded for their efforts. The rainbow are aggressive biters and scrappy fighters–an angler's delight.

This small lake is an ideal place to take kids fishing as it can be fished easily from either the shore or small watercraft. Most of the trout you will catch here are in the 25–35 cm (10–12 in) range but fish managing to avoid the frying pan for a season or two can get as large as 40 cm (16 in).

The lake is a little off the beaten track, so it does not receive a lot of pressure. Another bonus is the fact that the lake is high enough in elevation to maintain a decent fishery even during the height of summer. In most years, Stacey Lake is accessible and fishable from March to mid-October.

Fishing with a bobber and worm or Powerbait works well and is a kid-friendly method. For those with a little more patience, fly-casting small chironomids, leeches, Halfbacks or a Tom Thumb will bring plenty of action.

On the drive up to the lake you will most likely see hang gliders riding the thermals on a clear day. The glider launch is about 2.5 km (1.5 mi) up the gravel road. You also might see black tail deer, black bears, grouse and eagles in the area. An added bonus is the roadside wild huckleberries available in June and July.

Directions

Stacey Lake is found on Mount Woodside, which in turn is found north of the Lougheed Highway (Highway 7) between Harrison Mills and Agassiz. The turnoff to the lake is about an hours drive from Vancouver on the north shore of the Fraser River. Follow the Woodside Mountain Forest Service Road for about 7.5 km (4.7 mi) and watch for a small road to your left. Follow this road for 100 metres or so to the lake. A truck is recommended, especially if coming in the early spring or late fall.

Facilities

There is a small informal camping area at the lake. It also possible to hand launch small boats or float tubs from lakeside. Nearby Kilby Provincial Park offers a full service campsite and good access to Harrison Bay. During summer it is recommended to reserve a site through Discover Camping. For more luxurious accommodations the resort town of Harrison Hot Springs or at least the hot springs themselves are worth checking out.

Other Options

Further up the hillside, **Campbell Lake** is a difficult lake to get to. Despite being a true mountain lake, it offers a slow fishery for small rainbow trout. This is partly due to the fact the shallow lake winterkills over harsh winters. The lake has extensive shallows and a lot of shoreline debris making shore casting rather challenging. Best to bring a float tube for this one.

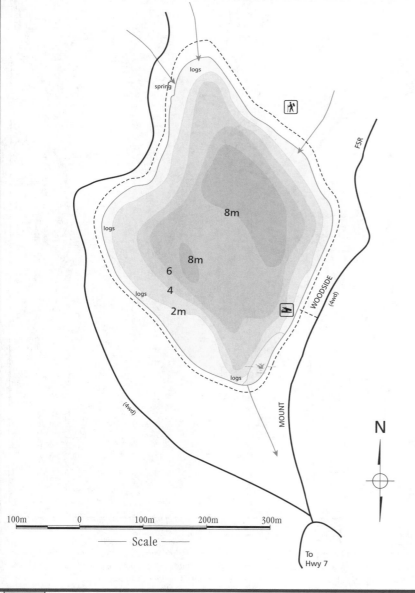

N

Stacey Lake			
Fish Stocking Data			
Year	Species	Number	Life Stage
2010	Rainbow Trout	750	Catchable
2009	Rainbow Trout	750	Catchable

100m   0   100m   200m   300m

— Scale —

To Hwy 7

Stake Lake

Location: 20 km (12 mi) south of Kamloops
Elevation: 1,320 m (4,331 ft)
Surface Area: 23 ha (57 ac)
Max Depth: 9 m (29.5 ft)
Mean Depth: 4.3 m (14.1 ft)
Way Point: 50° 30′ 53.0″ N, 120° 28′ 34.5″ W

Fishing

Stake Lake is a popular recreation destination. While it is best known for its Nordic ski trails, it is a popular spot for hiking, mountain biking and of course, fishing.

The State Lake fishing season begins in late April when the ice leaves the lake. There are fair numbers of rainbow trout that grow to 2 kg (4-5 lbs) but the average size of the fish is quite small.

You should expect to see other fishermen as the lake is often crowded, especially in the spring. State Lake is best fished, like most lakes in the area, in the spring and fall. However, the summer fishery does remain active. The lake has an aerator to guard against winterkill and it is stocked annually to counteract the heavy fishing pressure.

Gear anglers prefer to troll the lake with a Willow Leaf and worm or small lure such as a Flatfish or Dick Nite. However, fly-fishing should not be ruled out as the lake has some nice shoals and weed covered shallows to sample. Be forewarned, the crystal clear water makes the fly-fishing tough as the fish are harder to trick and are extremely picky. Try using a long, fine leader to counteract the clear water problem.

The caddisfly hatch at the end of May and into early June is a good time to fish with dry flies. A shrimp pattern, fished near the bottom, is also effective throughout most of the spring and the fall. Other hatches of note are the spring chironomid hatch, the spring mayfly hatch and the fall water boatman hatch.

The lake has some wide open areas, which shoreline fishers can access from the trails that circle the lake. Some spots will be more productive than others, as some points stick out closer to the drop off. Casting a small spoon or spinner from the shore can be productive, though many places are reedy.

For best results, use a float tube and cast near the shoals and drop offs, which are easily seen through the clear water. By casting this way, you are able to more effectively work the drop off and trout are more likely to follow your offering. The trick is to vary the speed and jerk the line so as to mimic a fleeing insect or baitfish.

Ice fishing is not recommended as the aerator makes the ice dangerously thin.

Area Indicator

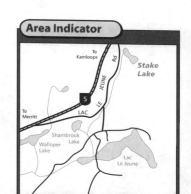

Stake Lake Fish Stocking Data			
Year	Species	Number	Life Stage
2011	Rainbow Trout	16,000	Yearling
2010	Rainbow Trout	16,020	Yearling
2009	Rainbow Trout	16,040	Yearling

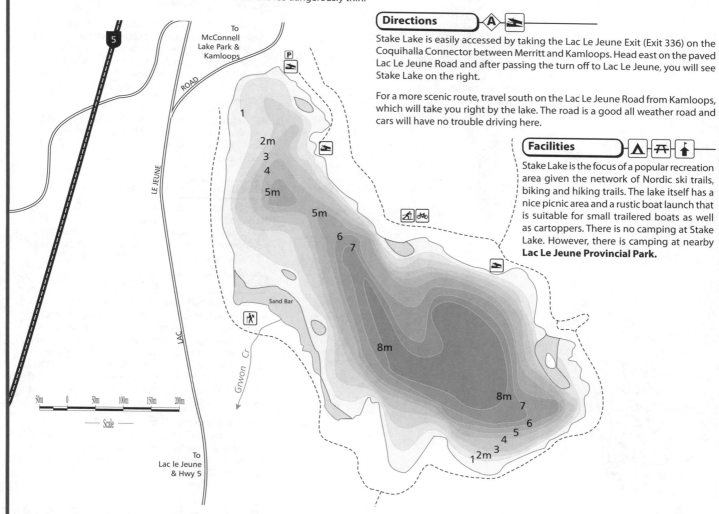

Directions

Stake Lake is easily accessed by taking the Lac Le Jeune Exit (Exit 336) on the Coquihalla Connector between Merritt and Kamloops. Head east on the paved Lac Le Jeune Road and after passing the turn off to Lac Le Jeune, you will see Stake Lake on the right.

For a more scenic route, travel south on the Lac Le Jeune Road from Kamloops, which will take you right by the lake. The road is a good all weather road and cars will have no trouble driving here.

Facilities

Stake Lake is the focus of a popular recreation area given the network of Nordic ski trails, biking and hiking trails. The lake itself has a nice picnic area and a rustic boat launch that is suitable for small trailered boats as well as cartoppers. There is no camping at Stake Lake. However, there is camping at nearby **Lac Le Jeune Provincial Park.**

© Mussio Ventures Ltd.

Location: 15 km (9.3 mi) north of Mission
Elevation: 214m (702 ft)
Surface Area: 5,858 ha (14,475 ac)
Maximum Depth: 101 m (331.4 ft)
Mean Depth: 34.8 m (114.2 ft)
Way Point: 49° 22' 9"N, 122° 17' 49"W

www.backroadmapbooks.com

Stave Lake

Area Indicator

Fishing

Stave Lake is one of a series of long, narrow and large lakes stretching back from the Fraser Valley into the Coastal Mountains. Like nearby Alouette Lake, Stave is a man-made, or rather, man-enhanced lake, created by building a dam Stave River in 1912, which roughly quadrupled the size of the original lake. Parts of the area weren't logged, especially the northern end and the lake still suffers from a large amount of debris and snags, some still standing above water and others snapped off just below the surface. These provide habitat for fish, but also create boating hazards.

The main arm of the lake is just over 20 km (12 miles) long and, as is typical with big lakes, trolling is the prime method of fishing here. Fluctuating water levels can create inconsistent fishing. Try working the inflow area from Alouette Lake, as well as the many stream estuaries, sandy beaches, rock cliffs and hidden coves.

Kokanee are best fished near the powerhouse, along the western shore. The oxygen rich water here attracts good numbers of these landlocked salmon in the spring. Kokanee can be caught by casting small lures and spinners along the edges of the current created by the outflow from the turbines. At this time, Dolly Varden, which can get to 5 kg (10 lbs) follow the kokanee. Dollies prefer to loiter around the bottom so be sure to get your presentation deep.

The lake also holds good numbers of wild rainbow and cutthroat. These are usually caught by trolling lake trolls, Flatfish or lures. At low water, the dam-controlled lake becomes almost river like at the north end of the lake. During these times fly-fishing can be quite productive, with rumours of 7 kg (15 lb) cutthroat caught on Doc Spratleys.

As is also typical with big lakes, it is prone to sudden strong winds that can make boating treacherous. Be sure to follow the warning signs and then stick to the deeper channel around the boat launch.

Directions

Most boaters launch near the Stave Falls Dam at the south end. The boat launch is found a short distance up the Florence Lake Forest Service Road from the Dewdney Trunk Road. The Dewdney Trunk can be picked up off the Lougheed Highway near Maple Ridge.

Facilities

BC Hydro maintains three facilities in the Stave Lake area and another one at Hayward Lake, just below Stave. The only camping in the area is at the **Stave Lake Lodge and Campsite**, a six unit campground. Also in the area is the **Stave Lake Boat Launch**, which is a day-use area with picnic facilities and the aforementioned boat launch. The **Stave Falls Interpretive Centre** is found off the Dewdney Trunk Road and tells a story of power generation in BC.

While the bridge to the former Cypress Point Recreation Site has been pulled and the site deactivated (victim of being too close to the Lower Mainland and too popular with the rowdies), it is still possible to access the site by boat. Intrepid explorers looking to stay on the lake can probably find better random camping spots elsewhere.

Stave River

www.backroadmapbooks.com

Location: West of Mission
Stream Length: 53.5 km (33.3 mi)
Geographic: 49° 10' 35" N, 122° 25' 20" W

Fishing

The Stave River drains Stave Lake, via Stave Falls, into the Fraser River, passing through Hayward Lake first. The actual "river" portion of the Stave is only a 1.5 km (0.9 miles), as the Ruskin Dam prevents the salmon from spawning any farther.

Despite its short length, the Stave is still a popular place to fish because it is easy to access and there are lots of fish.

Specifically, there are lots of chum salmon and in fall the river is usually crowded with people. In recent years, the river has seen an increase in the number of people fishing here who don't know what they're doing: fishing without a license, exceeding the daily limit and foul snagging fish is unfortunately quite common. Fortunately, there has been a strong grassroots effort to educate these anglers and it is a great place to learn how to fish properly, as the fish are usually quite willing to be caught.

For such a short river, the Stave is quite wide, with many islands and bars. Having a boat is a real bonus, as the banks can get quite crowded. Because the river is right below the Stave Dam, the water level can fluctuate greatly and, as a low-lying tributary of the Fraser, the Stave is a tidal river. All this is to say be careful when fishing here, as you don't want to get stranded by rising waters.

The Stave has a large return of chum salmon. These start showing up in October and peak in early November. There are thousands of chum, which are known for being aggressive and easy to catch. Chum are not a great salmon for eating, but they put up a good fight.

Fishing for chum can be done by drifting a float, bottom bouncing, using lures or spinners or even fly-fishing. Wool is probably the most common lure for fishing for chum, but fly-fishers can try working Woolly Buggers and leech patterns. Green and purple tend to be the best colours for chum. While wet fly-fishing is the most common, chum have been known to chase dry flies, too, so don't be afraid to experiment

The Stave also has a fair return of Coho that basically overlaps the chum return. Unlike chum, Coho are not aggressive and can be hard to find. Even if you are targeting Coho, expect to get more chum. You can increase your chances by targeting some of the quieter pools and back eddies. Coho seem to like silver or copper spoons.

Directions

To get to the Stave River from Vancouver, take the Lougheed Highway (Highway 7) east through Maple Ridge to 287 Street, just before the Stave River Bridge. This turns into Wilson Road and parallels the west side of the river. Turn right onto Hayward Street, crossing the single lane route over the Ruskin Dam and park at the BC Hydro day-use site. From here you can hike along the riverbank to find the perfect spot.

Facilities

There is parking and picnic facilities at the BC Hydro **Ruskin Dam Recreation Site**. You will also find public washrooms and a nice trail system. There is camping at nearby **Stave Lake Campground** and **Rolley Lake Provincial Park**, although these may be closed, depending how late in the year you go.

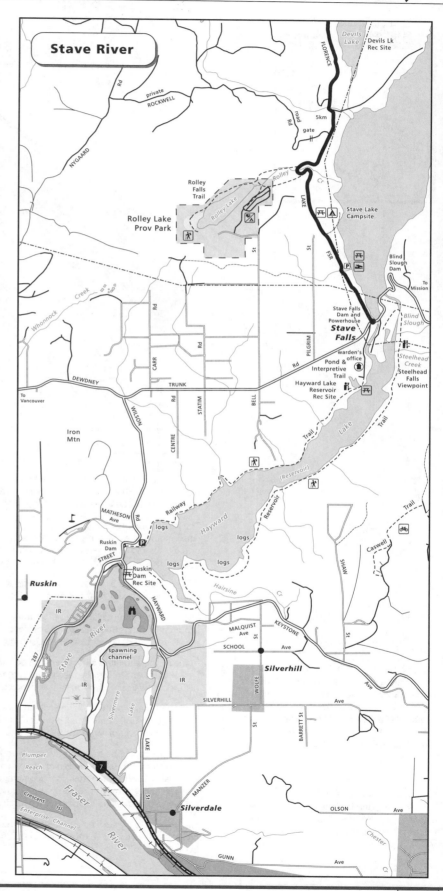

Location: 30 km (18 mi) south of Kamloops
Elevation: 743 m (2,438 ft)
Surface Area: 780 ha (1927 ac)
Max Depth: 21.3 m (69.9 ft)
Mean Depth: 11.6 m (38 ft)
Way Point: 50° 21' 37" N, 120° 22' 4" W

Stump Lake - Merritt Area

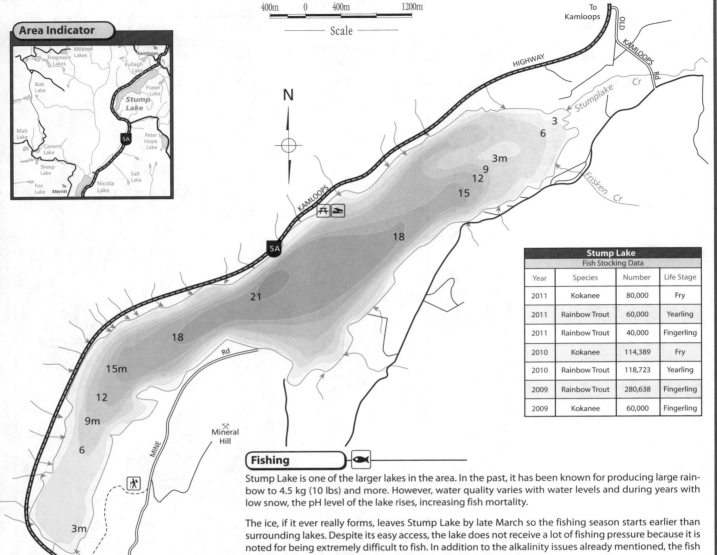

Area Indicator

Stump Lake			
Fish Stocking Data			
Year	Species	Number	Life Stage
2011	Kokanee	80,000	Fry
2011	Rainbow Trout	60,000	Yearling
2011	Rainbow Trout	40,000	Fingerling
2010	Kokanee	114,389	Fry
2010	Rainbow Trout	118,723	Yearling
2009	Rainbow Trout	280,638	Fingerling
2009	Kokanee	60,000	Fingerling

Fishing

Stump Lake is one of the larger lakes in the area. In the past, it has been known for producing large rainbow to 4.5 kg (10 lbs) and more. However, water quality varies with water levels and during years with low snow, the pH level of the lake rises, increasing fish mortality.

The ice, if it ever really forms, leaves Stump Lake by late March so the fishing season starts earlier than surrounding lakes. Despite its easy access, the lake does not receive a lot of fishing pressure because it is noted for being extremely difficult to fish. In addition to the alkalinity issues already mentioned, the fish are notoriously hard to catch and the wind can play havoc on boaters.

When the lake has a good inflow of water and is being flushed, the lake becomes very fertile with a lot of insect and aquatic invertebrates. It is at that time, a good fly presentation can be very productive.

Stump Lake produces large rainbow and brook trout to 2 kg (4-5 lbs) and kokanee to 1 kg (2 lbs). The productive waters help the stocked fish grow fast here. Since the lake is a lower elevation lake and is not that deep, it tends to warm during the summer so it is best to concentrate your efforts in the spring and fall.

In the spring and fall, trout anglers can do well by trolling a fly near the surface or the ever popular lake troll. If you want to fish the lake in the summer, try trolling a nymph pattern or a leech deep and slow. Also, a Willow Leaf and worm trolled deep continues to be a good choice.

In the summer months, kokanee fishing can be fairly good if you wait until there is a chop on the water and you then troll a pink Apex, pink Flatfish or Wedding Band near the surface very slowly. The trick is to find the cool layer of water the fish are hanging in (a fish finder helps).

Fly-fishermen will be most productive if you use a shrimp pattern on a sinking line dangled near the bottom. Damselfly or dragonfly nymphs cast near the reeds at either end of the lake works well particularly in the early spring when there is a good chance to hook one of the monster trout. Doc Spratleys or tied down minnow patterns should not be ruled out. In the summer months, black Idaho nymphs, 52 Buicks, chironomid pupae and halfbacks are particularly effective.

The lake is heavily stocked and in the last decade has seen hundreds of thousands of rainbow trout and kokanee stocked here. In the last couple of years, there have been a few hundred cutthroat trout stocked in the lake, too.

Directions

Stump Lake is one of the better large rainbow producing lakes in the Thompson/Nicola region. The lake is located next to Highway 5A northeast of Nicola Lake. Simply take the Highway 5A Exit off the Coquihalla Connector at Merritt. The lake is about 50 km (31 miles) from the turn-off. Alternatively, Highway 5A can be picked up from the Kamloops end.

Facilities

The lake has a public picnic area and a boat launch off of Highway 5A. There is a guest ranch on the lake for those looking to stay in the area.

www.backroadmapbooks.com

Stump & Edith Lakes

Location: 12 km (7 mi) north of Squamish

Fishing 🐟

These two pretty lakes are located in Alice Lake Provincial Park. It is a short walk into Stump Lake, while Edith Lake requires a longer hike if the gate near the park headquarters is closed.

Stump Lake is nestled in a thick, second growth hemlock/cedar forest. The trail circles the lake, offering access for shore fishermen. It is difficult to cast from shore except in a few limited areas where there are small clearings trampled by the volume of fishermen that visit the lake. Further, the shallows extend out a fair ways from shore making it best to have a float tube.

The lake is very inviting for fishermen despite the muddy bottom. There are number of large logs extending out into the murky water offering perfect habitat for fish. A picturesque island is also a good area to focus on.

Stump Lake contains rainbow (to 30 cm), although as of 2007 they are no longer being stocked. The lake is now stocked with cutthroat, but it may take a few years for these fish to become the main catch in the lake. The lake was also stocked with splake (a sterile cross between lake trout and brook trout) in the past.

Edith Lake is located on the opposite side of the park and doesn't see as much pressure, as it is a harder lake to get to. The lake contains stocked rainbow (to 30cm) and a few wild cutthroat. The fish tend to remain small.

A second growth forest surrounds Edith making fly-fishing very difficult from shore due to the encroaching vegetation and the expansive muddy shallows. Spincasters are able to pick their spots and cast a bobber and bait out far enough to get some action. There are some nice submerged logs, which can be seen in the murky water. Sink a wet fly next to one of the logs and you have a good chance for success.

As with Stump, a float tube is definitely helpful.

Directions Ⓐ

These lakes are located within the Alice Lake Provincial Park, which is found north of Squamish off the Sea to Sky Highway. Follow the signs into park and when you come to the big welcoming sign, stay left. You will soon come to the trailhead sign for the Four Lakes Trail. It is an easy 100 m (300 ft) hike to Stump Lake from the parking lot. Edith Lake is 4 km from here.

An alternative, shorter hike for Edith starts at the north end of Alice Lake at the parking area overlooking the wharf and a small beach. This parking area is reached by hanging a right at the sign welcoming you to Alice Lake Provincial Park and then driving to the end of the road. It is about 2 km (1.2 miles) from here to the lake.

Facilities 🏕 ⛱ 🚻

Although found in **Alice Lake Provincial Park**, there are no developed public facilities at these lakes. At Edith Lake, there are two private cabins with wharfs that extend into the lake. The **Four Lakes Trail** does link these lakes with nearby Alice Lake where visitors will find the main camping area and a beautiful picnic area.

Stump Lake			
Fish Stocking Data			
Year	Species	Number	Life Stage
2008	Cutthroat Trout	500	Yearling
2007	Cutthroat Trout	250	Fall Catchable
2006	Rainbow Trout	400	Catchable

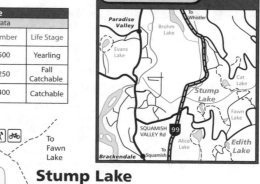

Stump Lake

Elevation: 217 m (712 ft)
Surface Area: 6 ha (15 ac)
Max Depth: 17 m (56 ft)
Mean Depth: 5 m (16 ft)
Way Point: 49° 47' 19" N, 123° 7' 20" W

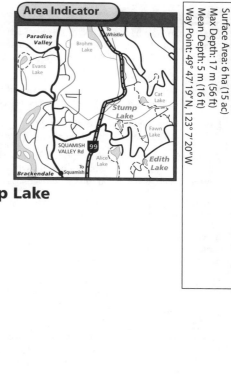

Stump Lake

To Fawn Lake

2m
4m
6m
4
8
2m 6m 10m
8
12
14
16m
14
12
10m
8
6
4
2m

To Parking Area

N

Alice Lake Provincial Park

Edith Lake			
Fish Stocking Data			
Year	Species	Number	Life Stage
2008	Rainbow Trout	800	Spring Catchable
2007	Rainbow Trout	800	Spring Catchable
2006	Rainbow Trout	800	Catchable

Elevation: 290 m (951 ft)
Surface Area: 2.6 ha (6.4 ac)
Max Depth: 9 m (30 ft)
Mean Depth: 4 m (13 ft)
Way Point: 49° 46' 33" N, 123° 6' 26" W

Edith Lake

Four Lakes Trail

To Alice Lake

private cabins

8m
6
5
3m
1

50m   0   50m   100m
— Scale —

Location: 23 km (14 mi) southeast of Hope
Stream Length: 30.16 km (18.7 mi)
Geographic: 49° 14' 51" N, 121° 10' 33" W

www.backroadmapbooks.com

Sumallo River

Fishing

The Sumallo River has its headwaters surrounded by towering mountain peaks just west of Skagit Valley Provincial Park. The river makes its way northwest, off the slopes of Mount Rideout to Sunshine Valley, where it takes a sharp right, flowing southeast for about 14 km (8.7 miles) to its confluence with the Skagit. The total length of the river is about 30 km (18 miles) and the closer you get to the Skagit, the better the fishing will be.

The Skagit is one of the most storied trout rivers in the province and the Sumallo, as one of its main tributaries, features some amazing fishing, too. However, the Sumallo is much easier to access than the Skagit since the Crowsnest Highway parallels the river from Sunshine Valley to the Skagit confluence. There are countless holes just begging to be tested in this stretch of highway.

Like the Skagit, the river is closed to angling for most of the year and is only open from July 1–October 31. There is a bait ban on the river, making it less popular with spincasters, but unlike the Skagit, you can catch and keep.

The river is best known for its rainbow trout fishing. These beautiful fish can get up to 50 cm (20 inches). The closer you get to the confluence with the Skagit, the bigger the fish are going to be. While the upper reaches of the river, accessed via the Sumallo River Forest Service Road, offer a much more remote feeling, you will find the fish here are usually much smaller.

The river features a rather healthy hatch of mayflies during July and on a July evening, fishing a Green Drake mayfly pattern can provide some amazing action. There are also caddis hatches early in summer.

In August when the weather is hot and the river is running low, try fishing small golden stonefly and mayfly nymphs near the bottom. Also try a Grizzly King or Royal Coachman. Other options include pheasant tail nymphs and small micro leeches in the afternoon. During the evening the fish start to rise again and dead drifting a size 16 mayfly on the surface can provide fast and furious action.

There are some Dolly Varden in the river. Dollies are piscivorous, which means they like to eat fish. Fishing a Muddler Minnow or something else that looks like a small fish will work well. However, they also seem to respond well to Woolly Buggers.

Directions

The Sumallo is the river that you follow driving along the Crowsnest Highway between Sunshine Valley and the Sumallo Grove Picnic Area in Manning Provincial Park. To get there from the Lower Mainland, take the Trans Canada to Hope, then take the Crowsnest Highway (Highway 3) exit towards Princeton.

At Sunshine Valley, you can turn right and follow the river up to its headwaters along the Sumallo River Forest Service Road or follow the lower stretch of the river along the Crowsnest.

Facilities

Outside of the **Sumallo Grove Day Use Area** and a second one at the West Gate of Manning Park, there are no facilities. The closest camping is to continue into Manning Park, where you will find four separate campgrounds.

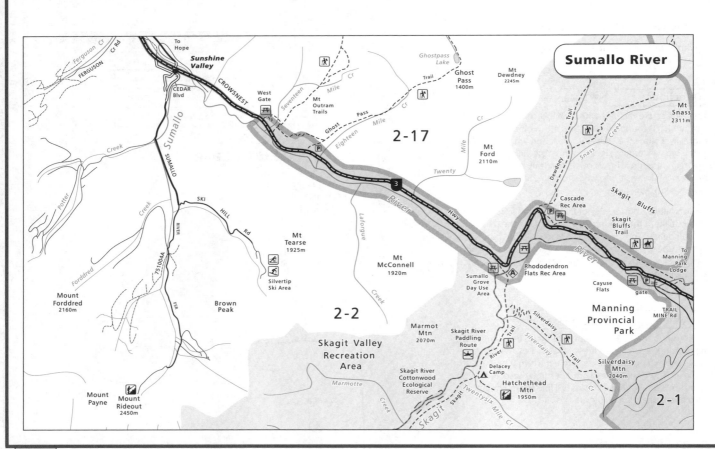

© Mussio Ventures Ltd.

www.backroadmapbooks.com

Sunrise Lake

Location: 21 km (13 mi) north of Harrison Hot Springs
Elevation: 413 m (1,355 ft)
Max Depth: 14 m (46 ft)
Mean Depth: 9 m (30 ft)
Way Point: 49° 29' 5.0" N, 121° 53' 29.3" W

Fishing

Located well down the west side of Harrison Lake, Sunrise Lake is a rarely visited gem of a lake.

There are two reasons the lake is rarely visited. The first is access. While the Harrison West Road is a nice gravel road (at least it is until the turnoff to the lake), the last few hundred metres are terrible. The Four Wheel Drive Association of BC, who maintain the site don't even recommend stock 4wd vehicles attempt getting in here.

The second is because the fishing is slow. Starting in the 1970s, the lake was stocked with cutthroat trout, but in 2001, they stopped stocking the lake. The hope was that natural reproduction would take over. And while there appears to be some of that happening here, the fishing these days is not as good as it used to be.

In early spring, spincasters can try working a small silver spoon, letting it sink down to near the bottom, then retrieve it with a slow, jerking retrieve. The bottom of the lake is fairly woody, so expect to lose a few hooks this way.

The shoreline of the lake is quite brushy, but there are some places where you can fish from shore. Focus on either the east side of the lake were there is a rocky outcrop or near the inflow creek on the west side of the lake. In both locations, the water drops off rapidly so you are able to cast to the drop-off and beyond.

If possible, bringing a float or small boat to the lake and cast towards the drop-off for better results. Trolling slowly can work well, too.

The cutthroats found here are generally small, with a 30 cm (12 inch) fish being a good-sized catch. The lake is also quite small and can get quite warm in the summer. In fact, the four wheelers have put a swimming platform in the middle of the lake. Obviously, the fishing slows during the summer.

Area Indicator

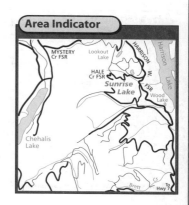

Directions

Sunrise Lake is found along the Harrison West Forest Service Road. To get there, take the Lougheed Highway to Harrison Mills. At the Morris Valley Road turnoff, head north and follow this road to the Harrison West Forest Service Road at about the 11 km mark. Continue north and shortly after the 26 km marker and the Hale Creek crossing, watch for a short spur road on the left.

The road in to the lake is steep and has many washouts making it a tough drive. Unless you have a modified high clearance 4wd you may wish to walk to the lake instead of driving. However, the Harrison West Road is a good, all season gravel road, so you can bring a car to the junction with the spur road.

Facilities

The **Sunrise Lake Recreation Site** has been maintained by the Four Wheel Drive Association of BC for years. There are four well cared for campsites here, along with a rustic boat launch that is suitable for canoes and small, hand-launched boats for those willing to lug a boat up the rough access road. In the summer, there is a small swim platform moored in the middle of the lake.

There is also an old campsite on the west side of the lake that is no longer maintained and is becoming overgrown. However, if the main site is full (rare, but possible), it is an alternative.

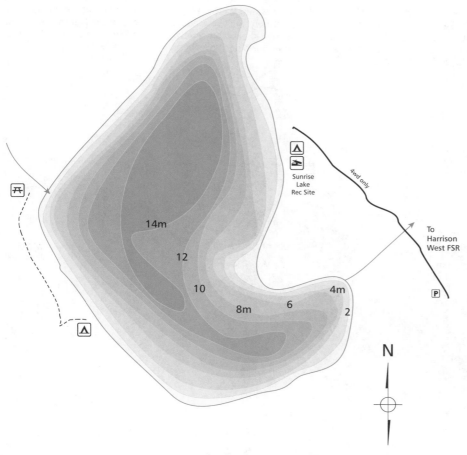

Location: 34 km (21 mi) southeast of Vavenby
Elevation: 991 m (3,251 ft)
Surface Area: 45 ha (111 ac)
Max Depth: 21 m (68.9 ft)
Mean Depth: 9 m (29.5 ft)
Way Point: 51° 26' 45.3" N, 119° 22' 40.8" W

Telfer Lake

Area Indicator

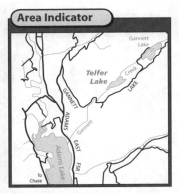

Fishing

The long drive into Telfer Lake all but guarantees that many anglers won't frequent the lake, especially now that the catch limit has been reduced to six.

Gannett Creek offers great spawning grounds and fry mortality is very low. This, coupled with the lower pressure, means that action here can be fast and furious, just don't expect to find anything big.

Smaller fish mean that even fewer people are willing to make the trip and the cycle continues. If the lake were easier to get to, it would be a perfect family fishing lake. The road up to the area is quite good except for the last bit and there are lakes that offer similar fishing much closer to home. So most people pass on Telfer.

While it is possible to carry a canoe or small watercraft to the lake, a float tube will be much easier to get to the lake. The last 30 metres (100 feet) into the lake is rough and muddy and nasty.

Fly anglers will be able to drag a red or green Doc Spratley pattern or mayfly nymph around the edges of the lake using a float tube. The lake has a good caddis hatch. Tom Thumbs and Nicola Sedge patterns around the lily pads work well when there is a hatch going on.

Spincasters can work the usual assortment of small spoons and spinners. If you're willing to go through the effort to get a boat to the lake, it offers some great trolling. Wedding Bands and Flatfish, especially the skunk pattern, work well, as do small black and yellow Mepps and bait and a bobber.

If you do go, bring lots of mosquito repellant, as they have been known to carry away anglers who came unprepared.

Directions

From the Trans Canada Highway (Highway 1) 5.5 km northeast of Chase, take the Squilax-Anglemont Road branches north. Turn left at the first major intersection past the bridge onto the paved Holdings Road. This road winds gently along the western banks of the Adams River to the south end of the lake. Continue along to the mill. From here, an excellent, well graded buy quite windy main haul logging road takes you to the end of Adams Lake.

At the 72 km mark turn east and then look for the Gannett Lake Forest Service Road at the 3.5 km mark of the Adams Lake East Road. The Gannett Lake Road is also in good shape and takes you up into the Gannett Creek drainage. Around the 13 km mark of this road, watch for a road on your left that heads back to the hidden Telford Lake. The last stretch is quite rough and may need to be walked. It is about 2.5 hours from Chase.

Other Options

If you are going to drive this far, might as well make it a weekend trip and explore other lakes like **Gannett Lake**. Surprisingly, this lake offers a slow fishery. But there are bigger trout here. It has expansive shoals throughout the lake and the same gear that works on Telfer should work here.

Facilities

There are no developed facilities at the lake, but there are a number of roadside pullouts where you can camp. It is possible to launch a small boat, but you will need to carry it to the lake. There is a recreation site at nearby Gannett Lake.

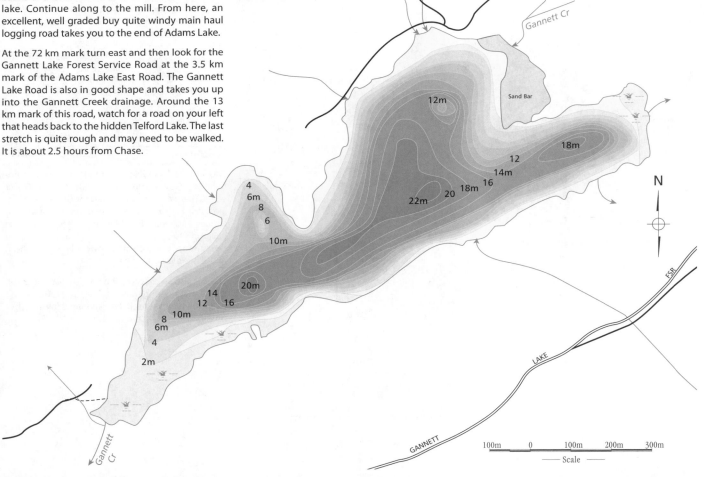

Tenquille Lake

Location: 25.5 km (15.8 mi) northwest of Pemberton
Elevation: 1,661 m (5,449 ft)
Surface Area: 27 ha (67 ac)
Max Depth: 37 m (121 ft)
Mean Depth: 14 m (46 ft)
Way Point: 50° 32' 5.9" N, 122° 55' 23.3" W

Fishing

Tenquille Lake is a beautiful lake set in a sub-alpine meadow surrounded by rugged mountain peaks. The area is extremely popular with backpackers, mountain bikers, snowmobilers and mountaineers. But that beauty comes at a price, which is a long, gruelling approach to the lake, especially on a hot summer's day.

The lake is popular, but still produces well for rainbow in the 20–30 cm (8–12 in) range. It is a small lake, set in a sub-alpine bowl which limits the fishing season. The lake is usually ice-free by late June and stays cold through summer until late October, when the snow starts to fly.

The lake has two deep pockets of water; one near the west end and one near the east end. Few people are willing to carry a float tube to the lake. Fortunately, there are plenty of open areas around the shore, making this a perfect lake for fly casters. This can be a double-edged sword, though, as fish are extremely leery of motion on the edge of the lake, thinking (quite rightly) that it could be a predator. Approach the lake slowly, taking time to observe the waters. The fishing is best during the early morning or late evening, when the trout are bolder and more willing to cruise around the shallows looking for food.

Because the lake is only ice-free for a few months, the fish can be extremely voracious and will strike most anything you cast at them. Spincasters will find that a bobber and bait (worm or single egg) is quite effective, although working a small spinner is preferred by some as casting these requires a bit more skill and effort. Fly anglers can try working dry flies like a Royal Coachman or Mosquito.

Speaking of mosquitoes, this area is thick with them and black flies. Bring deet and mosquito netting and possibly a few bottles of type O negative in case you need a transfusion.

Area Indicator

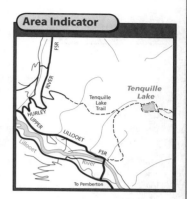

Directions

The lake can be accessed four ways. The easiest route leads from Branch 12 off the Hurley River Road gaining 450 metres over a 12 km (7.3 mile) return hike. The trail begins in an old cutblock and then crosses a creek before joining with the other trail leading from the Lillooet Valley. To get to the trailhead, you will need a 4wd vehicle.

An alternative route is to climb from the Lillooet Valley some 19 km (12 miles) return gaining a whopping 1,460 m (4,790 ft) along the way. The trailhead begins east of the Lillooet River Bridge and winds uphill through open forests. This is a popular mountain bike trail.

The other two routes, one from Owl Lake and the other from Tenquille Creek and the Birkenhead Lake area, should be left to the experienced backpackers. Whichever route you take, getting to the trailhead can be confusing. A copy of the Backroad Mapbook for the Vancouver, Coast and Mountains and GPS with the BC Backroad GPS Maps is highly recommended.

Facilities

At the west end of the lake you will find an open area with a few tenting pads and pit toilet. A cabin is also found at the lake. The original is in a state of disrepair, but rumour has it was being replaced in 2010. If camping, bring bug repellent and please respect this gorgeous alpine lake destination and pack out what you pack in. Better yet, leave the area even nicer than you found it.

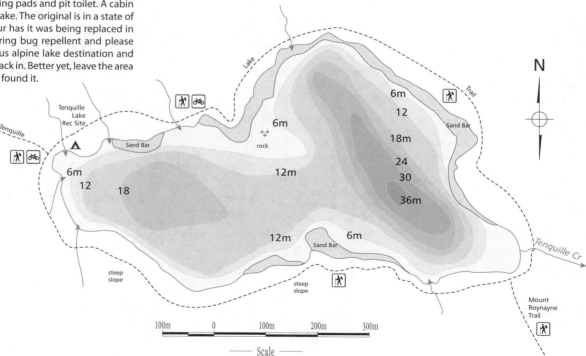

REGION 3

Location: Between Ashcroft and Lytton
Stream Length: 128.63 km (80 mi)
Geographic: 50°25'N, 121°19'W

www.backroadmapbooks.com

Thompson River

Thompson River

Fishing

The Thompson River carves its way through the arid high country of south-central British Columbia, passing through broad valleys and steep walled gorges as it makes its way across the province. The river drains 54,500 sq km (21,000 sq miles) before emptying into the Fraser River near Lytton. The river is named for David Thompson, a famous explorer in his own right and cartographer for the Northwest Company. Thompson never laid eyes on the river that bears his name; Simon Fraser named the river in Thompson's honour.

The Thompson River is comprised of the North Thompson and South Thompson River, which join at Kamloops. The Trans Canada Highway follows the Thompson from Lytton to Cache Creek where the river has worn its way though the mountains, carving out the Thompson River valley. This beautiful, rugged section of the river is often mistaken for the Fraser, as the section of the Trans Canada from Hope to Cache Creek is known as the Fraser Canyon.

The Thompson is known as a steelheader's paradise, with big fish that many will argue put up the best fight of any fish that you can catch. During fall, people drive for days from across the country to fish this river.

The first fish start showing up in river in late September, with the majority of the run arriving in October and November. The fish over winter in the river below Kamloops Lake and in May start making their way up the tributaries for June spawning.

The river is extremely popular with fly-fishers, especially the Spences Bridge area.

The average steelhead on the Thompson is around 7 kg (15 lbs), but you will find a fair number of fish that break 9 kg (20 lbs). There has even been a 14+ kg (30+ lb) fish pulled out of here that held the record for biggest steelhead for nine years. When these beasts hit your line, they can run you down to bare reel and have you scrambling to keep up.

The steelhead in the Thompson seem to respond well to surface flies, making this ground zero for some of the most spectacular fishing you will ever do.

Assuming of course, you can find the fish. It is a big river and hard to read and many people come here with grand plans of catching the big one and go home completely skunked. Even seasoned steelhead anglers who have never fished here can find the river difficult to fish. Historically, the river boasted returns of over 20,000 fish. These days, that number has plummeted to just over 2,000. A great day is catching one steelhead and sometimes people fish for days on end with no success.

Of Course, you can't say things like "world's greatest steelhead river" and expect to show up here and have the river, or even a part of the river, all to yourself. Even with the declining population, this is an extremely popular place to fish and on nice days, expect to be standing nearly shoulder to shoulder with other anglers, at least, if you want to fish the best spots, which include Rock Run, Martel Islands, Y Run and Flat Rock Run, the Grease Hole, Hotel Run, Murray Creek, Graveyard Run, Orchard Run and Big Horn Pool. Even on nasty, cold weekdays, it is rare to find a run to yourself except maybe near the end of the run, when the weather has turned and the steelhead are nearly through this section.

Because the river also holds plenty of small rainbow trout that like to feed on the eggs of spawning salmon, steelhead anglers often have to contend with the steelheads smaller, but nearly as feisty, resident cousin.

There are two ways of fishing the river for gear fishermen: float and bottom bouncing. Both techniques usually use the same terminal tackle, including single egg imitations, gooey-bobs, super goobers, Spin-N-Glos, corkies, red, pink and orange rubber worms and red, pink and orange wool.

However, the river is best known for its fly-fishing. There are five ways fly-fishers present flies to steelhead, of which three are used on the Thompson: floating line, skated or waked fly and sinking line. Learning which technique works best in a given situation is the essence of fly-fishing for steelhead. Floating line works best in the early season, while later in the season it works best in shallower water that is not moving too quickly. Later in the season, the fish are slower to react and if the fly is more than a few feet away, they're not going to react. Sinking line presentation works best when the water is deeper than say 2 m (6 ft) early in the season and 1 m (3 ft) when the water gets colder. Some successful fly patterns include Doc Spratleys, black Woolly Buggers, Black Speys, Black General Practitioners, Skunks, Grease Liners and the Eastern Canadian Atlantic Salmon Bomber.

In addition to the steelhead and rainbow, the Thompson River holds Chinook, Coho, pink and sockeye salmon. The Adams River sockeye run passes through the Thompson on their way back to their spawning stream, peaking every four years: 2010, 2014 and so on.

The most popular rainbow trout section is between Kamloops Lake and Ashcroft. This section of the river can be drift fished and provides some excellent dry fly-fishing for rainbow to 1.5 kg (3 lbs).

However, the river is best known for its fly-fishing. There are five ways fly-fishers present flies to steelhead, of which three are used on the Thompson: floating line, skated or waked fly and sinking line. Learning which technique works best in a given situation is the essence of fly-fishing for steelhead. Floating line works best in the early season, while later in the season it works best in shallower water that is not moving too quickly. Later in the season, the fish are slower to react and if the fly is more than a few feet away, they're not going to react. Sinking line presentation works best when the water is deeper than say 2 m (6 ft) early in the season and 1 m (3 ft) when the water gets colder. Some successful fly patterns include Doc Spratleys, black Woolly Buggers, Black Speys, Black General Practitioners, Skunks, Grease Liners and the Eastern Canadian Atlantic Salmon Bomber.

Of course, the Thompson isn't all steelhead, though it might seem that way. The river holds Chinook, Coho, pink, sockeye and resident rainbow trout. The Adams River sockeye run passes through the Thompson on their way back to their spawning stream, peaking every four years: 2010, 2014, and so on.

Rainbows are probably the second most common catch on the river and they can get up to 2.5 kg (5 lbs). The most popular rainbow trout section is between Kamloops Lake and Ashcroft. This section of the river can be drift fished and provides some excellent dry fly fishing.

The river features some prodigious hatches, with chironomids, caddisflies and mayflies. One of the best times to be fishing here is during June and July, when huge hatches of stoneflies occur. These stoneflies are like candy to the resident rainbows, which sip them under the water or off the surface.

In August and September, there are no hatches, but there are terrestrials such as black ants and more commonly grasshoppers.

The river also features a large run of Chinook salmon, although opening for Chinook are rare. Avid anglers check the DFO website daily, sometimes hourly, waiting for word of an opening of perhaps a couple of days and sometimes limited to only a few kilometres. Because Chinook don't feed in freshwater, your best bet is to irritate them into striking a lure. This usually involves throwing a garish, noisy lure right in front of them.

The Thompson has strict regulations to protect the monster steelhead and will occasionally experience special openings and closures, depending on returns. Drift fishing is illegal, bait is not allowed on most of the river and the river is managed as a Class II Protected River, which means a special Classified Waters License is needed to fish here.

Thompson River

Location: Between Savona and Lytton
Stream Length: 128.63 km (80 mi)
Geographic: 50°25′N, 121°19′W

Directions

Spences Bridge is found along the Trans-Canada Highway (Highway 1), 37 km (23 miles) up from where the Thompson flows into the Fraser at Lytton. While there are places upstream and down from Spences Bridge that can be fished with great success, Spences Bridge is ground zero for steelhead fishing. The town is 257 km (160 miles) from Vancouver.

Highway 1 continues to parallel the river all the way Kamloops Lake (and beyond). However, the steep canyon, private property or lack of side roads in most of these areas limits access. We have marked the popular steelhead holes on the map. Further afield, the best access is from the various provincial parks and road crossings. To be specific, Highway 97C in Ashcroft and Walhachin Road near Savona are other main road crossings. Drift fishers looking for rainbow often use these roads as access points.

Similarly, there are many roadside pull-outs for those simply casting from shore. Most popular holes will have a car or ten from dawn till dusk.

Facilities

Spences Bridge is a small town with a few hotels, a couple or three restaurants and a gas station. During the peak of the steelhead spawn, don't expect to find accommodations here. Even Ashcroft to the north and Lytton to the south become hoping little towns during the steelhead season.

At other times of the year, there are a couple nice places to camp when out on the river. **Goldpan Provincial Park** is a few kilometres south of Spences Bridge and offers 14 sites high above the river. You will need to drive down to the river if you want to fish from here. It is also closed after September 30. Farther a field, there is a nice campsite at **Juniper Beach Provincial Park** that is found between Cache Creek and Savona. This 30 unit site is preferred by rainbow trout anglers as it sits right on the river.It is open from April to December so some steelheaders do stay here. Of course we can't forget **Steelhead Provincial Park**. Resting at the mouth of the river on Kamloops Lake, it sports 44 campsites and a large beach.

In addition to provincial park campgrounds, there are also a few private campgrounds along the river.

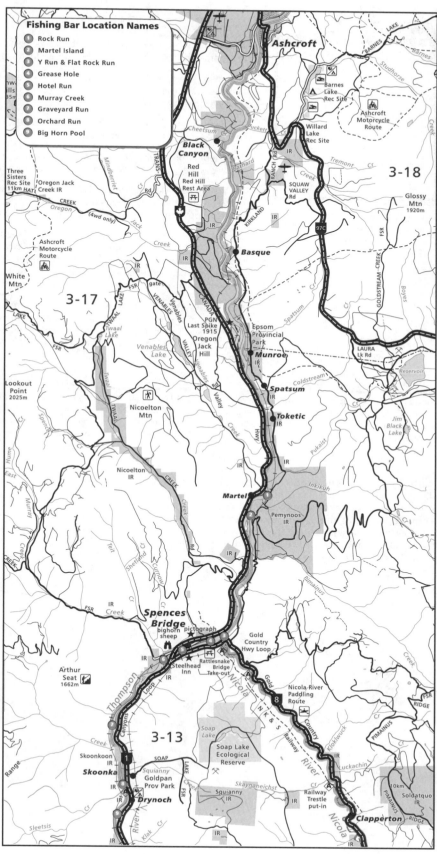

Fishing Bar Location Names

1. Rock Run
2. Martel Island
3. Y Run & Flat Rock Run
4. Grease Hole
5. Hotel Run
6. Murray Creek
7. Graveyard Run
8. Orchard Run
9. Big Horn Pool

Location: 36 km (22 mi) northwest of Kamloops
Elevation: 1,411 m (4,629 ft)
Surface Area: 58 ha (143 ac)
Max Depth: 13 m (43 ft)
Mean Depth: 6.6 m (22 ft)
Way Point: 50° 56' 7.9" N, 120° 34' 15.6" W

www.backroadmapbooks.com

Tranquille Lake

Area Indicator

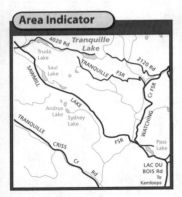

Fishing

The Tranquille Lake area is a popular winter recreation area and the Kamloops Snowmobile Club maintains a cabin in the area. The resort based lake is less known for it's fishing, although angling can be quite good at the lake.

Tranquille Lake, given its high elevation, is considered a good fishing lake throughout the ice-free season, even in the summer. The lake has rainbow to 1 kg (2 lbs) and some small kokanee. The fish are plentiful and are more than willing to bite your line but don't expect any big ones.

The deepest hole is towards the northwest end of the lake. The water drops off rapidly in that area. In the rest of the lake, the water drops off gradually.

Fly-fishermen use small attractor patterns like the Doc Spratley or leech patterns when searching for trout. During hatches, which are usually delayed here, it is best match the current hatch.

Trollers should stick to the standard Willow leaf, Wedding Band and worm or maggot combination. Spincasters do well with a Mepps, Panther Martin or Deadly Dick cast along or towards the drop off. Vary the speed and depth of your retrieve, being sure to jerk the line every so often to entice hits.

The kokanee are best taken on a very slow troll. They seem to really like the colour pink. A small Willow Leaf (from #1–00) is the most common attractor, often in tandem with a baited hook on either a Wedding Band or Dick Nite lure. Kokanee feed on plankton and are not going to go after large lake trolls. Trolling in a slow S-curve pattern, varying your speed and creating random motion on the troll will improve your success. For something different, kokanee can be taken on the fly with an egg-sucking leech, especially when the fish are spawning.

Kokanee are also active in the winter too. The lake freezes over by mid November and the ice is usually safe by mid December. At this time, you can catch both rainbow and kokanee by dangling bait (worms, maggots, corn or Powerbait) just off the bottom. The fish usually cruise the shallows so be sure to drill multiple holes. If you do not get a bit after 15 minutes move on. As an added bonus, the resort is open during winter making the perfect après fish experience.

Directions

Tranquille Lake is located on a plateau high above Kamloops. To reach the lake involves a long drive on a series of logging roads that most vehicles can negotiate.

From Kamloops, you will need to get to the Lac Du Bois Road. Take Halston Avenue east over the river from Highway 5 to hook up with Bachelor Hill Road, which turns into Lac Du Bois Road. Follow this road north past McQueen and Pass Lakes. When you get to the Y at the 21 km marker, stay left (west) and follow the lodge signs towards the lake. At the 40 km marker turn right (east) on the private road. It is about 9 km down this road to the lodge and lake access.

Facilities

The **Wendego Lodge** is found at the east end of the lake offering cabins and camping along with boat rentals and other amenities. There is a recreation site at Saul Lake, about 15 minutes away from Tranquille.

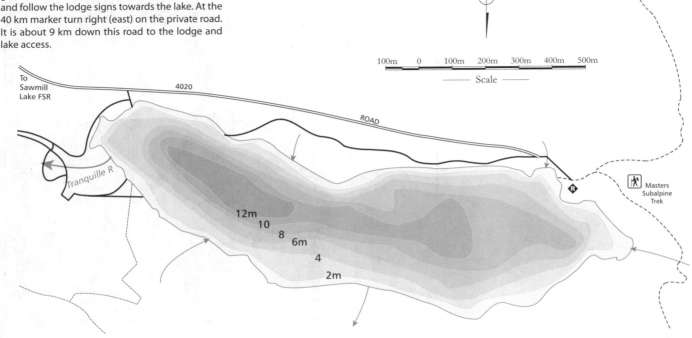

© Mussio Ventures Ltd.

Location: 10 km (6.2 mi) northwest of Sechelt
Elevation: 156 m (512 ft)
Surface Area: 7.6 ha (19 ac)
Mean Depth: 5.8 m (19 ft)
Max Depth: 17.4 m (57 ft)
Way Point: 49° 30' 30" N, 123° 52' 35" W

Trout Lake - Sunshine Coast

Fishing

Located northwest of Sechelt, Trout Lake is a popular fishing lake. It is found next to Highway 101, making it an easy destination to find. Its small size and plentiful fish make it a great place for the novice angler.

The lake is a low-elevation lake and can usually be fished year round. To ensure the fishery remains active, the Freshwater Fisheries Society of BC stocks the lake annually with cutthroat.

There is a great trail system around the lake, offering good access for anglers and scenic views for those more interested in biking, hiking or horseback riding. For shoreline anglers, try a traditional bobber and worm or spincasting with small lures such as a Krocodile or Little Cleo. Bottom fishing with a weight and worm also works particularly well in winter months.

The southwest shore has deeper water. If you use a boat or float tube, try trolling spoons, Wedding Bands or even a small Willow Leaf in this area.

For fly-fishing, use of a small boat or float tube is best. Blue duns, mosquitoes and dark olive chironomids work well in the early spring and there is almost always a black ant hatch sometime in May. This hatch is one of the best times to fish the lake and the action can be fast and furious. Getting the timing right for this hatch can be a challenge since they usually come out the first real warm day in late spring.

As the water temperature warms up, fish deeper. Try fishing wet flies like leeches, minnows, Woolly Buggers, Mickey Finns or dragonfly nymphs near the bottom, working around and across the drop-offs.

Traditional dry fly patterns for coastal cutthroat such as flying ants and caddis emergers also work well here. Always keep your eyes open for insects hatching. They are a great clue as what to try next. If you are in a boat try the northeast side of the lake, as it is consistently productive.

There is a new fishing platform being built on the lake, which will improve access for anglers. Anglers will also be happy to know that the average size of the fish stocked in the lake has increased over the last few years. Although there have been a few fish caught in the 30–40 cm (12–16 in) range, the likely hood of this happening more often is good.

The lake has an electric motors only restriction.

Area Indicator

Trout Lake
Fish Stocking Data

Year	Species	Number	Life Stage
2009	Cutthroat Trout	750	Yearling

Directions

Trout Lake is easy to get to. The lake is about 10 km (6.2 miles) northwest of Sechelt along the Sunshine Coast Highway (Highway 101). Watch for the lake on your right hand side. There is parking for vehicles at both the east and west ends of the lake.

Facilities

There is a place to launch small boats and float tubes at the parking lot at the west end of the lake. Another good place to try launching a float tube is from a point of land between the two parking lots, adjacent to the highway. The closest provincial park is north of Sechelt, at Porpoise Bay, where you will find 84 campsites.

N

50m 0 50m 100m 150m 200m
—— Scale ——

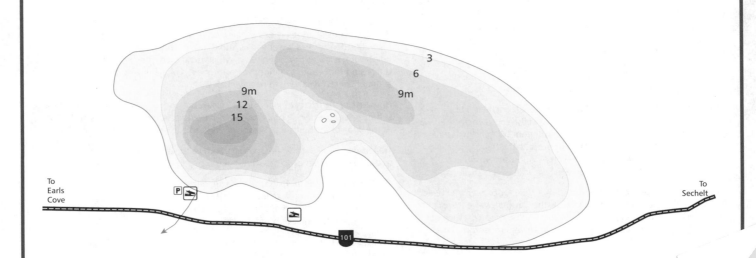

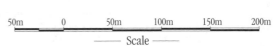

Tunkwa & Leighton Lakes

Leighton Lake

Elevation: 1,138 m (3,734 ft)
Surface Area: 53 ha (131 ac)
Max Depth: 5 m (16 ft)
Way Point: 50° 37'6"N, 120° 50'44"W

Area Indicator

Directions

From Merritt or Kamloops, take the Coquihalla Highway (Highway 5) to the Logan Lake exit and the Meadow Creek Road. This paved road leads west for about 24 km to the Tunkwa Lake Road, passing the town of Logan Lake along the way. Follow the signs for 14.4 km north along the Tunkwa Lake Road to reach the provincial park and its short roads leading to either Tunkwa or Leighton Lake. The route is paved for most of its distance and signs clearly mark the way. A car or RV can easily make this trip.

Facilities

Both lakes are found in **Tunkwa Lake Provincial Park**, a year round recreation area, noted for camping, fishing, hunting, horseback riding, wildlife viewing, cross-country skiing and snowmobiling. It is a popular destination and there are three separate campgrounds, Tunkwa, Leighton and Leighton North. Combined, the three campgrounds offer 55 typical individual campsites (for tenters or RV's) set in both treed and open grassy areas. There are also 220 informal sites for groups of four to camp together in the trees as well as the more exposed open areas. Camping is possible on a first-come, first-served basis year round, but full services are only available from May 1st to mid-October.

Visitors will also find gravel boat launches on both lakes and a separate day use area at the south end of Tunkwa Lake. Note the motor restriction. Trail enthusiasts and shore casters will also appreciate the trail around Leighton Lake. There are even ATV and snowmobile trails in the surrounding area.

If you prefer a bit more luxury like a roof over your head, be sure to check in with the **Tunkwa Lake Resort**. In addition to lakeside cabins and boat rentals, they offer visitors and guests a small convenience store.

Tunkwa Lake

Elevation: 1,143 m (3,750 ft)
Surface Area: 193 ha (477 ac)
Max Depth: 5.7 m (18.7 ft)
Way Point: 50° 36'32"N, 120° 51'23"W

Fishing

Tunkwa Lake is one of BC's most popular fishing lakes. In fact, it is one of the countries great fly-fishing destinations. It is found on a rolling plateau in the Interior grasslands and it offers beautiful scenery and a diverse but challenging sport fishery.

While Tunkwa Lake gets all the glory–even having the provincial park that encompasses both lakes named after it–Leighton is merely the lesser of two beauties, lacking notice only because it sits so close to its sister lake. If Tunkwa were not so close, Leighton would probably receive much more acclaim.

But that's okay, because here you don't have to choose. You can fish them both. It's okay. It's allowed. Leighton Lake is just a stone's throw away from Tunkwa Lake. The two are even connected by a dammed channel.

Each year, Tunkwa Lake is stocked with more than 35,000 rainbow trout. Catching fish to 4.5 kg (10 lbs) is possible, although 1–1.5 kg (2–3 lb) trout are more common. Leighton Lake also has a healthy population of rainbow trout and although it is stocked annually, many fish enter into Leighton from Tunkwa Lake via the spillway between the lakes.

Tunkwa Lake is essentially one big shoal, covered with aquatic vegetation that supports abundant populations of trout. Anglers target the lake's corners as well as the back channel at the west end. The productive capacity of the lake can make fishing a challenge. With so much natural food to choose from, anglers need to work hard to entice trout away from the real thing.

The action starts on May 1, when the lake officially opens. Ice-off usually occurs several days to a few weeks before, depending on the winter. Early spring fishing on Tunkwa Lake can be difficult because water temperatures are still cold. For the dedicated angler; however, there is tremendous opportunity as trout often congregate in shallow water to feed. Fish small chironomids and leeches tight to the banks, cast spinners from shore or dangle a worm beneath a float just over the bottom.

The action heats up as the sun heats up. By late May and early June, fly anglers can expect days with intense action as trout key in on the lake's abundant hatches of chironomids, mayflies, damselflies and dragonflies. Shrimp and leeches are also abundant. Chromies, black and red beadheaded chironomids in size #12 to #14 and maroon micro-leeches are good flies to start with. But watch carefully for insect hatches in different sizes and colours.

Fly-fishing slows during the hot summer, although anglers who troll flashers and big spinners still do well. These often attract the attention of big trout when fly anglers cannot. However, the tide turns in August when a big hatch of "bomber" chironomids rise from the lake bottom to take wing. Fly-fishers with flies up to 2.5 cm (1 inch) long can have spectacular days.

Late-season fishing is always good if anglers are hardy enough to brave the changing weather. It's common to hear Tunkwa mentioned in the Kamloops fishing shops as a prime destination well into November.

While the lakes may be similar–both have good hatches of chironomids, caddis flies and damselflies–they have their own unique qualities as well. Leighton Lake is smaller, deeper, has fewer shoals and different species of aquatic plants than its neighbour. It is also more sheltered, which makes it a good choice when the wind is frothing the waves to whitecaps on Tunkwa Lake. It is also harder to fish from shore at Leighton Lake than Tunkwa Lake.

However, tactics that work on Tunkwa Lake also work on Leighton Lake. Fly-fishers should keep their tackle box stocked with imitations in different sizes and colours. At the peak of the fly-fishing season, it's possible to encounter a variety of hatches.

Trollers do well with Dick Nite spinners, Ford Fenders and small Flatfish. Troll parallel to the lake's steeper drop offs, but make sure you go slowly.

Angling regulations for Leighton Lake are different than Tunkwa Lake. Anglers are prohibited from fishing with bait, barbed hooks or hooks with more than one point. At Leighton Lake, two areas are closed to fishing and anglers must not fish within 100 metres of the inlet or outlet streams.

Tunkwa itself has an engine power restriction of 10 hp (7.5 kw). Both lakes are closed to fishing from December 1 to April 30.

www.backroadmapbooks.com

Tunkwa & Leighton Lakes

Location: 13 km (8 mi) north of Logan Lake

Leighton Lake

Elevation: 1,138 m (3,734 ft)
Surface Area: 53 ha (131 ac)
Max Depth: 5 m (16 ft)
Way Point: 50° 37'6"N, 120° 50'44"W

Tunkwa Lake

Elevation: 1,143 m (3,750 ft)
Surface Area: 193 ha (477 ac)
Max Depth: 5.7 m (18.7 ft)
Way Point: 50° 36'32"N, 120° 51'23"W

Leighton Lake Fish Stocking Data			
Year	Species	Number	Life Stage
2011	Rainbow Trout	2,000	Yearling
2010	Rainbow Trout	2,000	Yearling
2009	Rainbow Trout	2,000	Yearling

Tunkwa Lake Fish Stocking Data			
Year	Species	Number	Life Stage
2011	Rainbow Trout	32,060	Yearling
2010	Rainbow Trout	41,492	Yearling
2009	Rainbow Trout	40,049	Yearling

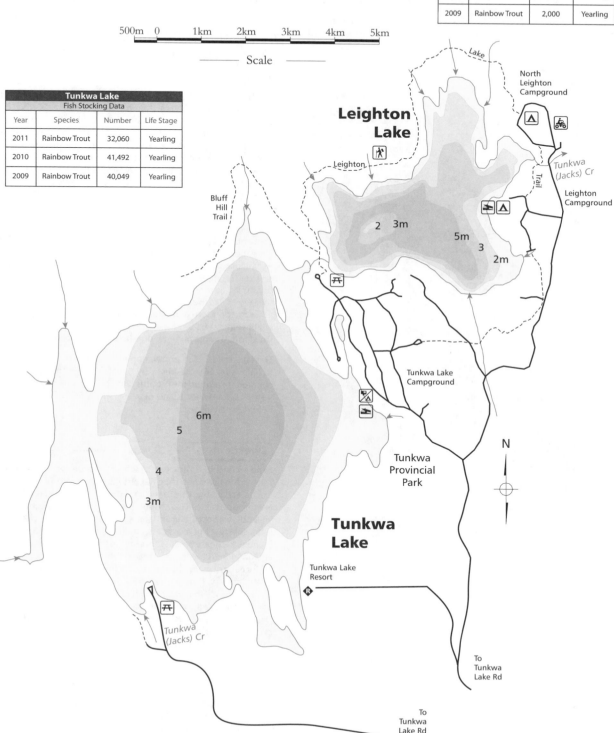

Location: 130 km (81 mi) northeast of Chase
Elevation: 663 m (2,175 ft)
Surface Area: 388 ha (959 ac)
Max Depth: 65 m (213.3 ft)
Mean Depth: 32.1 m (105.3 ft)
Way Point: 51° 52' 21" N, 119° 7' 11" W

Tumtum Lake

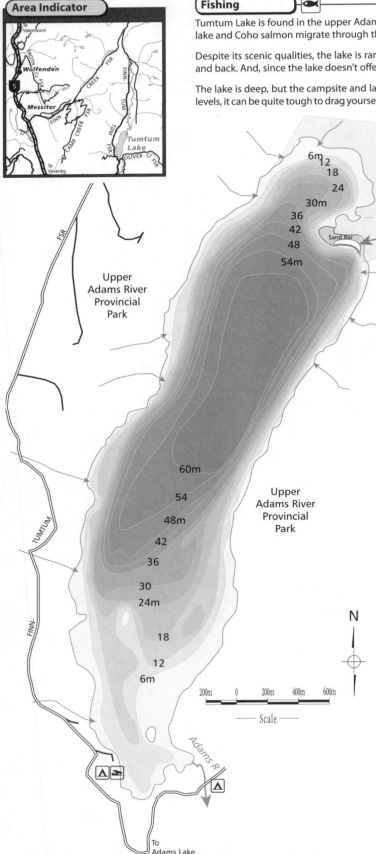

Fishing

Tumtum Lake is found in the upper Adams River Valley north of Adams Lake. The Adams River flows through the lake and Coho salmon migrate through the lake. It is a beautiful, wild, remote lake.

Despite its scenic qualities, the lake is rarely visited, as it is nearly a full day commitment just to drive to the lake and back. And, since the lake doesn't offer the best fishing in the region, most people give it a pass.

The lake is deep, but the campsite and launch is located on the shallowest part of the lake. Depending on water levels, it can be quite tough to drag yourself through this shallow, reedy section to get to the deeper parts of the lake.

If you can break through to the deep part of the lake, the lake is best fished on the troll, working along the drop offs on the east and west sides of the lake.

The lake holds fair numbers of Dolly Varden, Mountain whitefish and rainbow trout. The best time to fish for dollies is when the Coho are spawning in fall and again when Coho fry are migrating through the lake in spring. In fall, eggs float free from the gravel beds in the Upper Adams River and float downstream into the lake. Dollies feed on these eggs and are found in heaviest concentration around the inflow of the Adams. Spincasters will want to use single eggs as bait, while fly anglers will do well using an egg sucking leech pattern or other patterns that looks like a Coho egg.

In the spring, Coho fry begin migrating through the lake, and once again, the dollies feast, though this time, they are not as concentrated around the mouth of the Adams. While this is still a great place to fish, anywhere along the migration route of the fry will usually have good results. The fry will usually stick fairly close to the shore and will start to pile up near the outflow of the Adams. While the dollies probably won't come into the shallows at the very end of the lake, try working just off the shallows. Working a streamer pattern or minnow imitation will work for fly anglers, while spincasters have a whole arsenal of gear that resembles small fish. Using a minnow on a hook will work fantastic.

The lake holds a fair population of small rainbow trout. Again, trolling is usually the best way to catch them. They do tend to congregate around the mouths of inflow streams, as well as near a small underwater island near the south end of the lake, just before the shallows.

Directions

Sandwiched in a remote stretch of land between the North Thompson River and Lake Revelstoke access into Tumtum Lake can be a challenge due to the long stretches of gravel road. There are three possible access routes into the area. From Highway 5 at Vavenby, via Lost Creek and the Adams Lake Forest Service Road, is the shortest but most difficult drive. From Highway 5 south of Barriere, via Agate Bay Road and along the west side and northern end of Adams Lake, is more than double the length but the drive is a lot easier. Finally, the south route from the Trans-Canada Highway (Highway 1) near Chase and the Squilax-Anglemont Road is the longest. No matter which direction you choose, it is well advised to have a copy of the Backroad Mapbook for Thompson Okanagan BC, a GPS with the BC Backroad GPS Maps and a high clearance vehicle. Also use caution when travelling on logging roads as this is an active logging area.

Facilities

Part of the **Upper Adams River Provincial Park** there are rustic campsites at the southeast and southwest end of the lake. Small cartop boats can also be launched from the southwest end, but when water levels are low, it can be difficult. Please note this is a wilderness area and users are asked to pack out what they pack in.

Walloper Lake

Location: 25 km (15 mi) south of Kamloops
Elevation: 1,311 m (4,301 ft)
Surface Area: 43 ha (106 ac)
Max Depth: 7.8 m (25.6 ft)
Mean Depth: 2.9 m (9.5 ft)
Way Point: 50° 28′ 58.9″ N, 120° 32′ 7.0″ W

Fishing

At times, it can be a daunting task to get children hooked on fishing. Patience, while a virtue at many of the Kamloops area lakes, is not something that many kids possess. If they don't get a bite in the first few minutes, they're probably going to start getting bored. Sure, playing with worms will keep them occupied for the first few minutes, but then what?

That's when a lake like Walloper comes in. While the fish here are not big, it is stuffed to the gills with 0.5 kg (1 lb) rainbow that just love to be caught.

A 20 metre (60 foot) fishing wharf at the lake, which was built by members of the Kamloops and District Fish and Game Club, makes it easy for youngsters to drop a line without a boat. The water off the end of the dock is roughly 2 metres (7 feet) deep.

When the fish are nearby, which is pretty much all the time except when noisy people on the wharf drive them out, all it takes is a worm suspended from a bobber from 1–2 metres (3–6 feet) to get some action. Don't use big pieces of bait as your supply will quickly run out.

Walloper Lake is also a great place to introduce children to fly-fishing. These fish will quickly key in on chironomids, nymphs and leeches. Anglers with boats will find good action along the gently sloping shoals and at the drop offs near the lake's points. Deadfall along the shorelines can also hold fish, although fishing in the snags requires skillful casting.

Ice fishing is also popular on Walloper Lake. An aerator is on the lake to oxygenate the water and stave off winterkills, but caution is required as the ice near the aerator can be thin and unstable, even well back from the open water. Safety fencing is installed around the open water to keep anglers and animals out of harms way.

As long as they are bundled up nice and warm, kids will love ice fishing here. Hard water fishing is a different experience than fishing during the open water season. There is something magical about peering through that hole in the ice and into a different world and watching as a fish swims up to take your bait is one of those experiences that will keep kids coming back for more.

Walloper Lake is the perfect place to create a lifetime of memories with a young angler. Hopefully the great memories and thrill of fishing will carry those young anglers well into adulthood.

Area Indicator

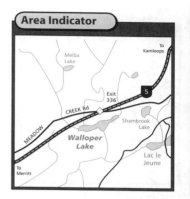

Directions

From Kamloops, take the Coquihalla Highway (Highway 5) south for 25 km (15 miles) to the Logan Lake exit (Exit 336). Cross the overpass and drive northeast for 0.6 km. Turn right to access Walloper Lake Provincial Park.

Facilities

The **Walloper Lake Provincial Park** is a day-use park situated on the northeast corner by the wharf. There is no camping at the park, but it offers a pit toilet, picnic tables and boat launch for cartoppers and small trailered craft. For people looking for overnight camping in the area, there are plenty of sites nearby, including Lodgepole Lake Recreation Site and Lac Le Juene Provincial Park on the east side of the Coquihalla.

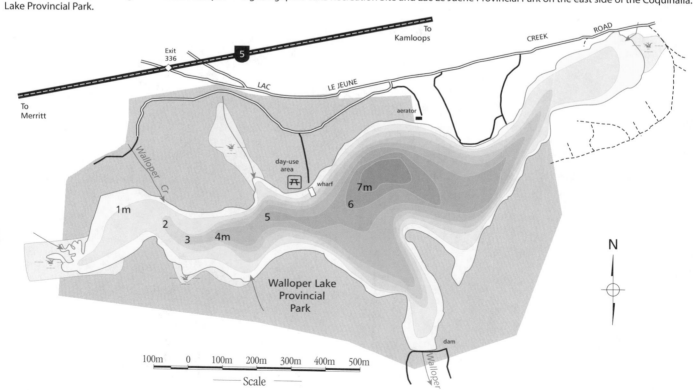

Location: 50 km (30 mi) northeast of Mission
Elevation: 261 m (856 ft)
Surface Area: 81 ha (200 ac)
Max Depth: 32 m (105 ft)
Mean Depth: 13 m (43 ft)
Way Point: 49° 21' 6.5" N, 121° 52' 32.7"

www.backroadmapbooks.com

Weaver Lake

Weaver Lake

Area Indicator

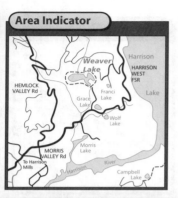

Weaver Lake			
Fish Stocking Data			
Year	Species	Number	Life Stage
2011	Rainbow Trout	6,000	Yearling
2010	Rainbow Trout	6,000	Yearling
2009	Rainbow Trout	6,000	Yearling

Fishing

Weaver Lake is found near the southwest end of Harrison Lake. It is a great place to fish, as the action can be consistent. It is also a great place for a family outing or weekend getaway.

The lake is surrounded by a dense forest and consists of two basins with small islands and numerous bays connected by a shallow passageway. As is typical with many coastal lakes, the shorelines are wooded with downed and submerged trees offering both habitat and refuge for bugs and fish.

The lake is well known for having lots of trout that really like to get caught. The rainbow range in size from 20–40 cm (8–16 in) and are aided by the Freshwater Fishery Society of BC annually stockings. Additionally, the presence of a man-made spawning platform at the lake outlet encourages spawning and natural recruitment, adding to the fishery.

Obviously, angling is closed in the spawning area; there are signs on the log booms denoting the closure.

The best time to fish Weaver Lake is during the spring and fall season. If you are a fly-fishermen, use a floating fly line to deliver a small brown, black or green chironomid or try trolling black or green Doc Spratley flies with a sinking line. For those with spinning gear, trolling a small Flatfish or Wedding Band tipped with a worm can be successful.

Fishing Powerbait or single salmon eggs on or near the bottom is a sure bet to some action. This method can also be productive in the summer as the lake temperature increases and fish seek cooler water temperatures. They usually retreat to the deeper sections in the western part of the lake.

In the fall, from mid-September to ice-on, which usually occurs in early November, the fishing will improve. Try using a small leech or damselfly imitation on a slow sinking fly line or trolling a small Flatfish or Hotshot. Trolling will allow you to effectively cover more of the lake as you search for fish. If all else fails, bottom fishing with bait seems to always provide some success.

Directions

Weaver Lake is one of several lakes found to the west of Harrison Lake off of the Harrison West Forest Service Road. To reach Weaver Lake from Mission, take the Lougheed Highway towards Harrison Mills. At the Sasquatch Inn, head north on the Morris Valley Road. You will pass the Weaver Creek Spawning Channels after about 11 km.

When the pavement ends, you are on the Harrison West Forest Service Road. About 1.5 km further along, you will come to the Weaver Lake Forest Service Road, heading left. If you pass Wolf Lake, you've gone too far. A short drive on a gravel road with a few rough spots brings you to the recreation site at the south end of the lake. From mid October to mid March, the road is gated, but you can walk in.

Facilities

Weaver Lake Recreation Site is set in a lush forest next to the picturesque lake. There are 29 well-spaced sites, a boat launch and dock to tie up small boats. Although access is a bit rough, small trailers can access the lake. The site is managed with fees from May to September and closed between October and March. New is the ability to reserve sites by calling M.G.C. Campsite Management Inc. at (604)796-0102, on Mon/Tues/Wed between 6-9 pm.

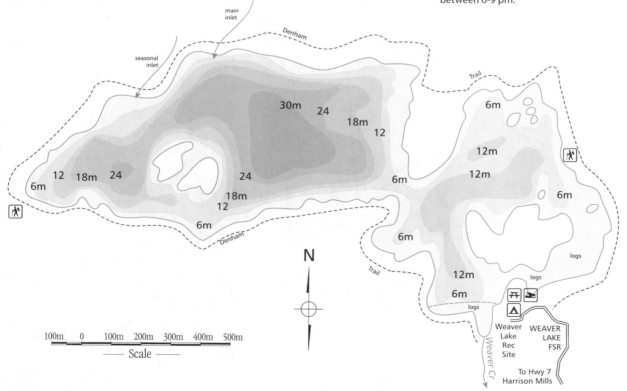

100m 0 100m 200m 300m 400m 500m
— Scale —

© Mussio Ventures Ltd.

White Lake

www.backroadmapbooks.com

Location: 20 km (12 mi) northwest of Sicamous
Elevation: 471 m (1,545 ft)
Surface Area: 570 ha (1,409 ac)
Max Depth: 40.2 m (131.9 ft)
Mean Depth: 23.5 m (77.1 ft)
Way Point: 50° 53′ 7″ N, 119° 15′ 42″ W

Fishing

In a land made famous for its great fishing lakes, White Lake is one of the standout lakes, with crystal clear water, large marl shores and rainbow trout to 4.5 kg (10 lbs) and more.

The lake is about 5 km (3 miles) long and about 1 km (0.6 miles) wide at its widest. This is a bit big compared to many of the other great Kamloops area lakes, but it makes up for its size with its many other traits. The lake gets its name because of the large white marl shoals that cover so much of the lake.

Each year, about 60,000 rainbow trout are stocked in the lake. While this is a lot of fish compared to other lakes, it is actually a fairly low-density population for this lake, which allows the fish to grow even bigger.

The lake is stunningly clear. So clear that traditional fly-fishing strategies are not going to produce as well. One of the best things you can do to improve your chances is to use a long leader with a dry line, especially when fishing bloodworm or chironomid patterns. Lines in the 5–7 metre (18–22 foot) range will improve your chances. Yes, casting with such a long leader is awkward, but with insects hatching as deep as 6 or 10 metres (20–35 feet), the long leader will help you get down to where the fish are.

White Lake is a low elevation lake and is one of the first lakes to be ice-free, usually by end of March. And it doesn't usually ice up until late December. This means that the aquatic life has a long time to grow, which in turn means the fish have a lot of food to choose from.

This is a mixed blessing. While it means that the fish get nice and big, it also means that convincing a fish to choose your chironomid out of millions can be difficult.

Because the lake is ice-free so early, it offers an early season fishery. But the low elevation lake creates a longer spring turnover. When the water is murky there is no sense fishing here.

By the end of April, the water has usually warmed up enough to stratify and by May, the fishing is hot again. The two most abundant food sources are Gammarus shrimp and water boatmen, but the fish tend to favour chironomids and bloodworms, dragonflies and damselflies. There are two sunken islands and lots of nice shoals at the west end of the lake.

While the water warms up during the summer, trollers can still do well. The trick here is a touch of red. Whether it is a lake troll or a lure, be sure to add red.

Area Indicator

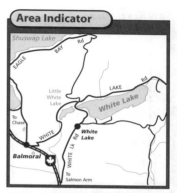

White Lake			
Fish Stocking Data			
Year	Species	Number	Life Stage
2011	Rainbow Trout	25,000	Yearling
2010	Rainbow Trout	25,000	Yearling
2009	Rainbow Trout	25,000	Yearling

Directions

White Lake is nestled in between two arms of Shuswap Lake a few kilometres off the Trans Canada Highway. From the town of Chase, drive 28 km east to the tiny settlement of Balmoral. Turn left onto the paved White Lake Road and follow that to the west end of the lake, 6.5 km beyond.

Facilities

There is a boat launch at the northwest end of the lake along with a commercial campground. About halfway along the north side of the lake is undeveloped **White Lake Provincial Park**. People do camp here, but there are no formal sites. There is however, a gravel boat launch, pit toilets and an old picnic shelter. At the east end of the lake there is a small parking area where people can hand launch a boat from.

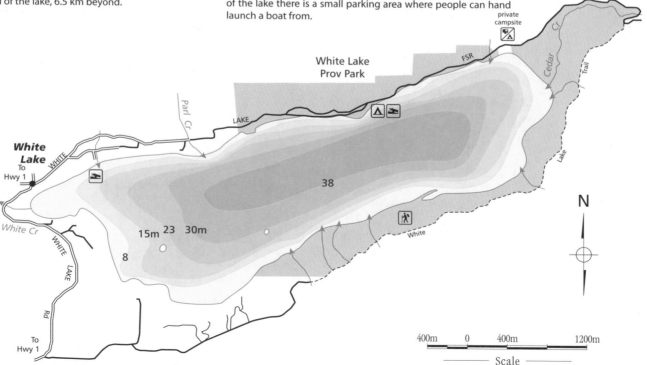

Location: 10 km (6 mi) east of Maple Ridge
Elevation: 173 m (568 ft)
Surface Area: 45 ha (111 ac)
Max Depth: 10 m (33 ft)
Mean Depth: 3 m (10 ft)
Way Point: 49° 12' 45" N, 122° 27' 00" W

Whonnock Lake

Area Indicator

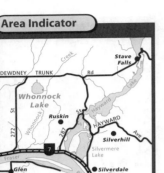

Whonnock Lake			
Fish Stocking Data			
Year	Species	Number	Life Stage
2011	Rainbow Trout	1,400	Catchable
2010	Rainbow Trout	1,400	Catchable
2009	Rainbow Trout	1,400	Catchable

Fishing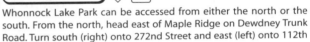

Whonnock Lake is a small, warm lake east of Maple Ridge. In the summer, it is a popular getaway for locals.

The lake is stocked with several thousand catchable-sized rainbow each year, which are best caught in the spring and the fall. The trout are aggressive biters and will chase most anything you toss at them, making this a great lake to take kids or new anglers for the first time. In addition to the trout, the lake holds good numbers of black crappie, ranging in size from 15–25 cm (6–10 in).

When introducing kids to fishing, remember, they may need to be both entertained and active so if the fish are not fully cooperating, you can always take them on a nature walk around the lake or explore the shallows for what are rumored to be the "World's Biggest Tadpoles" and other aquatic life.

Most of Whonnock Lake is fairly shallow. A boat or float tube will be very helpful, as you can cover more water and access the deeper holes. If you don't have a boat or a tube, the best place to shore fish is the north end.

If you are fishing from shore, a simple setup with a bobber and worm or Powerbait is a sure way to get some action. Adjust your float so it suspends your offering just off the bottom so fish cruising by will not only be able to smell it but see it as well. If you are out in a boat, try trolling a Flatfish or Wedding Band tipped with a worm. You can also anchor in the deeper parts of the lake and try the bobber and worm setup. Or cast a small lure or spinner such as a Krocodile or Mepps Silver Fox. It is always a good idea to be prepared with different types of tackle and bait because you never know what is going to work for those fish at that time.

Fly anglers can try working a small green or brown chironomid suspended on a dry line in the springtime. In the fall, the trout tend to favour larger food as they begin to prepare for the long, lean months of winter, so try working a dark-coloured leech fished on a slow sinking line.

Black crappies have small mouths, so you will need some small gear to catch them. Try small jigs, flies, or worms. Crappie usually feed mid-water, which can make them an infuriating fish to find consistently. Vary the depth you fish at from just below the surface to near the bottom.

Directions A

Whonnock Lake Park can be accessed from either the north or the south. From the north, head east of Maple Ridge on Dewdney Trunk Road. Turn south (right) onto 272nd Street and east (left) onto 112th Avenue and follow the signs to the lake.

From the Lougheed Highway, turn north (left) on 272nd Street and follow it almost all the way to Dewdney Trunk Road. Turn east (right) on 112th Avenue and follow the signs.

Facilities

Whonnock Lake Park is a popular summer destination for swimmers and boaters. There is a barbecue pit, concession stand, picnic tales, a playground, washrooms and paddleboat rentals. Camping is available at nearby **Rolley Lake Provincial Park**.

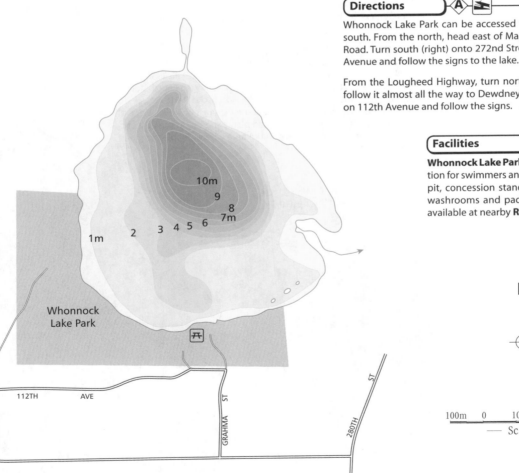

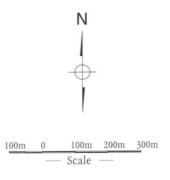

www.backroadmapbooks.com

Widgeon Lake

Location: 23 km (14 mi) north of Port Coquitlam
Elevation: 786.4 m (2,580 ft)
Surface Area: 221 ha (546 ac)
Max Depth: 141 m (462.6 ft)
Mean Depth: 52.6 m (172.6 ft)
Way Point: 52° 10' 00" N, 125° 51' 00" W

Fishing

Widgeon Lake is quite possibly the most difficult lake to get to in this entire book. It is also a place of astounding beauty. The lake is set in the mountains east of Pitt Lake. Although very difficult to access, the lake makes an excellent choice if you want a secluded backcountry fishing adventure.

Just getting to the lake is an epic adventure that only a few hardy souls are willing to undertake.

Because the lake is so difficult access, it provides good fishing for rainbow trout rumoured to reach 2 kg (4.5 lbs). The fish have been stocked in the past and are best caught by packing a float tube into the lake and spincasting or fly-fishing.

However, it has now been a decade since the lake was last stocked and since the lake is so infrequently fished, there are few reports on how well the fishing is holding up. The lake is a low nutrient lake, meaning there is not a lot of food for the fish to eat. The most recent reports we've seen have said that there are quite a few rainbows. But they are only in the 25–30 cm (10–12 inch) range.

The lake is very deep and has a rugged shoreline making shore fishing difficult. The water, due to its depth, drops off rapidly so stick near shore for best success. Also, there are two inflow creeks near the east end of the lake and two outflow creeks towards the south end of the lake where the fish tend to hang out. Therefore, try casting around those areas.

Spincasters can use small spinners and lures, while fly anglers will have the most success with attractor patterns like Doc Spratleys and Woolly Buggers. However, because it is a mountain lake that sees few anglers, the lure of choice is not a big concern.

Area Indicator

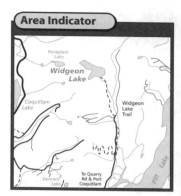

Directions

The first part of the trip is the easiest. From Grant Narrows Regional Park (see the write-up for Pitt Lake on how to get there), paddle a canoe (you can bring your own or rent one there) across the sometimes-windy Pitt Lake into the Widgeon Slough. Follow the left channel through the slough to the Widgeon Lake Recreation Site.

From here, it is an 18.5 km (11.5 mile) return hike to the lake that will test the endurance of even the hardiest of hikers. It isn't the distance that's the problem, but the elevation gain. The trail initially follows an old logging road, but at a washed out bridge it heads up to the lake, climbing nearly all of the 786 m (2,578 feet) in elevation in the last few kilometres.

Of course, some people fly into the lake, but in our minds, getting there is half the fun.

Facilities

An undeveloped camping site with space for maybe one big group is located at the south end of the lake where the trail first meets the lake. The actual **Widgeon Lake Recreation Site** is a peaceful site found at the end of a grassy slough at the start of the hike up to the lake. It makes a great launching off point for the hike, which will take most people the better part of a day. It is a flat grassy area that can hold up to 10 tenting parties and is very popular with canoeists, hikers and those looking for water-fowl viewing opportunities.

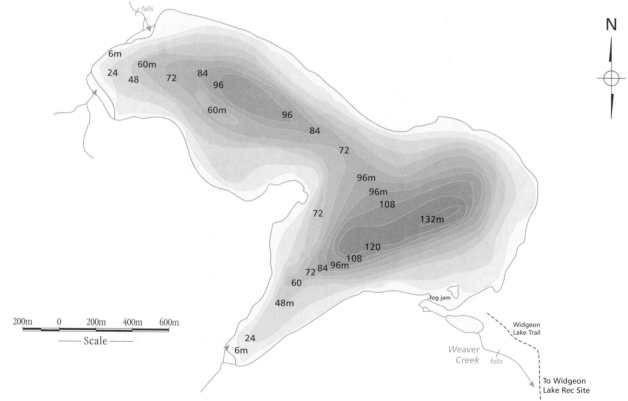

Location: 21 km (13 mi) northwest of Harrison Hot Springs
Elevation: 164 m (538 ft)
Surface Area: 5 ha (12 ft)
Max Depth: 14 m (46 ft)
Mean Depth: 5 m (16 ft)
Way Point: 49° 27′ 32.7″ N, 121° 51′ 21.2″ W

Wood Lake - Harrison Area

Area Indicator

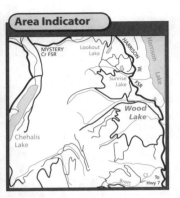

Fishing

Wood Lake is a small, shallow lake. Not much more than a pond actually. It is found a fair ways down the Harrison West Forest Service Road and does not see as much pressure as lakes that are easier to access. This is not to say that the lake isn't popular. It is, just not as popular as lakes closer to the main highway. This helps keep the trout population up and you will find lots of fish here.

The lake is stocked annually with rainbow. These trout are typically found in the 25–30 cm (10–12 in) range. However, the occasional fish reaches the 40 cm (16 in) range because the lake is nutrient rich compared to other coastal lakes.

Because the lake is so small and low, it does get quite warm in the summer and fishing falls off in July and August. On the other hand, it opens up fairly early in the season and can be fished as early as March if you're willing to brave the cold.

There are two prominent deep-water pockets, one in the western most part of the lake and one in the northern most part. Grab your boat or float tube, head out to the deep pockets and start casting a nymph or suspending a chironomid imitation towards the drop-off.

The chironomids are usually quite small, ranging in size from 14–20. They usually start hatching near the end of February and last until late May. To fish chironomids, double anchor a small boat to keep your line as still as possible since the way you present the fly is as important as the fly you present. Trout feed on chironomids in the nymph stage, usually near the bottom of the lake. Retrieve slowly and if you're not having much luck, retrieve slower, pausing frequently. The colour of the hatch can change several times over the few months, but brown, black and green are the most common.

In the fall there are fewer hatches and the fish are usually looking for bigger food to help sustain them through the lean winter months. A black leech or Woolly Bugger pattern as well as various nymph patterns can work at these times.

Spincasters will want to work a variety of small spoons or try suspending a worm or Powerbait just off the bottom. Trolling a Wedding Band tipped with a worm can work quite well, too.

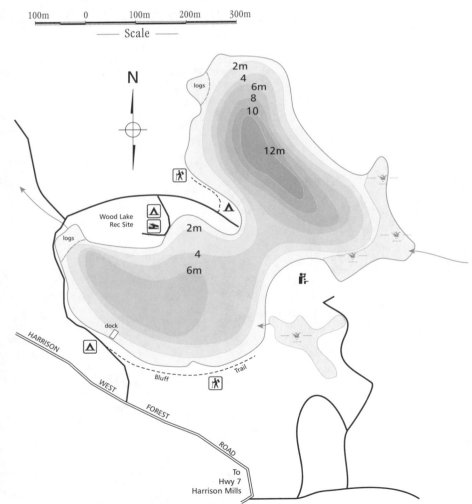

Directions

Wood Lake is located next to the Harrison West Forest Service Road. The road to the lake is gravel but in good enough condition to bring a car to if you wish.

From the Lougheed Highway at Harrison Mills, turn north on the Morris Valley Road. This road turns into the Harrison West Forest Service Road around the 11 km mark. Continue on the logging road crossing Simms Creek and then Walian Creek. Watch for the first turnoff to the lake on your right about 32 km (19.8 miles) from the Lougheed Highway. There is a second turnoff to access the north side of the lake a few hundred metres beyond. If you come across the 20 km marker or Hale Creek on the Harrison West Forest Service Road you have gone too far.

Facilities

Wood Lake Recreation Site is a popular destination that has recently been enhanced. There are now 30 partially treed campsites in two different sites on each side of the lake. The northwest site is the nicer location and offers a boat launch for non-motorized boats. New is the ability to reserve sites by calling M.G.C. Campsite Management Inc. at (604)796-0102, on Mon/Tues/Wed between 6-9 pm. Camping is available during long weekends and between May 1st and the Labour Day long weekend in September.

Wood Lake			
Fish Stocking Data			
Year	Species	Number	Life Stage
2009	Rainbow Trout	500	Yearling

Fishing Tips & Techniques

Bait (Still) Fishing

Probably the simplest way to catch fish and introduce young people or novice anglers to sport fishing is by a technique known as still fishing. When still fishing from the shore or a boat, the angler casts out and waits for a bite. Still fishing can be done with or without the use of float. Floats (bobbers) can be attached to the line so the baited hook stays suspended in the water. The depth can be adjusted by simply sliding the float up or down the line.

In smaller lakes, a one metre (3–5 ft) leader with a size 8–12 hook is recommended. Weights should be avoided if possible, as they tend to scare off the fish. Most fish tend to bite on worms and a single egg or roe. Other effective baits include maggots or artificial bait such as powerbait. Use the lightest line and smallest hook possible for the size of fish you are trying to catch.

Ice Fishing

Many of the large, low elevation lakes do not ice up, and many high elevation lakes are not accessible. However, there are still quite a few places to try ice fishing in the area. Generally speaking, ice fishing is possible from the end of December through to early March as long as the ice is safe (there will need to be at least 15 cm/6 in of ice to bear weight safely). Jigging a small spoon or other attractant lure up and down has become one of the most popular fishing methods since live bait is not permitted in BC.

While rainbow slow down in cold water, burbot and eastern brook trout need less oxygen and remain active throughout the winter.

Jigging

Jigging can be an effective method of fishing if you can find where the fish are congregating. Jigging is essentially sitting in a prime location, such as near underwater structure and working a jig head and body up and down to entice strikes. Outside of the traditional jig head and (where permitted) bait set up, you will also see anglers jigging spoons and other similar type lures.

Spincasting

Spincasting is another popular and effective fishing method for all types of water. Essentially, spincasting is the process of casting a line from a rod with a spinning reel. The set up is quite simple making it easy for anyone to learn how to fish and have fun at it. The key is to have line light enough to cast and tough enough to withstand fighting and landing some fairly large fish. A good idea is to get an open face reel with removable spools. One spool could have light line (6 lb test or lighter) for small lakes and another have heavier line (8 lb or higher) for rivers and trolling.

Trolling

Trolling is the mainstay of bigger lakes, but also a popular alternative for many smaller lakes. Ideally you should use a longer, stiffer rod than traditional spincasting set ups. Eight-pound test is okay for small lakes but you will need heavier line for bigger lakes, especially if using a downrigger.

It is best to troll near structure, along the drop-off or near a mid-lake shallow, such as a sunken island. On larger lakes, trolling for rainbow is very effective. Concentrate on points, inflow creeks or bays. A depth chart or depth finder will help you pinpoint these locations.

Lake trolls are popular because of their effectiveness and ease of use on both big and small lakes. These usually consist of a Willow Leaf or Ford Fender with a short leader and a small lure like a Wedding Band or similar along with bait where allowed. There are many shapes, sizes and colours of lures that have proven effective trolling for trout and dollies. Some of the most common trolling lures include Flatfish, Krocodile or Little Cleo spoons. Fly fishers usually troll a leech pattern, particularly in murky water. Other all purpose trolling flies are Carey Specials, Woolly Buggers, and Doc Spratleys. Work the area just off the drop-off

In addition to the tips under each fish species, we have provided more tips and techniques below. This section is designed to give you a better understanding of the various types of fishing styles as well as a much more elaborate breakdown on fly-fishing. Whether new to the sport of fishing or a wily veteran, we recommend reading through this section to pick a few tricks. We also recommend stopping in at the local tackle shop before heading out. They are the ones that know the local tricks and what has been producing well recently.

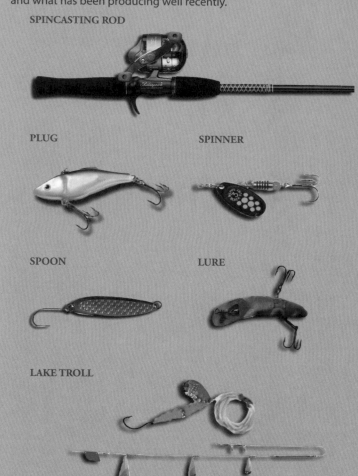

SPINCASTING ROD

PLUG

SPINNER

SPOON

LURE

LAKE TROLL

in a figure-eight pattern to vary the direction, depth and speed of the fly.

When trolling for cutthroat, try a silver Muddler Minnow or other baitfish patterns. In the fall or winter, troll a streamer type fly pattern like a bucktail quickly behind the boat. As the water warms, try an Apex, Lyman plug or flasher with a hoochie in the 10–30 m (30–90 ft) depth for bigger fish.

On larger lakes, trolling for rainbow is very effective. Concentrate on points, inflow creeks or bays. In the fall or winter, troll a streamer type fly pattern like a bucktail quickly behind the boat. As the water warms, try an Apex, Lyman plug or flasher with a hoochie in the 10–30 m (30–90 ft) depth for bigger fish. For deep trolling, downriggers with the aid of a heavy weight will enable you to troll your lure deep enough to find holding areas. Alternatively, lead core line or similar set-ups allow you to get your presentation down deeper without having to use downrigging equipment.

Fly-fishing is easily the most popular or at least most talked about fishing method of fishing in BC. It is also the hardest technique to master. Perhaps it is the challenge that attracts so many people to devote so much time. Or maybe it is the fact that once you have caught a fish on fly gear, everything else pales in comparison. Whether it is a small trout or an acrobatic salmon, the shear excitement of landing a fish with fly-fishing gear is exhilarating.

FLY FISHING ROD

BEAD-HEAD NYMPH   **CAREY SPECIAL**

CHIRONOMID   **ELK HAIR CADDIS**

DOC SPRATELY   **MUDDLER MINNOW**

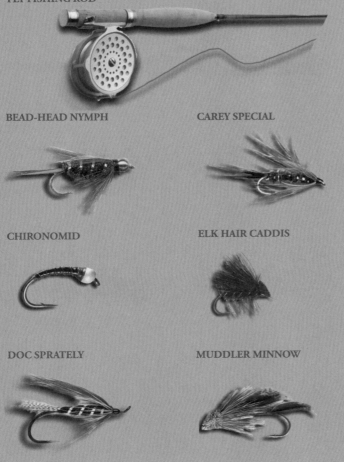

Fly-Fishing

Fly-fishing is easily the most popular or at least most talked about fishing method of fishing in BC. It is also the hardest technique to master. Perhaps it is the challenge that attracts so many people to devote so much time. Or maybe it is the fact that once you have caught a fish on fly gear, everything else pales in comparison. Whether it is a small trout or an acrobatic salmon, the shear excitement of landing a fish with fly-fishing gear is exhilarating.

Fly-Fishing Equipment

Basically, there are three parts to a fly-fishing outfit: the rod, the reel and the line. Rods come in a variety of lengths and weights, depending on your size and the size of the species you intend to fish. As an example, a 9 ft, 6-weight rod would be an ideal set up for everything from trout to salmon up to about 5 kg (11 lb) in size. Longer rods are helpful in casting and helping manipulate flies into position on streams, especially on rivers and streams.

To handle bigger fish, fly anglers need a much heavier rod such as an 8 or 9-weight rod. Many fly anglers will have at least two if not three or more rods of different size and weight in order to maximize their fishing experience. Essentially, a smaller size and weight rod would be used for fishing small trout or panfish, while the longer heavier rod would be used on rivers for big salmon.

When picking up a fly reel, the vast majority of reels (or any that are worth buying) will be weighted similar to the way rods are weighted. The reels are actually made to fit the appropriated rod. The difference in the weights of reels is mainly the size of the reel, since larger rods will be loaded with thicker line; therefore, the reel has to be a little larger to hold the increased line size. Also, the reel itself is often physically weighted to suit the rod weight so that the casting motion is balanced properly when casting your fly line.

When fly-fishing lakes, it is necessary to have a floating line in addition to a medium or fast sinking line. The floating line presents dry flies, as well as sub-surface wet flies. Dry line can also work well with weighted wet flies. However, a more popular subsurface option is using sink tip line, which is a combination of sinking and floating line where just the end of the fly line sinks. This type of line has a number of advantages, one being the ability to present subsurface flies while retaining the visibility of the fly line on the surface. This helps dramatically in spotting strikes, especially when fishing for trout. One of the best times to surface fish is during the mayfly and caddis hatches, however, trout usually prefer streamers and subsurface flies since they are very reluctant to strike the top of the water.

Medium sinking lines are ideal for fishing wet flies such as nymphs or chironomid pupae near the bottom. The medium sinking line offers the best control when attempting to fish a specific depth. If you do not have a medium sinking line, you can use a longer leader with some weight on your dry line. With a properly weighted fly or leader, this method can produce similar results. This type of presentation is ideal for working a particular depth, such as along a drop-off or along weed beds. Dragonfly, damselfly and even leech patterns can be worked quite effectively this way.

Fast sinking lines are ideal for trolling. If you are not familiar with the lake, trolling a fly is a good way to start. This allows you to cover a lot of distance searching for the ideal spot on the lake. Also, trolling is most effective on lakes with a low population of fish or during the summer doldrums. Woolly Buggers, streamers and leeches are all good all purpose trolling flies. Work the area just off the drop-off in a figure-eight pattern to vary the direction, depth and speed of the fly.

Regardless of which line you run with, you will also need backing and leader. The backing is designed to fill up the spool, as well as to act as reserve for when that fish goes on a 100 metre dash. Most people keep 100–150 metres of backing on their reel. The leader is a thinner monofilament line that attaches to the thick fly line to the fly. Leaders have a thicker butt that tapers to a thin tippet.

Flies

There are numerous books on fly-fishing techniques and how to choose the best fly for the particular season; however, it is really quite simple. Match the hatch! What you want to do is use a fly that most approximates the insect or baitfish on which the sportfish are feeding.

To determine this, spend some time observing the aquatic insects at the lake and try to determine what the fish are rising to and how the insects are moving in the water. If you can not see the adult insect on the water surface then try using a small fine net to scoop up the insects. If you catch a fish, you can also use a throat pump to physically see what the fish are eating. Once you have discovered what type of insect the fish are feeding on, you should try to determine how the insect moves in the water so you can imitate it. For example, is the adult insect sitting motionless on the water or is it rapidly flapping its wings?

Here is a list of recommended flies to include in your fly box. By no means is this exhaustive, but rather a good base to work from:

Bead Head Nymph is a variation of the halfback or pheasant tail nymph patterns, but is often a little more versatile. The fly is already weighted so it can be fished easily in streams and lakes with either sinking or floating line. The bead head also is an attractant that often glistens in the water attracting attention of predatory fish.

Carey Special is versatile enough to be used in both lakes and streams. Try size 4-8 for trout or 6-12 for salmon in red, green or brown. One of the most popular lake patterns in BC, it is a great searching pattern that can simulate many insects, including dragonfly, mayfly and caddis nymphs, as well as leeches. Smaller flies using a simple strip retrieve with sinking line is best in lakes, while moving water requires a bigger fly that is drifted with quicker strips.

Chironomid (Midge) has quickly become one of the most important flies in the fly box of a BC lake angler. Many anglers have a special box dedicated to them. Chironomids can be found in every lake in the BC and varies in size and colour depending on the lake and time of year. The fly must always be worked very slowly in the part of the water column that depends on what stage of the main hatch is taking place. The big hatches are mainly in the spring, although they are present all year round.

Doc Spratley is a general-purpose fly that can imitate most insects and a number of leeches. Perhaps the most popular fly in BC, the large sizes can imitate the dragonfly or damselfly nymphs, while smaller versions are like chironomid pupae. Black is the most versatile, but red, green and brown work, too. Depending on what you want to imitate dictates the method of presenting this fly. If you are looking to imitate a dragonfly nymph, stripping the fly in a consistent manner would be appropriate. On the other hand if you are looking to imitate a smaller nymph pattern, a shorter stripping retrieve may be required.

Dragon and **Damselfly Nymphs** vary in size and colour. Since they are found everywhere, they should certainly be part of every fly box. There are literally dozens of patterns that are used throughout the province and your best bet to know what works is to inquire locally before you head out. These nymphs are often worked deep and even off bottom for cruising trout.

Elk Hair Caddis is a fly that revolutionized top water caddis fly fishing. Depending on the time of year your presentations will vary with this type of fly. In the early part of the season, hatching caddis will often flap along the surface attempting to break away. Therefore, your presentation should imitate this. Later in the season when caddis are laying eggs, they will literally smack the water and trout will pounce on them. They key is to be observant of the hatch and what the flies are doing.

Leeches are a definite must in every fly box since they are found in virtually all lakes in BC. Leech patterns are versatile and great for searching lakes. At times, this is all trout are feeding on. Even if they are feeding on something else, they will rarely pass up a well-presented leech.

Mayfly patterns vary dramatically in size and colour. During a hatch, trout can sometimes be so picky that they will literally pass up your mayfly if it is a size or two too small or a wrong colour. However, the mayfly hatch is a big part of the open water season and a good variety of this fly is needed in your box, especially early in the season.

Muddler Minnow imitates a minnow in distress and is the ideal meal for a wide variety of fish. In general, larger fish seem to like bigger presentations of this fly. The fly is mainly worked below the surface although some anglers have been known to put floatant on them and work them on or just below the top of the water for big aggressive fish.

Scud (Shrimp) patterns, similar to chironomids, vary greatly in size and colour depending on the lake. A good rule of thumb is to use whatever colour the lake bottom is. Working the fly needs patience. It should be allowed to sink close to the bottom and retrieved with slow short strips followed by a short pause. Working closer to shore is better, since shrimp are most often found frolicking here.

Salmon and steelhead prefer bigger and bolder patterns. Although the names may be the same as those used for trout, it is often just the size that changes. Of course adding a bit of sparkle or brighter colours never hurts as many of the streams run murky.

COLORADO SPINNER

JENSEN EGGS   MICKEY FINN

DOC SPRATELY   MARABOU

SPIN-N-GLO   WOOLHEAD SCULPTING

Streamer is a good versatile pattern for all sportfish species as it imitates baitfish or larger meals that most sportfish thrive on. This fly can be of almost any size and colour, but the key is that it should have a long sleek profile in the water and is used to fish subsurface. While you will see bright coloured streamer patterns out there, typically for Ontario lakes you are looking for a pattern that imitates baitfish.

Tom Thumb is one of the more popular dry flies in British Columbia. Size is very important to match the current hatch, especially if surface fishing. While the fly can imitate a number of different insects, it is most commonly used as a caddis imitation.

Woolly Bugger is a good versatile pattern for salmon, steelhead and trout. This fly imitates larger meals such as a baitfish or leeches and can be effective in both streams and lakes. While the most popular colours are olive and black, other colours and variations, such as a bead head, can create a unique fly for that unique situation.

Southwestern BC Hatches: From ice-on to ice-off, fly patterns of choice should coincide with these major hatches. Remember that hatches are weather dependant. At higher elevation lakes, hatches occur later than at low, and hatches occur sooner closer to the coast. But as a general rule, chironomid (midge) hatches start in April, peak in mid May and continue through June before returning at the end of September and through October. The next insect to hatch is the mayfly, which traditionally runs from May through to mid July. Damselfly patterns are effective in June to August while dragonfly patterns can be used from June to the end of September. Evenings from mid-June to early July can produce some exciting top water action for caddisflies, while terrestrials, such as ants and grasshoppers, hatch in the mid-summer. Water boatman or water bug patterns are best right after ice-off and again in August through October. Finally, shrimp and leech patterns can be productive all year round, as there is not a set hatch period for them.

Feb & March:
· All chironomid stages
· Shrimp
· Leeches

April:
· All chironomid stages
· Shrimp
· Leeches
· Dragonfly nymph

May:
· All chironomid stages
· Mayfly nymph
· Shrimp
· Leeches
· Dragonfly nymph

June:
· All chironomid stages
· Mayfly nymph
· Damselfly nymph
· Shrimp
· Leeches
· Dragonfly nymph

July:
· All chironomid stages
· Mayfly nymph
· Damselfly nymph
· Caddisfly/Sedge
· Shrimp
· Leeches
· Dragonfly nymph

August:
· All chironomid stages
· Mayfly nymph
· Damselfly nymph
· Caddisfly/Sedge
· Shrimp
· Leeches
· Dragonfly nymph

September:
· All chironomid stages
· Dragonfly nymph
· Shrimp
· Leeches
· Water boatman

October:
· Shrimp
· Leeches
· Water boatman

Fishing Small Lakes

On smaller lakes, the predominant fish species are rainbow, brook and cutthroat trout. If you are looking for more success and less size on your day out on the water, small lakes are a good bet as there is less water to cover. Fishing near structure such as logs and weeds, shoals or at the edge of a drop-off produces the best results. Food sources also congregate around weeds and inflow or outflow streams and in the thermocline. The thermocline is the area of the lake between the warm surface water and the cold water. Concentrate your efforts in these areas to improve your chances of angling success.

A good way to explore a new lake is to use searching type lures or flies and work them near the subsurface structures. Along with your depth chart map, it is a good bet to invest in a depth finder. Depth finders can give even more detail to the underwater structure that maps simply cannot provide. Another tool that can help when fishing lakes or streams is a good pair of polarized glasses. Polarized lenses will help you spot fish or underwater structure that may not show up on a map or depth finder.

A universal set up that will attract all species is a lake troll with a short leader and a Wedding Band or similar with bait. Flatfish, Krocodile or Little Cleo spoons are trolled, while fly fishers usually troll a leech pattern, particularly in murky water. Other all purpose trolling flies are Carey Specials, Woolly Buggers, and Doc Spratleys. Work the area just off the drop-off in a figure-eight pattern to vary the direction, depth and speed of the fly. When trolling for cutthroat, try a silver Muddler Minnow or other baitfish patterns.

If you are fishing from shore, try casting along the shore or towards a fallen log, weed bed or drop-off. Use the countdown method to find where the fish are holding. Casting almost any small spinner or spoon with some bait (worms are preferred) can prove successful, but watch for bait restrictions. Favorites are the Panther Martin (silver or black), Mepps Black Fury or Blue Fox. As for lures, a Deadly Dick, small Dick Nite, Flatfish or Kamlooper also work well. The good ol' fashion bait and bobber can be very effective, while fly anglers should pay attention to the current hatch.

As the water warms up and the fishing slows during the late spring, move to a higher elevation lake. By continually moving to higher elevations you can continue to fish the first few weeks of prime time period right until the lakes begin to cool down in the fall. And as the water gets too cold up high, begin moving down to the lower elevations. Most of the high elevation walk-in lakes offer good fly-fishing during their limited season, which lasts from late June until October. Another nice thing about these lakes is the fish are more active when the light penetrates the water. This makes an 11 o'clock arrival a good thing. If the water is murky, you might as well move on, as the lake is experiencing turnover and the fish will rarely bite.

Many of the lakes in the southern interior feature gin clear water. This means that insect life happens deeper, and that the fish are much easier to spook. Fly anglers in this region use long leaders (up to 7 m/35 feet) to get chironomid and other patterns down to where the action is happening.

Fishing Bigger Lakes

Big lakes can be intimidating. This is where the map comes in really handy. Study your map for structure and devise a game plan prior to arrival. Once at your spot, use your depth finder to hone in on those really unique structure areas and work them hard before heading on to another area.

On larger lakes, trolling for rainbow is very effective. Concentrate around creek or river mouths. Fish seem to hold around the drop-offs in these areas because of the large amount of feed available. Drop-offs near cliffs or rock walls are also good areas to focus your efforts. In spring, fall or winter, troll a streamer type fly pattern quickly behind the boat so they skim off the surface can produce some big trout. Muddler Minnows, Polar Bear or bucktails are popular choices. As the water warms, try an Apex, Lyman plug or flasher with a hoochie in the 10–30 m (30–90 ft) depth. For deep trolling, downriggers with the aid of a heavy weight will enable you to troll your lure deep enough to find holding areas.

If fishing from shore, working the drop-off around creek mouths is your best bet. Bait balls (a large cluster of worms or eggs and a hook) can be fantastic for Dolly Varden and sometimes rainbow. During the summer a float with a grasshopper can also land you a nice trout.

Fishing Streams & Rivers

Rivers and streams can be a challenge to fish, but at the same time they offer other opportunities that lakes do not. Most notably, hot spots in rivers can be very easy to find as they are often at the bottom of a small waterfall, or the slack water next to the fast water. The main problem with bigger rivers is getting your presentation out far enough from shore to where the fish are holding. The easiest way to overcome this problem is to use a boat if possible. This way you can find seams and pools where fish are holding and get your presentation to where the fish are instead of fighting the current with your cast from shore. You can also access some of the more remote areas that shore anglers are not fishing to find some of the more productive holes.

Of course getting a boat onto smaller streams is often not possible. In these cases, a good set of waders and river shoes can make a big difference in being able to get to the good holes. To work these streams effectively, you need to sneak up on holes to avoid being detected by trout. Work every pocket, pool or seam no matter the size. Some of the biggest fish are hiding in the most unlikely places. Many of the smaller rivers in the area run quite warm in summer and wading can be a refreshing break from the heat of the day. Bring along a hat that you can dip in the water, too.

Please Note: There are regulations imposed for many of the lakes and streams in order to preserve the quality of the resource. Always check the regulations before fishing!

Releasing Fish - The Gentle Way

There is a growing trend among anglers to catch and release, unharmed, a part of their allowable catch. As well, more restrictive regulations on specific waters can severly limit the angler's allowable harvest.

A fish that appears unharmed may not survive if carelessly handled, so please abide by the following:

1- Play and release fish as rapidly as possible. A fish played for too long may not recover.

2- **Keep the fish in the water as much as possible.** A fish out of water is suffocating. Internal injuries and scale loss is much more likely to occur when out of water.

3- Rolling fish onto their backs (while still in the water) may reduce the amount they struggle, therefore minimizing stress, etc.

4- Carry needle-nose pliers. Grab the bend or round portion of the hook with your pliers, twist pliers upside down, and the hook will dislodge. Be quick, but gentle. **Single barbless hooks are recommended**, if not already stipulated in the regulations.

5- Any legal fish that is deeply hooked, hooked around the gills or bleeding should be retained as part of your quota. **If the fish cannot be retained legally, you can improve its chances for survival by cutting the leader and releasing it with the hook left in.**

6- If a net is used for landing your catch, it should have fine mesh and a knotless webbing to protect fish from abrasion and possbile injury.

7- **If you must handle the fish, do so with your bare, wet hands (not with gloves).** Keep your fingers out of the gills, and don't squeeze the fish or cause scales to be lost or damaged. It is best to leave fish in the water for photos. If you must lift a fish then provide support by cradling one hand behind the front fins and your other hand just forward of the tail fin. Minimize the time out of the water, then hold the fish in the water to recover. If fishing in a river, point the fish upstream while reviving it. When the fish begins to struggle and swim normally, let it go.

  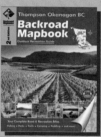
 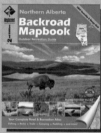 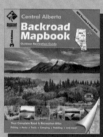
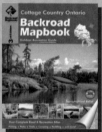  
  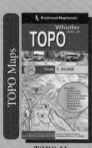 

Index

Important Numbers

Fish and Wildlife
BC Fishing Information.. www.BCFishing.com
....www.sportfishing.bc.ca
Freshwater Fisheries Society of BC...www.gofishbc.com
Department of Fisheries and Oceans ....www.pac.dfo-mpo.gc.ca
Current salmon and steelhead regulations ....www.env.gov.bc.ca/fw/
....www.pac.dfo-mpo.gc.ca/recfish/default_e.htm
E-Licensing..www.fishing.gov.bc.ca
BC Wildlife Federation...www.bcwf.bc.ca
Observe, Record and Report 1-877-952-7277

General
BC Ferries ....www.bcferries.com
....1-800-223-3779
Highways Report ....www.drivebc.ca
....1-800-550-4997
To Report Forest Fires 1-800-663-5555
*5555 (cellular phones)
Tourism BC ....www.hellobc.com
....1-800-435-5622
Updates...www.backroadmapbooks.com
Weather Conditions........... www.weatheroffice.ec.gc.ca/canada_e.html

B.C Forest Services (Road Conditions)
Ministry of Forests ....www.for.gov.bc.ca
    Ministry of Forests ....www.for.gov.bc.ca/
    Chilliwack Forest District 604-702-5700
    Merritt Forest District....................250-378-8400 or 1-800-665-1511
    Squamish Forest District...604-898-2100
    Sunshine Coast Forest District 604-485-0700
    Okanagan Shuswap Forest District (Salmon Arm)....250-558-1700
    Southern Interior Forest Region ....(250) 828-4131
    100 Mile House 250-395-7800
    Arrow Boundary Forest District..................................250-365-8600
    Cascades Forest District 250-378-8400
    Kamloops Forest District 250-371-6500

Parks
BC Parks/Ministry of Environment ....www.bcparks.ca
Park Reservations ....www.discovercamping.ca
....1-800-689-9025
Kamloops 250-371-6200
Thompson River District 250-851-3000

Advertisers